A CELEBRATION

"an amphitheatre of hills of stupendous grandeur
clothed with wood" Jonathan Williams (1905) [1]
Photo 2010

Roger Coward
Cwm Bedw
Abbeycwmhir Community Council

ABBEYCWMHIR

History, Homes and People

"...betwixt ii great hills in a bottom, wher rennith a little brook...." - John Leland (1540)[2] Photo 2010.

Dear Reader,

It is with great pleasure that I write this introduction to the Abbeycwmhir Community Book, a book which began with the Millennium Celebrations in the community enjoyed by all from Abbeycwmhir, Bwlch y Sarnau and the surrounding area.

So some fourteen years after these celebrations The Community Book has become a finished current history of the local community. It was through the initial efforts of the late Willie Griffiths of Devannor and the then working group that brought together considerable detail of people and places from our area, detail that unfortunately lay fallow for some time following Willie's sad passing.

Happily the information was not lost but held by the Community Council waiting to be dusted off and re-energised by an enthusiast; a champion was found in Roger Coward of Cwm Bedw who has over the past six years searched, sifted, coaxed and assembled the Book that you now hold in your hands.

We live in a beautiful part of Wales, our home, and are surrounded by many characters, a rich history and tales to be told. Roger has brought together much of the richness of our community and presents it for our delight and that of our children and grandchildren.

Read, enjoy and again celebrate
                - our community.

Keith Powell
Esgairwy,

Chair (May 2011)

Abbeycwmhir Community Council
Alan Bennett, (Crossgates) Llanerfraith; Brian Rees, Penbrynccnna;
Dai Jones, Llwynon; Glyn Powell, Waen Farm;
Julie Evans, Clewedog Bungalow; Gareth Rees, Brondrefach;
Clerk to the Council; Peter Kirk, Sunnydale.

"A Wild and Mountainous Place" [3]
Photo 2010

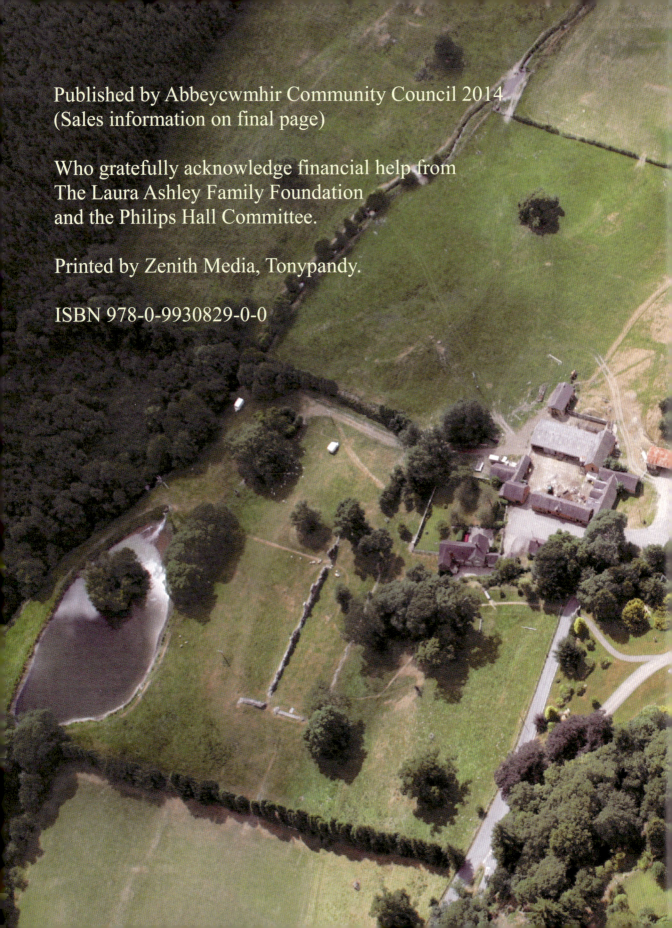

Published by Abbeycwmhir Community Council 2014
(Sales information on final page)

Who gratefully acknowledge financial help from
The Laura Ashley Family Foundation
and the Philips Hall Committee.

Printed by Zenith Media, Tonypandy.

ISBN 978-0-9930829-0-0

Abaty'r Cwmhir Central
C 2006

Preface

"Root Deep and Spread Wide" - Radnorshire Saying

This book is a celebration of life in a tiny community, in beautiful Mid-Wales, which through the ages has been associated with some of the main events in Welsh History. Abbeycwmhir was protected and visited by English Kings and Marcher Lords, had the longest Cistercian Abbey in Europe and saw the squire-archy's tenants become freehold farmer owners. The history extends into the twenty first century since the book started as a Millennium Book with contributions from and about each household. It has been written by people living in the Community drawing together new research and the most respected authorities for the first time. Pages of Appendices help with research, family genealogy and ideas for regional walks for adults and children

In the words of another Radnorshire saying -

"Carry the morning in your face".

Roger Coward MA
Cwm Bedw, Abbeycwmhir.

Acknowledgements

This book is written by the local residents - which makes it a very special community book. A history from the beginnings and documents for a social history right up to the twenty first century - the contemporary period. Each household has written a piece and provided a photograph for the *Homes & People* section and most of these are in colour, so we have a history printed in colour too. It was written by Julian Lovell of Tyr Ehedydd, Diana Berriman of Little Plock and Noel Price, author of *Tales of a Welsh Postman,* who lived at Keepers Cottage and wrote much of the *In Living Memory* section and myself, Roger Coward. Thanks go to the many community members who have contributed information in conversations and emails - and provided photographs and documents without which the project would have been inpossible. Only three pages were written by somebody outside the community and that was Dr Adrian Humpage from the British Geological Survey.

The information for the history section has been gathered from the most reliable sources and put together for the first time with a focus on Abbeycwmhir. A great deal of personal help was given by Paul Remfry, the independent historian; Dr John Davies, Chair of the Abbeycwmhir Heritage Trust; Revd. Dr David Williams, much published Cistercian and seal expert; Neil Thompson, Archivist, State Library of South Australia and Professor Flavia Swann, grand-daughter of Colonel John Lionel Philips. To all of them we are very grateful.

We have featured the wonderful Tapestries made by the women of the village for the Millennium 2000, now in the Community Hall, and the *Bwlch y Sarnau School Then and Now* painting. The frontispiece to the *Homes & People* section was especially painted by Angela Lewis of Cwmffwrn.

A full list of acknowledgements for permission to use pictures and other help is in the Appendix (p 272) but here I would like to especially thank Peter Kirk of Sunnydale, the Clerk to the Community Council and Wendy Kirk, the Community Councillors, Powys County Library Service - for the extremely efficient and helpful provision of journals and books, also Powys Archive and Powys Training; the National Museum, Cardiff and the National Library of Wales, Aberystwyth. All these institutions were vital. We also thank the Queen for permission to use pictures from the Royal Collection.

Introduction

Contents

1) A Celebration & Introductions...................... 1
2) As Time Goes By, Whats in a Name?............ 10
    a - The Abbey of Cwmhir.... 12
    b - Before the Abbey
        - Geology.....................45
        - Pre-History.............. .48
    c - After The Abbey............ 50
        - Abbeycwmhir Bible.. 52
        - The Fowlers.............. 54
    d - The Church...................58
    e - The Chapels................... 61
    f - The Hall
        - Wilson...................... 68
        - Philips..................... 76
        - Others..................... 88
    g - The Happy Union...........89
    h - The Mill........................97
    g - Homes No More............ 105
    h - The Forestry....................114
3) Village Group Photographs 1893,1993,2002... 120
4) Millennium 2000 Celebrations and Projects... 124
5) In Living Memory – the 20th Century............. 138
6) Homes & People................................168
7) Index to Appendices 271

   which include: Picture Acknowledgements & Permissions; Sources of Information; Granges; Castles; Keys to Tapestries, Painting & Village Photographs; Index to Personal Names; Welsh Property Name Translations and much else.

8) A Celebration - mainly of Bwlch y Sarnau..... 314

Top right: Abbeycwmhir 1578 on a map of Radnorshire from Camden's Britannia published in 1607.

9

Forethoughts on:
As Time Goes by..

You must remember this….
The fundamental things apply,
As time goes by…"[1]

Everything and everyone has a history - whether we like it or not. You may say the past is just the past but the past is also present and it could be our future too - for better or worse. History includes everything right up to the present moment and so is not limited to official publications. After all, everybody knows some - but few write it down. This history attempts to see around some of the corners through the memories of living people and other original documents not seen before.

Researching family history and genealogy is a way of knowing and valuing our journey whether personally, as a family or as a community or nation. It would seem that for most people things were usually worse in the past despite our nostalgia and love of old things. There was a great deal of physical violence, short lives and death from battle or illness, but these were the result of the attempts of people, often in complex and inconsistent ways, to organise their lives materially and to have ideas and beliefs to make them make sense. History could be where we learn to be nasty. But we can also see that in the past people were often highly intelligent, clever and strong and always with faith in a better future - on earth or in heaven. We are not today starting from the beginning of human life although some people's actions might make you think so.

There is so much change going on in history that it can be annoying and frustrating to follow - it is often true about the present as well. By taking an over-view of past change perhaps we can learn to assess which new changes are more fundamental and worth encouraging.

An Abbey with its idealistic and altruistic spiritual aim still had to organise its economy with local farms. Money to make payments for services had to be raised. It also needed protection from attack and contracts with wool merchants and so there is the necessary development of fairness and justice, and law to ensure it, mainly through the King's travelling Courts often surprisingly nearby at Hereford, Gloucester and Rhuddlan. All this led to contracts, property deeds and writing it down on vellum and people to do it - originally in Latin. Seals were used to prevent identity fraud. Our problems are not new. All this needed to be paid for. The development of taxation over the years can be seen through the payment of fealties (loyalty, military service, hospitality), tithes (a tenth of produce originally for church purposes) and heriots (death duties).

Princes of Wales and Kings of England also needed to guarantee security by keeping people on side. They did this often by giving them jobs and by giving them property or estates which included daughters in marriage to potential enemies such as King John's daughter, Joan, married to Llewleyn Fawr (The Great) - not that we hear much of her as written history tends to be His-story rather than Her-story.

In this brief account we have tried to go back to the calves skin (vellum), to the original documents and to the rock and artefacts that tell the story of our Community. **History belongs to us all.**

Always bear in mind the date and what is happening all around. When our Abbey was being established from 1176 cathedrals and abbeys were popping up all over Europe; America hadn't been discovered (except by its native people;[2]) Thomas à Becket had just been murdered in Canterbury Cathedral, the Crusades had reached Jerusalem; and Richard the Lionheart was about to become King of England; Ghengis Kahn was invading China and the temple of Angkor Wat was being completed in Cambodia!

What's in a name?

You wouldn't think there was so much in the history of one very small place.

We might tease the monks for not calling their abbey *"The Convent on the Babbling Brook"* or *"Abbey Babbly"* for short. After all they built their Abbey on the Clywedog (the Welsh *Clywedig* meaning *audible* or *heard*) but often translated in English as *babbling* or *murmuring*). On the other hand, they might have called it *"The Abbey of Gollon"*[i] - the name of the Home Grange by 1537 or even *"Hot Abbey"* as the monks would have taken their *cold* water from the Poeth (*hot*) stream running through their enclosure. Instead they borrowed the name meaning 'long valley' from the brook further up the valley and gave it to the longer valley - that of the Clywedog stream re-naming it in true Cistercian style "The Abbey in the Long Valley". The translation "the long dingle" has no Welsh basis and was introduced by the Rev WJ Rees MA FSA, Rector of Cascob & Rural Dean of Lower Melenith, in the first publication about the Abbey in 1849, "An Historical and Descriptive Account of the Ruinated Abbey of Cwmhir".[3] It became fashionable amongst tourists in the 19th Century.

850 years ago, it is obvious that this area was not called *Abbey* Cwmhir. We know that two territorial units were here at the time of King John's charter of 1215 - *Kenepawel* (Cefn Pawl) which it could have been called and *Dynanner* (Devannor) which it is unlikely to have been called since the name means "main" or "manor house"[4]. Prior to the Abbey the focus of the community would have been Bylch y Sarnau with it's ancient Bronze Age ridgeway across Cefn Crin and Camlo Hill going later to the Roman fort of Castell Collen at Llanyre and in the other direction to Newtown or Caersws. Also crossing it at Bylch y Sarnau in Roman times was a road from Llanidloes to Llanbister going through Tyn y Berth. Cross roads are good places for settlements.

In the Abbeycwmhir Bible *(cf page 52),* William Fowler signs himself in 1590 as "Lord of the Manor of Golon" and "Monarchide (monks house) Golon". As late as 1857 Francis Aspinal Philips created an Inclosure of the Township of Gollon - including some of Cefn Pawl. It is difficult to be sure of the meaning of Gollon (or Golon) as there is no farm of that name. It is probably a corruption of the Welsh word *collen* meaning *hazel* and may have been adopted because of the *relatively* close Roman Fort of Castle Collen at Llanyre. At the time of the inclosure, the township of Gollon was on the North bank of the Clewedog from Buddugre to New House & Upper Dolau with the township of Cefn Pawl on the south bank from the farm of that name along the Cwmhir Valley to Cwmffwrn. The name Gollon disappeared after the 1861 census.

In 1644 the village was referred to as Nant Cwm Hir - *Brook* of Cwmhir.[5] In various documents it has also been called *Kwmhir* (earliest 1198) *Cumhyr, Comby, Combehire, Combishire, Cumhire, Comehyre, Comehere, Cumhyre and Comhire*! The present name may have been adopted as late as 1831 when the Parish of Abbeycwmhir was created. Certainly Thomas Wilson (here 1824 -1837 cf p 68) called it "Abbey-Cwm-Hir". In 1833 The Topographical Dictionary of Wales said of Abbey Cwm Hir that it is "a parish in the union of Rhaiadr, comprising the hamlet of Cevnpawl, in the hundred of Kevenleece, and the hamlet of Gollon, in the undred of Knighton, county of Radnor, South Wales, 5 miles from Rhaiadr, containing 589 inhabitants."[6]

The fair tapestry of human life reflected in the images on this and other pages[1] *are jewels from the four Abbeycwmhir Tapestries made by the women of the community at the time of the Millennium 2000 (cf p 128-131). There is a key to the subjects and their makers in the Appendix on page 297.*

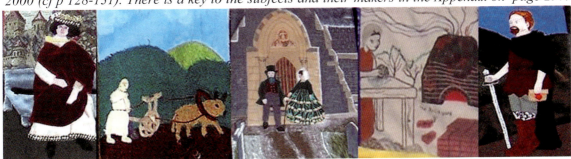

CWMHIR, MAELIENYDD - 'TWIXT WYE & SEVERN

Today's Rural Deanery of the Church of Wales has the same name as the Medieval Cantref of Maelienydd from before the time of the Abbey of Cwmhir. With its neighbours, Elfael and Gwrytheyrnon, it is the origins of the County of Radnorshire and goes back to the ancient Welsh Kingdom between the Wye and Severn - Rhwng Gwy a Hafren - founded in the Tenth Century.

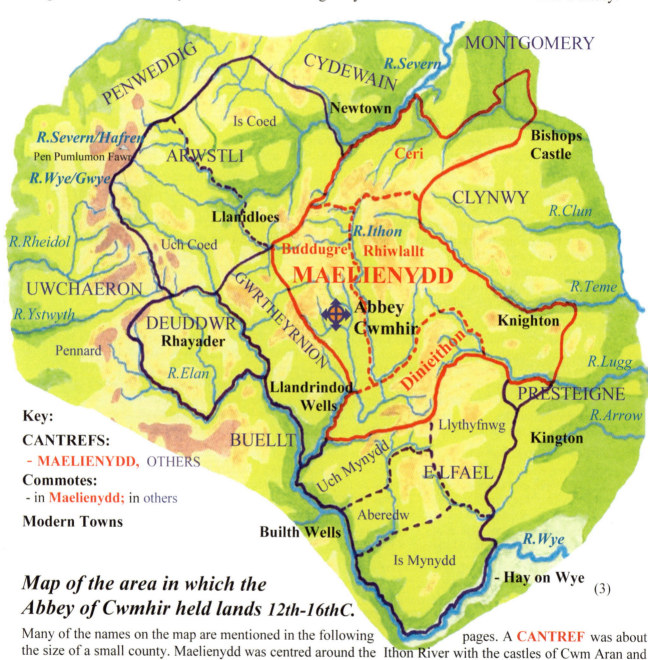

Map of the area in which the Abbey of Cwmhir held lands 12th-16thC.

Many of the names on the map are mentioned in the following pages. A **CANTREF** was about the size of a small county. Maelienydd was centred around the Ithon River with the castles of Cwm Aran and Tinboeth as political centres (cf map p 40) and Cwmhir Abbey as spiritual centre. The boundaries would frequently change. The Kingdom of Rhyng Gwye a Hafren sometimes included Buellt and Commote Deuddwr across the River Wye. A **Commote** was similar to a parish or modern community.

Note: Not all rivers and streams are shown on the above map - mainly only those with boundaries along them. However the boundaries changed frequently - if not the rivers and brooks.

The Abbey of Cwmhir

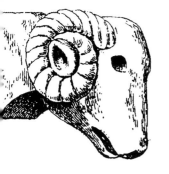

The Mystery of Abaty'r Cwmhir

Imagine our tiny village dominated by a huge cathedral-like building bigger than St.Davids with up to sixty male monks living here permanently; chanting and praying inside and one hundred more working outside in the forests and fields. Carts rattling past bringing food from the farms and horses neighing, bearing visitors riding in from France - from the Cistercian Mother House of Citeaux, in the Cote d'Or of Burgundy - or emissaries from the Vatican in Rome delivering Bullae or mandates from the Pope. Then the great bell would toll - and all would be silent save for the sound of evensong filling the deep long valley. The purpose of this huge building and complex international organisation was to know God.

It is hard for us at the beginning of the 21st Century to imagine this "Sumptuous Building" as it was described already in 1231 by Roger of Wendover.[7] The length of the nave was 78 mtrs, one of the longest in all Britain (Westminster a mere 71.5mtrs, Strata Florida a tiny 41 mtrs) and the longest Cistercian Abbey in all Europe. Its sumptuousness can be seen in the intricacy and depth of some of the carvings of foliage on the capitals on top of the pillars and the eight bundles of *triple sandstone shafts* on each column under each arch - fortunately preserved for us at St Idloes Parish Church, Llanidloes and in the terrace wall of Abbeycwmhir Hall. Imagine fourteen of these arches four feet taller than at Llanidloes with a row of windows above on both sides of the nave and topped with a fine wooden roof! The mystery is, "Why was it so grand?" Its patron must have been a person of the very greatest ambition.[8]

Cistercians deliberately chose locations "removed from the conversations of men"[9] in the hope of finding God in the silence. Here, at Cwmhir, the *"Longae Vallis",*[10] a "wild and mountainous place",[11] came together with the ambitious Lord of Maelienydd and a French Saint - Bernard of Clairvaux. Cwmhir Abbey was to be the highest - above sea level; the longest Cistercian nave in Europe; the most isolated; have unique spiritual duties to the local population - and have a Royal Prince entombed in its building.

Cadwallon ap Madog ab Idnerth ap Cadwgan ab Elystan Glodrydd - great great grandson of the founder of one of the five Royal Tribes of Wales - the dynasty of Rhwng Gŵy a Hafren (between Wye & Severn), was prince of Maelienydd (Llandrindod - Knighton - Bishops Castle area) and was also called "Rex de Delvain" - *King* of Elfael (Builth - Cascob - Hay-on-Wye area) *(cf map p 12).*

The lower drawings on this and on adjacent pages are of the Abbey Ruins made between 1997- 2000 by CPAT. (4)[12] *There is a masons mark on the drawing on page 21 for which there is a key in the borders of pages* 36-7.

Pillar base

Why would a man like this want a French monastic order to build a cathedral sized Abbey on his field and allow them to farm up his Welsh valleys especially when French Normans were already threatening from the Marches to the East? Not that Cadwallon's first abbey was as big as the eventual 13th century edifice.

Cadwallon was no ordinary Welsh *squire*. Although loyal to his dynasty, as Lord of Maelienydd,[13] he also kept the peace with the King of England thus bringing an era of stability and prosperity to this war-like country. The year before he founded Abaty'r Cwmhir he and his brother, Einion Clud from Elfael, attended the King's Council at Gloucester as part of the entourage of their uncle Lord Rhys from South West Wales to negotiate a peace deal and was able to offer tribute of a massive £333.6s.8d in cash to the king instead of the usual 1000 head of cattle (worth over £1 milllion in 2014!). As well as being in touch with the King of England and having cash available he was also in contact with Churchmen. A few months before founding our Abbey he protected Giraldus Cambrensis, the Archdeacon of Brecon, from attacks by local clergy (!) and supported him in a conflict between bishops over Ceri. The next year, after his brother's mysterious death, Cadwallon met Henry II, the English King at Oxford as Prince of most of the land between Gwye and Hafren (Severn) like his great grandfather. "At the end of the twelfth century the area between the Severn and Wye was at its zenith, a golden age (*ruled by*) the greatest native prince who held sway in the precariously positioned lands of the old Welsh kingdom"[14] Tinboeth Castle (cf p 199) just to the north of Llanbister would have been his major military defence and he probably built our local Castle on Beddugre Hill for the same purpose.

Stone carving of crowned head - perhaps of Cadwallon?

These were turbulent times. The next day you could be dead or married to your enemy's daughter. Wealth and power were acquired by the simple but effective means of taking it by force - and what was won by the sword could just as easily be lost by someone else's sword. Cadwallon was murdered a few years after he founded our Abbey by Roger Mortimer and his men in 1179 whilst under Royal Protection after another visit to King Henry II's Court. For this deed the King threw even Roger Mortimer into prison - which was the law, but also reflects the status that Cadwallon had with the King. Cadwallon's court was, perhaps, held to the south across Maelienydd at the uniquely naturally defended Cwm Aran Castle (cf p 177), on the stream of that name, and along the Llanbister Road road. Poets had always been welcomed there.

The upper drawings of escavated stonework from the Abbey were made in 1894 for Stephen Williams (5)

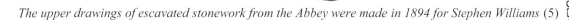
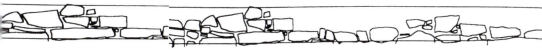

Coat of Arms of Cadwallon from Elystan Glodrydd

On his death in 1179 a long elegy was written by Cadwallon's own resident bard, Cynddelw Brydydd Mawr who wrote:

> *Since now, by stroke of battle-axe cut down,*
> *Our princely lion-monarch is laid low,*
> *A chief supreme, from ancient sov'reigns sprung;*
> *Since our dispenser is in truth no more,*
> *Lord God! the friend of all the poor,*
> *Pillar of Britons, and their sheltering shield…*
> *Let angels guard him to Heav'n's bright abode.*[15]

Ironically, we know of Cadwallon's benefaction of land for the Abbey only by report[16] and have no copy of his original deed of endowment. It would seem that the Norman Roger Mortimer made sure that Welsh Cadwallon's Foundation Charter disappeared and didn't mentioned it in his own bequest of 1200! (cf pic 19) Later, after a Welsh Resurgence in 1215 the English King John confirms only the gift of Maredudd ap Maelgwyn,[17] Cadwallon's grandson which, however, certainly included Cadwallon and his brother Einion Clud's gifts.

The Cistercians were rapidly expanding right across Europe and were welcome in Wales because their monasteries seemed like the old Celtic *Clasau*. Each abbey was directly responsible to the head Abbot in Citeaux, Burgundy, France, whereas those of the French Norman Benedictines were governed by the local abbot and so subject to the corruptions of the local powers that be - and the English King (cf page 44). The Cistercians were called the White Monks because they wore undyed sheeps wool suggesting innocence. They also set out to be self sufficient growing their own food rather than take tithes or death duties from the general population. As part of their estate management skills they also developed sheep farming and the wool trade. They were worth having around.

There were already at least half a dozen Cistercian Abbeys in Wales including Strata Florida (1164). So the idea of having an Abbey on your land was current. But all so far were founded by incomer Normans. However, as Rhys ap Gruffydd strengthened his hold over Y Deheubarth (South Wales) as well as Ceredigion he assumed responsibility for the premier Welsh Abbey of Whitland in Pembrokeshire. He was also cousin and neighbour to Cadwallon at Cwmwd Deuddwr. There was a need for Welsh Founders and if the 1143 attempt to found Abbey Cwmhir had succeeded it would have been the first Welsh Abbey. In 1176 it was second to Strata Marcella (1172) north of Welshpool and Cwmhir's first known Abbot was the Welshman Meurig (d.1184).

The fact that the Cistercians welcomed Welsh Abbots and monks (you could say provided employment) and also educated the sons of Welsh freemen meant they contributed much to the local area. Their monasteries also provided a consecrated burial place for family members of the Welsh Lords. In 1234 a descendant of the founder and a monk/benefactor, Cadwallon ap Maelgwyn was buried in the Abbey as was Mabli, or Mabel, whose coffin lid was found in the Abbey and is now kept in St Mary's Church. She would have been a member of an influential Welsh Lord's family perhaps

The square holes are for scaffolding crossbeams or putlogs and may have been filled with wood after use.

living at Perth Mabli (today Berthably) close to Castle Hill in Nantmel. (There was also a female Welsh Saint Mabli with a church dedicated to her still today at Llanvapley near Abergavenny[18]). The Floriated Cross down the centre of her tomb from the thirteenth century has beautiful Lombardic style letters on each side which are often difficult to decipher. It also looks as if the local stonemason ran out of space for his letters and had to abbreviate some of the words in the lower part – although contractions were common in medieval documents:-

Engish:	here	lies	M a
Latin:	h I C I A C E T		M A-

(6)

ntractions:	- B L I	c A I e P P I C I E T	D E O
tin:	- B L I	cujus Animae Propi c I e - tur	D E O
glish:	- b e l	on whose Soul, merciful,	may God be

How historians worked this out see page 293

The earliest reliable record (1849) by Rev CW Rees has no doubt about the gender of Mabli. He writes in his record of the first escavation, "It is not known who this Mabli was, there not being any particulars of *the lady* recorded".[19] There is no known Abbot of the name Mabli[20] (cf p 300) and in his article in Archaeologia Cambrensis, Rees is very clear that Mabli's coffin lid was found on the west side of the north-easternmost pier. It was already broken into two parts and was 18"- 24" above the tomb suggesting that the lid had been previously removed.[21] Also that "Not far from that spot, were also the remains of several monks". We know for sure of two burials in the Abbey (above) and there could have been other benefactors and local lords - not to mention many of the Abbots, and we know of sixteen, who could have been buried there. Rees also says "The workmen also turned up a great many human bones[22] - so there were originally many burials. Wilson's new Hall was finished in 1833 and made from the clearance of the Abbey site so it is unlikely that there would have been any tombs un-opened in 1836[23] in which an Abbot's skeleton could be found.

Rog Mortimer (active 1174 - d 1214) - Marcher Lord

Roger Mortimer was the first Marcher Lord to have an influence on the Abbey of Cwmhir as political power swung from the Welsh Princes to the Marcher Lords for the first time. Having killed its founder in 1179, he attacked Maelienydd bringing it under his control, reinforced by rebuilding Cym - Aran Castle and assuming the patronage of Cadwallon's foundation at Cwmhir. As a result, three years later, the monks upped and left. According to the *Brut y Tywysogyon* (History of the Princes*)*, "the community of Cwmhir went to reside at Cymer" (*cf p 31)* where 'Grifini'[24] a cousin of Llywelyn Fawr wanted to found an abbey. Cymer was officially a daughter house of Cwmhir.

However Roger Mortimer appointed his own, but Welsh, Abbot Rhiryd to Cwmhir Abbey and confirmed the rights of the Abbey giving lands in the north west to support the monks "for the salvation of the souls not only of himself, his parents, his wife Isabel, his sons and daughters and his followers, but also of those of his men who lost their lives in this very conquest".[25] The lands, towards Llangurig may have been chosen to provide a defence against Welsh invaders from the West. Roger Mortimer was an extremely wealthy man[26] with three Abbeys under his patronage: Wigmore in Herefordshire, St.Victor-en-Caux in France and now Abbeycwmhir in Maelienydd so there is the possibility that he was the provider of the building here that went up in the next three decades and whose ruins remain today. Could it be that his spiritual interests and concern for the "men who lost their lives" included this form of attonement for his murder of the founder?

The family name "Mortimer" means 'dead sea' or 'dead pool' - so called either because they came from the Norman French town of Mortemer sur Eaulne - which overlooks a stagnant bend in the River Eaulne, or because a knightly family Crusader had been to the Dead Sea. Eventually Roger became gravely ill and bought the right from King John for his son, Hugh, to inherit his estates before he died which he did in June 1214. When Hugh himself died in 1227 his brother Ralph inherited Wigmore and married the Welsh *Gladys "Ddu"* ferch Llewelyn (who had *"dark-eyes"*), the daughter of Llewelyn ap Iorwerth and Tangwysti ferch Llymarch - which didn't stop him going to war against her father and his nephew Llywelyn - ap Gruffydd!

- Close up of Roger Mortimer's seal.

The charter states, towards its conclusion, that *"the grantor has given to the monks all the land within the aforesaid defined boundaries together with the woods, meadows, streams and pasture and every liberty saving only the beast and birds of his forest, and also common pasture in the whole of Maelienydd and Gwrtheyrnion (cf map p 12), saving only the grantor's fortifications and saving the ancient vills, meadows, and cornfields of grantor and his men. The monks are to be for ever free of every kind of tax and annoyance and secular custom throughout the grantor's lands"*.[27]

As Time Goes by - The Abbey

The earliest charter of Cwmhir Abbey to survive - 1200 AD
- nearly a lampshade!

Rog de Mort Mary

Maelienydd

Ecclesiie beate Marie

- hir

Cwm -

Crychel

Clywedog

Haber Nant Llanerch Fraith

Some parchment bought to make a lampshade in Battle, Sussex in 1956 was fortunately considered to be too small - measuring only 200 x 230 mm. But suspecting that it might be important it was given to University College Library, London where it was recognised as the earliest known charter of the Abbey of Cwmhir.[28]

It was the grant by Roger Mortimer in 1200 AD (modern date) the first regnal year of King John. It actually says *"the Sixth day before the Ides of March of 1199"*. Much of it confirms the lands already held by the Abbey which it describes in great detail using mainly river and stream names to indicate the boundaries - most of these are recognizable today. The Charter is in Medieval Latin in which the monks were literate but perhaps because of the high cost of parchment, shorthand was used in the form of super and sub scripts and abbreviations. For example **Rog de Mort Mari-** Means *Rogerus de Mortuo Mari* the Latin name for Roger Mortimer. Another shorthand is ***ecclie bate marie*** (Top Right) which when expanded in Latin means *ecclesie beate Marie in Cwm Hir* or Church of the Blessed Mary in Cwmhir. Names were also spelt differently in the past, often making understanding difficult or impossible. Here we find *Melenid* for Maelienydd, *Cum Hyr* for Cwm Hir; *Clawedauc* for Clewedog; *Haber Nant Llanerch Freit* for Llannerchfraith and *Kregel* for Crychell. Sometimes you just have to guess!

(7; Calligraphy 8)

The charter was counter signed by the Abbot of Wigmore and the scribe or scrivener was Welsh!

19

The Turbulent History

1176 — Cadwallon ap Madog, Founder. (d 1179) Brothers & Sons.

1215 — Llywelyn ab Iorwerth, *The Great* (d 1240) Gwynedd

1262 — Llywelyn ap Gruffydd P*rince of Wales* (d 1282) Gwynedd

1401 — Owain Glyndwr (d 1416) Gwynedd

1537 — Abbot John Glyn (1535-7)

1644 — Charles I (d 1649) and Royallist Sir Richard Fowler (d 1686)

1200 — Roger Mortimer (d 1215) Wigmore

1240 — Ralph Mortimer (d 1246) Wigmore

1282 — Edmund Mortimer (d 1304) Wigmore

1405 — Henry IV (d 1413) England

1536-9 — Henry VIII (d 1547) England

1644 — Oliver Cromwell (d 1658). Attack led by Colonel Myddleton.[29]

[10]

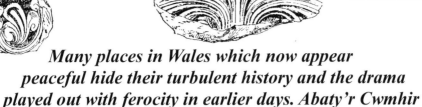

As Time Goes by - The Abbey

Many places in Wales which now appear peaceful hide their turbulent history and the drama played out with ferocity in earlier days. Abaty'r Cwmhir is one of these places still haunted by old spirits - John Davies, Abbeycwmhir Heritage Trust.[30]

On the chart opposite the Tympanum of Christ Ascending (upper right) represents the Abbey which was fought over for centuries. It is now in the wall of Home Farm.

The arrows show the main changes of political hands influencing or controlling the Abbey as they followed each other (Left-Right, Right-Left). Green represents the Welsh Princes and the Abbey itself, Blue the Mortimer Marcher Barons, Red the English Kings and Brown the Parliamentarians. (A fuller account follows on the next pages and on heraldy in note 29 on page 279).

Here is a summary:-

Cadwallon ap Madoc founder of the Abbey in 1176 was murdered by **Roger Mortimer** in 1179 who then invaded Maelienydd, confirmed the Abbey's lands and gave some of his newly conquered territory in his Charter of 1200 (cf p 19).

In 1215 Llywelyn ab Iorworth, The Great, (d 1240) (cf p 20) eventually brought peace with the Marcher Lords and the King of England. It was in his lifetime that the Abbey building whose ruins survive was built. On his death the Welsh Lords rebelled and King Henry III imposed **Ralph Mortimer** on Maelienydd in **1240**. However he died a few years later and in the same year (1246) as Llywelyn's son and successor, Dafydd.

It would be a few years - until **1262** - for **Llewleyn ap Gruffyd, *Ein Lliew Olaf* Our Last Leader,** (cf p 24) to gain control and be acknowledged as Prince of Wales. He was not the son of Dafydd but the grandson of Llewelyn the Great by a different wife, Tangwystl. He was killed in **1282** allowing **Edmund Mortimer (d 1304)** & others to rout the Welsh army (cf pp 27-30).

In **1401** there was a new uprising by **Owain Glyndwr** (cf p 32) who "spoiled and defaced" the Abbey for its loyalty to the Mortimers. He, in turn was defeated by **Henry IV's** army in **1405.**

At the time of **Abbot John Glyn, Henry VIII** initiated the Dissolution or Supression of the Monasteries starting with the small ones like Abbeycwmhir from **1536/7** and moving on to the larger ones in **1539**. Three monks stayed till the end living in a Monaughty or Monks House somewhere.

In the next Century, the **Royalists** ensconced themselves in the Abbey owned by **Richard Fowler** in **1644** where they were successfully attacked by the **Parliamentarians** led by Colonel Myddleton. Afterwards **Richard Fowler** (cf p 55) worked for Oliver Cromwell and the Parliamentarians. The Abbey remained in Fowler hands for nearly 266 years. Richard Fowler built a hunting Lodge at Devannor.

Masons mark 9 *cf Key around pages 36-7.*
robbed pillar *robbed pillar*

An Abbey sometime in Marchia Walliae which helped develop the idea of Welsh Nationhood (Pura Wallia).

As Time Goes by - The Abbey

The Marcher Lords

Part of Wigmore Castle in 2008 (13)

Roger Mortimer 2nd Earl of March (d 1360) in the Robes of the Order of the Garter (14)

After Edward I's conquest of Wales in 1282 "the March or Marches, the long North-South border, stayed fully independent for a further three hundred years. So for five hundred years in all it was outside the king's rule with a make-up unique in Europe. The March consisted of a group of forty or so fiefdoms administered as huge private mini-states or feudal demesnes by individual Marcher Lords, rebellious military adventurers who could establish local parliaments and courts, create forests, confiscate estates at will, maintain private gaols and gallows. Marcher Lords could even build castles, elsewhere a jealously guarded royal privilege, and mint their own coins. Indeed, they could wage private wars, against the Welsh and also against one another. They were miniature kings, administering laws, establishing market-towns, maintaining chanceries. Only when there was no heir did royal writ obtain, for their lordship then reverted to the Crown. Even on the Anglo-Scottish border...there was no equivalent...The Welsh Marcher Lords believed (falsely) their liberties derived from William the Conqueror's royal grant." [31]

Above Left: *Cwmhir Abbey ruins Circa 1994 - 5*

Below Left *Cwmhir Abbey ruins 2010*

Right: *'Wigmore Abbey in 2008* (15)

Llywelyn ab Iowerth - *Fawr* - "The Great" (Active 1200 - d 1240)

Since the building of Offa's Dyke the awareness of being 'in Wales' had increased and the reputation of Rhodri the Great (active 844 - d 877) who had ruled from Anglesey to Gower anticipated the possibility of a united Wales. But one of the main difficulties in doing so was the Welsh Law of inheritance which decreed that an estate must be democratically divided amongst all sons which resulted in disunity and dispersion. But without some unity there could be no peace or prosperity. It was fortunate for Llywelyn son of Iowerth Drwyndwn, of the all important Line of Rhodri the Great, that he was an only son. But the previous generation were still alive - for a while.

Llywelyn's climb to greatness started by disposing of his uncles Rhodri and David. After trying to marry Rhodri's widow he gained greater political advantage by marrying Joan the illegitimate daughter of King John of England in 1209, which, later on, didn't prevent him allying himself with the barons who forced John to sign the Magna Carta, the beginning of democracy and the principles of human rights.

"Leolin(us) moriens" Llywelyn dying - with his two sons. The eldest, Gruffudd by Tangwystl, and the father of Llywelyn ap who became Prince of Wales and Dafydd by Joan, daughter of King John of England who he nominated as the future Prince of Wales. (Drawing by Matthew Paris in Chronica Majora) (16)

Llywellyn only allowed himself to be called Princeps Norwalliae - Prince of North Wale or Gwynedd and sometimes Lord of Aberffraw where he held his court. He was also the first to call himself Lord of Snowdonia. But by 1218 he was supreme in most of Wales as well as in his hereditary lands and was so recognised by King Henry III of England. He was therefore able to bring a period of relative peace and prosperity to Wales (1213 to 1240) especially after King John's death in 1216.

Under him building and literature flourished brilliantly - including the building of the longest Abbey in the country at Cwmhir *"No chirch in Wales is seene of such lengh"*[32] - also described as "sumptuous" by a contemporary[33]. The main construction period of the building whose ruins survive is likely to have been between 1200 and 1231. The only grant we know Llywelyn gave to Abbeycwmhir was in 1226 of land at Cause Castle, Montgomery and Caer Eionion near Welshpool.

One item the Abbey provided for Llywelyn Fawr was horses, "two colts of their superior breed", possibly Spanish crossed with Barb Arabs or Andalusians. Introduced to Powys a century earlier, they were light, clever and sure footed and part of Llywelyn's military strategy to invest in cavalry.

The Abbey certainly had many monks at this time. It is documented that in 1227 the Abbot took fifty senior advisors from Cwmhir Abbey to New Radnor to resolve a dispute with Strata Marcella Abbey, north of Welshpool, over adjacent lands around Cwm Buga near Staylittle. The Abbey was planned for sixty[34] but how many were left behind? A few years later in 1239 a Ralph Tosny, having failed to establish an Abbey in Devon, provided for thirteen additional monks at Abbey Cwmhir.[35] That makes seventy three monks plus, say, 150 lay brothers which makes 223 mouths to feed. Those carts of produce would have been rattling into the village.

As this great abbey grew towards completion the English King Henry III gave it a good deal of attention. This has been interpreted as an attempt to thwart Lywelyn's plan to make Cwmhir Abbey his national cathedral where his son Dafydd would be crowned "Prince of Wales. In 1214 and 1229 King Henry curried favour with the Welsh Abbot ("A") by giving Royal Writs of protection to the Abbey but in 1231 burned the Grange of Carnaff and threatened to burn down the Abbey itself because a "friar" or monk had directed English troops into an ambush near Hay-on-Wye allegedly at the behest of Llywelyn. "....the King speedily went to the Abbey, whose friar had betrayed the soldiers and in revenge for such criminal conduct, plundered and burned the grange belonging to the Abbey, and ordered the abbey itself to be similarly plundered and destroyed by fire. But the Abbot of the place, that he might save the buildings, which had been erected to such very great expense and labour, gave the King three hundred marks, and thereby assuaged his indignation."[36]

The Abbey was saved but the money to complete it was gone - as the ruins show to this today. The coronation of Dafydd was moved to Strata Florida in 1238 - to which Abbey Llewelyn gave funds and help. In 1232 King Henry III gave Abbey Cwmhir a more generous Writ of Protection in an attempt to buy its support against Llywelyn Fawr. Ironically it was in the same year that the Pope gave the Abbey the right to administer the sacraments to the local lay people because it is "in a mountainous district, remote from parish churches" [37] – also giving it more of the function of a Cathedral!

Shortly afterwards, in 1234, the last descendant of Cadwallon ap Madog, Cawallon ap Maelgwyn of Maelienydd who had become a monk here[38] died and was buried in the Abbey.

Llywelyn Fawr spent his last two years at Aberconwy Cistercian Abbey having taken the monastic habit and where his body was *honourably entombed*. A Cistercian source wrote that "he kept peace for men of religion" [39]

This was a fruitful time for Wales: the Mabinogion was probably composed during his era and the poetry of ten Bards has survived and many others are known. Prydydd y Moch (The Great Maker) wrote of Llywelyn:

Seal of Llewelyn the Great
(17)

Well known it is that thy long hand never falters

As it bestows the red and the yellow gold.[40]

God made thee braver than any man that breathes -

Most liberal, too, as far as the sun's course extends:

And in thee the generous deed is reborn. [41]

Base of Llewelyn's sarcophagus now at Gwydir Chapel, Llanrwst (18)

Abbeycwmhir Community Book

Llywelyn ap Gruffydd - *Ein Llyw Olaf - Our Last Leader* - "The Last" (active 1246 - d 1282)

Coronet of the Prince of Wales. Llywelyn's was assimilated into the English Crown Jewels in the shrine of Edward the Confessor in Westminster Abbey (19 Royal Collection)

Llewellyn ap Gruffydd, whose death on December 11th is remembered every year[42] around the *carreg goffa* or memorial slate in the Cwmhir Abbey ruins, was the second and last Welshman to be acknowledged as the Prince of Wales (*Tywysog Cymru*) by all the Principality of Wales and the English King, Henry III. Llywellyn Fawr had never called himself by that title but had arranged with the Pope and the King for his son David to be so called. But it was Llewellyn ap Gruffydd who became the last Prince of an independent Wales before it was conquered by Edward I and he was buried at Cwmhir Abbey - probably. Abbeycwmhir is thus able to play a part in the creation of the idea of the nation of "Wales" and through the annual celebration of his life and death. (cf p 138)

The first Prince of Wales, David ap Llywelyn, only lived for six years after his father's death and had no heir and so in 1246 came the chance for Llywelyn ap Gruffydd (The Last). Inheriting the "fiery & enterprising spirit" of his father[43] (who had recently died trying to escape down the Tower of London on bed linen) he set out to do battle with and then imprison his own brothers, Rhodri and Owain on his way to supremacy. By 1258 he had received the homage and fealty of the minor Welsh chieftains and styled himself "Prince of Wales".

In 1262 he re-took Cefnllys Castle while Roger Mortimer's (d 1282) men were rebuilding and adding to it after an attack by the men of Maelienydd.[44] He then went on to take the castles of Bleddfa, Knucklas, Norton and Presteigne continuing south to make his final southern boundary just outside Abergavenny. They were described as "the jubilant men of the hills" in a private letter of the time.[45]

In 1263 the last Welsh prince, Gwenwynwyn of Powys, submitted and in 1267 in the Treaty of Montgomery, King Henry III acknowledged Llywelyn's right to the title of "Prince of Wales" having already received his homage and fealty in the presence of the Papal Legate Ottobon who wrote of his great rejoicing at the reconciliation of the king and this "great and puissant member of the English realm"[46]. Llywelyn also had to pay 25,000 marks up front with annual installments of M3000!

"The unity of the Prince"[47] lasted for nine years - the longest period Wales had ever been under

The Situation after the Treaty of Montgomory
Llywelyn ap Gruffudd's principality;
territories he conquered; his vassals;
Marcher Barons; King of England.

As Time Goes by - The Abbey

(21)

the rule of a single prince. This "Wales" was the "The Principality" which excludes some lands along today's Hereford and Shropshire border and also excludes South Wales, though not the Valleys[48] - from Chepstow to Pembroke and Carmarthen which was still under the control of Marcher Lords or the English Crown. (cf map opposite)

1274 was the crucial turning point as it was the year Edward I was crowned King of England. Llywelyn didn't go to the Coronation nor did he swear fealty to the new king in retaliation for his harbouring his escaped and rivalrous brothers in his court. Llywelyn also provoked the King by arranging to marry Eleanor de Montfort from one of the most powerful baronial families in England. Trouble was also brewing with the church, Llywelyn was in dispute with his distant cousin Einion, Bishop of St Asaph, an appointee of the English King over some land, and in conflict with the Archbishop of Canterbury defending the rights of the *Walenses* (Welsh) to be judged by *Welsh Law*[49] This led to an official curse on *Welsh Law a*nd Llywelyn's excommunication for disobedience to the King.

In his support the Welsh Abbot of Cwmhir Abbey wrote, with others, to the Pope in 1274 asking him to order the Archbishop of Canterbury not to excommunicate Llywelyn because "*the prince, has shown himself protector, not only of the Order (Cistercians), but of each and every order in Wales*". An excommunicated person cannot be buried in an Abbey or any sacred ground.

In 1277 Edward invaded Wales followed by a new castle building spree - even as far West as Aberystwyth. Llywellyn was obliged to give way and signed the Treaty of Aberconway and paid homage and his dues to Edward. But he was not crushed and still held a position which many English earls might have envied, including the respect and honour of Edward who hosted his wedding to Eleanor de Montfort at Worcester Cathedral in the presence of the Queen and a *brilliant asssemblage* of English magnates. "Edward bore the cost of festivities and conveyed the bride's luggage as far as Oswestry"![50]

Edward I's rule through his agents and the use of English Law was very unpopular and when he made incursions in Gwynedd in March 1282, Llywellyn's brother, Dafydd, responded successfully - inspiring much of Wales down through Ceredigion to the South Wales Vallies.[51] But it wasn't until June that Llywelyn himself joined in and set out to consolidate his rule by seeking homage and fealty from the people of Breconshire and the Valleys and perhaps also with the his family relations, the Marcher Lords, meeting at Builth Castle.

It is recorded that he came to territory "situated between an Abbey of the Cistercian order called Cwmhir and a town called Inlamake (Llangamach (Wells)[52] - Cefn-y-Bedd (old name for Cilmery) on the Irfon with Llangaston (Church) on the corner. "He sent his men with his steward to receive homage of the men of Brycheiniog and the prince was left with a few men with him."[53] All he needed for a meeting at Builth Castle where he had been led to believe he would receive homage.

The Dolgellau Chalice - made from the melted down matrices of seals and other regalia of Llywelyn and family. He'd left some at Cymer Abbey, Cwmhir's daughter house, befor his last-campaign. National Museum of Wales. (22 Royal Collection)

27

There are many conflicting reports about what happened next - most of them written some time afterwards and some from the distance of East Anglia where Llywelyn's daughter was imprisoned as a nun. Although one says he was killed in battle and another beheaded in front of his army, there is a concensus that he was killed away from his army and the battle field.

There were three forces present around Builth: the Welsh defenders and Llywelyn's army; the son's of his cousin Roger Mortimer (d 1282), Edmund and Roger (of Chirk) heading the Marcher Lords and the Royal Montgomery Army representing the King of England. Which side the Marcher Lords would be on was uncertain.

Builth Wells is marvellously defended by its natural position behind three rivers, the Wye, the Irfon (or Orewin) and the Duhonw across which there would have been bridges or fords; and from behind the castle the Garth and the Eppynt hills. Llywelyn would have come south either through Gwertheyrnion or west of the Wye skirting away to Cilmery; the Royal Montgomery Army would have come down the ancient trackway above the Ithon and camped at the site of the Royal Welsh Show ground; the Herefordshire Marchers would have approached above the Wye from Clifford and Hay in the South. The area was swarming with soldiers.

An extremely powerful group of Marcher lords were present including the new Constable of Builth Castle, Lord John Gifford of Clifford. It was not unreasonable to expect that they might be on Llywelyn's side and one account says that he may have been tricked into thinking this. He, his chief minister and a few men may have approached them at Builth Castle on the evening of the 10th December, 1282, but either the negotiations failed or they were turned away - and so he was separated from his army base. A local story says he visited the blacksmith, Madoc Min, to have his horse's shoes reversed to fool any following troops and then set out for the safety of his own Aberedw Castle. As this might be anticipated by his enemies he hid in St.Cewydd's hermitage cave nearby - which has since been known as Llywelyn's Cave. It is claimed that on the morning of the 11th he attended Mass in St.Cewydd's Church (although not necessarily taking the sacriments because he was excommunicated) and then headed back towards his army at Cilmery but had the problem of getting across the rivers, past Builth Castle and all the troops in the area.

It was known that Merlin had prophesied that Llywelyn would ride, crowned, through the middle of West– Chepe, London. So Edward ordered the head to be ironically crowned with a silver coronet. A Crown of Ivy would have made him a King of Outlaws. (23)

He was killed by a Shropshire soldier Stephen Francton who didn't know who he was. Later he was recognised and beheaded by Robert Body but his head was taken to Rhuddlan in North Wales to show the King by Roger Mortimer of Chirk. From there it was sent to Anglesey to boost morale from there to be paraded in the streets of London. An important victory for the King. A major defeat for the leaderless Welsh who were completly routed the next day somewhere between the Orewin (Irfon) Bridge and Cefn-y-Bedd or Cilmery two miles away.

What happened to Prince Llywelyn's Body?

According to the Chronicle of Florence of Worcester "the body of the prince, headless and *dismembered*, was buried in the Abbey of Cwmhir by the Cistercian Order",[54] but this is not corroborated by any of the many other contemporary reports. There seems to be some doubt at least in the mind of the Archbishop of Canterbury since he wrote several times to the Arch-Deacon of Brecon "to inquire and certify if the body of Llywelyn had been buried in the Church of Cwmhyr?"[55] His recent excommunication may have been on his mind and there is no record of a reply.

If evidence could be found that he repented at the time of his death then the request for his absolution from excommunication could be granted. The result seems ambivalent as evidence that he did receive last rights was found but so was an incriminating letter traitorous to the King of England hidden in his clothes - along with the matrix for his privy seal.

The head, we know, ended up on a spike at the Tower of London where it was said to have lasted *incorruptably* for fifteen years. The body could have ended up in several places - like a saint's relics.

There are some good reasons why his body may not have been buried at Abbeycwmhir. Firstly, Builth castle already had a pro Mortimer Constable now loyal to the King and after the routing of the Welsh army the area around Builth would have had a very strong Royalist presence. How could the Welsh monks, who were on the losing side, have obtained the body? Secondly, for the Royalists to allow a Welsh Abbey to entomb their most popular leader would be politically unwise as it would be creating a shrine to him and a rallying point for Welsh independence.

Edward I, as well as being ruthless towards the Welsh princes and their children, was a pious king and would have insisted on Christian burial and probably in Wales, but preferably somewhere private in a monastic building, perhaps, where the owners were the King's friends. Another tradition has grown up around Llanrhymny Hall in Cardiff where a stone coffin in the basement has long been attributed to Llewelyn[56]. Supporting this is the fact that in 1404 Owain Glyndwr, whilst destroying many Abbeys, spared Llanrymny but had sacked Abbeycwmhir in 1401 - which would be unlikely if his predecessor, a Prince of Wales, was buried there.

Llywelyn the Great was buried before the high altar at the Abbey of Aberconway and his son David nearby. Out in the old Abbot's garden, not sacred land, is a stone to the memory of "Lewelinus

Llywelyn ap Gruffyd, Tywysog Cymru.

The Carreg Coffa close to the position of the high altar at Cwmhir Abbey.
(cf p 138) (24)

The common procedure of dismemberment, by a doctor, of the bodies of saints and aristocrats was at its peak at this time and was forbidden by the Pope in a decree a few years later.[58] Devout and noble people at this time (and for many centuries to come) often had their hearts removed after death and their body's dismembered to enable them to be buried in several places, often near a saints *many* relics [59]; perhaps this last Welsh Prince was laid to rest throughout all Wales with his essential life spirit still circulating from the Heart of Wales at Abbeycwmhir:

> "... *his blood, and the blood of his Wales,*
> *The Wales of St David and King Hywel and God.*"   Gwennallt [60]

"It is said that had Llywelyn lived for just two days more all those of the Welsh tongue would have turned to his cause."[61]

Llywelyn had no male heir and his wife Eleanor de Montfort had died whilst giving birth to their daughter Gwenllian whom Edward imprisoned as a nun at Sempringham Abbey in Lincolnshire for the rest her life.

His still rebellious brother, Dafydd, was pursued to the side of Cadr Idris and then dragged or *drawn* behind a horse to Shrewsbury where he was *hung* until nearly dead, then castrated and disembowled, beheaded and then cut into *quarters* - a traitors death. Goliath won.

Coronets and Possessions

Edward was determined to stamp out all signs of princely independence especially it's most potent symbols. King Edward, himself went to Abbeycwmhir's daughter house, Cymer, to seize Llywelyn's Coronet which he had left there in the care of the monks on the way to his last campaign. The coronet was then put with the English Crown Jewels in the Shrine of Edward the Confessor at WestminsterAbbey.[62] Llywelyn's wealth was confiscated and guarded by "40 men from Shropshire" [63] at Castell y Bere just south of Cymer. The vital symbols of his identity, his and his family's seal matrixes, were also seized and sent to London to be melted down by the King's goldsmith, Nigel [64] who commisioned his neighbour, Nicholus from Herford near Chester, to create one of the largest and finest medieval chalices still in existence today (p 27) and stamped his name on the base.[65] He was commissioned to take it to the King, then at Caernarvon, but somehow it went missing and found its way to Cymer Abbey. There it was safely kept until the dissolution of the monastery in 1536 when the quick thinking monks hid it amongst boulders on the mountainside outside Dolgellau. There it remained until 1890 when some miners discovered it and sold it for 50 shillings. It has since been known as the Dolgellau Chalice and is now kept in the National Museum of Wales in Cardiff - but it is still owned by the Queen from whom we had to get permission to reproduce it in our book!

25. Cymer Abbey's Abbots Seal showing the Abbot with Crook and Book - The Rule of St. Benedict .

Other regalia from the House of Gwynedd was also seized by Edward who based his army near Cymer Abbey as Llywelyn had done: the family jewels, the Crown of Arthur, and above all the most cherished relic in Wales, the piece of the true cross known as Y Groes Naid (Cross of Neath) symbol of the Divine protection of the House of Gwynedd. This was taken and paraded through London with the King and Queen and their children in the procession as well as many magnates, the Achbishop of Canterbury and fourteen bishops. Edward prized it so much he took it on his own itineraries.

Cymer

Ruins of Cwmhir's daughter house of Cymer Abbey just North West of Dolgellau. Half the lengh of Mother! (26)

In 1198 'the Community of Cwmhir went to reside at Cymer" states the "History of the Princes" (*Brut y Tywysogyon*) [66] where for several years "Grifini" - as his name appears on the petition to the Cistercian Order - or Gruffudd ap Cynan (d1200), his brother Maredudd and son Hywel had wanted to found an Abbey. So the threat to the Welsh monks from Roger Mortimer, who had killed Cwmhir's founder twenty years before and was invading Maelienydd again, synchronised with that wish. It is unlikely that all the monks left Cwmhir or some may have returned when it was given a new charter and Abbot already by 1200 - by Roger Mortimer.

Cymer is in Gwynedd and it is likely that it's founding was encouraged by its Prince, Llewelyn ab Iorwerth (The Great) who gave his support to that monastery himself in a generous charter in 1209. Later, Llewelyn ap Gruffyd used one of it's Granges as somewhere to stay - some of his chattels being found there after his death, even basing his army there, as did Edward I after him.

An impression of daily life in a Cistercian Abbey (27)

Ora et Labora at Cwmhir Abbey

- The whole of the book of Psalms was recited every week and the day's timetable "Opus Dei" was based on Psalm 119: *"At midnight I will rise to give praise to thee - Because of Thy righteous judgements (Verse 62) and "Seven times a day do I praise thee - Because of Thy righteous judgements"(Verse:64)* making an eight stage <u>Horarium</u> of: **Matins** at Midnight; **Lauds** at dawn - about 3am; **Prime** or first hour - about 6 am; **Terce** at Mid morning - 9am; **Sext** at Midday -12 Noon; **None** at Mid afternoon -3pm; **Vespers** - at the lighting of the lamps - 6pm and **Compline**, night prayer before retiring - at 9pm. In between: manual work!

Owain Glyn Dwr

At the Millennium in AD 2000, Glyndwrs Way, which passes through Abbeycwmhir, was declared a National Trail even though it wasn't opened until 2002 and had been a Powys long distance path since the late 1970's. It was an expected Millennium 600 years before this that inspired Owain Glyndwr to start a Welsh revolt from England, declare himself Prince of Wales - and pay us a visit.

"A thousand years of blessedness" following the Second Coming of Christ *(Revelations 20)* was just what people in Europe longed for after a century which included the Black Death, the Schism of the Church - with one Pope in Rome another in Avignon, the Muslim Turks invading the Balkans, the Peasants' Revolt and recently, at home, the killing of the English King, Richard II, by Bolingbroke who declared himself the new King Henry IV (1399). There was a great deal of unrest.

Welsh Bards were predicting 1400 as this kind of Millennium land mark. Glyndwr declared that he was "appointed by God" to "release the Welsh from Bondage"[67] and had his own "Master of Brut" a professional prophet involved in what Shakespeare's Bolingbroke calls "skimble-skamble-stuff".[68]

Great seal of "Owain by the grace of God, Prince of Wales" enthroned and with the arms of the Gwynedd dynasty - four lions rampant - which he had assumed.(28)

When Glyndwr's neighbour, Sir Reginald Grey of Ruthin, stole some of his land saying "What care we for barefoot Welsh dogs?", the time had come. After taking castles in Denbighshire and being defeated in 1400 his campaign became, for a time, guerrilla warfare by small bands of angry Welshmen and this may be how it came to be that already in Autumn 1401 at Cwmhir Abbey "Al the house was spoilid and defacid" - according to John Leland in 1538.[69] Most Cistercian Abbeys in Wales were damaged by either Glyndwr or King Henry IV over the next twelve years of revolt and suppression, depending on which side they were perceived to be on. Many Cistercians, clergy and local people were initially active supporters of Glyndwr but Abbeycwmhir was a Mortimer Abbey and so was presumably considered an enemy.

However by the next year Glyndwr was sufficiently organised and with a local general, Reece Gethin of Llanwrted,[70] to defeat Edmund Mortimer, representing the King, at the Battle of Bryn Glas at Pilleth close to our Grange of Monaughty. Soon Machynlleth was declared the capital of Wales and his parliament was held there in 1404.

How seriously damaging to an Abbey the *"spoiling and defacing"* of its large stone building can be is doubtful. In the same year the Bishop of Hereford ordained ten monks from Cwmhir abbey, four as Deacons, three as Sub-Deacons and three as Priests in his diocese.[71] Perhaps they left because they saw trouble coming; certainly no more were ordained until Glyndwr was in decline.

Owain ap Gruffyd was a descendant of the Royal House of Powys, Deheubarth and a relative of Gwynedd and derived his name Glyn Dwr from his family estate Glyndyfrydwy in the Dee Valley. Nearby was his main home and Court at Sycharch towards which a bridle path crosses the Berwyn Mountains which, ever since he rode it, has been called Ffordd Owain Glyn Dwr[72]. However the National Trail stops short of this at Welshpool!

After 1412 Glyndwr disappears. Like King Arthur he isn't known to die, but enters the world of myth - of the "men whose time had been - but were yet to be" [73]

As Time Goes By - The Abbey

Corporate Seal of Cwmhir Abbey 1533 (29)

Identity Fraud C 1533

You can just make out in the centre of this damaged seal the Blessed Virgin Mary holding the infant Christ with her right arm and sitting under a gothic style canopy. This is the only Cwmhir Abbey common seal known to have survived. The coat of arms underneath bears the emblems of those who gave financial support to the Abbey after Owain Glyn Dwr's atack[74]. It is particularly elaborate for such a poor monastery and includes the arms of France, England, Anne Mortimer (& de Burgh), her husband, Richard of Cambridge and her son, the Duke of York, as Barons of the March. On the left, in a niche, stands either the Abbot of Cwmhir or St.Bernard, founder of the Cistercians, holding a pastoral crook. The seal matrix was one of the most valuable items in an Abbey and might have a working life of two centuries and was made of copper.

The document the seal was attached to (*below*) was from Abbot Geoffrey Davys (1532-4) to Roger Vaughan of Clyroo, esquire, and his sons appointing them to the office of steward of the lands in the lordships of Elveld (Elfael) and Huntington (Herefordshire) and the parish of Brilley, with an annuity of 13s. 4d.[75]

A seal impression in wax was made with a matrix made either of wood, clay, silver, stone or slate and after 1335, for Cistercian Abbeys, of copper.[76] These were very precious and were kept under lock and key and destroyed on the death of the bearer or in the case of a Cistercian Abbot sent back to Citeaux. So important was an Abbey's seal that it's design had to conform to Regulations laid down at various times by the Cistercian General Chapter and after 1307 English Law required that the Common Seal be kept by the Prior and four monks under the seal of the Abbot. The Corporate or Common Seal was essential for the running of the estate: for agreements with wool merchants or the leasing of land. The Abbot's seal was used as well or separately for major purchases, agreements and charters.

(30)

A Matrix

Cwmhir breaks the Rules

Already by 1522 Cwmhir Abbey had broken the rule by having just two keys and locks to the chest in which the seal (matrix) was kept and so just one monk was required to use it.[77] Just after this the Abbot, Richard Vaughan (or Vayn) was accused of using "the seal secretly, without the assent of the community" to lease out the granges of Carnaf, Mynachdy Poeth, Nant-yr-Arian and others. Nobody did anything about it![78] (31)

Papal Lead Seals from Bulls found at Cwmhir - what was their message?

St. Paul and St Peter on obverse side of all papal bulla - this one found at Abbeycwmhir (32)

In today's Wales dotted with Non-Conformist chapels and disestablished Welsh Churches it is hard to imagine the power of the Roman Pope in the Middle Ages here. But Llywelyn the Great and his successors saw the Pope as their protector against the power of the English crown and as a guarantor of their independence. He obtained Papal support in his bid to make his son Dafydd Prince of Wales and Dafydd himself even attempted to become a vassal of the Pope in the hope of making Wales subject to the Papacy rather than to England! A little later it was the papal legate Ottobuono who negotiated the treaty of Montgomery in which the English King Henry III acknowledged Llywelyn the Last as Prince of Wales in 1267.

Abbeycwmhir reflects some of this relationship through the lead Papal Seals, called bullae (Latin: stud, knob, boss), which were found by Col. John Lionel Philips (Squire 1932 - 1959 cf p 79) who gave a seal of Popes Honorious III and Alexander IV to the National Museum of Wales in 1962, and Thomas Wilson (here 1824-37) who wrote that in 1827 he had found seals of Honorious III & IV. Popes came and went like shops in Middleton Street - in the Thirteenth Century there were 17 Popes and 2 interregnums totalling 5 years when there was no Pope because the Cardinals couldn't agree! One Pope lasted sixteen days.

Pope Honorious III (Papacy:1216-27) in the time of Llywelyn the Great, was a heavy weight who addressed a letter of affection to the Cistercian Order only two days after his installation as Pope. He sent white monks to reform other monasteries and a monk of Rievaulx praised him in verse "Because of him the Order of Citeaux more than others shines."[79] In his speculative poem "The

Far Left: reverse side of the actual seal found at Abbeycwmhir from Papa Honorious III . On the right Giotto's painting illustrating his reputed kindness, indulgence and patience. (33 a,b,c)

Abbot of Cwmhir", Thomas Wilson has Honorious III give Abbot Rhiryd permission to bury next to him in the Abbey his love Mabli (cf p 15) (renamed Orpah) - inspired by his discovery of her tomb close to which he found his seal:

> *'Twas granted, and by Rome's behest*
> *Within the abbey walls should rest*
> *The form of her he loved the best,*
> *And his be placed beside."* [80]

Honoriouis initiated the Fifth Crusade to regain the Holy Land, continued the repression of the Cathar heresy in the south of France, rewarded Simon de Montfort for his inquisition and purportedly wrote a Grimoire of occult knowledge on how to invoke demons, once in the possession of John Dee, whose family lived at Nant y Groes, Pilleth.

As Time Goes by - The Abbey

It was in the reign of the Pope after Honoriuos III, Gregory IX (1227-1241), that the only known and recorded papal bull came to Cwmhir in which the Abbey was granted the privilege of administering the sacraments to the general public - like a cathedral and a parish church, in 1232.

Left: reverse side of the actual seal of Papa Alexander IV found at Abbeycwmhir which was sent by Col. John Lionel Philips (cf p 79) to the National Museum or Wales, Cardiff in 1962.

(34 a, b)

Alexander IV (Papacy:1254 – 1261) during the middle years of Llywelyn the Last. On April 12, 1261 he issued a papal bull for Henry III of England, absolving Henry of oaths taken in the Provisions of Oxford thus causing the Second Barons' War with Simon de Montfort which weakened Henry so that he was obliged to acknowledge Llywelyn as Prince of Wales. He also continued with the suppression of the Cathars and tried to unite the Eastern and Western Churches.

Far left: a cast of the reverse side of a seal of Papa Honorious IV, a cameo and a cartoon.

(35 a,b,c)

Honorious IV (Papacy 1285 – 1287) - whose bull was found in the Abbey in 1827 according to Thomas Wilson. His election was one of the speediest in the history of the papacy due to the urgency of dealing with the Sicilian Vespers - which he did. Otherwise his papacy brought peace to Italy and Europe. Earlier he held the benefice of rector at the church of Berton in the Diocese of Norwich in England, a nation he never visited.

Actual "Henry" denier reading HENRICVS REX from the Cwmhir Hoard (in background right) (36 a, b)

A hoard of coins has also survived and was found in a package inscribed "Anglo-Gallic coins c.1190 from the Abbey" probably when Col. John Lionel Philips was clearing out The Hall around 1959. They are now in the National Museum of Wales, Cardiff. A total of 13 deniers including eight in either the name of Henry II or III and 3 in the name Richard I - all issued in their capacities as Dukes of Aquitaine, Western France, Europe - *and* Kings of England. Perhaps Henry III had them in his pocket when he came to burn down Cwmhir Abbey? The value in the 12th Century would have been 2 -3 contemporary English pence, about a day's pay for an artisan at that time.[81]

Architecture and Design

St Idloes is not a small space. Imagine a building nearly three times as long and much higher
- in our Valley.

(37)

There was a different type of carving of the capitals on each of the columns under each arch of the Abbey and above each of the triple sandstone shafts now to be seen at St Idloes Church at Llanidloes. (cf pp 39 & 50)

The inspiration for the carving came from the south western workshops centered on Wells Cathedral and the Great Church at Glastonbury which were reaching completion at this time.

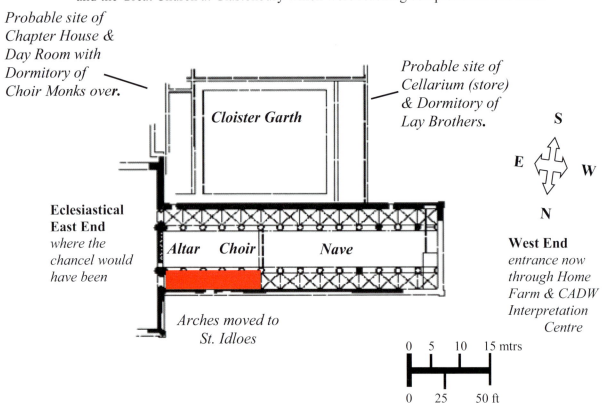

Plan of the Abbey as viewed from the modern village road . (38)
This followed the usual Cistercian plan devised by St Bernard. but it was unusual to build the nave first rather than the chancel - which was never built.

36

As Time Goes By - The Abbey

"A construction of quite astonishing conception.."

It is likely that the first building around 1176 would have been either made of wood or have been a simple stone building in the form of a chancel for the monks to recite the *Ora* but after 1200 this "otherwise poverty stricken community at this remote house was able to embark upon a construction of quite astonishing overall conception….as first laid out the Cwmhir nave was a staggering fourteen bays (*or arches*) in lengh." [82] How did this come about ?

Computer artist's impression of Cwmhir Abbey after 1232 when sacraments like baptism were authorised. The Choir monks would have sat behind the screen at the far end for services and the lay monks would stand in front. No evidence has been found of stone vaulting so the ceiling would have been wooden and flat as at Abbeydore. It was the longest Cistercian nave in Europe and one of the longest in England and Wales. (Computer artist - David Bennet) (39)

The geometric designs around the page are masons marks from the building of the Abbey and can be seen in the ruins at Abbeycwmhir and at Llanidloes. Mark number 9 is on page 21. Clywd -Powys Archaeological Trust has drawings showing the position in the ruins of the others.[83]

Abbeycwmhir Community Book

Devannor Corbel

(40)

Stephen Williams, escavating at the end of the Nineteeth Century,[84] claimed that Grinshill Triasic Sandstone was used for all the dressed stone work and carvings. However recent research suggests that this may not be so.[85] After all it did have to travel some 88 Kilometers on 1215 trackways. Lime came from Dolyhir, Walton, as it does today. But supplies were not always reliable.

Details of pictures on page after next p 42.

(41)

(42)

Fowlers cave - source of the main building stone - Yr Allt Formation (Ordovician) - photographed circa 1953 (43)

Abbey Stones

- Llanbister Princess

Saint Tecla

A Cwmhir door - now the South entrance at St Idloes.

Five arches were taken to St Idloes Church, Llanidloes in 1542

(44)

Abbeycwmhir Community Book

The Lands of the Abbey of Cwmhir
Granges, Farms, & Tracks Connecting
in the context of Castle Power Politics

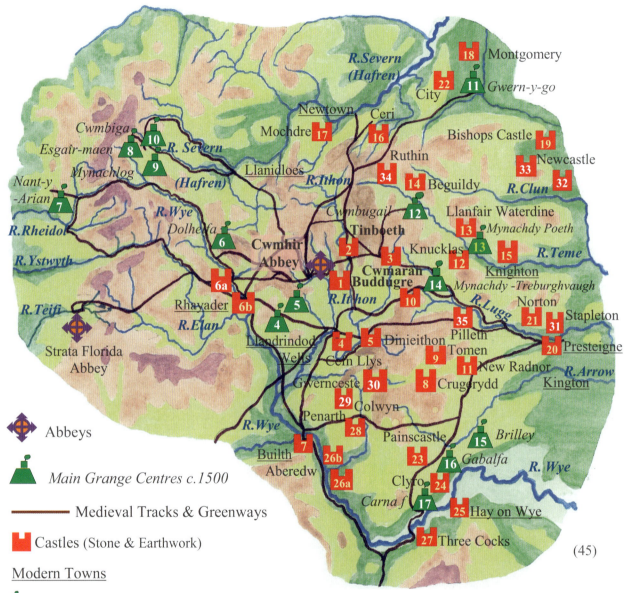

Due to scale of map, Granges 1- 3 are not shown but were at Cwmhir (1) Home Grange of Gollon; (2) Ty Faenor; & (3) Cefn Pawl. Not named are (4) Nantymynach & (5) Rhymney. All would have been groupings of land in each area given to the Abbey since 1176. A list of the lands given up to 1232 are included in the Granges Appendix (cf p 290). Closest, but not all, castles are shown. All listed with Ordnance Survey References in Appendices on pagecs 290-91.

Note: *this map doesn't have every river or stream on it - mainly only those running along medieval boundaries cf map on **page 12**. Modern roads are not shown and only key modern towns.*

(45)

As Time Goes by - The Abbey

The lands of Cwmhir Abbey made a huge triangle straddling the sources of the rivers Wye and Severn close to Plynlimon (Pumlumon) in the north west, across to the south of Montgomery in the north east and then down to Hay-on-Wye in the south.

A Grange could be anything from a mini-monastery with a chapel and even a court as well as a huge estate complex, to a single farm, a small holding or an individual building like a mill or a forge - or even a sheep run. Many were the model farms of the day. The Cistercians requirement for self sufficiency to feed their monks meant they developed into extremely efficient farmers bringing improvements to sheep farming and land and estate management The Granges were called *mynachdy* meaning, in Welsh, monastery from *mynach* meaning monk. In English it becomes *Monaughty* with examples today near Bleddfa or Monaughty Poeth on the Lugg just north of Knighton. [86]

Cwmhir was the highest above sea level of all Cistercian Abbeys in Europe (250 mtrs.) but this meant that the farming at the home grange, called Golon by the 1500s, was limited to sheep rearing and oats so the Abbey had to have a mixed economy and so leaned heavily on the more low lying granges such as the Gabalfa-Carnaf complex in the south on this side of the Wye across from Hay and stretching up to Michaelchurch. (Some farmers here follow this principle today.) There were also productive clusters of lands around Mynachty Poeth north of Knighton and around Hopton, centered on Gwern-y-go. Another significant pastoral property was Nantyrarian Grange in Ceredigion. These were the bread-baskets.

Abbeycwmhir Tapestry, circa 2000.
(46)

This *empire,* all within a day's travel, was managed by the Cellarer who organised the farming to provide food and drink for the monks and for the hospitality of guests. Also for sales, especially of wool, to merchants to raise income. All the business of the Abbey went through his office or *Cellarium*! He also over-saw the hundred or more lay monks or *Conversi* who worked on the farms. This was more like the work of a Chief Executive of a large corporation. No wonder he is often pictured in manuscripts of the time taking a nip from a barrel of wine - for which he was also responsible - in all senses. The spiritual life of the lay brothers was cared for by a spiritual mentor or confessor - a monk appointed as *"Master of the Converse"*. Most of the *conversi* lived and worked on the granges ideally returning to the Abbey for worship on Sunday and great festivals. Some granges had oratories or chapels for the monks - but not open to the public. Perhaps Chapel Field or Chapel Close & Chapel Meadow at Gwern-y-go. Some had Courts of Justice (perhaps Court Farm near Gabalfa, Clyro). [87]

Each Grange had a *Conversus,* or *Granger* or *Master of the Grange*, who was in day to day charge. Each Grange would have accommodation for the conversi to eat and sleep, there would also be agricultural buildings such as barns and water mills as at Nantyarian. Sometimes the Choir Monks helped out. In 1231 at harvest time *"monks and brothers"* reaped the corn" at Cwmhir's Carnaf and Gabalfa Granges by the River Wye.

The Grange farms closest to the Cwmhir Home Grange mentioned as early as 1215 were Cefn Pawl (Kenepawel) which had a fish pool and Ty Faenor (Dynanner) which, it is recorded, paid rents in cash and 28 bushels of oatmeal (valued at 8 old pennies) each year. Llanerchfraith is mentioned as being on the boundary of the estate in Roger Mortimer's Charter of 1200 (cf p 19). The next closest granges were over Camlo Hill at Rhymney Farm and Nant y Mynach(dy) Caravan Park. A little further away were farm granges at Buddugre, Laithdu, Dolygarn and Cwm Nant-du near Llanbadarn Fynydd, Old Neuadd Bank towards Dolfor & Llyngwyn north of Rhayader. (cf pp 290- 291).

The Cistercians practised transhumance - the moving of cattle to higher pastures in the summer- which was common in medieval Wales The term 'hafod' occurs frequently on their lands and the evidence from Cwmhir is that it's Cwmbuga Grange was able to support four hundred kine in summer but only thirty in winter. In Tudor times "summer houses' or 'dairy houses for summer' are described on the former lands of Cymer Abbey. Later the word "hafod" was often used to describe these.

Castles were often close to Granges. They were like Police Stations, but the justice was rougher and the penalties harsher and rival police forces kept taking them over - yesterday! Cadwallon ap Madog may have been the original builder of Buddugre Castle (on the next page).[88] It is a typically Welsh choice of site - on top of a hill. *Buddugre* means *victory* [90] - perhaps over the Normans. There is also the tradition that it comes from Bedd Ygre or "Grave of Ygre" possibly an ancient British chieftain who fell and was buried near this spot. [91]

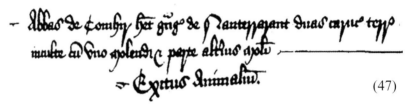

(47)

From the Taxatio Ecclesiastica 1291 which listed the stock of each Grange. You can just make out on the top row:"Abbad de Comby her granges Nant-y-Arian......"

Abbey Stones on the page before last - 38 - 39
Soon after the Dissolution of the Abbey (1537) the destruction of the building began in earnest when five arches from the east end of the northern arcade were removed and taken to Llanidloes in 1542. Inevitably the partially dismantled Abbey became an opportunity for the re-cycling of its stones in neighbouring buildings.

On left hand page 38 :-
Top Left: (40) *Three pictures of the Devannor Corbel - found by Jack Griffiths in some rubble at Devan nor and given to the Radnorshire Museum in 1970. As the face is carved in the Romanesqe style of the 12th century it pre-dates the final building at Cwmhir and so could be the only solid evidence of an earlier stone building.*
Left Centre: (41) *Tympanum from over a door in the Abbey now in Home Farm photographed in 1952*
RCAMHW.
Bottom Left: (42) *Surviving pillar in ruins of Cwmhir Abbey - exterior wall side of southern arched arcade.*
Bottom Right: (43) *Fowlers cave - source of the main building stone . Photographed circa 1953 by Teddy*
Bennett of Tynycoed..

On right hand page 39 (all 44): -
Top Centre: *Carved Female face on a large building stone found under the foundations of Old Vicarage Farm at Llanbister.*
Top Right: *Corbel with carving of a woman's face from above a side door at St.Tecla's (Llan - Degla) Church at Llandegley. St Tecla was a female saint in the 4-5th Century.*
Centre Right: *carvings of foliage on the capitals on top of the pillars at Llanidloes cf pages 28 & 48.*
Bottom Left : *A Cwmhir door - now the South entrance at St Idloes.*
Bottom Right: *One of the five arches taken from Cwmhir Abbey to Llanidloes.*

Some of Cwmhir's Medieval Granges - farms still today.

Cwmbiga Farm now in the Hafren Forest close to the source of the Severn. (48)

Cabalva Farm on the northern bank of the Wye opposite Hay (49)

Nant-y-Arian Grange Mill in the 1980's. The outline of the mill wheel is visible on the right and the leat is traceable on the ground.(50)

Nant-y-Arian Farm near Ponterwyd in 2011. Leat still traceable. (51)

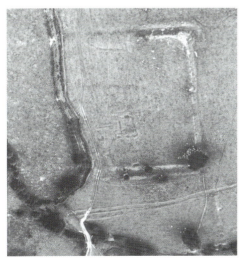

Mynachdy moated enclosure on lands near Llangunllo belonging to Cwmhir Abbey. Aerial photograph 1949. (52)

The dam holding the monks fishpool until 1932 at Fishpool Farm, Abbeycwmhir 2011 (cf p 153 & p 212). (53)

ST BERNARD - ST BENEDICT - BENEDICTINES AND BURGUNDIANS

The Cistercians (cf p 16) were a reform movement from the Benedictines who were founded by **St. Benedict of Nursia** (c.480–547) whose *"Regula Benedicti"* or *Rule* had become the basis of Western monasticism for monks living communally under the authority of an abbot. Several centuries later, perhaps because each abbey was independent, the **Benedictines** had become quite worldly and were used by the Normans for political purposes - and they made a liqueur.

About 500 years after their founding a group of monks from the Benedictine monastery of Molesme moved away to found Cîteaux Abbey in 1098, with the goal of following more closely the Rule of Saint Benedict. They became the **Cistercians** – *Cistercium* being the latin name for the village of Cîteaux, near Dijon, **Burgundy,** eastern France. In the early 1100's **Bernard** entered the monastery with several relatives and friends. An Englishman Stephen Harding, one of the first Abbots, chose Bernard to found the new Abbey of Clairvaux from where he caused the rapid proliferation of the order (300 in all Europe) in which every abbey was the daughter of another with Citeaux at the centre. All Abbeys were dedicated to "Our Lady the Blessed Virgin Mary".

Abbeycwmhir's local motte and bailey castle - Beddugre Hill in 1995 (cf p 42)   (54)

Choir *Monks* and Lay *Brothers*

The Cistercian "Charter of Charity" said of the Conversi or Lay Brothers, "We hold them to be our brothers and, equally with our monks, sharers of our goods both spiritual and temporal". Sometimes benefactors of land became lay brothers. Nevertheless it was a two tier system with the lay brothers doing most of the physical work so that when the Choir Monks helped with the harvest in 1231 it was especially recorded.[92] In 1195 the Cistercian General Chapter was told that the lay brothers of Cwmhir had stolen their abbot's horse because he had forbidden them to drink beer.[93]

Before the Abbey......................

Oceans, Mountains and Ice

- the formation of the landscape and geology of the Long Valley

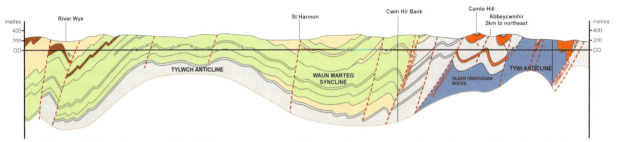

When Wales lay south of the equator on the northern margins of a continent called Avalonia that included Europe and Russia, 440 million years ago, Abbeycwmhir was a deposit at the bottom of a deep-water ocean - in the form of silt and sand, which later became the grey mudstones and thin sandstones that we have today.

Dr Adrian Humpage of the British Geological Survey, Cardiff, writes:

Like much of mid-Wales, the rocks and landscape of Abbeycwmhir record a long history of deep oceans, episodes of mountain building and fault movements, and millions of years of erosion by water and ice to form the incised topography of the Long Valley seen today.

All the rocks which underlie the area of Abbeycwmhir Community Council are part of the Lower Palaeozoic "Welsh Basin", which were deposited in a deep water ocean (called the Iapetus Ocean) between 440 and 428 million years ago. At this time, known as the "Ordovician", Wales lay south of the equator on the northern margins of a continent called Avalonia, which included all of southern Britain. If you look carefully around Abbeycwmhir, you may be able to find traces of strange deep water creatures called graptolites (related to corals and with species names like *Didymograptus*, *Glyptograptus* and *Triangulatus*), which floated in the deep water, and as they died their skeletons were preserved as fossils in the great thicknesses of grey mudstones with occasional thin sandstones which were deposited on the ocean floor. Over time, plate movements caused the area which was to become Wales to migrate northwards, the deep water began to shallow and ultimately, the ocean basin was infilled with more sandy sediment, these younger rocks being deposited during the "Silurian Period".

The British Geological Survey, with its remit to serve government, industry and the community through its national strategic geoscience programme, has a long history of working in Wales, and much of the area surrounding Abbeycwmhir was mapped in the late 1980's as part of a programme to study the Rhayader district, whilst the northern edge of the Community Council area rising onto Hirddywel was studied as recently as 2007 whilst surveying for the Llanidloes geological mapsheet.

However, this was not the end of the story! The continent of Avalonia collided with another continent to the north-west, called Laurentia, and just as is happening between India and Asia today, a great mountain chain began to form. As these mountains, called the Caledonides, formed, so the rocks of the Welsh Basin were subjected to great pressures as they were squeezed together in the heart of the new mountain chain. As a consequence, large folds formed and the rocks began to crack and faults developed across central Wales. South from Abbeycwmhir, a large fold called the Tywi Anticline formed, which pushed up older Ordovician rocks into the surrounding younger Silurian sandstones. The faults which formed often ran parallel to the line of the growing mountains, and were oriented north-east to south-west, a trend that is still visible across Abbeycwmhir Community today. Some, such as the Cwmysgawen Fault are important regional local structures, causing big offsets within the rocks, whilst others are much smaller but can still be seen at the surface, such as one exposed on the right side of the roadside quarry on Bailey Hill, just beyond Bwlch y Sarnau. Although long inactive, occasional crustal movements cause some slight movement on some of these faults and small earthquakes occur, such as the magnitude 3.0 tremor on 20 September 1996 with an epicentre 14km below Beddugre Hill, three kilometres east of Abbeycwmhir village. Very rarely, a significant tremor occurs on these faults, such as the magnitude 3.6 earthquake at Sennybridge on 25 October 1999 which was widely felt across mid-Wales.

Over long periods of time, a new ocean, the Atlantic Ocean opened up, splitting the continents apart once again. The high Caledonide Mountains were eroded away and crustal movements and changes in sea levels all played a part in this process. Today, their remnants form the mountains in Scotland, Wales and Ireland in Europe, and the Appalachians in North America.

By about two million years ago, the landscape was not dissimilar to that seen at present, and the upland plateaux and the courses of some of the major rivers we know today could be recognised. However, this time period, called the "Quaternary", marked the start of rapid and repeated environmental and climatic changes as the planet went through a succession of cold and warm

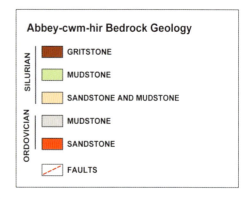

which were reflected in the waxing and waning of huge ice sheets which may have been up to 2km in thickness on the land surface over mid-Wales.

Across Abbeycwmhir can be seen the influence and deposits of the last Ice Age, which reached its maximum extent approximately 20,000 years ago. Ice sheets formed on the Cambrian Mountains to the west, and spread eastwards. Glacier ice flowed either side of Cwmysgawen Common, over-deepening the valleys of Cwm hir and the Clywedog Brook to leave the classic steep-sided U-shaped valley of a glacial trough. Most of the ice continued to flow eastwards down the main axis of the valley, but a lobe of ice crossed the col of Rhiw Gam into Cwm Bedw south of Llywy Hill where the ice was able to erode the soft mudstones and exploit lines of weakness in the rock. The sudden change in direction at Upper Cwmhir (north-eastwards) towards Abbey-cwmhir village centre, and the side valleys such as Cwm Farsley and Cwm-poeth, reveal the position of faults. Similarly, a small rise in the road outside the old Forestry Offices by Cwmysgawen Farm on the ice-scoured valley floor picks up a "step" in the bedrock along the Cwmysgawen Fault where it crosses the valley.

The depth of the U-shaped valley may be due to the pressure of unmelted snow called *firn* (somewhere between loose snow and glacier) which gathered thickly above the hill tops pressing down into the bedrock which remains today close to the surface and enables the valley sides to "hold-up". Other lower valley-side slopes are often mantled in thick drift deposits of till and glacio-fluvial deposits. When the ice melted for the last time about 11,500 years ago at Abbeycwmhir, the sediment carried by the glacier was dumped as only a veneer of boulder clay across the valley floor, whilst meltwater from the decaying ice deposited glaciofluvial sand and gravel.

Nevertheless, the over-steepened valley sides were in some places unstable when without the support of the ice, and landslides occurred, as can be seen on the south side of the valley near Lower Cwmhir. With the end of the last Ice Age, rapid climatic warming soon led to the establishment of thick deciduous woodlands in the valleys and on to the hilltops, peat developed in low-lying boggy areas, and rivers established narrow alluvial floodplains along their courses. However, that is not the end of our story. From about 9,000 years ago, humans arrived in Wales and began to modify the landscape to suit their purposes, a process which still continues today!

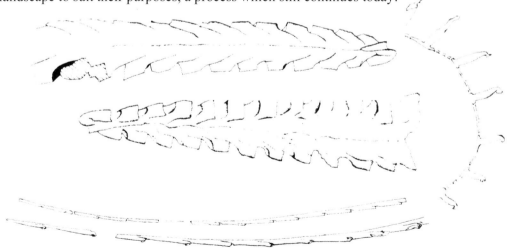

Fossils called graptolites, related to corals and with species names like Didymograptus, Glyptograptus and Triangulatus, may be found around the Community area.

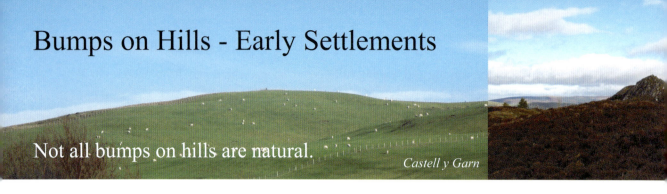

Bumps on Hills - Early Settlements

Not all bumps on hills are natural.

Castell y Garn

When is a Cairn - a Mount or a Round Barrow - a Tumulus?

Red deer and boar hunting, fishing and plant gathering nomadic people left their tools at Cwmtelma Farm[1] (**1** *on map opposite*) in Mesolithic prehistory (**Middle Stone Age** about 9,000BC) long before Stonehenge and the Pyramids were built and whilst Britain was still physically connected to Europe by "Doggerland". Harpoons and spears were common tools and were made by fixing tiny flint stone barbs (microliths) in rows along the spear. It was these flint barbs and the core they were struck from that were found. From the much later Neolithic (or **New Stone Age** - about 4000BC) a flint axe head (**2**) was found in Abbeycwmhir village centre[2] and a hide or woodworking thumb scraper (**3**) at Devannor[3] - used by people who were beginning to domesticate plants & animals on farms and develop early villages. There is a visible enclosure from the prehistoric period near Cwm Pistyll (**4**). Did this territorialising have anything to do with the earliest incidents of warfare also discovered from this time? Few were found anywhere during the Early Bronze Age.

Most of the early earthworks in the Community are from the **Bronze Age** (2100 - 750 BC Megalith building continuing elsewhere - Stonehenge and Pyramids recently started). The climate during the Early Bronze Age was warmer so most of the earthworks are on the higher ground of the community where the best views are still spectacular - from Domen Ddu (553 mtrs) - cairn and round barrow (**5**) to Crugyn Llwyd (571 mtrs) round barrow and ring cairn below (**7**), Banc Du's Fowlers Armchair stone circle and cairn (**6**), and in between, the Fuallt settlement: hut, stone and enclosure (**8**). Then following the Bronze Age ridgeway south there is Castell y Garn[4] by Cefn Crin (**9**) above the Creigiau, the Hynod Cairn built on rocks (**10**) and on to Camlo Hill with its Llwn Dwr standing stone (**11**), and barrow and The Devils Apronful of Stones cairn (**12**). The latter's name is a Victorian *purification* because aprons full of stones are associated with Celtic hag Goddesses. A large stone carving of one, Sheelah--na-Gig, was found nearby under the old Parish Church in Llandrindod Wells where she can be seen in the Radnorshire Museum.

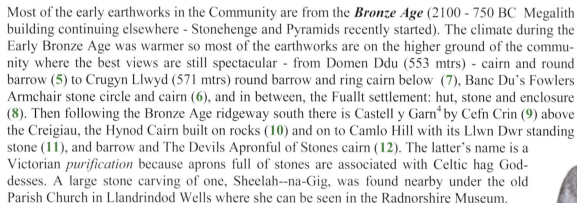

Microlith barbs

These sites are mainly used today for displaying fencing but originally would have been used either for religious rituals or as burial places for the community leaders and council. Unlike the Neolithic *communal* long barrows, the mound of earth of a Bronze Age round barrow - or the stones of a cairn - covered the burial place of an *individual* either placed in a crouching position or cremated and placed in a pottery urn or small stone slab chest - or cist. All may be labelled on a map *Tumuli* - the latin for mound of earth. As Bronze Age weather became wetter burials may have taken place more on lower ground such as "The Mount" (**14**) behind Maes y Gwaelod sometimes called "Bedd Garmon".

Agriculture started in the New Stone Age and continued through the Bronze Age - for example at the field system at Blaen Trinnant (**13**) and perhaps on a hill above Abbeycwmhir village where a Bronze Age stone axe-hammer was found .[5]

Iron Age (1100BC – 700AD) Camp Wood (**15**) a place name suggesting an Iron Age hill fort.

Axe head or

Thumb scraper

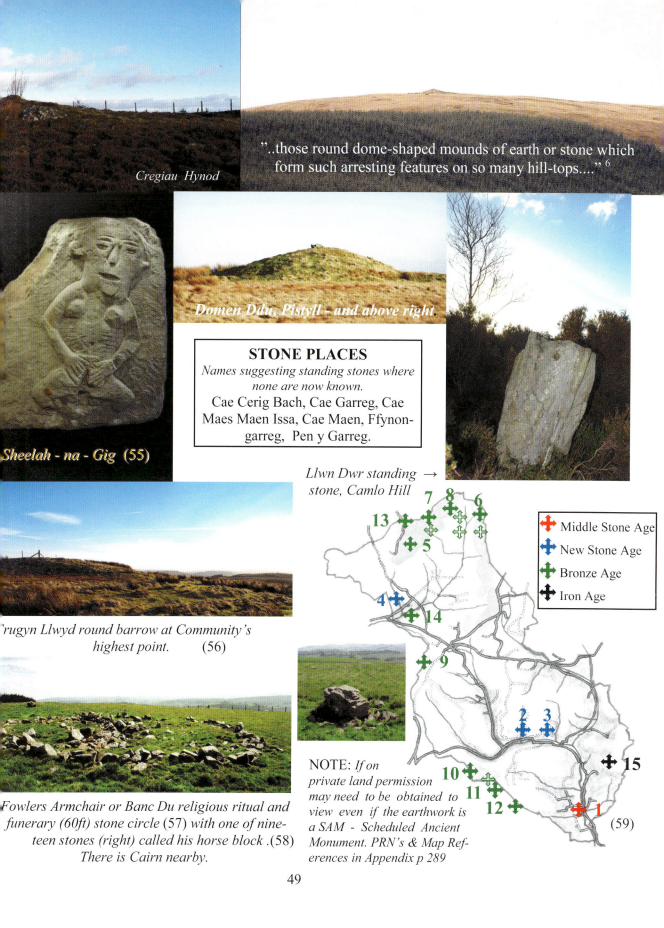

Cregiau Hynod

"..those round dome-shaped mounds of earth or stone which form such arresting features on so many hill-tops...." [6]

Domen Ddu, Pistyll - and above right

Sheelah - na - Gig (55)

STONE PLACES
Names suggesting standing stones where none are now known.
Cae Cerig Bach, Cae Garreg, Cae Maes Maen Issa, Cae Maen, Ffynon-garreg, Pen y Garreg.

Llwn Dwr standing → stone, Camlo Hill

Middle Stone Age
New Stone Age
Bronze Age
Iron Age

'rugyn Llwyd round barrow at Community's highest point. (56)

Fowlers Armchair or Banc Du religious ritual and funerary (60ft) stone circle (57) with one of nineteen stones (right) called his horse block .(58) There is Cairn nearby.

NOTE: *If on private land permission may need to be obtained to view even if the earthwork is a SAM - Scheduled Ancient Monument. PRN's & Map References in Appendix p 289*

(59)

Abbeycwmhir Community Book

Five arches were recycled by St Idloes Church, Llanidloes in 1542. St Idloes is not a small space. Imagine a building with 28 arches - nearly three times as long and much higher - in our Valley. (60)

The Abbey ruins before the clean up by Clwyd Powys Archaeological Trust 1994 - 1998 (61)

AFTER THE ABBEY.........
The King's most Royal Majesty - being Supreme Head on earth, under God, of the Church of England*

1534 Act of Supremacy*

1535 Thomas Cromwell publishes Valor Ecclesiasticus after the general visitation in preparation for the Dissolution of the Monasteries.

1536 Act of Dissolution of smaller Abbeys under twelve persons. Cwmhir's Day of Sup - pression was 2nd March 1537.

1537 Act of Dissolution of larger Abbeys like Strata Florida - Day: 23rd Feb 1539.

Pope Clement VII refused Henry VIII's biblically based argument for annulling his marriage to Catherine of Aragon so Henry broke with Rome and had Parliament declare him Supreme Head of the *Ecclesia Anglicana* - and thus in control of the Abbeys and Monasteries. This was the beginning of a series of events known as the English Reformation. By this time there were just three monks left at Cwmhir even though twelve monks were required even by the Cistercian Order to perform the "Ora". The "Labora" was now done by the ex Conversi tenants who now had leases or mortgages on the Abbey's land.

A sign that the abbeys were no longer performing their spiritual function, although having a big effect on the economy, was that the last Abbot of Cwmhir, John Glyn, appointed at the last minute in 1535, had been deposed from two previous houses for "misguiding and decaying them" and was clearly after an Abbot's pension.[1] The suppression had been anticipated by many and abbey land was transferred to friends who might look after abbots and monks after the big day. Henry VIII was aware of this and made "utterly void and of none effect" any transactions made in the previous twelve months.[2] Sir *John* Price of Newtown, a commissioner of dissolved abbeys, authorised the conveyance of five of the Abbey's arches to Llanidloes.[3] A *James* Price was able to build his new house at Monaughty on the lands of the former monastic grange of Treburgh stradling the Llangynllo-Bleddfa parish boundary in the Lugg valley.[4] The three remaining monks could have ended their days here, or at Mynachdy Poeth on the Teme north of Knighton or even at the *monaughty* or *monks house* at Cwmhir4.

The vast Cwmhir Abbey estate went through five transactions and seven hands before William Fowler and Edward Herbert of Powys Castle bought it 23 years later in 1558. The property market was surely booming.

The Great Bell of the Abbey was sold to a grocer in London but spent twenty years at Chepstow waiting for the ferry[5]; the picture of Christ was sold to the Abbot of Strata Florida; and the people of Llanidloes started the "robbing" of the Abbey by arranging to remove the stone of five arches - perhaps John Glyn sold them off?

Abbeycwmhir Community Book

The front cover of the first Welsh Language Bible of 1588 translated by Rev William Morgan.

Individuals should make up their own minds about God based on their own reading of his Holy Book, the Bible. This was the argument of the Reformation sweeping across Europe and used, in part, to justify the creation of the Church of England. This meant that churches and individuals needed copies of the Bible in their own language - rather than in the antique Latin of the Catholic Church which could only be interpreted by authorised, and possibly corrupt, ordained priests.

Printing made it possible, since 1450, for more people to read and the first book to be printed was the Bible - but in Latin - by the printer Johannes Gutenberg. In a troubled world of sickness, plague, and endless wars, lay folk looked for answers, and failing to find them from the churchmen, they looked for them in the scriptures. Vernacular bibles were appearing across Europe.

Luther had published his New estament in German in 1522 and William Tyndale printed his English New Testament in 1525-6 also in Germany. Even though Henry VIII was spiritually conservative and before his break with Rome had been made a "Defender of the Faith" (*Fidei Defensor*) by Pope Leo X in 1521, he supported the publication of Miles Coverdale's complete *Great Bible* in English in 1539 and ordered that only English Bibles be used in churches - including in Wales. Although there had been two recent Acts of Union of Wales and England (1536 & 1543) enforcing English law and language, most people in Wales only spoke Welsh and so there was a need for a Welsh Bible as well. When the protestant Elizabeth I came to the throne in 1588 (also the year of the Spanish Armada), Wales was ready with a complete Welsh Bible dedicated to her - and Abbeycwmhir had its own copy already in 1590. It was translated by Rev (later, Bishop) William Morgan. He was born at Tŷ Mawr Wybrnant, Penmachno, where our Bible can be seen today. Morgan's bible is considered a major literary achievement in the Welsh language.

The first carer of the Cwmhir Bible was also the first Fowler to own the Abbey estate - William. He was apparently so pleased with the bible he signed it three times - even though, being himself English, it was unlikely he could read it. How he came to possess it and why he signed it in Abbeycwmhir which was not

Above: William Fowler of the Manor of Golon of the Aby Cumheer - by mee Ed: Da. 1590 Top Right: Willi Fowler.....(unclear)

a parish at this time when the English Parliament had ordained that every parish in Wales should have one, is not known. It might suggest that Abbeycwmhir did have a church - perhaps built into the remaining twenty three arches left in the ruins - between the dissolution of the Abbey and the building of the first church here in 1686 by Willi's successor Sir William.

In a letter which the first William Fowler wrote in 1564 describing 'my poore howse at Cumheere' there is the suggestion that there was also a "howse" in the Abbey ruins which may or may not have been the Abbots Dwelling - possibly now Home Farm.

As Time Goes By - After the Abbey

This is the first Bible that ever was in Abbey Cwmhir Church

The last page of the Old Testament with the hand written words probably by William Lewis.

Elswhere in the Bible is enscribed:

"I William Lewis late of Abbeycwmhir do present this Holy Bible to his nephew George Lewis of Cwmscawen and has a particular wish that the said George Lewis will take care of it in his life time and at the end of his to let it go on by Heirship.
    Written this 10th day of August 1840.
                 - William Lewis"

"Willi Fowler. Monarchidy Golon"
(Mynach + Ty = Monks House, Golon).

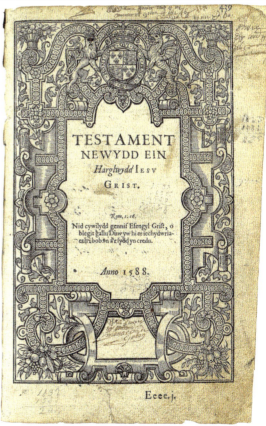

Frontispiece of the New Testament section with William Fowler's two signatures above and one centre below. Why so many? (64)

Abbeycwmhir Community Book

The Fowlers for 266 Years
- *here and there - Revolutionary Revolving*
- Brondrefawr - Devannor - Bart & Decline

The Fowlers were an ancient Norman family who could trace their history back to medieval times - no doubt working as fowlers! A Richard Fowler went on a Crusade to the Holy Land in 1190, at his own expense, and provided a company of bowmen all of whom were his own tenants. For this he received a knighthood from King Richard I. There developed a tradition of service to King and Country in the family. Later, another Sir Richard Fowler, was Chancellor of the Duchy of Lancaster.

By the middle of the 16th Century a William Fowler had purchased Harnage Grange, previously part of Buildwas Abbey estate He also had a large holding around Oswestry which once belonged to the Benedictine Monastery of the Apostles Peter and Paul in Shrewsbury.[1] He extended his interests in previous Abbey lands around 1562 when he paid £19,000 for Cwmhir Abbey which had passed through many hands since it was seized by King Henry VIII in 1537. This payment was made in two halves, one on the Feast of the Annunciation of the Blessed Virgin Mary, the other at Michaelmas, both at the Belfry door of the parish church of Burfield, Berkshire. In this purchase William Fowler was joined by Edward Herbert of Powys Castle.[2]

William Fowler was a man of considerable wealth, which was in part old family money, partly the profits of his trading as a merchant in Shrewsbury and the considerable revenue in rents, tithes and herriots from his huge estates. His Will, proved in the Prerogative Court of Canterbury after his death in1597, shows that he owned land in the counties of Radnor, Montgomery, Merioneth, Stafford, Chester and Derby. Fowler was an important and influential man in the affairs of Shropshire. He was a Freeman and a Burgess of Shrewsbury and as Steward, he effectively ran it. He presided over the Great Sessions, the principal court, dispensing the summary justice which was normal in those times.

The Cwmhir Abbey estate[3] which William Fowler purchased was much larger than the later Abbey-cwmhir estates created in the 19th Century by Thomas Wilson and Francis Philips. Measured in tens of thousands of acres, it took in the Manor of Go<u>ll</u>on and the Township of Cefn Pawl in Llanbister parish, all of Llananno parish, most of the extensive parish of St. Harmon and a considerable part of Llanbadarn Ffynydd parish. To this could be added property in Nantmel, Disserth, Cefnllys, Llangunllo, Kerry and the more distant Clyro in lower Radnorshire. It has to be remembered that this was only one of a number of sizeable estates which Fowler owned in various counties on both sides of the border. They would have kept him busy, together with his duties as Steward of Shrewesbury.

Management of the estate would have been the responsibility of the estate Steward assisted by a Bailiff, probably more than one Bailiff for an estate this size. The Manor of Gollon had its' own Manorial Court which was responsible for dealing with matters of tenancy, rents, tithes and herriots, as well as settling disputes. It also had power to deal with local petty crime. As Lord of the Manor of Gollon, William Fowler would have to be present at meetings of the manorial court, known as the Court Leet. The court had its origins in medieval times but there is evidence that it survived well into the 18th century. Documents show that it met in 1720 and again in 1760 in order to walk the boundary of the manor and deal with encroachments. Where the court met in the early

Fowler years is not known for certain[4], but in the second half of the 17th Century it might have met in the present building of Ty Faenor, **Devannor**, which had been built by the Fowlers as a hunting lodge,[5] set within a great park in time for a Richard Fowler to give it as his address in 1656 and an Edward in 1715 when they were High Sheriffs.[6] The house remained in the family until 1769 when Charles Gore finally purchased it and the Manor of Golon from the estate of the late Sir William Fowler, 4th Baronet (d 1760) (cf p 57).

There is nothing to suppose that the first William Fowler and his family resided at Abbeycwmhir, neither is it known exactly where he stayed when he visited his estate. In a letter which he wrote in 1564 from 'my poore howse at Cumheere' to his wife and family back at Harnage Grange, he laments the poor state of the house in which he is staying and the conditions he has to endure. His accommodation may have been a building which had survived on the Abbey site. A stone-built house, similar in appearance to the old Brondrefawr, was known to exist near the site of the present Home Farm. It might have started life as a single-storey hall-house, constructed of timber, but later, like many others, built around with stone and with a storey inserted. The building seems to have spanned the Fowler years and it has been suggested that this was where the business of the Manor was conducted. The 'mannor howse of Cumheere' is referred to in 1600.

William Fowler represented Shrewsbury on the Council of the Marches, a body set up to deal with complaints, legal matters and enforcements along the border between England and Wales. Owning estates on both sides of the border and actually on the border, he would have had a particular interest in the smooth running of affairs. However, he may have seen the Council as a source of conflict with the Manorial Court of Gollon. In 1562 he complained to the Council that his tenants had been indicted at the Quarter Sessions for 'overpressynge the common of Hirddywel,' an offence 'wiche always hathe bene heretofore presented in the courte and lawdaye of the Abbey'.[7]

The ownership of large tracts of land gave the Fowlers both status and influence, together with a substantial income. Having money tied up in land made it more difficult for hard-up monarchs like the Stuart kings of the 17th Century to sequester the wealth of others. As with the first William Fowler to own the Abbeycwmhir estate, ensuing generations held important positions in the counties of Radnor and Shropshire and indeed, in national life. In 1611, one William Fowler was described as being 'Secretaire to the Queen's Majestie', that is to say secretary to the wife of James I. Much later, in 1682, a Richard Fowler was an Equerry to the Queen of Charles II.

> "Radnorsheer, poor Radnorsheer,
> Never a park and never a deer,
> Never a squire of five hundred a year
> But Richard Fowler of Abbey Cwmhir"

It is said that this rhyme was invented by a disgruntled Commissioners who had been sent by Parliament to collect fines from Royalists after the Civil War.[8] Perhaps they were disgruntled because the richest man in the County was now working for Parliament's Puritan Commission for Peace. The rhyme lends itself to revision including of the name and title of the Fowler concerned. At least the Commissioners and Richard Fowler put Abbeycwmhir on the map.

Revolving in the Revolution

The middle years of the 17th Century were turbulent ones as civil war raged between Royalists and Parliamentarians, King Charles I was executed in 1649 and Oliver Cromwell's puritan Commonwealth ruled throughout the 1650's. The Fowlers were fundamentally Royalists. William was a Commissioner of Array for the county of Shropshire and Abbeycwmhir was regarded as a Royalist stronghold, home to a garrison of over 70 troops. Radnorshire did not experience the major battles

Fowler Memorial St. Peter's Church, Cound, Shropshire - to the Fowlers of Harnage Grange. (65)

which took place in the English counties but still the local Gentry took sides, militias were raised and skirmishes took place.Fortifications were built at Abbeycwmhir, but in December of 1644 it fell to the forces of Sir Thomas Myddleton of Chirk Castle.[9] The Abbeycwmhir garrison, under the command of Colonel Barnard, mainly consisted of men from Shropshire and Staffordshire. After a spirited defence, lasting for an hour and a half, they were overcome. Today, metal-detector enthusiasts have been known to recover musket balls from the fields around the village.

Both William and Richard Fowler were captured in Shropshire by the Parliamentarians but escaped any serious punishment. Unlike many of their Royalist compatriots, they managed to avoid having their assets sequestered by their opponents. At the end of the civil war Richard was to be found serving on the Puritan Commission for Peace as life began to return to some sort of normality.[10] Had he changed sides?!

The office of High Sheriff was an important one dating from 1541 in Radnorshire and seven Fowlers discharged that duty between 1600 and 1765.[11] The Sheriff was responsible for the maintenance of law and order in his county on behalf of the King. The appointment was made on the basis of the ownership of land in the county and influence, not necessarily of long-term residence. The fact the office-holder was sufficiently wealthy to pay his own expenses whilst serving was also a consideration in the appointment. For example, Charles Gore, who purchased Devannor and other properties from the Fowler estate in 1769, was made High Sheriff for the County of Radnor in 1771, although he lived in Southampton at the time and had previously been a resident of Lincolnshire.

Brondrefawr

It is difficult to establish which of the Fowler family lived for any length of time at Abbeycwmhir. The balance of evidence suggests that they were more likely to be resident at Harnage Grange, their home in Shropshire. The Llanbister Parish register records only two Fowler burials and two baptisms. John Fowler, who lived at Brondrefawr from about 1680 and died in 1697 and his son Edward, also of Brondrefawr, who died in 1722, are recorded. The baptism of William Fowler, son of the third Baronet is recorded in 1734 and that of his daughter Letitia in 1736.

By contrast the registers of St. Peter's Church, at Cound in Shropshire, the parish in which Harnage Grange lies, records more than a dozen Fowler baptisms, marriages and burials in the 17th and early 18th centuries. Others appear in the registers of the Shrewesbury churches.[12] St. Peter's also contains a fine mid-18th century monumental inscription to the Fowlers of Harnage Grange (picture above).[13]

To return to John Fowler of Brondrefawr, it is possible to argue that his was a settled family. He was born in 1629, the third son of William and Anna Fowler and as such would have been apportioned part of the estate. He was a successful merchant in his own right, with considerable estates and business interests. His grandchildren had a number of children who all married into families from the counties of Montgomery and Cardigan. This represents an interesting cultural shift from the very English Fowlers, to the Welsh speaking families into which they married.

Bart & Decline

The status of the Fowler family was boosted at the beginning of the 18th Century. On the 1st November 1704 a William Fowler was created a Baronet by Queen Anne, thus he and his successors became styled 'Sir' William etc.

The fourth Baronet, Sir William, died of illness in 1760 at the age of only 26 [14] whilst serving in a Dragoon regiment in Germany. [15] He was unmarried and had no heir and so the Baronetcy passed to Hans, a brother of the third Baronet. However, Sir Hans, styled himself as 'of Abbey-cwm-hir' which suggests that he lived at Abbeycwmhir during the 1760's and claimed Ty Faenor as his residence for being High Sheriff in 1765. Evidence from Shropshire shows that by 1760 the Fowlers were no longer in possession of Harnage Grange.

Sir Hans Fowler memorial, St Mary's Church, Abbeycwmhir.(66)

From this point on the Fowler estates in Radnorshire were in decline. In 1769 a large area around Abbeycwmhir had been sold to Charles Gore, including the historic Devannor, which eventually became part of the Penybont estate. At the same time Jonathan Field bought Bryn Camlo, Esgairwy and a number of farms around Llaithdu. Other sales followed between 1781 and 1828. Not all the sales were immediately successful. The Sale Particulars of the time tell a story of many run-down farms, low rents, decayed buildings and poor management of the estate.

It is recorded in the Llanbister Parish register that Sir Hans died in 1771.[16] He died without an heir and the Baronetcy became extinct. He was buried under the altar in the old church at Abbeycwmhir and there is a plaque to him in the modern church. The Abbeycwmhir estate passed to his sister Sarah who was married to a Colonel John Hodges.

The Fowlers were linked by marriage to the Earls of Huntingdon in the late 17th century. Several generations later a Hans Francis Hastings was determined to prove that he was the legitimate heir and was eventually successful in proving his claim through the Courts, but the cost was enormous and almost bankrupted the family resulting in the remaining Fowler estates in Radnorshire being sold on orders of the Court of Exchequer. He changed his name to Thomas Hodges Fowler, styling himself 'of Abbey-cwm-hir', indicating that he might have lived at Abbeycwmhir between 1790 and his death in 1820. However, he also possessed his wife's family home, Court of Hill, in Shropshire. Although the church at Abbeycwmhir contains a fine monument to Thomas Hodges Fowler, the work of a London monumental mason, he is buried at Burford, Shropshire. His death witnessed the final severing of the Fowler links with Abbeycwmhir after a period of two hundred and sixty years.

Thomas Hodges Fowler memorial. St Mary's Church, Abbeycwmhir (67)

The above section "The Fowlers for 266 years" was researched and prepared by Julian Lovell of Tyr Ehededd.

St Mary's Church, Abbeycwmhir

As the Abbey had the responsibility of administering the Sacraments to the people living nearby the Dissolution of March 1537 meant this was taken away. Already in mid - April 1537 letters were despatched from London saying that an "Edward Beawpe and another planned to "build a chapel in Maelienydd in the honour of Jesus, where they intend to have the sacraments and sacramentals administered"[1]. With this in mind, they sought the return of the Abbey's framed picture of Jesus from Strata Florida whence it had been already sold. The present picture (right) evokes the original and is similar to a painting by Coreggio with the same title.[2] Thomas Wilson gave it for use as the altar piece in the old church and possibly had it painted by John James Hall one of his close artist associates.[3]

The Agony in the Garden (68)

DH Williams says that "The the chapel was built but the division of Abbey Cwmhir remained extra parochial".[4] Perhaps it was built into the nave of the Abbey as much of it would have been still standing, or even built on the site of the present church - somewhere for Willi Fowler's Welsh Bible to be kept - despite it not being a parish church.

The first known separate chapel or church in Abbeycwmhir was built in 1680, closer to the road but on the site of the present church, during the time John Fowler lived at Brondrefawr. He was succeeded in 1696 at Brondrefawr by his son Edward, who died in 1722. Both John and Edward were buried at Llanbister, according to the Llanbister Church records. However, a recent uncovering of the will of John's daughter Jane, dated 1720, states she would like to 'be laid as near as may be to the coffin of my father and mother at the chapel of Abbeycwmhir in the County of Radnor'.[5]

The church was initially a Chapel of Ease or Convenience to Llanbister, and joint records were kept. 'GOL' was inserted next to an entry which related to Abbeycwmhir Church (short for Golon), so it is possible that this was omitted in relation to the burial of Jane's parents. Abbeycwmhir parted from Llanbister in 1831, and the first Abbeycwmhir registers therefore start from this time.

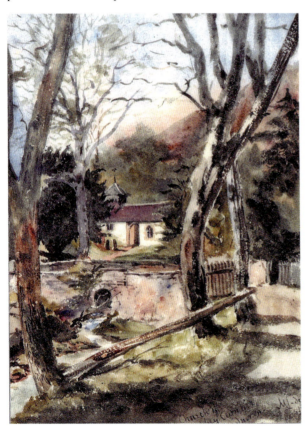

The 1680 St Mary's Church built in the time of John Fowler. Here painted by Mary Leighton [6] in 1858 while her brother Rev. John Parker preached inside.(69)

As Time Goes By - The Church

Before the Lych Gate of 1900 in memory of Mary Beatrice Philips 1828 -1898 (70)

Over the years the church became quite dilapidated, and in 1824 Thomas Wilson, who was the new owner of the Abbeycwmhir estate, carried out repair work. He wrote, 'I found it in a wretched condition and have prevailed on the parish to repair it. I have paid for ceiling it, and have provided an organ and bell, and the parish new pewing and flooring, and furnishing the gallery, and a new pulpit.'[7] He also installed the lid of Mabli's tomb in the floor towards the west end and left a mobile secretaire chest of draws converted from a Gentleman's Chest (with a brushing slide) with his initials on it - which is still in the vestry.

In the 1840s, Francis Philips, together with the Rev. Evans of Nantmel, brought a court case against the first curate of Abbeycwmhir, the Rev. George, for dilapidation of duty, i.e. a failure to carry out his duties as minister and take services as required.[8] The reason for the curate's absence was that he had found himself a better appointment in Pembrokeshire where he became Vicar and accordingly earned a higher salary. Philips and Evans sought legal opinion on the case, as was the custom in such circumstances. The two barristers differed. One felt Francis Philips and James Evans had a good case, the other that they did not. When it went to court the curate triumphed because his salary was very low, under £8 a year, and, according to the rules, when on such a low salary, it was not necessary to give notice and resign in the usual way. The legal wrangle lasted for several years and Philips and Evans had to pick up the costs - in excess of £500. Francis Philips, who held the patronage of Abbeycwmhir, complained to the Bishop that it would be impossible to secure the services of a good minister at such a low salary. His fears, it seems, were groundless, for the Rev. James Evans of Nantmel accepted the office and served as perpetual curate from 1847 to 1891. At the same time he held other appointments as Vicar of Nantmel and Llanfihangel Heligan with Llanyre. He was also a local magistrate.

In the 1860s it became apparent that a new church was needed. Miss Mary Beatrice Philips, sister to the Squire, Mr George Henry Philips, built a new church at her own expense in 1865/6. Her portrait used to hang in the vestry[9] but has since disappeared. The old church was demolished, and a new one built a little further back from the road. Cost (£2,000) appears to have beeen no object. The stained glass windows are considered to be the best in Radnorshire. The rose window to the west (bottom left next page) is unique in the county and is the work of Clayton and Bell of London , circa 1866.[10]

Todays Church, built in 1868, in 1900 but still in the days of coaches and horses. (71)

The Church and Chapels sections were written by Diana Berriman of Little Plock.

Abbeycwmhir Community Book

The Crucifixion and the Resurrection

I am the Good Shepherd

Scenes from the Gospels with the twelve Disciples and Virgin Mary.

The other windows in the chancel are by another well-known London firm of glass artists, Heaton, Butler & Bayne. The firm was founded in 1855 and was producing windows well into the 20th Century. Their work of the 1860s is considered to be outstanding and an example was used as a cover illustration on the definitive book 'Victorian Stained Glass' by Barrie and Jenkins. A richly moulded arch on columns of Peterhead granite separates the chancel from the nave. The choir stalls are beautifully carved, the flooring encaustic and sacarium tiles. The altar is from Caen stone and the pulpit of Bath stone with decorative carvings. The Church has a bell tower and spire, organ chamber and vestry. An organ blower was employed from March 1879.

The entrance, under the tower, has the tympanum above (a copy of the original from the Abbey, which was intended to be used but was damaged in transit. The original is in the garden wall at Home Farm). The tympanum depicts the Ascension of Christ.

The new church, dedicated to St Mary, was consecrated by the Bishop of the Diocese of St. Davids on 14 November 1866. The Church remained in that Diocese until 1926 when the Swansea and Brecon Diocese was formed.

The present Broad Oak (there was an older Broad Oak Cottage further down the hill) was built as the vicarage until Ernest Hermitage Day became the vicar in 1891[11] (cf p 166). He apparently did not wish to be so close to the Baptist Chapel. So, Brynmoel was built in 1892, by Anna Theophila Philips, widow of George Henry Philips. It was designed by Stephen Williams of Penrally, Rhayader, County Surveyor to Radnorshire. This was the last house to be built in the area until 1953 when the Forestry Commission built one for the head forester near Cwmysgawen.

The Lychgate was erected in 1900 by the inhabitants of Abbeycwmhir in memory of Mary Beatrice Philips (d 1898) who built the church.

In 1955 the church was grouped with the parish of Llanddewi-Ystradenni, Llandegley and Llanfihangel Rhydithon as the Lower Ithon Valley Parish. In 2009 it was further grouped with the parishes of the Upper Ithon Valley, Llananno, Llanbister, Llanddewi and Llanbadarn Fynnydd, creating a group of 8 churches. An assistant vicar, was recruited to assist Canon Loat with this larger grouping.

> *"Join me at the gap, stand with me in the breach,*
> *So that we may retain for the ages to come*
> *the beauty that has been.*
> *And this, my Lord, is the vineyard of your beloved:*
> *The clearing full of faith, from Mary's church to Mary's church"*
>
> - Saunders Lewis *Buchedd Garmon* [12]

Portrait of Chrystine Anna Philips (d 1958) hangs in the sanctuary. (72)

I am the Light of the World

The Baptism of Christ and Agony in the Garden (73

As Time Goes By - The Chapels

The Baptists in - Bwlch y Sarnau

Bwlch y Sarnau Chapel, built in 1901, is the only remaining place of Baptist worship in the parish. Over the centuries, however, there has been a huge amount of Baptist activity in the area, with open air preaching and worship held in many farmhouses throughout the parish.

It all appears to start with a man named Vivasour Powell, born in Knucklas in 1617. He trained for service in the Anglican Church and around the year 1650 was preaching wherever he could gather a congregation, under a tree, in the street or in a farmyard. Whilst preaching in Newtown he met a staunch Baptist named Thomas Edwards and soon afterwards he left the Anglican Church, was baptised by immersion, and began converting hundreds of people in Mid Wales to the principles of the Baptist faith. It is known that he preached in the farmhouses of **Brondrefawr** and the **Hendy**, and this is the beginning of the Baptist Movement in the Bwlch y Sarnau area. After the Restoration in 1660 and the Act of Uniformity (1662), the Baptists were persecuted for being 'Dissenters from the Orthodox Church', and upon capture by Royalist forces would be tortured and imprisoned. Many Radnorshire Baptists (and other non-conformists) fled to North America to escape this persecution and founded churches over there.

Vivasour Powell's portable pulpit still kept in Bwlch y Sarnau Chapel. (74)

Whilst preaching at Brondrefawr, on what was to be his last visit there, Vavasour Powell learned that Loyalist forces were in the area seeking his arrest. Throughout his journeys he carried with him a small mobile pulpit which he would erect whilst preaching. He left it at Brondrefawr to travel less conspicuously, but a few days later he was arrested in South Radnorshire and spent many years in prison. The mobile pulpit has remained in Bwlch y Sarnau and can be seen today in the Baptist Chapel.

Meanwhile, early Baptists also worshipped at **Cwmfeardy**, possibly from as early as 1660. The farmhouse was occupied by a Peter Gregory, and a Henry Gregory from Llanddewi was the Minister. Henry Gregory died in 1700. In 1721 the Annual Meeting of the Welsh Baptist Association (which stretched throughout South Wales) was held at Cwmfeardy, which indicates its importance as a church. The farm was at that time occupied by a Nathan Davies. In 1722 a church was built at Rock, near Cross Gates, and Nathan Davies was buried there upon his death in 1726. The Cwmfeardy farmhouse in which the services were held has long since gone and been replaced by the

Baptism in the River Marteg Rev Ivor Brown and John Davies (75)

The old Bwlch Sarnau Baptist Chapel built in 1829 and demolished in 1900 (76)

current house, built in 1875.

In 1807, a Stephen Pugh from Cwmderw was baptised at Nantgwyn Chapel (founded 1792). He preached regularly in the farmhouses of Bwlch y Sarnau, and in 1817 moved in to Brondrefawr, where he lived for the rest of his life. His preaching was very popular and soon the farmhouses were not big enough for the number of people wishing to hear him. Many people were converting to the Baptist Faith, and in 1826 and 1827 many baptisms took place - the first recorded in the Bwlch y Sarnau district were in a stream by the Hendy and later in the River Marteg.

In May 1828 building of a chapel began on a site central to the village obtained from one of the Deacons, Mr Josiah Pugh of **Beili Bog**. The chapel was of basic oblong design and constructed using local stone, slate roof and a clay floor. It used the natural contours of the land from east to west, with two doors in the south facing wall, one entering by the pulpit on the lower end, one at the back at the upper end. The chapel had no form of heat or light, the latter being provided by tallow candles. As many came to worship on horseback, a stable and horseblock were also built, both of which are still there today, in the wall next to the old school.

The chapel was opened for worship with a service on

The new 1901 Bwlch y Sarnau Baptist Chapel built by farmers men. (76)

As Time Goes By - The Chapels

21st May 1829. It cost less than £100 to build. A couple of years later, one of the congregation, a Mary Williams, who had come to live at Pantglas in 1770 from Nantmel, bequeathed her cottage Ffosyfaen and land for the use of Bwlch y Sarnau chapel for ever. A Manse was built on this land in 1894 at a cost of £210.

The Rev Stephen Pugh was the minister of the chapel until his death in 1872, aged 87. Rev David Davies then became joint pastor of Nantgwyn, Beulah and Bwlch y Sarnau.

In 1870 the members of the church built a school, which, in 1924, due to the hefty maintenance costs, was sold for £400 to the Radnor Education Authority.

The Baptists in Abbeycwmhir

Meanwhile, in Abbeycwmhir, worship took place in Cefn Pawl Farmhouse. Mr Pryce Pugh, a deacon of Bwlch y Sarnau, occupied Cefn Pawl for a short time until his death in 1843 aged just 37. His brother Josiah Pugh then lived there for the next 40 odd years, during which time he kept the house open for regular worship. He longed to see a chapel built in the area, but sadly he died before this happened, on 9th May 1885, aged 76. However, his son, Thomas Pugh of Llwyn Onn, travelled to London to see Squire George Henry Philips of Abbeycwmhir Hall, the owner of the Abbeycwmhir Estate which included Cefn Pawl Farm, to ask for a site on which to build a chapel and graveyard. Squire Philips immediately returned and generously gave the land and later paid the conveyance costs. Josiah Pugh was laid to rest in the graveyard, the first to be interred there, before the chapel was built. The foundation stone of the chapel was laid on 6th November 1885 by the Rev J

Headstone of Josiah Pugh, the first burial in Cefn Pawl's graveyard - still is use today. (78)

Prickard of Rhayader, a clergyman of the Church of England. The chapel cost £600 to build, most of which was raised by Thomas Pugh.

By 1900 Bwlch y Sarnau Chapel was too small for the congregation - it had been felt for some years that a bigger and better building was needed, so a 'Building Fund' was launched for a new chapel in May 1900 and work started to pull down the old one. Donations were collected from all over Mid Wales, and the farmers pledged to release a man for a day a week during the year of construction to help with labouring jobs and carting materials. In August 1900 two commemorative stones were laid in the foundations and inscribed silver trowels were presented after the ceremony. One of these trowels was presented back to the chapel in 1977 where it is now on display.

The new chapel was completed and opened for worship in June 1901. It cost £1000 to build, easily covered by the £1060-8-3 collected in the Building Fund. It is of solid construction with stone walls and slate roof, and the cost included fixed seating. It is built in the shape of a cross with box channel ceiling in the main body of the interior for good acoustics.

Cefn Pawl Baptist Chapel in 1995. (79)

In 1886 Bwlch y Sarnau Chapel severed its connection with Nantgwyn and Beulah churches and joined with the newly erected Cefn Pawl Chapel, sharing ministers for 59 years until they decided to separate in 1945. Thereafter, Cefn Pawl was without a full time minister, relying on lay preachers for the Sunday services. From 1952 Frank Price, the Chapel Secretary, conducted many of these services.

Bwlch y Sarnau Chapel joined with Rock Baptist Church in 1972, and with Rhayader Baptist Church in 1980.

In 1922, there was a dispute between Major Philips and the Local Education Authority which resulted in Abbeycwmhir School being shut for one year. The tiny Chapel vestry at Cefn Pawl served as the village school for 23 children from October 1922 until October 1923.

A centenary service was held at Cefn Pawl Chapel on 6th November 1985, led by Rev J.C. Jones who had first preached there some 40 years earlier.

At the time of the centenary, the church officers were Mrs Nora Bennett, Treasurer (whose father Edward Morgan founded the Sunday School in 1914 and was treasurer himself from 1926; Mrs A Price, Secretary (whose husband Frank Price and father-in-law Edward Price were trustees and lay preachers); and Miss V. Price, Organist.

Declining member numbers and rising maintenance costs of the building led to the sad decision to close the chapel in 1995. The building was deemed unsafe, so had to be demolished. The last sevice took place on Sunday 20th August 1995, led by Mr Ken Gabriel. The footprint of the chapel remains, together with the foundation plaque. The graveyard is maintained by the members of the chapel, and is still in use today.

The last service at Cefn Pawl Baptist Church 20th August 1995 led by Mr Ken Gabriel. (80)

Cefn Pawl Graveyard in 2010 (81)

Methodism in Abbeycwmhir

Methodism in Abbeycwmhir has been contained almost entirely within Devannor farmhouse for a period of nearly 200 years. It began in 1818 when Thomas and Sarah Griffiths moved to Devannor from Llanbister parish with their three children, Evan (20), John (7) and Anne (4). They started holding Methodist services in Devannor house almost immediately, and regular meetings and services were held for the next six generations until 2003.

Between 1891 and about 1920 services and meetings were also held at Cwmgringlyn, where Evan (above) had gone to live and have a family. Devannor was in the Rhayader Circuit initially, then in the Kington Circuit, then transferred to the Knighton Circuit when that was formed in 1861 and there it remained. In 1860 the Kington Circuit had 38 Chapels and Societies from Radnorshire, Shropshire and Herefordshire, (Devannor was a Society) and 54 preachers, two of whom were John Griffiths of Devannor (the John above), and his nephew Evan or Thomas from Cwmgringlyn .

The preachers travelled between chapels and were greatly scrutinised to ensure they met the requirements for Methodism – non-smoking, tee total, non-gambler, attentive to discipline etc. They travelled on horseback and often stayed overnight at Devannor whilst taking services at the chapels in the vicinity. In 1864 the journey was made easier with the advent of Central Wales Railway Line. Penybont could be reached by rail, preachers would then walk, borrow a horse, or more often be collected by pony and trap on Saturday after noon by someone from Devannor.

The last Service at Devannor in 2003 with *Willie Griffiths in the foreground.* (82)

Mrs Clarice Griffiths, who came to Devannor to live in 1919 upon her marriage, would frequently take the trap to meet the preacher at Penybont, until 1929 when her husband, James John Griffiths bought a motor car, one of the first people in the valley to do so, primarily for the purpose of conveying the preachers. Interestingly, Clarice Griffiths above, nee Lewis of Troedrhiwfelen, was the great-grand daughter of Rev Stephen Pugh, Brondrefawr, who converted so many to the Baptist faith in Bwlch y Sarnau in the early 1800s.

Devannor had 'society meetings' on Sundays and monthly class meetings on Thursday evenings (this had changed to Friday by 1891). Cwmgringlyn held meetings on alternate Sundays and Llanbister had its monthly class meeting on Monday evenings. The same preacher, from Knighton

Methodist's loved the Word of God and Singing Hymns. (83)

or Clun, did all these services and meetings, walking from Devannor to Cwmgringlyn to Llanbister and back, and so probably stayed at Devannor from a Friday eve until Tuesday morning. A lot of walking and a lot of extra work for the household with meals to prepare and sheets to boil.

In the Wesleyan Methodist Magazine of 1913 the Rev. Isaac Page reminisces over incidents occurring in "A Riding Circuit Fifty Years Ago". He kept a journal and for Thursday 15th September 1863 wrote:-
'That first service at Devannor will never be forgotten. It was held in a spacious farm kitchen, with open fire-place and blazing wood fire. A congregation numbering about thirty was arranged around the room, several sheep-dogs occupying the centre of the floort. In one corner was a preacher's desk, with a wooden block to stand upon, and a lighted candle, the only one in the room. When the service began, hymn books were produced and a young woman carried around a bundle of peeled rushes, soaked in fat, one of which served two persons. These were knocked out with the fingers when the hymn was finished, to be re-lighted for the next. A novel sight for the young minister, accustomed only to town life!'

In the circuit each year there would be Annual Circuit Teas and Public Meetings, where members from each place were encouraged to attend every other place to develop the spirit of the circuit. In June 1893 there was a 75th Anniversary Celebration Tea at Devannor, and the Methodist Magazine said:-

"We propose arranging for a Brake, or more than one, for the Devannor Tea. We can scarcely imagine a finer outing than to drive to Devannor. The picturesque Abbey-cwm-hir, the glorious view, north, south, east and west, from the splendid hills at the back of Devannor House. Should the weather be sufficiently fine we expect to have tea under the trees, with the splendid valley down which the Clewedog finds its way to the Ithon below Penybont, and Llandrindod in our view."

The Brake referred to is a four wheeled open carriage, drawn by horses with two lengthwise seats facing one another behind the driver's crosswise seat. It would have brought people from Knighton. The write up in the magazine the following month said a good time was had by all; some walked in the dingle, some climbed the hills, some visited Abbey-cwm-hir 'to see the Hall and visit the ruins of the old Abbey. Upwards of 100 sat down for tea and we had a crowded place afterwards for the Public Meeting.'

The write up in the magazine the following month said a good time was had by all; some walked in the dingle, some climbed the hills, some visited Abbeycwmhir 'to see the Hall and visit the ruins of the old Abbey'.

In the 1950s some ministers would spend holidays at Devannor while their wives visited family elsewhere; others with a sporting interest would come over mid week to shoot rabbits or play cricket. One minister, who had trained as a civil engineer, designed and supervised the construction of a concrete cricket pitch on a flat riverside meadow (which still exists today).

1918 saw the Centenary Service, and on Saturday 24 July 1993 a special celebration for the 175th

Anniversary. Basil Howard, who was 'stationed' in the Knighton Circuit fifty years earlier after graduating from Wesley College in 1942, and who happened upon the celebration by chance after booking a caravan holiday in Brecon, wrote:- *"some 150 people came, from nearby places and a few, like me, from a distance. A service was held in the kitchen and relayed to a large overflow in a marquee. And then, of course, there was tea for everyone."*

Harvest Festivals at Devannor were big celebrations, held the third Sunday in October, with usually over 100 people attending and sitting down to tea afterwards. Devannor teas consisted of bread and butter, cheese and homemade jam, and a wide variety of homemade cakes and tarts.

In the 1960s joint services with St Mary's Church were introduced, on the third Sunday of each month alternating between the Church and Devannor.

Devannor was never registered for weddings, but christenings have been taking place there across the generations, the latest two being 7th generation Griffithses, Abraham and Reuben Berriman, in 2000 and 2002, who now live next door.

Services ceased here in 2003, with the last being held on 16th February 2003, a joint service with St Mary's.

One of three benches used for services at Devannor. (84)

The people knelt
At the sturdy bench of the yard of their neighbourhood farm,
With easy generosity, it gave them
A barn to shelter against bishops.
The resolve of its children will not bend
neither to a lord nor all his machinery.
- Waldo Williams [13]

THE HALL

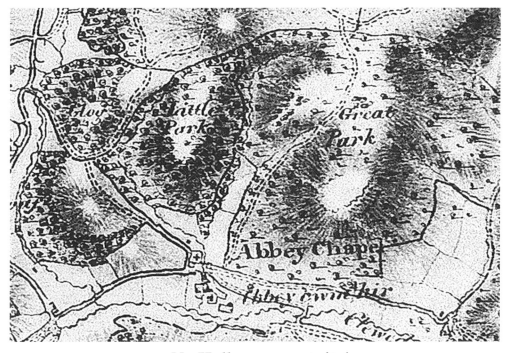

No Hall on present site!

The above is the oldest detailed map of Abbeycwmhir - an 1817 Surveyors sketch for the Ordnance Survey - there is no Hall but only parkland under the words Abbey Chapel. The road goes straight across the present hall's garden, without a bend, to the Abbey Chapel of Ease (Convenience) of Llanbister Parish. The only houses are where Home Farm and the Abbey ruins are today. (87)

"The situation of these ruins like that of many other monastic remains evinces the classic taste and superior judgement for judicious selection of the ancient ecclesiastics.

Embosomed in the centre of a fertile valley, encompassed by hills of no mean elevation. and grandeur, it seems to have been designed for the abode of satiating affluence, and indolent repose. From these hills surrounded by scenery of bold and romantic aspect the eye expatiates with delightful satisfaction over a country beautifully diversified and of wide extent, till the view is terminated by a northern horizon, formed by the venerable Snowdon, the Plinlimon and Cader Idris, whose lofty summits majestically mingling with the clouds seem to prescribe a limit to the boundaries of space". The sales pitch of Wilson's Estate Agent, Layton Cooke. [1]

Above left: *the watercolour painting seems to be an artistically elongated version of Home Farm (below) with similar windows. It was painted by the Canada based Scotsman George Herriot during his only known travels in Wales between 1796 and 1799 - before the time of Wilson. (85)*

Below Left: *Home farm and the ruins in 2010. (86)*

Thomas Wilson

Thomas Wilson's brief thirteen years of ownership of land in Abbeycwmhir created some of the biggest beneficial changes to the Community since the Cistercians. Not only did he build the first Hall on the present site, he made the roads function, improved most of the main institutions of the village: the Church, the Pub, the Mill, the Blacksmiths – and the Forestry (see the relevant sections of this book). He also rebuilt or repaired most of the farm houses.

Wilson was a practising solicitor and a manager of the huge Lord Portman's Estate in Marylebone, London,[2] so he knew a bit about estates and also who knew even more than him. Layton Cooke, styled a Land, Tithe and Timber Surveyor, was also an active and published agriculture and trade researcher in Europe and the UK (cf p 301) he was the top man to write a report about Abbeycwmhir. It has been assumed that Wilson commissioned him to make this very detailed and comprehensive report but the properties most featured were those the Fowlers sold him directly later on – so they could have been behind it.

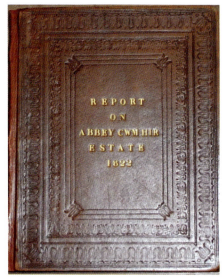

Wilson's leather cover for the Layton Cooke Report 1822 (88)

Also the Report is dated 1822 but it wasn't until April 1824 that Wilson actually bought twelve farms in the Community area totalling 1282 acres.[3] A few days later on the 10-12th April he successfully petitioned Parliament to allow him to clear the abbey ruin. *"That the scite of the Monastery of Cwm Hir be dissolved by Authority of Parliament"* where he made excavations *"soon after"*.[4] But curiously he didn't purchase the Abbey site, the Great Park and sixteen other properties amounting to 2128 acres until 1828 - directly from the Fowlers.[5]

Thomas Wilson, Gent, was probably introduced to the area by Samuel Woodburn who owned Cadwgan Hall, Llanbadarn Fawr, (Crossgates), and was the art

Left: Thomas Wilson (1787 – 1863). *A photograph of a lost painting by J.J. Halls, Exhibited at the Royal Academy in 1832.* (89) *"....he is blessed with a pair of such singularly active legs, as seemingly to annihilate distance and space, his presence in chambers, in the council room, in his own offices, and at the extremities .... being apparently coeval in point of time'.* South Australian Magazine, Adelaide, (where he moved next and became Mayor) published in November 1841, three years after he emigrated.

As Time Goes By - The Hall

Haymaking over the years at Abbeycwmhir

Left: *"Airing the Millinery" at Upper Esgair 1976. Top left: Shirley Stephens & Rose Davies. Below: Ken Davies, Glyn Davies & Gwynne Stephens.* (90)

Centre Left: *"A Load of Hay - before tractors" outside Beilibog.* (91)

Below Left: *"Harvest Home " Davies Family, Beilibog, 1950.*(92)

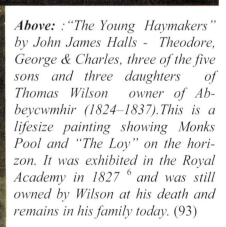

Above: *:"The Young Haymakers" by John James Halls - Theodore, George & Charles, three of the five sons and three daughters of Thomas Wilson owner of Abbeycwmhir (1824–1837).This is a lifesize painting showing Monks Pool and "The Loy" on the horizon. It was exhibited in the Royal Academy in 1827* [6] *and was still owned by Wilson at his death and remains in his family today.* (93)

dealer who had helped him create his impressive art collection in his home in Dulwich, London.[7] Two Rembradt prints are acknowledged as his donation to the British Museum today.[8] He also commissioned several paintings of Abbeycwmhir. He probably wished to have a country seat, to which he could retire with space for his ever-growing art collection in a Hall he was finally to build. He was truly a *Renaissance Man*, at 37 years old he had a country estate, was somewhat experienced in the ways of the world, had a unique art collection, and went on to publish his own poetry,[9] and lecture and write about art: especially engraving, music: organ building, and natural history: entomology (insects).

His signature on the mortgage of 29th July 1834 (94)

The 63 pages of the Layton Cooke report are written in a fine copper plate handwriting, but apparently bound in leather by Thomas Wilson whose personal copy has his hand written notes in – mainly from 1833 after he had made many improvements to the Estate and thereby giving us much information.[10] After a purple sales passage (cf p 67), the report, offers extremely detailed advice on what needs to be done to improve the estate and make it profitable to a future owner. "In contemplating the improvement of this magnificent property, amongst the various objects that crowd upon the mind, that which firsts solicits attention by its individual importance, and by its intimate connection with every other branch of improvement is the state of the roads!"[11]

Wilson notes in 1833 that these are now "...all perfectly level and of good width, it passes by Hamptons Cloth Mill under Cwm Verdy wood and enters the Estate at Cuckoos Nest and thence to the Dwelling House".[12]

Soon after the Parliamentary Authority came through Wilson writes, "I contracted to have the interior of the ruins cleared to the floor.....of the ruined building itself I have not disturbed a stone"[13] He talks of *clearing* rather than excavating but the science of archaeology was in its infancy. Only a few years before, in 1803, the Earl of Elgin had *cleared* the "Elgin Marbles" from their original place on the Parthenon in Athens, Greece and taken them to the British Museum in London! James

A Summer morning after the ruins had been cleared painted by Frank Howard (C 1827). Thomas Wilson claims to have planted the trees in the background on the left. (95).

Purchase & Sale information researched and summarized by Julian Lovell of Tyr Ehedydd.

Lewis of Cwmscawen thought a good job had been done and wrote, that "… the ruins of the Abbey... (have) lately been tolerably excavated" in a letter dated 25 March 1825[14]- thus giving a date for the start of the work which probably wasn't finished until 1827.[15] Wilson was very excited about the discovery of Mabli's tomb (cf p 17) the Papal Seals (cf pp 36-7) and some silver pennies of Edward II (1284 – 1327).

It has been said that Wilson was the biggest influence on Abbeycwmhir since Henry VIII implying that much was lost by his clearance of the ruins. However, he clained that it was, "the <u>un</u>-ornamented freestone I have used to build a good substantial dwelling house, introducing some of the ornamented pieces; The other stone (many hundred tons) I have had broken up and used for the roads". [16]

"Near the new Dwelling House I have turned the high road to obtain more lawn, and have cut down the banks, filled the hollows way in front of the public house, and built a stone bridge

Cwmhir Lodge, Wilson's home in Kensington, Adelaide, South Australia. Now demolished. The family still have a Cwmhir Farm near Adelaide. (96)

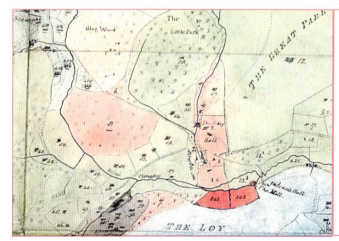

1837 Sale Map. Wilson "inclosed about 30 acres of land including the Ruins & Old Orchard for private use & pleasure Ground." (97)

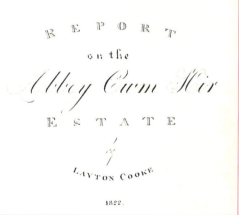

Report Frontspiece. Note copper plate handwriting (98)

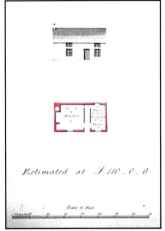

Plan A

over the little stream. Below the ruins I have formed the river into a lake which much adds to its beauty." (Ibid) The Dwelling House cost £2,000 to build. In the 1837 Sale document it is described as "a recently erected elegant and commodious residence built of freestone in the Elizabethan style".[17]

"On Fishpool Farm I have restored the Monks pool and planted the banks, making a walk around – I have formed the waste waters of the river over the head into a cascade whence the river flows down the valley. This pool contains about 3.5 acres" Also,"A walk is formed to the summit of the plantation on the Sugar Loaf Hill and round its base a walk is now continued along the foot of the adjoining hills and of the Globe Wood to the Upper Pool".

Layton Cooke lists all the farms on the Estate that Wilson bought in 1828 [18] describing repairs and improvements that needed to be made. Also plans and drawings to replace several houses as one of three types of two story houses A, B & C. Plan A was recommended for Lower Escair and three *Homes no More*: Galenein, Llanerch Dirion, Curckoos Nest (cf p 106); Plan B was recommended for Upper Escair and *Home no More* Cwm Lleyst (cf P 118) and a larger version of Plan C was built at Cefn Pawl.

All have a Kitchen, a Parlour, a Dairy or Milk House – Cefn Pawl had both plus a "Best Parlour" – and a Cellar. Wilson writes "Almost all the farms have been rebuilt....The dwelling houses have been whitewashed and the buildings coal tarred....All the leases are either expired or in my hands". Part of his motive was to attract better quality tenants so that he can increase the rents and thereby the value of his estate. The "Tenantry" are much criticised by Mr Cooke, "it would be most desirable to introduce habits of cleanliness..." But in 1833 Wilson writes that "the present tenants of the Abbey and Cefn Pawl farms are good farmers...." Of Abbey Farm he writes, "The whole House, Barns etc have been completely rebuilt". Layton Cooke, during his survey of the estate spotted "brick earth of good quality is found on Cefn Pawl land" presumably at The Brickyard and Wilson confirms "Bricks have been made and ...used to rebuild the farm houses". He also attended to drainage - mentioning work on The Rossy (above Wennalt Barn) - and to the defining and marking out boundaries between farms and sheepwalks. He took Rhiw Gam Farm (below the hill of that name) away from Cefn Pawl and added it to Wennallt Farm.

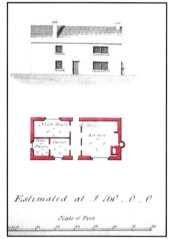

Plan B

Plan C (99)

The Smith's shop was taken down from opposite the Bailiff's cottage and rebuilt with dwelling house and nine acres of land near Loy Hill.

As Time Goes By - The Hall

The amount of money-borrowing, mortgaging and complex deals that went on in early Nineteenth Century Georgian England seems more like the scandals of the early twenty first. Not surprisingly CW Rees writes[19] "in 1824 the property, *notwithstanding its several defalcations by previous sales*....was purchased by Thomas Wilson Esq..." "*Defalcation*" means misappropriation of funds entrusted to someone or "embezzlement". The 1824 purchase had originally been sold by the Fowlers in 1816/17 and there was an attempted resale in 1820 (by Layton Cooke!)[20] between London solicitors and their stationers - property speculation was rife. Wilson eventually reunited parts of the estate in time for Francis Philip's to purchase it!

At the same time as investing in Abbeycwmhir he was also putting money into property development in London - on his employers land. The Portman hay and vegetable market scheme whose grand buildings were built some distance to the north of the Portman Estate across the Marylebone Road in Church Street at Paddington Green (picture cf p 193) was expected to rival Covent Garden Market, but it didn't work and so he and his family were seriously in debt. A year after he completed the first Hall in Abbeycwmhir he re-mortgaged it and had to sell three years later to settle his debts. "He gradually sold his house in Dulwich, his Abbey in Wales and his collection of Rembrandts in order to be able to satisfy his creditors. Poor man!" [21]

Wilson discharged all his financial obligations, according to his nephew Alfred Russel Wallace (the other discoverer of Evolution) and then set sale for Australia to get away from that world. Lord Portman was raised to the peerage (Baron 1827; Viscount 1873).[22]

Wilson clearly loved Abbeycwmhir and named his Adelaide house after us and kept his paintings of the ruins all his life, even in his late sixties he wrote the poem about Abbot Rhirid and Mabli.

Ironically one of the two of his Rembrandt etchings still in the British Museum collection is called 'The Goldweigher' with the subject title: "Banking" - but the other is "Tobias & the Angel"!

Cut Bench Mark (height above mean sea level on Ordnance Survey maps)on the Bridge over the Cwmhir. Hunt the others cf page 303. (100)

The Rev William Evans "was for several years in the 1830s Curate in charge of Abbeycwmhir and lived at the Hall of which he was lessee, when the property was purchased by Mr Frances Phillips in 1837." [23] William Evans and his son started the skeleton in the grave story.

Abbeycwmhir Community Book

(101)

(102)

As Time Goes By - The Hall

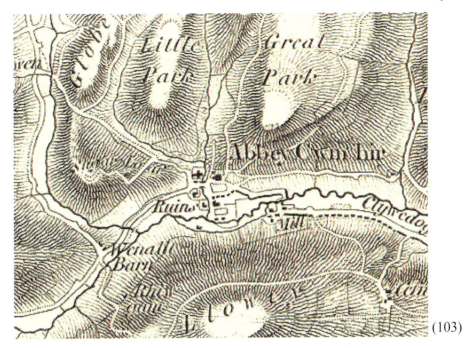

(103)

1833 Ordinance Survey Map showing a Hall in it's present position with extensive gardens behind - and the kink in the road. This is in the time of Thomas Wilson. Note the mill leet curving around the Clywedog and the pond (cf page 100).

***Top Left*: Thomas Wilson's Hall** or "Dwelling House" as he described it finished in 1833 in time for the Ordnance Survey map above. The Sales Document of 1837 describes "THE HOUSE which is built and finished in the most perfect manner and consists: *On the Ground Floor* - of an Entrance Hall and Vestibule, a Dining Room 16ft 16", including bow, by 15 feet 10"; Drawing Room 23ft 8" by 17 feet; a Library, a Ladies Store Room, Kitchen and Scullery. *On the Upper Story* - are Four Bed Rooms, Two Dressing Rooms, Ladies Boudoir, Linen Closet and Water Closet supplied by running stream from the hills behind the house. At a convenient distance are a Coach House, 2 Stall Stables, Yard & Piggeries; also adjoining is a Bailiff's Cottage containing five rooms".[24]

***Lower Left*: George Henry Philips' Hall** photographed around 1901. Note the Chimneys and windows are in the same place but the wings and roof have been replaced. Dated 1868 although masons, joiners and decorators were still at work in April 1870 when Kilvert visited. It was re-designed by architects Poundly & Walker of Liverpool with builders Porteous of Welshpool - who also built the Church.

The rebuilt Hall is in the Gothic Revival style and is Listed Grade II and has 52 rooms including a polygonal ended Billiard Room added on in 1894. Clad in Ashlar stone with polychromatic bands it has three stories with six bays on the south front and three on the east. There are four high gables ornamented by bargeboards which run deeply into the steeply pitched slate roof. On the east front there protrudes a single storey recessed Tuscan style porch with half marble columns and a tiled floor. The windows are embellished above with slate and brick detail. The retaining wall on the south side is set with corbels, and other stone work, from the Abbey.[25]

The Philips - *elegance in simplicity*

Francis Philips (1771 -1850) Squire from 1837 - for 13 years Engraving from a painting. (104)

Francis Aspinal Philips (1793-1859) Squire from 1850 - for 9 yrs and his wife Jane Jackson (1792 - 1857). Paintings by Augustus Henry Fox in Radnorshire Museum, Llandrindod Wells. (105)

George Henry Philips (1831 - 1886) Squire from 1859 for 27 years (106)

Anna Theophilia Prescot (1836 - 1915) his wife - outlived him by a further 27 years. (107)

Mary Beatrice Philips (1828 - 1898) his sister - not maried.108)

← (10
114) -

SQUIRES PHILIPS, WIVES - SISTERS & BROTHERS

From *Further details on Page 82*

1837 **Francis** (Age 66) (Son of John who bought Bank Hall, Heaton Norris, Manchester, (in 1777). Cotton Mill Owners descended from Philips of Heath House, Staffs. "Of Bank Hall & Abbeycwmhir". Would have stayed in Wilson's Hall.

1838 DAY & SUNDAY SCHOOL STARTED by his son Francis Aspinal & Jane.

1846 STARTED INCLOSURE NEGOTIATIONS

1850 **Francis Aspinal** (Aged 57) of Bank Hall & Abbeycwmhir - would have Stayed in Wilson's Hall. OBTAINED INCLOSURE ACT AND BUILT SCHOOL HOUSE IN 1857.

1859 **George Henry** (Aged 28) lived at Abbeycwmhir and buried here.

1867 Married *Anna Theophilia Prescot* & had six children. Buried at St Mary's.

1868 ENLARGED THE HALL, GAVE LAND FOR CEFN PAWL CHAPEL, BUILT A NEW SCHOOL AT PICCADILLY & FITTED THE LAUNDRY.

1868 *Mary Beatrice* sister to George Henry. RE-BUILT ST.MARY'S CHURCH Buried at St.Mary's - Lych Gate in her memory (1900).

1886 *Anna Theophilia* ran the estate & 6 children. Mary Beatrice living in The Hall.

1893 VICARAGE BUILT; 1894 Billiard Room added to The Hall.

1915 **Major Francis, George, Prescot** (Age 42 - wounded) Not married. Buried here (*note his and Anna Theophilia's equipment branding irons - left*).

1918 Attempted Sale, also in 1919 and in 1932.

1932 **Lieut. Colonel John Lionel*** (Age 54). DSO Squire for 27 years. Buried here.

1937 BUILT COMMUNITY HALL Youngest brother of the Major and "of Abbeycwmhir". *Chrystine Anna* (Middle Sister) Church Organist & repair funder, People's Warden and Church Benefactor. Buried at St.Mary's.

1959 Sale of Hall to Nicky and Martin Fenner - the hairdressers - and farms to farmers and Forestry - moved to Ivy Lodge "Little Abbey", Hereford City.

1975 Colonel John Lionel buried at St.Mary's, Abbeycwmhir.

ate branding irons leather, tools and es kept at Home rm today. Impress-s below & left (110)

Major Francis George, Prescot Philips (1873-1932) from 1886 - 46 years. Eldest son of GHP (111)

Chrystine Anna Philips (1870-1958) elder sister of the Major. Church Benefactor (112)

Lieut.Colonel John Lionel Philips DSO (1878- 1975) from 1932 - for 27 years. Youngest brother of the Major (113)

✝ SACRED TO THE MEMORY OF FRANCIS ASPINALL PHILIPS

Abbeycwmhir Community Book

As Time Goes By - The Hall

George Henry Philips's sitting Room at The Hall - restored today by the Humpherstons. (114)

THE CHARMING FREEHOLD, HISTORICAL, RESIDENTIAL AND SPORTING ESTATE.

THE GLASS HOUSES CONSISTS OF ONE COLD PEACH HOUSE, ORNAMENTAL CONSERVATORY (HEATED) **THREE VINERIES AND ONE PEACH HOUSE ALSO HEATED**, GREEN HOUSE, CUCUMBER HOUSE, MELON HOUSE, MUSHROOM HOUSE, VEGETABLE STORE ROOM, BEHIND WHICH ARE SITUATE VEGETABLE FRAMES, LARGE POTTING SHED AND FURNACE ROOM AND SOFT WATER TANK AND PUMP. THE POST OFFICE TELEPHONE AND TELEGRAPH IS IN THE VILLAGE 100 YARDS AWAY. AT PRESENT THE HOUSE IS LIGHTED WITH LAMPS BUT ELECTRIC LIGHT COULD BE AT SMALL COST SUPPLIED FROM THE DYNAMO NEAR THE FARM BUILDINGS BELOW, WHICH NOW PROVIDES THE ELECTRIC LIGHT TO THE HOME FARM AND BUILDINGS. THE MANSION IS CENTRAL HEATED FROM THE BASEMENT. - *DRIVER, JONAS & CO.*[26]

Above Left: *Glass houses behind the Hall where they remained until the 1970's* (115) *and the village centre.* (116) *(There is a more recent picture of The Hall in Homes & People p 220).*

Right: *The 1894 Billiard Room restored by the Humpherstons.* (117)

Below Left: *The village centre as it is circa 2010.* (118)

The sons of George Henry Philips: John Lionel (the Colonel), Francis George (the Major) & Charles Kenrick. Eton Photo. (119)

Three of the Philips Squires went to Eton and Oxford - two to the army. All held public office.

Francis was a Justice of the Peace & a Deputy Lieutenant (DL still today it is a military commission guiven by a Lord Lieutenant who is the personal representative of the British Monarch in a *Lieutenancy* - an area similar to a county. In England, Lieutenancy areas are colloquially known as the *ceremonial counties* and in Wales, as the *preserved counties of Wales*. Francis was "of Bank Hall and Abbeycwmhir".[27] He *"employed a great many labourers in improving the estate especially by means of spade husbandry, for the extension of which he was a great advocate."* From his Obituary in the *Gentleman's Magazine*.[28]

Francis Aspinal was a Justice of the Peace and in 1851 High Sherriff (- or shire reeve - theoretically the sovereign's *judicial* representative in the county. An annual appointment at your own expense). He was "of Bank Hall and Abbeycwmhir". His first son, Francis Philips stayed at Bank Hall and was also "of Lee Priory" cf pictures p 86).

George Henry MA, Oxon was his second son "of Abbeycwmhir" and buried at St.Mary's. He was a Justice of the Peace, Deputy Lieutenant and High Sheriff in 1860 - *"an Eton man, and a great sportsman....very pleasant and hospitable...shy and reserved"* according to Kilvert in April 1870.[29]

Major Francis (Eton and New College, Oxford). Justice of the Peace, Deputy Lieutenant; Major in Hereford Militia and Volunteers and the Kings Shropshire Light Infantry. Won the Military Cross in France 1915. High Sheriff in 1906. He was "of Abbeycwmhir" and buried at St.Mary's.

Lt.Col. John Lionel went to Eton and New College, Oxford. Served in World War I (Royal Artillery) and was mentioned in four despatches. DSO - Distinguished Service Order (1917). A Justice of the Peace. High Sheriff in 1935. He was "of Abbeycwmhir" and buried at St.Mary's.

Anna Theophilia, wife of George Henry caught the roving eye of Kilvert when he popped in for lunch, "cold mutton, bread and butter, sherry and some splendid Burton beer". He described Anna, then 34 years old, as *"Young, lively, girlish and rather pretty"* in April 1870. According to local legend she road about the village on a tricycle and when she came to the rise between the blacksmiths and The Hall she would call out to the blacksmith and his assistant to leave their work to push her up the hill. Similarly if there were any children nearby she would call upon them for help.[30]

The children were required to bow or curtsey and say, "Good Morning Ma'am" to her if she passed them. One day Anna Theophilia was not satisfied with the depth of the curtsey of a little girl and so made her retrace her steps to repeat her greeting. A keen churchgoer she would also wait in the porch until she had seen how many of her tenentry were absent and then visit them during the following days - also a chance to see if there was any of the squires' game stewing in their pots whose lids she was known to lift. In 1905 Williams described The Hall as *"the seat of Mrs Philips"*[31] although The Major (32 yrs) was officially the Squire. "She is buried at St Mary's, Abbeycwmhir. Kilvert also commented with prettiness in mind again on *"the pretty new church, which has free open seats and a good deal of stained glass."*[32]

(120)

The six children of George Henry and two of their partners on the occasion of the marriage of the eldest sister, Mabel (Mabli?)Florence Mary (centre) on Thursday October 27th 1892 to the son of Henry Plantagenet Prescot Phelips (deceased), Harry Vivian Majendie Phelips - with moustache, whose uncle - the vicar centre left - Rev Arthur Majendie Phelips conducted the marriage ceremony with Rev Hermitage Day assisting. The other children are Francis George, the future Major (age 19) holding the arm of his eldest sister - for whom he was Best Man, On the left is the middle son, Charles Kenrick; behind him is Doris Elinor who will marry Rev. Hermitage day (far right) standing . On his left is the 14 yr old John Lionel - the future Colonel. The central bridesmaid is the middle sister, Chrystine Anna, who, like the Major, didn't marry.

The photograph was taken at 2.30 after the wedding by Llandrindod Wells Photogrpaher, Mr T.Roberts.

Not all is black and white. The bride is wearing a dark blue travelling dress and a yellow wastecoat. The bridesmaids wear white dresses but the two on the left have blue wastecoats and the one on the right, a cousin, has a pink wastecoat! A huge crowd waved them off on their honeymoon from Penybont Station. They travelled by train to Hawkestone Park, near Wem where they stayed before boarding the P&O ship Peshawur for India where they lived and worked.[33]

But nobody looks very happy! At the back left is the only person looking reasonably content - Doris Elinor, the younger sister, who is going to marry, the next year, the young Rev Dr Ernest Hermitage Day (top right - note his face). Local legend records that he was in love with the beautiful Mabel who has just married the other young man! To help his pain the Philips build him a very wonderful Vicarage – still there today.

BACKGROUND

The Philips are an old Staffordshire family who have held manors there since the Sixteenth Century and since the early 17th Century at The Heath House, Tean, which is still owned by the family today. In the mid 18th Century they built the innovative Tean Hall Ribbon Mills and five Mills in Manchester (*Dorcas bed linen*) whence the Abbeycwmhir, Bank Hall, branch originated. The family were major cotton and sugar[34] importers with a branch, a town (Philipsburgh), and a Merchant Bank (Boddington, Philips & Sharp) in America.

The Abbeycwmhir Philips also owned many acres in central Llandridod Wells as it was developing. George Henry and Anna Theophilia bought in the 1870's and sold in the 1890's land which became Middleton & Temple Street & the Pump House Hotel now the site of the present County Hall.[35]

The wedding party of the eldest sister, Mabel Florence Mary on Thursday October 27th 1892 after she had married Harry Vivian Majendie Phelips. This picture also shows Francis Philips of Bank Hall and Lee Priory, (sitting far left) brother of the late George Henry who led Mabel down the isle. Next to him is Mary Beatrice who had St.Mary's Church built at her own expense. Sitting on the far right is her mother Anna Theophilia who gave her away and to her left sisters Doris and Chrystine Anna (standing). (121)

In the front row of the photo above, sitting, from the left: Francis Philips of Bank Hall and Lee Priory; Mary Beatrice (St. Mary's) and Francis's wife Caroline Mary.

In front from left to right: Chrystine Anna, Anna Theophilia and Mabel Florence with Harry behind with their new family & Ayah - in Hyderabad, India.
(122)

Centre right of the above photo: Rev H.Day - still looking glum- behind his future mother-in- law Anna Theophilia and future wife, Doris.

Abbeycwmhir reaches the Indian Raj - at high speed
From right to left: On the bicycle in front is Chrystine Anna Philips; on the horse is Mabel Florence and on the bicycle at the back is her husband, Harry Majende Phelips. (123)

THE SQUIERARCHY is now a largely historical British social class, consisting of land owners who could live entirely off rental income - they were commoners in the British sense because they didn't hold inheritable titles. *"The landed gentry, or what used to be called the Squirearchy, is a particularly British institution. Nothing quite like it exists in the world.* (Except in China, India and Korea - Ed.) *Its members have no constitutional title or* (inherited) *privileges, the duties they take on are, broadly speaking only those they give themselves...strictly speaking three qualifications were considered necessary before the title could be properly used (1)There should be a mansion or residence; (2) There should be a farm attached to the residence. (3) There should be an estate no matter how small or how large".* (Maddox [36])
A prolonged agricultural depression in Britain at the end of the 19th century, together with the introduction of increasingly heavy levels of taxation on inherited wealth in the 20th century, put an end to agricultural land as the primary source of wealth for the upper classes. Many estates were sold or broken up, and this trend was accelerated by the introduction of protection for agricultural tenancies, encouraging outright sales, from the mid-20th century. Abbeycwmhir estate was finally dismembered in 1959.

Burkes Landed Gentry in 1952 was sponsored by South African Sherry (South African Wine Farmers Association) perhaps because many of their readers ended their days in South Africa. Doris went with the Rev Hermitage Day to Pinelands, Cape Town, South Africa where Mabel and Harry were also living by 1952. The Indians and Africans were probably better *"tenants"* than those in Abbeycwmhir!

Abbeycwmhir Community Book

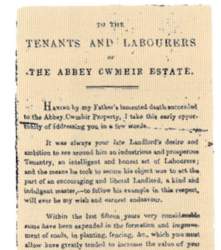

Left: The four page printed letter sent to the farmers and labourers by George Henry Philips - the new man at The Hall in 1859 .just after the inclosure of the estate. He signed it "Your Affectionate Friend, GH Philips. (124) This letter illustrates the values of the Liberal Landlord:

"It was always your late Landlords desire and ambition to see around him an industrious and prosperous Tenantry, an intelligent and honest set of Labourers; and the means he took to secure his object was to act the part of an encouraging and Liberal Landlord, a kind and indulgent master.....

Bearing in mind these and other liberal acts of your two former Landlords, I beg each of you ask himself the questions - Have I done all I can to improve my farm, my Cattle and my Sheep? Have I tried by increased exertion to show that I appreciate the many, acts of kindness that have been offered me? Or have I been content to farm in the same way as my ancestors did for the last hundred years or more, without taking advantage of modern experience?....

I am very thankful to say that with the last few years there has been a great advance made among many of you; your farms look neater, your crops cleaner and more prolific; and rest assured it is by your increased energy, your skill and perseverance in improving your Farms that you can alone expect to retain possession of them for any length of time, owing to the gradual approach of railways, the easier access to the great manufacturing districts of England as your markets, and the consequently enhanced value and demand for the larger class of your Farms....

As your Landlord. I shall be willing to build, drain, and carry out other improvements....and as the cost of draining is now reduced by the manufacturing of pipes on the Property, I hope to see a great spirit of improvement going on in this most necessary of all agricultural undertakings....

You have had a school provided for you, affording the advantages of a good education for your children, but I much regret the lukewarmness there is among some of you in sending your children to it ......I hope it cannot be the few pence you have to pay, for then you surely are not in a fit position to hold your Farms.....Let me beg of you to send your children to School, and above all let me impress on you the necessity to send them regularly.[12] (Full text is in Appendix on Page 299)

The Philip's enclosure at St.Mary's Graveyard. Foreground: George Henry & Anna Theophilia; to the right: the Major; right again: Lieutenant Colonel John Lionel; to the left the standing cross is for Mary Beatrice and to the right of her is a ledger stone slab to Chrystine Anna. (125)

As Time Goes By - The Hall

The Colonel and the second Mrs Philips, a Canadian, Shearne Van Kaugal playing with Rufus the dog - and guests. (126)

Mrs D. Prosser of Llwynon, the oldest tenant, gives to Col. Philips the key and an engraved silver plate for the writing desk they gave him as thanks for 100 years association & generosity.(127)

Times May 8th 1959 (P15, Col.G)
"Virtually the whole of the Abbey Cwmhir estate, which extends to about 2,200 acres...has now been disposed of privately, mainly to tenants, but with a portion going to the Forestry Commission, who already own land near. The property includes four major farms, a public house, a large number of cottages and a considerable area of woodland. The Hall itself was sold separately. Messrs. Strutt & Parker, Lofts & Warner handled the sale. [37]

"When my father was going to the village school, there was a Major Philips at the Hall. My father used to tell of harvest time at Home Farm. They would be hay making down on the meadows below the village, and this one day, he was going home from school when he counted twenty people on the field. Apparently it was looking like rain and so the Major had every available person on the field to help get that hay in. Servant girls from The Hall as well as the carpenter and stone mason, Blacksmith, Wheelwright, Miller, as well as his regular farm hands".

And we knew that just over the high garden wall, was a large strawberry patch – and every now and again, along the wall, was a pole that took the electric up to the gardener's cottage (that was the first electric - not the mains). In the summer evenings we would be playing football using the church gates as one goal and the alley going down to the Union as the other. And we would wait for Mr & Mrs Mytton to go to the pub, wait for perhaps another ten minutes for him to get a pint and perhaps start a game of darts, and off we would go, climb up one these poles onto the wall. Then it was only a small step down on the inside. Being summer we would be wearing just shirt and trousers, filling our pockets we would slide back down the poles. What a mess. One way of making strawberry jam in one minute flat!

*In the early nineteen twenties when the chap who was then the blacksmith came back from the war, he asked the Major about electricity – the Major had heard of it. This man, by the name of Jack Went, a very clever chap, knew his stuff. He told the Major if he would get the equipment needed, the blacksmith would do the rest. Borrowing the Carpenter to make a shed and the blacksmith started making a small water wheel to fit into the hole. So it was done. The little home made waterwheel drove the dynamo. And so electricity came to Abbeycwmhir. Years before it came to Llandrindod Wells, we had electric light through the village and up as far as the school". **NP** *[38] But it would be turned off when the Major went to bed!

Some of the members of the eleven families which took part in the scheme to bring effective television to Abbey Cwmhir.

Mrs Chamberlain (centre) and members of the eleven families after she switched on the TV for the first time at Abbeycwmhir. (128)

After the Philips:

1959 -1962 Jimmy **Fenner** from Lincolnshire, wig-maker & hairdresser; ran a Chinchilla "Ranch" in centrally heated Squash Courts. [39]

1962 - 1995 Mrs Mary Ethel **Chamberlain**
The *mysterious and extraordinary* [40] Mrs M.E. Chamberlain acquired a fascinating collection of paintings, furniture and works of art in her attempt to restore the Hall to its former glory. At her death in 1995, 111 items were auctioned in Cardiff and expected to raise in excess of £50,000. They included a 17th C carved oak court cupboard estimated at £4,000 and Portugese painting of Madonna with infant Jesus surrounded by 15 vignettes of the life of Christ estimated at £2,500. Her money came from the Daytech Missile Guidance Company.

1995 - Nov 1997 **Reynolds.**

1997 **Humpherstons** Paul & Victoria Humpherston bought The Hall, spent nine years restoring it - and many more sharing it.

"..the sometimes crotchety manner of the Major concealed a kind heart. Paddy Larkin, a casual labourer, had been out in the woods collecting firewood, and was homeward bound with a bag of wood chips slung over his shoulder when he ran into the Major who asked him what the bag contained, "Wood Chips, sir" was the reply. Asked if he had obtained permission to collect the wood Paddy replied, "No Sir," whereupon he was ordered to tip out the contents of the bag. As Paddy disconsolately made for the Happy Union, the Major went to Home Farm where he ordered the waggoner to take a horse and gambo into the wood, collect a load of firewood, and deliver it to Paddy".[41]

Every year at the Abbey School, or at least, every Autumn, we would be working hard on our Christmas Concert as well as learning the usual things. At about 5pm there would be a tea party and The Colonel and Mrs Phillips would give each child a small gift. Then we would play games until the concert started at 7pm.

Children would sing, recite poetry. Some of the bravest would sing solo, some in pairs and we had a choir of sorts. We would do sketches and all sorts of things for two hours or so. Then it would be home, happy and very sleepy. The money we made on concert night would be kept safe and then in Summer it would pay for school trips to Aberystwyth – another evening when we would go home tired and happy. I used to think that the best part of the day was stopping for fish and chips in Rhayader – a treat we only had once a year.

Then came the Italians and the one that came to work for the Colonel stayed here, Greeno Barbaretto, or something like that. He worked at Home Farm until the end of the war, and some time after. They were allowed to go home. He asked if he could come back to this country and the Colonel said yes. He went to try and find his childhood sweetheart – and he found her. I can't remember if he brought her back on the next trip or not - but he brought her over soon after. And then he was made Gardener and lived in the Gardeners Cottage. NP

THE HAPPY UNION INN

(129)

The Happy Union Man on Goat

What could be better than there being at the centre of our Community a pub whose name evokes Happiness and Unity with a jewel[1] of a sign symbolising the depths of Welshness and Good Cheer?

Such a name, the Happy Union, begs a question as does the very unusual sign. Who originally conceived and painted the sign? It is claimed by John Jones, the present publican, to have had →

the date of 1858 beside the signature - this was the last year of Francis Aspinal Philip's life. There is a story that about this time the artist came to stay at the great house over the way and he, like many others, was struck with the curious name of the inn, and so he endeavoured to express *The Happy Union* in the inn sign which he painted"[2] But who was the artist? Major Francis Philips, claimed in the Estate Sale Brochure of 1919 that it was painted by ↓

George Morland - but the famous Morland died in 1804 so either the date or the identity of the painter are wrong! Morland was much imitated and although the subject – country folk, animals not to mention pub scenes – are the sort of subject he would have painted it would certainly have been mentioned by Thomas Wilson (here between 1824 and 1837) who commissioned several paintings of Abbeycwmhir (cf pp 71-72), some exhibited at the Royal Academy He was a significant art collector, including of Rembrandt Etchings, and would have known of the late Morland and so would have certainly mentioned a painting or Inn sign by him in his published lists of his own collection.[3] The sign was necessarily repainted in 2003 by Mary Strong of Broad Oak and not for the first time in living memory - Stephen Dexter of Laithdu repainted it in the 1980's (centre top on previous page).

But why would a publican want a sign like this and why would a painter choose to put these elements together?

They may have been influenced by cartoons about the Welsh which had appeared in London with the discovery of printing from a copper plate (intaglio) in the eighteenth century. Satirical cartoons began to appear like *St David for Wales* (left) riding a goat (1781) and *Taffy and Hur Wife, Shentleman of Wales* (1786) (right) showing the then Prince of Wales, future King George IV, with his mistress Mrs Fitzherbert - also riding a goat.[4] Note the Wenglish, the Anglicisation of Welsh which was spoken throughout Wales at the time (1747) on the cartoons opposite. *Poor Taffy,* riding to London on his goat, was a familiar motif and is probably an influence behind the Happy Union sign.

(*Top 130, above 131*)

The Happy Union Inn

Typically, Taffy wears or carries a leek, a round cheese (cf caws pobi –Welsh Rabbit or Cheese on Toast) and often a red herring.[5] This tradition would have influenced the original painter of the sign even though it was originally a lampoon of a Welshman. Of course the leek symbol goes a long way back in Welsh history .[6]

With Leek

It was said that hiring of workers took place at the Knighton May Fair where the plant you wore in your hat signified your preferred work .[7]

Shon-ap-Morgan Shentleman of Wales, on his Journey to London.

But what tasks would an out of season leek signify? Perhaps the leek was worn by mercenary soldiers seeking employment? (cniht - knight/soldier; tūn - town/settlement = Knighton) Shakespeare refers to the custom of wearing a leek as an "ancient tradition" even at the time he wrote Henry V (1598/9). In Act 4 Scene 7, Fluellin (Llewellyn) says to the King, "I do believe your majesty takes no scorn to wear the leek upon Saint Tavy's Day?" King Henry replies," I wear it for memorable honour: for I am Welsh, you know, good countryman." Fluellen replies, "All the water in Wye cannot wash your majesty's Welsh plod our of your pody, I can tell you that; God pless it and preserve it, as long as it pleases his grace, and his majesty too!"

*Unnafred Shones.
Wife to Shon-ap–Morgan.c 1747*

Although the leek has been recognised as the emblem of Wales since the 16th century, The Red Book of Hergest at the end of the thirteenth century states that leeks are good for healing wounds if mixed with salt and even for healing fractured bones. Perhaps that's why it is considered protection against wounds and therefore to symbolise victory.

Its smell was regarded as similar to the smell of striking lightening.[8] Not surprising its association with the military. As far back as 633 AD, when, at the battle of Heathfield, a monk apparently suggested the Welsh soldiers wore leeks in their caps to distinguish them from their Saxon opponents - and they won the battle. The Welsh Guards to this day have a golden leek as their cap badge. There is also a painting by Richard Caton Woodville (1856 -1927) entitled "Eating the Leek" set in the Officers Mess of the Royal Welch Fusiliers around 1815. (page 108) The Goat is also shown being paraded. (This page *132, 133, 134.*)

Even today at the St.David's Day parade all soldiers must wear a real leak in their hats and the youngest soldier is required to eat a raw leak and then wash it down with a pint of beer.

The association to Wales seems to go back even further to Dewi Sant, Saint David, or Taffy, (d.589 AD) who it was said lived on bread, water, leeks and watercress. He lived to an old age and his last sermon contained the words, "Be joyful and keep your faith and creed. Do the little things that you have seen me do and heard about." Which presumably implied a recommendation to "Eat Leeks"?

The Goat and Wales

In 1857, the year before the sign was probably first painted, Queen Victoria made the Goat the mascot of what became the Royal Regiment of Wales as a result of incidents during the Crimean War (1853-56). The soldiers in the Crimea killed and ate the goats they saw roaming about for fresh meat. But one evening, outside Sebastopol, a goat entered the trenches and, as it was very cold, a soldier, probably a Welsh farmer's son familiar with wild and herded goats, took the animal and put it inside his coat to keep warm. Treble turns on sentry duty in exposed forward positions were commonplace, and this was to be the lot of the soldier concerned who, having placed the kid inside his greatcoat to provide extra warmth, found himself positioned well forward of the advance trenches and close to the Russian position. Unable to move about much during his long vigil, he was drifting into a state of hypothermia when a bleat from the goat alerted him to the Russian advance and he was able to warn the troops behind and so saved the day. The Russians were defeated. After this he protected the goat and even took it on parade with him from which he was not discouraged by his

Cloth leek worn on Busby. (135)

(136)

Royal Welch Fusiliers "Eating the Leek" c 1815 by Richard Caton Woodville 1856 –1927 showing goat (left) & leeks. being eaten (137).   (138,139,) →

The Elements
The Leek

The Goat

Welsh Guards leek forage badge.

Royal Welsh Goat and Goat Major

The Happy Union Inn

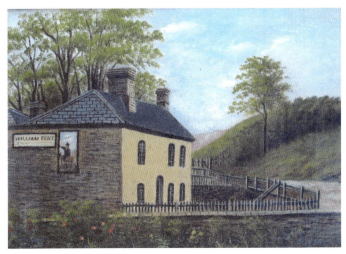

"The Union" a painting showing the sign in 1894 (140)

superiors. The soldiers refused to kill or eat this goat.

When they returned to England and paraded this brown goat before Queen Victoria she designated it the regimental Mascot and offered a white Cashmir goat from the Royal Parks to replace the brown goat when it died. The soldier in charge of the mascot is styled the "Goat Major" but is a corporal. All this was recent history and a likely influence at the time the Happy Union sign was first painted.

A goat had also served with the Royal Welch Fusiliers during the American Civil War since 1775. Official documents state, "The Royal regiment of welch Fuzileers has a privilegeous honor of passing in review preceded by a Goat with gilded horns, and adorned with ringlets of flowers" and "*the corps values itself much on the ancientness of the custom.*"[9] The two regiments with goat-mascots combined as the Royal Welsh in 2006.

| *Merlin with a leek and a goat - a 3D pub sign in Pontypridd, 19th C.* | **King Arthur rides a goat**
Welsh King Arthur, of European fame, riding a goat and carrying a leek seed sceptre depicted in a mosaic in Otranto Cathedral, Sicily, 1165. | *Santa Claus riding the Yule Goat found in Scandinavian folk traditions deriving from the Norse god Thor who rode through the sky in a chariot drawn by two goats. In Sweden the Yule Goat was thought of as an invisible spirit guarding the Yuletide preparations.* |

Flag of St David

Welsh leek Stamp 1999

Welsh Coin of 1985

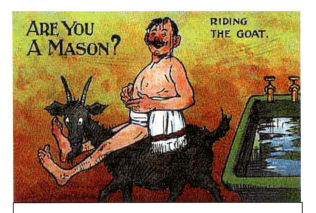

Masonic Associations

"Our first experience upon entering the Lodge as apprentices is to be warned about the Goat. Even before we are informed of 'in whom we should put our trust', we are given knowing looks followed by such comments as; " he's going to get the goat" or " you are going to ride the goat" or even "look out for the goat". It is a good thing that we are informed that we place our trust in God, since some poor unfortunate apprentice could understandably be forgiven for replying," in the Goat".[10] (142)

The doctor's been here seven times
Since father rode the goat.
He joined the lodge a week ago —
Got in at 4 a.m.

There must have been a lively time
When father rode the goat.
He's resting on the couch to-day!
And practising his signs —

But, somehow, when we mention it,
He wears a look so grim
We wonder if he rode the goat
Or if the goat rode him.

*Edited by James Pettibone, 1902
& Roger Coward 2009
From The Masonic Bulletin Oct 2006*

When did The Union become Happy?

Did it always have the same name? Thomas Wilson referred to it as The Happy Union in a handwritten note on his copy of the Estate Sales Catalogue of 1837 [11] as does Kilvert in 1870[12]. But later, William Price, the publican, was less happy when he died in 1887 only claiming to be "of *The Union Inn of this village*" according to his gravestone inscription in St.Mary's churchyard (above -143). However, before 1822 it was known as "The Public"[7] (cf Historical Note p 95) so it became The Happy Union between 1822 & 1837 probably first so called by Thomas Wilson.

Pub names which include the name *The Union* usually commemorate one of the Acts of Union with England. Wales was the first in 1536 & again in 1742, Scotland in 1707 and Ireland in 1801. As the first Welsh Act abolished Welsh Law codified by Hywel Dda (the Good) and the Welsh Language in official documents it is unlikely this would be commemorated. Neither are there are known events at the Happy Union which coincide with these dates. The fact that Abbeycwmhir was in the front line of the wars between the King of England, the Marcher Lords and the Welsh Princes might make the idea of a "happy union" very welcome and our Inn's name may well resonate with that wish. The County of Radnorshire was often considered to be the most anglicised of Welsh counties so a truly Welsh sign like this would be a reminder that we are in Wales.

The Happy Union Inn

The word *union* has another meaning of course. There is an Union Inn in Staffordshire whose sign shows a man and a woman of medieval times being married. A union of hearts and minds. So was there an important marriage in the community, the Hall or nation at this time?

What's in a Name?
- Does the sign explain it?

Perhaps the explanation of the name is in the painting of the sign? A Welshman riding a goat is in happy union? At one level it could be that goats were a familiar and traditional means of transport and a source of food and milk very much to be *in union* with - especially with a tankard of beer in hand!

Or, the eating and drinking man dressed in everyday clothes is happy if he is in control of, and in union with his goat nature. The Goat-Gods, Pan and Dionysius in Greek mythology represent unbridled nature; lust in the case of Pan and drinking and fertility in the case of Dionysius. Hence we have the term for a lecherous older man; "you old Goat".[13] Pan is represented as being half human, half goat with horns, and would later be used in medieval times to represent the devil based on St.Matthew's distinction between the good sheep and the bad goats who go to hell (Matt. XXV:32). So goats can represent vitality, nimbleness and fecundity as well as destructiveness.

Top Hats were worn by all classes in the Mid - 19th Century – including rat catchers, gardeners & fishermen. (144)

In modern terms, a person is in union with themselves if they know and can live comfortably with all sides of their character - including their goat - rather than making a condemned devil out of it or playing the giddy goat. This might be their eating-to-destruction side, or their obstinacy or their sexuality. Whenever the Happy Union sign was painted, whoever created it and whatever influences came to bear, it is undoubtedly a rich human jewel at the centre of the Community of Abbeycwmhir.

Historical Note:

In 1822 The Happy Union was referred to as "The Public" and was a cottage divided into two tenements which had been illegally built as an encroachment on common land by the tenant of Abbey (or Home) Farm, a Mr Lewis.[14] By 1833 it had been "rebuilt" as one building "with a front and back garden and a small piece of Land" - according to a handwritten note by Thomas Wilson of work he had done in his copy of the Layton Cooke Report. [15]

Perhaps the **Happy Union** was at the simple practical level of the union of the two tenements into one building?! Are the two roofs in the picture on page 89 relevant? It is now a grade II listed building (one roof in picture - page 222).

Pewter Tankard Held High

Not just saying "Cheers" but held high to signify that we sell our ale in pewter jugs as the law prescribes, for right measure - that's why many pubs today have such mugs on display - left over from the those times *(1632 & 1649 Pewterers Petitions)*.[16]

"The Advowson of the Chapel adjoining the Abbey Hall, as also The Public House ("The Happy Union') are part of the Property (145)

First written record of the name "The Happy Union" in Wilsons handwritten note on the 1837 Sales Prospectus.

Abbeycwmhir Community Book

THE WAGES OF LABOUR 1871—1898

1892 Jobs on the estate farms

1897 Jobs at the Hall

1897 Pensions too…..

Excerpts from the Ledger of Home Farm during Anna Theophilia's time - she also provided the pensions. (146)

The Mill

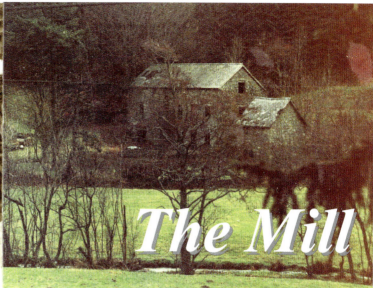

Interior workings of Abbeycwmhir Mill showing the great spur wheel and drive to the millstones which were on the floor above - in 1958. (147)

Abbeycwmhir Mill circa 1976 (148)

The Mill just prior to demolition in 1987 (149)

The Cistercians had nearly 90 mills in Wales and there were at least six belonging to Cwmhir Abbey. There is documentary evidence that this Abbey had two mills in the Manor of Golon at the time of the Dissolution. One was called Guellanissa[1] (possibly *Golon - isa'* or Lower Golon Mill) and the other was probably on the site of the present Mill[2] - plus four at its Granges at Gwernygo, Gabalfa, Buscuant - and Nant-yr-Arian in Ceredigion[3] where the outline of a wheel emplacement could be seen until recently (cf p 43).[4]

With at least sixty male monks to feed, the means of converting grain to flour was essential to make bread - not to mention animal feed. All medieval mills, like those belonging to Cistercian Abbeys had wooden wheels. In its final years, the waterwheel at Abbeycwmhir was made of iron with wooden buckets and the water went over the top (overshot) and was positioned inside the building on the South side. It was about 16 feet in diameter and 5 feet wide. The Mill had two stories and an attic with a wooden pulley and hoist.[5] There were two sets of French burr (quartz) stones on a stone floor, one with a square box and the other with a circular box around it for grinding flour for human consumption. There was also a wooden lean-to building to the west with another grindstone in it probably from Anglesey or Monmouth used for animal feed stuffs.

Abbeycwmhir Community Book

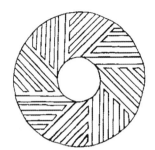

A Quarter Dressed Millstone like those remaining at Abbeycwmhir which are the finely grinding French burrstones, not one piece of stone, but built up from sections of Marne Valley quartz, cemented together with plaster, and bound with iron bands.

Part of the mill and Pony Stable 1968 (150)

A Mill Pick used for dressing the millstones.

Before and after the Dissolution of the Abbey the corn mill was an essential part of the community without which the population could not survive. Whosoever owned or controlled the mill therefore effectively controlled the population within that area whether it was the Abbey or the Squire. Usually you had no choice as to where you ground your corn.[6] The Miller would normally be a tenant of the landowner and had some land attached so he could keep a couple of pigs (fed on chaff, waste corn or meal) & his own pony for delivering sacks of flour and mead.

Because of the damp climate of mid-Wales some grain had to be dried before it was ground. By 1829 the Abbeycwmhir Mill had "come into hand" or reverted back to Thomas Wilson who installed an "iron Dyring Kiln"[7] - cast iron sheets with holes in, there are still some lying about, with a fire underneath. Kiln houses were popular places for the village lads to gather and talk on cold winter nights when the cosy atmosphere was very welcoming.[8] Wilson also installed a Dressing Machine probably operated via a cog off the great spur wheel. (Picture on previous page -147).

With the rising cost of flour and rising populations in the cities, the protective Corn Laws (*Importation Act 1815)* were repealed by the *Importation Act 1846.* The price of grain was central to the price of the most important staple food, bread, on which the working man spent much of his wages. By allowing the import of grain from France, Russia, North America and Australia prices came down down as imported grain could be milled in huge purpose-built industrial mills at the ports of entry so the need for the rural mills went out of use.

Abbeycwmhir's Mill was partly dismantled by 1940 although the wheelwright continued to live there. By 1976 The Old Mill was owned by Jack Griffiths of Devannor who tried to sell it to Durlot Ltd for £9000 with a view to developing the site but the deal didn't go through. A Mr Day bought the Mill and a Mrs Cashmore the Mill House Barn. Later, Mr & Mrs Moore bought both and pulled the old mill down in the summer of 1987 to prevent it being developed next to their house.

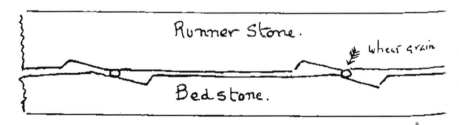

The grain was ground between the similarly patterned bed stone (stationary) and runner stone, the rotary action of which drove the flour to the outer edge.(151

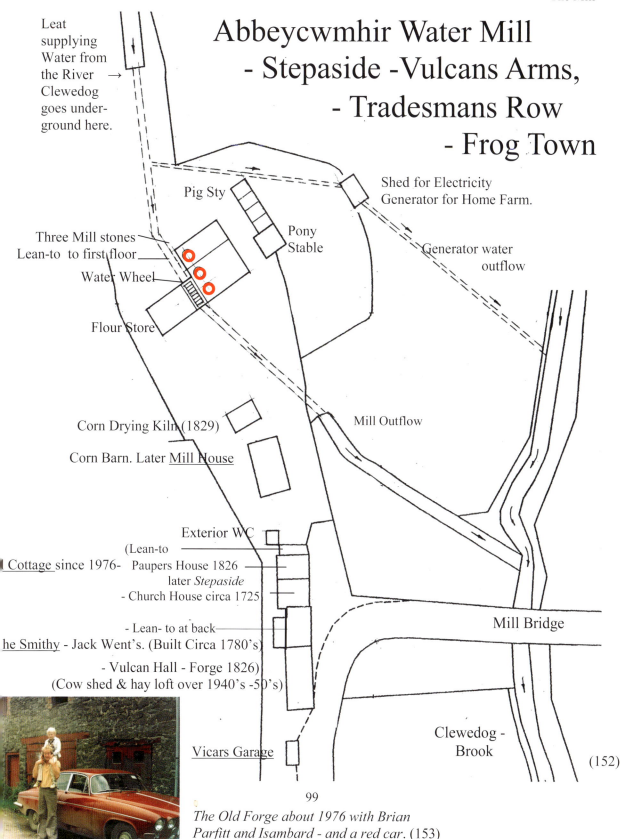

The Old Forge about 1976 with Brian Parfitt and Isambard - and a red car. (153)

Abbeycwmhir Community Book

The outflow to the Clywedog from the Home Farm Pool - not water for the Mill. (154).

Flem, Race, Weir, Leat - the route of the water

When Thomas Wilson wrote in 1833 "Below the ruins I have formed the river into a lake which much adds to its beauty".[9] He was able to do this because the Clywedog then ran more centrally in the valley and so could flow directly into the pond (cf above from page 69) with an outflow (pictured left) - over a cascade or weir. The leat itself branched off the Clywedog further upstream opposite the Philips Hall and ran behind the pond where the river now runs. Signs can still be seen of the red brick dam & weir, close to the south east corner of the pond which used to hold the water for the mill. Only when water was low in the leat was the pond used to top it up through a sluice gate.

1903 map showing new route of Clywedog (155) with water piped into the pond. Note plural weirs. cp with route of 1832 map above (& p 75)

Other Mills on the Clywedog and its tributaries

By the end of the nineteenth century virtually every river and stream in the country could boast at least one waterwheel or turbine which powered a corn mill, a farm threshing machine, a saw mill or a fulling mill which cleansed and thickened the woollen cloth.

George Lewis writes, "As far as I can discover there were five and possibly six mills in the vicinity (of Henfryn), two of them within a hundred yards of each other. A small stream flowed past Cwmfaerdy farmhouse and passed under the road, ...before it reached the river (Clywedog) its power was once used by a mill, a fulling mill. Where the Pandy (stream) joined the Clywedog ... there was another mill—Pandy-yr-Oedd, the Mill of the Cotton.

The outlet from the water wheel in 2009. The square slot to the left was where an external machine -- a chaffer, root cutter, timber-saw or grindstone could be connected.

The story goes that a Mr. Meredith, a cotton factor from Manchester considered that there was a market for his goods in the area and to further this purpose purchased three adjoining farms to secure a permanent supply of water to drive his mills. The Pandy (stream) supplied water in the first instance, and there is some indication that this supply was augmented by water brought from a little higher up the river Clywedog and brought to the mill by a Mill *Flem*—the local name for a man-made stream for this purpose. After the water had worked this mill, it was returned to Pandy (stream) to travel a few yards before being dammed and diverted southwards by another *Flem* in the direction of Coedtrewernau where there were two mills. The first was an undershot mill, a working corn mill in the early twentieth century, the last miller being a man by the name of Sam Brown. From here the water was taken on a raised channel to an overshot wheel, and thence back to the Clywedog. The water was again used after it had joined the Clywedog at Coedgwgan Hall mill".[10]

THE MILL, THE BLACKSMITHS AND THE FROGS' TOWN

As you drove up the Abbey Road, one hundred years ago, first there was a cow shed (John the Union's Shed, 2008). The field at the back belonged to the Blacksmith and he used to keep a cow or two. Then there used to be four cottages, next was the prentice where the horses used to be shod and then The Forge, where the fire was and the horse shoes used to be made. Adjoining was the Blacksmith's two-up-two down, then the Wheelwright's two-up-two-down. And then the Shoe-makers' or Menders' two-up-two down. And then, I think, was a weaver in his two-up-two-down. Four dwellings there and not much more than a dozen yards further was the Mill House. It was known as Tradesman's Row. I don't know how it came to be, but somehow it was called "Frog-Town". (Because of the large number of frogs - even circa 2008 Ed.) Noel Price.

"The Smith's shop has been taken down which was erected opposite the Bailiff's cottage and a new one near the Hill has been built for the Smith with a dwelling house and 9 acres of land inclosed from the Lloy....There is also a cottage not noticed by Mr Cooke called Stepaside let to the Parish for 2 old paupers."[11]

Also in a Deed of 8.3.1831 we read, *"cottage with forge called Vulcan's Hall."*[12]

Lewis's plan of the Mills along the Clywedog.
Below: Coedtrwernau Mill exterior in 2001 (157)
Coedtrewernau Mill interior in 2010 (158)

The Marteg. Bwlch y Sarnau in distance far left

The lower Cwmhir

Junction of Clywedog (right) and Cwmhir. 19th C site of a dam?

Below Beili Hill - one of the sources of the Clywedog

The Clywedog and its valley - looking towards Abbeycwmhir

The Bachel (top right) joins the Clywedog

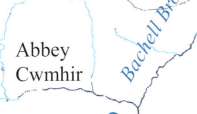

Clywedog outside Ty Cartreff

(159)

How London nearly stole the Clywedog and Bachel Brooks

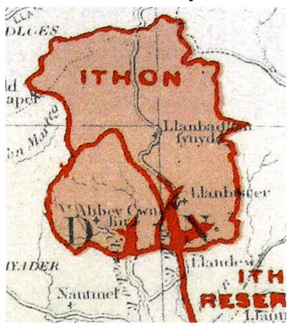

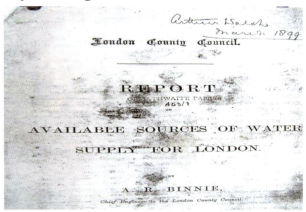

Report to the London County Council by it's Chief Engineer Sir Alexander Richardson Binnie in 1894.

Abbeycwmhir section of London County Council map showing Reservoirs (Deep Red) and Gathering Grounds (pink) in Radnorshire. (160)

Decades of work went into surveying and planning to take 415 million gallons of water everyday from Mid-Wales to London at a cost of £38 Million. The flooding of part of the Abbeycwmhir Community area would provide back up or "compensation" to the Ithon dam at Llandewi providing 38 million gallons a day for Londoners. Ours was one of the smaller reservoirs in the general scheme which stretched from the Upper Wye and Ithon Rivers across to the Towy and down to Llangorse lake and the Usk.

The Clywedog dam would have been somewhere between Broad Oak and Cookoo Bridge and built to hold 2,200 million gallons at a water level of 240 metres above sea level. The water would have reached just below Mill Bridge and well up the Bachel Brook just skirting Devannor.

415 million gallons is rather more than the 75 million a day which goes to Birmingham from Elan and the 40 million that goes from Lake Vyrnwy to Liverpool - and all by gravity.

The report recommended building ten large dams and twenty smaller ones plus two aquaducts all the way to London. One from the Ithon area to Banstead, in North London and the other from Llangorse to Elstree in West London. Throughout Mid-Wales 488 square miles of land were to be purchased, flooding villages, schools, chapels, churches, graveyards and farms. As a result of public protest a Royal Commission and Parliament stopped the scheme requiring London to take it's water from the Thames Valley instead.

The London County Council chief chemist had travelled to Wales to test the water which he described as of exceptional purity and softness, the *soap test* showed only one degree of hardness whereas the London water was fifteen to twenty degrees of hardness.[1]

Homes No More

Hendy Old Farm with classic Welsh external chimney (161)

Prysgduon in 1913. (No 13 on Map p 106) Later derelect & demolished (162)

Over forty five *homes that are no more* have been identified in the Community reflecting the huge economic and social changes which brought an end to a way of life which included the availability of common land. In Medieval times open fields of ridge and furrow planting in strips for different crops or meadow are known to have existed in the centre of Abbeycwmhir Village, at Cwm Bedw, Cwm Geifer and Pysgduon (cf map p 106 no "2") [1]. Whether they were common fields with different tenants cultivating each strip, as in the rest of the UK, is unclear.

The appearance of the landscape was also different because there would have been far fewer fences and hedges. In 1822 Layton Cooke describes "an imaginary line" possibly with a few stakes driven in[2] to mark the boundaries and natural demarkations such as the rivulet between the Cwm Bedw and Cefn Pawl sheepwalks.[3]

He says that most of the boundaries "are pretty well ascertained"[4] but amusingly describes a particular spot which was claimed by William Lewis for Abbey Farm and by Edward Lewis for Cefn Pawl. However when they later swapped farms the dispute continued but with each claiming the opposite!

He also says "The Cattle of the different tenants do not run in common here as in many parts of the Kingdom, the stock of each being limited within certain boundaries, which have been defined by ancient usage".[5] In fact there were already "2070 acres of inclosed land, divided into sundry farms, and 972 acres of common or hill ground".[6] Both cows and sheep were grazed here in the early Nineteenth Century. Cwmyscawen Common, still noted on the map, is a relic from these times and Penybont Common is one today.

Living in homes close to the common, it was possible to be self sufficient and subsist without selling much produce or working for another person. With a small patch of ground and using a common field people could raise some vegetables, keep a cow, a pig or a goose, gather firewood or have fun - on the common.

Even of the farms, Layton Cooke, an agricultural improver and reformer, laments in 1822, that there is "no more Land being planted (with potatoes and corn) by the Farmer than is calculated to be sufficient to supply his own and his Labourers families till the next season."![7]

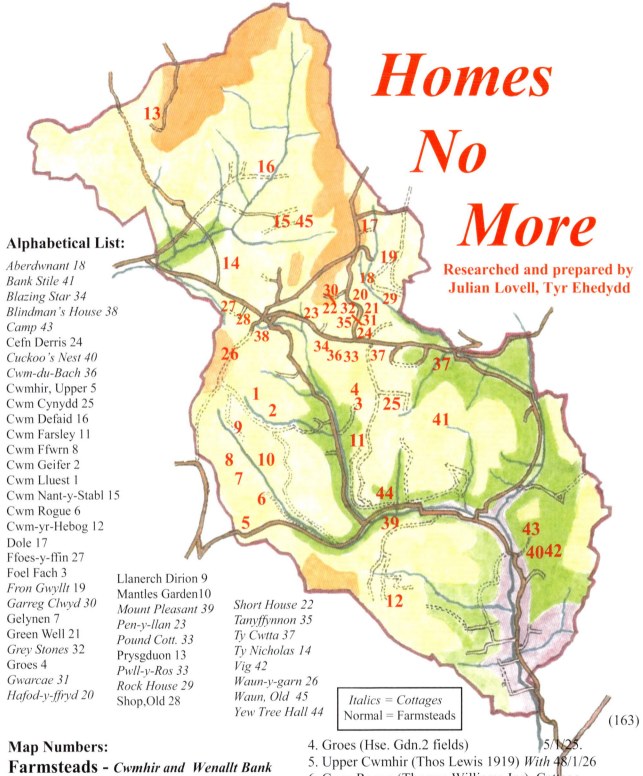

Homes No More

Researched and prepared by Julian Lovell, Tyr Ehedydd

Alphabetical List:

Aberdwnant 18
Bank Stile 41
Blazing Star 34
Blindman's House 38
Camp 43
Cefn Derris 24
Cuckoo's Nest 40
Cwm-du-Bach 36
Cwmhir, Upper 5
Cwm Cynydd 25
Cwm Defaid 16
Cwm Farsley 11
Cwm Ffwrn 8
Cwm Geifer 2
Cwm Lluest 1
Cwm Nant-y-Stabl 15
Cwm Rogue 6
Cwm-yr-Hebog 12
Dole 17
Ffoes-y-ffin 27
Foel Fach 3
Fron Gwyllt 19
Garreg Clwyd 30
Gelynen 7
Green Well 21
Grey Stones 32
Groes 4
Gwarcae 31
Hafod-y-ffryd 20
Llanerch Dirion 9
Mantles Garden 10
Mount Pleasant 39
Pen-y-llan 23
Pound Cott. 33
Prysgduon 13
Pwll-y-Ros 33
Rock House 29
Shop, Old 28
Short House 22
Tanyffynnon 35
Ty Cwtta 37
Ty Nicholas 14
Vig 42
Waun-y-garn 26
Waun, Old 45
Yew Tree Hall 44

Italics = Cottages
Normal = Farmsteads

Map Numbers:
Farmsteads - *Cwmhir and Wenallt Bank*
1. Cwm Lluest (John Lewis 1840)   59/1/35
2. Cwm Geifer stone cottge.
          Owner: Miss A. Evans 1919) 1/1/02
3. Foel (Vale) Fach (Homestead & Gdn. 32/0/03
4. Groes (Hse. Gdn. 2 fields)   5/1/25.
5. Upper Cwmhir (Thos Lewis 1919) With 48/1/26
6. Cwm Rogue (Thomas Williams Jnr). Cottage
          & land Disapeared by 1900. With 6/1/25.
7. Gelynen, Hstead. (Hugh Jones) With 49/2/19
8. Cwm Ffwrn (Thomas Williams Snr.) 55/2/24
          (Ruin in front of present house.) 36/3/18

(163)

Homes No More

Map Numbers continued

9. Llanerch Dirion Hse.&Gdn. (Thomas Lewis)
10. Mantles Garden. No documents found.
11. Cwm Farsley Homestead & Farm   50/3/09

To the South

12) Cym-yr-Hebog. 1840 James Price; 1851 Ebenezer Hamer; 1861 no record, *with* Llwyneuadd.1891 building on OS map in use incl. as a blacksmith   48/3/36.

To the north – Bwlch y Sarnau

13. Prysgduon. Timber box frame house of 1711. Last to be built in Radnorshire. Demolished.   344/1/30
14. Ty Nicholas. With Penlanole Estate.   6/1/15
15. Cwm Nant-y-Stabl (William Wozencraft) part of Brondrefach. Stable still stands   /1/20
16a. Cwm Defaid Cott. Gdn. & Field. 1840 on Brodrefawr (Anne Williams)   1/3/33
16b Cwm Defaid. Adjacent to Brondrefawr also Cwt (Richard Dakin 1840)   4/0/27
17. Dole, Upper & Lower Dolau. 1841 Two Home-steads Garden & Field   0/1/3
18. Aberdwnant, on ancient routeway footings & collapsed barn remain. Occupied into 20th C. 6-22 acres. Amalgamated with Fron Gwyllt.
19. Fron Gwyllt/Cerrig Llwydion. On ancient routeway Hse. empty by 1851. Outline and Boundary barely visible. Area unknown.
20. Hafod-y-ffryd. Name suggests "Summer Farm". Home to 2 families in 19th.C   4/0/17
21. Green Well 1841-51. Thomas Hughes & Family "Clover Field" abandoned by 1900.   6/1/3
22. Short House. sheep walk & house. (Evan George 1840)   7/1/32
23. Pen-y-llan, Bwlch y Sarnau Fm. Occupied into 20thC. Low walls visible.   **36/3/17**
24. Cefn Derris. H.stead & Fld (John Lewis 1840)   10/0/7
25. Cwm Cynydd. Sold to Forestry Commission in 1939. Area as 1847 (Incl.) & 1919 Sale: 461/1/12
26. Waun-y-garn (or Gwern Garn) Garden & Field above Cwmydea. 1/3/16
27. Ffoes-y-ffin. (Mary Williams 1894 gave part to build B-y-S Chapel Manse.   3/3/7
28. Old Shop, Bwlch y Sarnau. Gdn. & Field.

Cottages

29 Rock House (Penycraig).
  (1861 Thomas Crowther (94 yrs) Tailor)..
30. Garreg Clwyd, (1851)
  Four Pugh Brothers Age 7-15 No parents.
31. Gwarcae, Home throughout 19th Century
32. Grey Stones, (1891)
33. Pound Cott or Pwll-y-Rhos Hse. & 1 acre plock by Hendy field Turnpike Gate. 1850 Jane Jones bought for 10s. Sold to GH. Phillips of The Hall for £5 in 1859. Then moved to:-
34 Blazing Star, Jane Jones leased from above for 6d pa. Name suggests a Ty'r Unos (p108)
35. Tanyffynon, 17th c stone barn at Ffynnongarreg. Jane Jones, now a "pauper", was living here in 1861.
36. Cwmdu Bach, let with Hendy Farm 1919.
37. Ty Cwtta or Te Cota. Built 1860 by Thomas George. Exact location uncertain.
38. Blindman's House, rented by parish for use of poor. 1851 by Edward Owens (77yrs).
39. Mount Pleasant, Ralph Robinson, Agent for Philips Estate lived here 1841—1853.
40. Cuckoo's Nest, Encroachment of 1790. Bought on "Mr Fowlers Account" 1808 - £18. L. Thomas Pugh Jun 1822. Disappeared 1841
41. Bank Stile. Encroachment till 1850's. Then enclosed above Waun Gaseg - disapeared.
42. Vig 1872 Eliz. Edwards. Family Ex tenants of Fowlers. Moved to Troedrhiwfelin till 1882.
43. Camp, 1841 James & Bufton Families Occupied in 20thC.
44. Yew Tree Hall next to St. Mary's Church. Poss. on site of Cross Cottage (The Laundry p 192).
45. Old Waen - (Brondrefach cf p 178).

Left & above: name of property, tenant or owner & date of record. **Figures at end of row** are Acres/Roods/Poles (or Perches). **1 Acre** = 4 roods or 10 sq chains or 4840 sq yards or a statute acre (0.40 hectare) eg. a good-sized football pitch. **1 Rood** = ¼ acre = 1,210 sq yards = 40 sq poles. Sq **Pole** = 30¼ sq yards often simply referred to as a **P**ole or **P**erch in land measurement. **"With"** means amalgamated with next. **L**=Lease.

Continued →

The number of homes in the Community of Abbeycwmhir has varied enormously over the centuries. The list on the previous pages cannot be a complete list of dwellings that have appeared and disappeared - since records of any kind only began about a thousand years ago and most of these properties have physically disappeared.

Types of homes no more

There was a tradition that if a family could erect a dwelling on the Common in one night and have smoke coming from the chimney by dawn and enclose a small portion of land they had earned the right to stay and would not be evicted. This was called a "Ty'r Unnos" or "House of one night".[8] The name "Blazing Star" (map:34) suggests that it was one of these although there is no documentary evidence for it. However one leaseholder had very good terms from George Henry Philips. Jane Jones, a spinner of hemp, had bought Pound Cottage (map: 33) for 10/- in 1850 - and sold it to Mr Philips for £5 (the amount being offered by the Crown for Encroachments) nine years later. Then she rented "Blazing Star" for 6d a year! Quite a star.

A number of small **farmsteads** and cottages existed in the area to the east of Bwlch-y-Sarnau, especially around Ffynnon-garreg. Most of these would have been of a poor standard and built of materials which would not last such as small stones, rubble, soil, timber and turf. For this reason little trace of them remains today.

Some may have been "Hafoddai", for example Hafod-y-ffryd, (map:21) the **summer farms** which belonged to the valley farmers who stayed on the hills with their cattle and sheep during the summer. Lluest (map:1), meaning Camp, also indicates a summer farm. Under the old Manorial law, the Hafoddai could only be occupied from the end of May until the 15th August. Frequently they were quite close to the main farm, even less than half a mile.

Most of the **cottages** which have disappeared were located on the high ground to the north of Abbeycwmhir. They were here for several reasons. The earliest houses would have been the Ty taeog, the poor turf-roofed serf's hut. Historically, some would have their origins as the hafoddai and llyestydd, the summer farms and camps, belonging to the valley farms. In the sixteenth century the Llyest was commonly referred to as the "dairy house", indicating its main purpose.

NOTE ON MAP & LISTS on previous page and these pages 97-98

Researched by Julian Lovell of Ty'r Eheydd (2010) from documentary evidence and excludes buildings replaced by occupied new ones (except Prysgduon & Hendy) and also where houses have been combined into a new one or renamed like Church House & Stepaside becoming Mill Cottage. If no acreage is given it is because it is not known and in the case of cottages would have been very little. The dates do not normally reflect periods of occupancy but only the date they appear in the records, (cf p 286)

1841 –1911 is the every ten year Census; **1840** is Tithe Map and the Tithe Commutation Act Survey, The Manor of Gollon and Township of Cefn Pawl: 13th May 1839. William & Morris Sayce, Surveyors. Kington. **1894** is Tax Rebate Application, Collection of Mel & Anita Hamer, Home Farm; **1919** is attempted Estate Sale Document of Major Philips.

Any inconsistencies in the information given is because of what is available. As work has continued since the map was assembled the names of the following homesteads have been discovered:- the farm Rhiew Gam, The Llether, Vale Fach, Baxter's Bank, Stepaside, Gwern Garn and empty farm houses at The Fron and Cwmyscawen.

These date back to Tudor times and occur in local place names (Welsh: Llaethdy). Others would have been the upland homes of stockmen, the shepherds and cattlemen who tended the herds. Still more would have been built as a result of encroachment on the Commons and upland sheep runs by people who were homeless. Quality was poor and many disappeared with the inclosure of the sheep walks.

The survival of any building depends on location, contemporary relevance and need and the quality of the original structure. In earlier times houses and farm buildings were thought of as purely functional features of the upland landscape and may have been altered or demolished after a short period of time, maybe as little as twenty years. Timber-built farmhouses of the sixteenth century were converted for use as barns when re-building in stone became fashionable towards the end of the eighteenth century.[10] A number of houses of this period are found around Abbeycwmhir, as well as new-build houses from the seventeenth century.

A number of **old farmhouses** have disappeared or fallen into dereliction in recent times. In the 1970's grants were available for the building of new farmhouses in upland areas as part of attempt to revitalise hill farming. The attraction is obvious: a grant-aided new house or an old one in poor condition to be repaired at the owners expense.

The further down the social scale, the cheaper and poorer was the build. As a consequence, the chances of an old cottage surviving are poor. In Wales generally, there are comparatively few cottages remaining from before 1850 and Abbeycwmhir is no exception. Many of the cottages found today are houses built by the Estate in the nineteenth century, usually constructed of brick. The bricks were either made on the estate at the Brickyard or brought in from further afield by railway to Penybont. The local stone is mostly unsuitable for building.

Today there is little remaining of the significant number of dwellings, and their large families, that once existed on these uplands. Throughout the nineteenth and early twentieth century they supported a large population. As already stated, changes in farming practices reduced the need for manpower. Social changes and different attitudes, especially after 1918, made this system unsustainable. Added to this, from mid-Victorian times onwards the developing industries of South Wales and across the border in England saw a steady migration of population from mid-Wales, as people sought a better life and improved wages elsewhere. As a result of this process of depopulation, compared with many parts of the United Kingdom, the number of people in Radnorshire has hardly changed in the last hundred years. The number living in the parish of Abbeycwmhir has fallen as people have moved away and families become smaller.

In the heather, in the heather
(on the common)

Let the stranger, if he will,
Have his way with the glen;
But give us to live
At the bright hem of God
In the heather, in the heather.

Anonymous folk stanza
translated by RS Thomas[11]

If you own land that is subject to rights of common, they could include some or all of these rights:
- **'right of herbage'** - to graze sheep or cattle
- **'right of turbary'** to take peat or turf
- **'right of estovers'** to take wood and gorse
- **'right of piscary'** to fish from water ways
- **'right of pannage'** to allow pigs to eat acorns or beechmast.

Commons Act 2006
which *allowed statutory commons councils to be established for UK's 1.3 mil. acres.*[12]

Abbeycwmhir Allotment

Act of Parliament 9-10 Vic. c. 5 1846.
Award 1857.

Common and waste: 7000 acres

Principal allottees: John Cheesement Severn, Francis Philips, and Jonathon Field.[13]

The pressure to inclose came from the fact of food shortages for a rising population. Between 1700 & 1900 the population of the UK sextupled from 5 to 30 million. The Napoleonic Wars and the Corn Laws prevented imports so food was short and extremely expensive so there was a great pressure on agriculture to be more productive by using machinery (Jethro Tull and others), to improve the breeding of crops and animals, to control stock and to improve techniques of agriculture (Turnip Townsend etc) or in other words - be more "efficient". Often a lot of the villagers agreed with these ideas. It was a nuisance to have scattered strips a long way from each other. If one strip was ill-tended and grew weeds, neighbours would suffer. Any kind of selection of good varieties of food crops was difficult. If all the village livestock grazed together, selective breeding was impossible and there were lots of scraggy animals of indifferent quality - often more than the land could adequately support.

However even Arthur Young, Secretary to the Board of Agriculture and pro inclosure, wrote, "By nineteen Inclosure Acts out of twenty, the poor are injured, in some grossly injured."[14]

Probably the main cause for the abandonment of the homes around the high ground around Abbeycwmhir was their inclosure by Act of Parliament in 1857[15] which allotted the land to the above three persons who lived elsewhere much of the time. Although acknowledged tenants (cf map on next page) were rented a small parcel of land and even a turbarry these were not of enough acreage to enable subsistence without access to a common. So, unable to survive, people left their homes and went to work in the expanding cities and coal mines as wages earners - or got hopelessly drunk on any compensation they received.

"Inclosure" was the process by which land which had formerly been used in common by many people was "privatised". Industrialists who had saved capital or could take out mortgages from the fast developing Banks made these purchases and wanted a return on their money. As a result, by 1900 agriculture had mostly been reorganised from a subsistence-based occupation into something more akin to an industry where productivity and profit were the goal and the wages for the village labourer were very low. "Inclosure was a plain enough case of class robbery" asserted the Hammonds in *The Village Labourer*, in 1911.[16] The Landowner elite tended to be Anglican and the Tenants tended to be Welsh speaking Non-conformists.

The fact that it took eleven years and 119 court cases to achieve the local Inclosure is an indication of the reality of these tensions. Claims, objections and counter-claims had to be heard and adjudicated. Sometimes a generous allotment of Turbary peat was the temporary compensation.

The rise of grouse shooting as a popular sport and an economic opportunity for landowners was realized and this was advertised as a benefit of the Abbeycwmhir Estate in the attempted sale of 1919

(cf p 149).

Homes No More

The occupation of land was not simply a means of gaining a livelihood, but was also a way of securing social status. The tenant's lack of secure tenure rendered him vulnerable to bullying at election times - the price of a 'wrong' vote in Wales, was eviction.

Before enclosure the cottager was a labourer with land, after enclosure he was a labourer without land. Families that had lived for centuries in their valleys or on their small farms and commons were driven away. Landless, the agricultural labourers who remained were powerless to prevent exploitation and were therefore forced to work for long hours for meagre, irregular wages.

Attempts to fight back, notably through trade unions from the early 1870s, failed. The wonder is not that so many left, but that so many stayed. [17]

They hang the man and flog the woman Who steals the goose from off the common. But let the greater criminal go loose Who steals the common from the goose.[18]

Increasing productivity with a harvesting machine at Cwmfaerdy c 1920 (165)

THE TURBARIES

In Radnorshire most land made available for public allotments amounted to just 1% but in Golon 240 acres were allotted for turbaries - that is 3.4%. Peat and turf were important fuels in Radnorshire, given that coal and timber were expensive, and one wonders if this generous turbarry allotment was a concession to win over a deeply sceptical public opinion and a recognition that the turbaries would be useful supplementary source of income to some. [19]

Peat was cut soon after "Colan Mai" (May Day). Six or seven skilled men would cut in teams. A wide spade used for first cut, a narrower spade for the lower rows and depths. After nine days the women and children would turn the peat over where it was laid by diggers to "cure" for a further nine days. When dry it was taken by barrow, sledge or cart to the peat shed where it was stacked near the farmhouse for winter use. A family would need 600 yards of peat for a winter. It would take a man one day to cut sixty yards. [20]

Any peat surplus to requirements was sold. In 1868, after the coming of the railways, turf and peat from such parishes as Llanano, Llanbister and Llanbadarn Fynydd is known to have been sold in the Penybont, Knighton and Newtown markets.

In 1894 at the first Parish Council Meeting, the first item on the Agenda was Marking out the Turbaries. Alas this was 37 years too late as the Turbarries had been allocated to specific farms by the Inclosure Act of 1857 and were no longer a commons right. (cf next page).

"The rabbit had not where to make his den, And labours only cow was drove away, No matter - wrong was right and right was wrong - Inclosure, thou'rt a curse upon the land
- John Clare (1793-1864) [21]

Note: Layton Cooke (cf p 70) was involved with these issues and wrote *"Bread for the people! : secured by the skilful cultivation and efficient supervision of estates"* 2 editions published in 1855 (cf p 301).

Abbeycwmhir Community Book

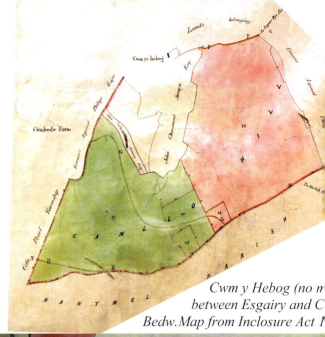

Francis Aspinal Philips probably painted just after the Inclosure Act was passed. Painting is in Radnorshire Museum, Llandrindod Wells.(166)

Cwm y Hebog (no m
between Esgairy and C
Bedw. Map from Inclosure Act 1

Cwm Rogue (no more) at the top of the hill on the Rhayader Road. Map from Inclosure Act 1

Waun y Garn (no more) North East of Castell y Garn. Turbury to left. Map from Inclosure Act 1857.

Close up of sealed document held by Francis Aspinal Philips (above) - either a letter or perhaps the Act of Inclosure for the Community? (167)

112

Some Abbeycwmhir Inclosure maps 1857

Homes No More

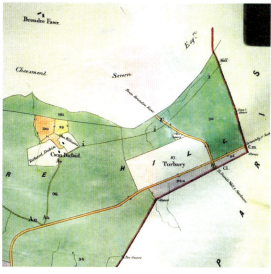

Cwm Defaid (no more) Turbury on the right. Near Brondr Fawr. Map from Inclosure Act 1857.

Turbury Spades on display in the Radnorshire Museum, Llandrindod Wells. (168)

> "Fence now meets fence in owners little bounds
> Of field and meadow large as garden grounds
> In little parcels little minds to please . . ."
> from "The Mores" - John Clare (1793-1864)

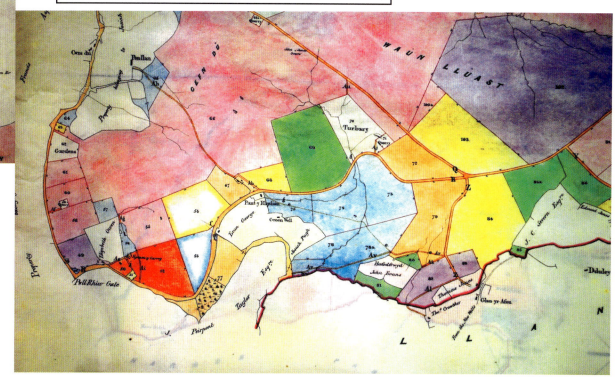

Pant y Rhydian above Ffynongarreg with turbary to the right. Map from Inclosure Act 1857. (169)

COED SARNAU
The Forestry

Forest removed and awaiting collection - opposite Waun Pistyll (170)

"Embosomed with Wood"

"Numerous groves of majestic oaks formed the grand and beautiful characteristic of their domain" wrote Edwin Davies of the monks of Cwmhir, in Jonathan Williams's *History of Radnorshire* (1905).[1] Williams was originally researching around 1818 when he also wrote, "oaks of immense size …. grew in the parks of Abbeycwmhir within the recollection of many persons now living".[2]

And just a few years later (1822), Layton Cooke confirms, "The estate bears manifest traces of having been once amply supplied with timber, and most of the tenants are old enough to remember when at "one fell swoop" four thousand trees, principally oak, were sacrificed for the sum of three hundred pounds!"[3] Wilson set about re-planting "on an extensive scale" and by 1833 his notes in the report state that, "The Sugarloaf Hill was fully planted in 1823 [4] and is now in a most thriving state. The various dingles are also planted and the rabbits in great measure destroyed….an extensive nursery was at the same time planted behind Mount Pleasant." (39 on map p 105)[5]

Layton Cooke was also a Forestry surveyor and writes at lengh about the value of an adequate timber supply for profit, hedging ("live fence"), and shelter. Also to provide "a variation of tint and foliage" for the beauty of The Great Park.[5]

'When I first came hither, the great valley you see was a wooded glen, and a race of men came thereto and it was laid waste. And the second wood grew up therein, and this wood is the third.'

— The *Owl of Cawlwyd* in The Mabinogion [7]

'A town amongst the Britons is nothing more than a thick wood'

— *Julius Caesar*, De Bello Gallico.[8]

The Cistercians and the Forest.

Gerald de Cambrensis wrote of the Cistercians,"Give them a wilderness or forest, and in a few years you will find a dignified Abbey in the midst of smiling plenty".[9] This inevitably involved cutting down, or assarting, forest that had been there for centuries to make fields - "changing an oak wood into a wheat field"[10] - or to build buildings and gather firewood.

Nevertheless when Cwmhir Abbey leased the whole Forest of Maelienydd from the Mortimers in 1357 they not only had the right to timber but also nuts (hazel, beech, chestnuts) and wild honey[11] together with beeswax for candles and making seals. Other forest product were bark for tanning leather and charcoal for heating or burning incense - as well as the opportunity for *pannage* or pasture for pigs. Not to mention game. However, earlier in 1241, the Abbey allowed Roger Mortimer (d 1282) to hunt in its woods and make enclosures.

Our daughter house, Cymer, faired better. In 1209 Llywelyn ap Iowerth granted them the "birds and wild beasts and animals of every kind" and in 1348 their abbot laid claim to take "falcons, sparrow hawks and all other birds and beasts of the forest".[12] All this despite an early injunction (1158) by the General Chapter discouraging hunting and the "working in skins of wild beasts, neither wild cats, rabbits, squirrels, nor miniver"[13]. (*Ermine* or winter white fur of a stoat).

Our granges also had forests. Coed-yer-ynys at Carnaf Grange (14 on map p 42); Coed-yr-Abbot (12 acres in Brilley - (15 on map); Coed-y-Mynach at Bleddfa (14 on map); Coed-y-Abbot (11 acres at Mynachty Poeth - 13 on map); 34 acres at Ysgubor in Llanfair Waterdine and Coed Ceri in Montgomery - where the locals had to be prohibited from wasting or destroying the abbey's wood in 1252.[14]

Abbeys with much woodland would appoint a "Forester" from the *conversi* or lay brothers and he might have *corrody* or free accommodation in a grange - as well as a horse on which to ride through the forests. A *keeper of the woods* might also have to look after the rabbit warren.

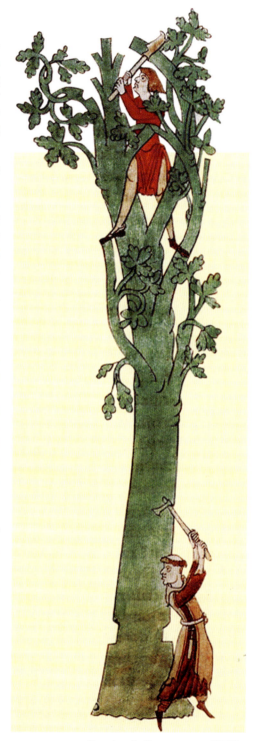

Brotherly Love (171)

Abbeycwmhir Community Book

NATIONAL & LOCAL FORESTRY DATES

Plaque on Forest Lodge house in Abbeycwmhir Village (172)

1607 First Surveyor General of Woods, Forests, Parks and Chases.
1810 Changed to Commissioners of Woods, Forests and Land Revenues
1919 The Forestery Act sets up The Forestry Commission. Wood stock was very low due to First World War and trench warfare. Heavy industry was dependent on coal and mines needed pit props.
1939 Forestry started at Abbeycwmhir - felling on the Wennallt and planting of Cwm Cynydd.
1940 - 46 51 million cubic feet of timber cut for war effort; employees increased from 14,000-44,300 including Women's Timber Corps or "Lumberjills". After the war, agriculture was Depressed so the Forestry Commission was able to buy land cheaply.
1953 Foresters House built at Abbeycwmhir on Bwlch y Sarnau road. The single storey part was the Forestry office until the depot next door was built. The Manager of the forestry lived in the house up to about 1982. (cf p 214)
1959 Colonel John Lionel Philips sold some Abbeycwmhir estate farms to the Forestry.
1959 - 70's National forest estate doubles, investment soars.
1960 Forest Lodge in the village built as a supervisor's house for the Coed Sarnau forest. In those days all supervisory staff were 'mobile' and could be posted, often at very short notice to any part of the country. So each forest had sufficient houses for its staff, the larger forests even having small villages, housing supervisors and Forest Workers.
1965 Loy Hill Planted. (Cut in 2014 - ed..)
1966 Wenallt Hill planted.
1970 Dutch Elm Disease. 30% of Elm population lost - especially in central & southern England.
1984 Closure of Coed Sarnau office at Abbeycwmhir on Bwlch y Sarnau road. (March 1984).
1987 October Gales ("The Hurricane") 50 mill trees blown down. Most salvaged and marketed
1992 Forest Enterprise started. (April 1st)
2008 Forestry Commission cancels right to purchase a licence for collecting firewood.
2013 Natural Resources Wales formed combining Forestry Commission Wales, the Environment Agency Wales and Countryside Council for Wales. (April 1st). Forest Enterprise abolished.

right of estovers: to take wood and gorse.

Log Schism (173)

Monkish Forestry (174)

"Forestry started in 1939, wasn't it - They fell all this timber on the Wenallt bank for the war. Sam Nichols was working on it. Rifle butts. Working on it opposite the Pheasants wood." - Albert Philips

Cregiau
(172)

"The Forestry Commission's origins are in the First World War, and difficulties Britain had meeting wartime demands on timber. Woodland resources had been declining since the middle ages, but reached an all time low in the wake of the Industrial Revolution. With the outbreak of war the country was no longer able to rely on timber imports, and in July 1916 Minister Herbert Asquith appointed the Acland Committee to look at the best ways of developing woodland resources. The Committee reported to Asquith's successor, David Lloyd George, in 1918. They recommended a state organization the most effective way of co-ordinating a re-afforestation plan to meet timber needs for the foreseeable future. " (FC Statememnt)[15]

First World War

Losing so many of our men in the First World War, there were Portuguese men felling the timber in the 1920's. They had a camp between Llywneuadd turn and the Cookoo Bridge..... One is buried in the Churchyard – a tree fell on him. NP

Right: "Timber Workers at Abbeycwmhir about 1919-1921. They corriger (corrody?) at Fishpool & Cwmyscawen and in The Village."[16] Man on far left is Bert Smoutt of Llwy Cottage .
(176)

Abbeycwmhir Community Book

1500 trees a day planted by hand and foot. Pay: £3 per thousand
- interview with Albert Philips of 2, Cwmhir Cottages.

When I retired I could easily put a thousand trees in. I used to plant a lot for farmers until 2005. I could put a thousand trees in - start at 9 O'clock. Dinner about twelve for fifteen minutes and have a thousand in by three O'clock. No problem. I used to like planting, mind. I used to love planting. Planting hedgerow was: Spade in, push it out, tree in, spade out, heel on. Next one. Alternate strides. You know. Fifteen in twenty minutes. We had a special spade with a little curve on it. ……
We (Lindsey and I) used to do 1500 trees a day at £3 per thousand - along the furrow. A few extra for another day if it was wet.

Planting in the winter

I was up on the top, there. see, planting by myself. And who should come along but Byron's father, Abe, he was taking the sheep down. He shouted at me, "Hey, boy, he said what the hell are you doing here? He said, "Its freezing". It was freezing, the mist was coming. My coat, my waterproof jacket it was, it was freezing. It was breaking all up as it fell off. He said, "I'm taking the sheep down, if its too rough up here for them, you shouldn't be here." But I carried on. Lindsey came up there and he got out of the van, he only went three or four yards. He said, "Bloody Hell!", he said, Its too cold here for me" and he ran back in, shut the door and away t'go. I was left out to blighty. Dinner time come and the Head Forester got on to me, "Whats the ground like?" I said, "Its like concrete". "Oh you better come down and meet my boys at Abbey Turn."
....I had a job to go down. I went in the van and rolled the window down and there was another window there - of ice. There was - complete from top to bottom. I've never seen that before - and the wind was blowing like.... The track was a complete sheet of ice - I was going about 5 miles an hour all the way down. By heaven, I thought, if I go off the side, I've had it, like. I got to the bottom, anyway. He told me another higher-up boss had stopped his men planting in Red Lion.

Albert Philips & Lindsey Williams planted these ploughed forestry furrows - for the first time in July 1970 at Cwm Bedw - part of the Forestry Commission's expansion at this time. - Photo: Alan Gayse. (177)

Training & Pay

We had a lot of training on the chain saw even just before I retired. I'd used one since the seventies when we started using them. Every two years we had a week. Then we did courses on the buzz-ball as we called it - the strimmer, saws for clearing small stuff, courses for spraying. We had less pay when on a course - by damm until I got onto the Union then we had average pay. Usually we were on piece work. Most of the time. Like, Wet Time we'd have day work. That was no good to no-body - day work: that was too low, you see. Aye.

You could only have two hours Wet, you see, you couldn't have one hour Wet. If you had one and a half hours wet in a day, it wasn't counted - you wouldn't get paid and had to make it up with

The Forestry

piece work. Make it up making stakes or weeding. You'd have to do a bit extra to cover that wet day. If you had two hours wet, like, they'd pay you. It was a bit rough we had to work. We were employed by them, by the Forestry and got a pension. Christ, man, we'd be down the road if I didn't. We couldn't live on £90 - the wife uses that shopping for one week in Llandod. And Oil has to be paid for. Telephone. Electric. Poll Tax.

The amount you got paid varied every week and depended on what job you were doing and how much you did, you know? They'd have prices for each job, like. Oh aye. It had been worked out to a fine art. On wet days we'd have day work at Coed Sarnau offices in the workshop, making bird boxes, anything, owl boxes. Wet Day Work. Not paid so much.

Tariffing

"Tariffing" was measuring trees - their height and circumpherence to estimate their cubic capacity. You'd do it in different ways depending on whether you were thinning or clear felling amd how many trees there were. Three of us would be blazing or taking off the bark. of each tree with a slashing hook and there's a bloke on the book, see. At every tenth tree after the second swipe he'd shout "Girth" then we'd have to measure the girth at chest height, see. Put a tape round it. Wouldn't we? Sometimes you had to get somebody to help you if it was a big tree. You'd be shouting "pole" every time you measured one. "Pole". Then I shout 4/3 - and he shouted 4/3 back. Put it in a book. Next ten do it again.

You had to completely measure every 100th tree. Had to cut it down to do the length. Can't use a machine in a forest because of the branches. How long it was and mid-girth if over 3ft girth. Put it in a book. Then sell it.

I was supposed to be a forester, sometimes we did it.

I was a forest worker.

Tariffing Book 1888 -1890
(178)

Spruce Bark Beetle

We used to go up to Hafren a lot and in Kerry and down to Builth - Edw Forest which was then joined to this one, Coed Sarnau - and then there was Radnor Forest used to do a lot of work there. A lot of planting there. We went to Aberedw and all the way down to Hay when they had the Spruce Bark Beetle - it was eating the spruce trees, see, going in under the bark, like, and growing in them and killing the tree. We'd find the beetle, fell the tree and then spray the bug. 1981-2 on farms and in forests. We went up nearly as far as Machynlleth and Kerry and up as far as the Elan Valley and down as far as Hay.

If there was beetle in the top of the tree you could see tracks of them down the bottom. A light powder - grey crumbly stuff, like. Sometimes it would be all joined together. You could tell exactly, especially if you'd seen a bit of it before, like. Low down, they'd bore in and leave the white stuff sticking out with a hole in the middle of it. Came here first to Cwm Bedw on the bed of a lorry - that's where the Spruce Bark Beetle came first in 1981-2.

> ## Cymru
>
> The dust of all the saints of the ages
> And the martyrs lies in your bosom;
> It was you who gave them breath,
> And you who took it from them.
>
> The angels would be walking here,
> Their footprints on your roadways,
> And the Holy Spirit nested
> Dovelike in your branches.
>
> Poets heard on wind and breeze
> His cry of sacrifice, His gasp of pain,
> And in the middle of your forests
> The Tree of the Cross was seen.
>
> D. Gwenallt Jones (Gwenallt) [16]

1893
Village of Abbeycwmhir
Happiness to the Rev Hermitage Day and Doris Philips on the occasion of their marriage. He was particularly popular with the school children who bought him an ink stand when he finally left the area. (cf page 166 "In Living Memory") (179)

1873 Celebration of birth of Philip's son

George Henry Philips *(1831-1886)* and Anna Theophilia (1836-1915) were clearly very worried that after the birth of two daughters (Mabel Florence and Chrystine Mary) they still had no male successor to the Estate. When Francis George, the future Major, was born there was great celebration, "*a procession was formed, headed by a band, followed by gaily dressed wagons containing two magnificent beasts, after which came the whole of the tenantry on horseback. The beasts were cut up and distributed among the workpeople, the menfolk dined at the local inn, and tea was provided for the labourers' wives and children in the schoolroom. There were fireworks and balloon ascents in the evening and dancing and conviviality continued to a very late hour*". [1]

"To mark the occasion spruce trees, interspersed with larch, were planted on Sugar Loaf Hill in such form that they spelt out the Major's initials "F.G.P.P." They remained in being until shortly after the First World War." [2]

Village Group Pictures

1993

(180)

Whose Who? Names put to numbers on page 298.

Abbeycwmhir Community Book

The Village at The Hall for th

Village Group Pictures

Queen's Golden Jubilee 2002

Whose Who? See Appendix page 296-297. Photo by Paul Humpherston, The Hall (181)

Millennium Celebrations

In the summer of 1998 a meeting was called, to which everyone in the Community was invited, to discuss the forthcoming Millennium and decide what activities the Community of Abbeycwmhir wanted to do to celebrate the occasion. The meeting was well attended and many ideas were suggested, out of which the following were short-listed to take forward:-

A Party
A Book
A Wall Hanging
A Village Green
Bwlch-y-Sarnau Seat
Mugs
A Time Capsule (which was never realised).

Meetings were held every month, alternating the venue between the Philips Hall in Abbeycwmhir and the Community Room in Bwlch y Sarnau. Working groups were set up to develop different ideas and fundraising events were held to cover the costs. These operated under the constitution of the Community Council and a savings account was set up (linked to the main bank account) into which all the funds raised went.

The Village Green

The piece of land which now forms the Village Green was sold to the Community Council by Vernon Gibberd, previous owner of Cross Cottage (the first village school and school house, from 1857 to 1864). The land formed the original garden for the Teacher at the school, and in 1998 had become very overgrown, the thick hedge overhanging the road creating a very dark route for people walking between the church, pub and Philips Hall.

The ground was sold on the provision that it would be for community use as a Green, and never be built upon. The legal fees for the transfer were covered by the parish and then began a series of working parties to clear the land etc. The first such working party, in October,1999 was a gathering of men with Chain saws, and the bulk of the overgrown mass was removed, and used to build the village bonfire ready for Bonfire Night. Before this, we consulted one or two local landscape gardeners, to get an idea of which trees were worth retaining. Gradually, over the period of 18 months or so, the ground was transformed to the site you see today using the voluntary labour of the villagers. The land was cleared, the design finalised, the area ploughed and seeded or stoned, the flower beds put in and then planted. Trees were obtained under Powys Council's tree Planting Scheme for National Tree Week and the area fenced. Thorn trees were purchased for the hedge on the Forestry track side of the site. The Forestry Commission donated a Picnic table, other picnic tables were bought.

(182)

Millenium Celebrations

Funding

The project cost over £3000, including costs such as purchase of the land, fees for the legal conveyancing, land registry and planning permission, fencing materials and gates, and stone and grass seed. A Social Development Grant from Powys County Council was awarded for £1400.00, and the rest was raised through local events: pub quizzes, parties etc throughout the period.

The Village Green was officially opened by our local Assembly Member Kirsty Williams and local County Councillor David Evans in May 2001. It has become a well used and focal point of the village, hosting barbecues, parties, a Christmas Tree (power was installed in December 2001 so that the tree could be lit up), with the shed on the Green housing Santa and his elves.

The pavement between the village square and the Philips Hall, by the side of the Village Green, was added in 2003 by Powys Council, making the passage between the two safer and much less muddy!

Before and After: Village Green being opened by Assembly Member Kirsty Williams and local County Councillor David Evans in May 2001.

Mugs

St Mary's Church, Abbeycwmhir, bought mugs for all of the children in the parish. There were two designs, one of the Baptist Chapel in Bwlch y Sarnau, and one of the Happy Union in Abbeycwmhir. Mercy Griffiths of Piccadilly Cottage drew both of the designs, a lady in Penybont made the bone china mugs, and sent them elsewhere for the printing of the design onto the mug. The first batch came back with the wrong captions for the pictures, however these still proved very popular and all of them were sold!   ***Continued on page 128***

Abbeycwmhir Community Book

126

Millenium Celebrations

MILLENNIUM NEWS 1999-2000

CHRISTMAS EDITION

Are you ready for the Millennium party? Tickets are now being distributed. If you have not recieved your ticket by the 20th then call the ticket hotline on 851776.

To recap events:-
- 6pm Church Service at St Marys, Abbeycwmhir
- 6.45 Beacon bonfire and mulled wine at Philips hall
- 7pm firework display at Philips hall
- 7.15 Bar opens in hall, all alcoholic drinks 50p - £1 (bring plenty of change) soft drinks are free
- 7.45 first sitting of evening meal in hall
- 8.45 last sitting of evening meal
- a delicious buffet will be available later
- 11pm Service at Baptist Chapel at Bwlch y Sarnau
- MIDNIGHT Toast- bubbly and millennium cake..........
- followed by disco, singing, dancing and general merryment until the wee small hours.....zzzzzzzzz.

Someone said to me.....that this has been the warmest year on record. By contrast the coldest year in living memory has to be 1947. It froze on the 20th of January and didn't thaw until April- quite a contrast. I am told that the school only closed for 1 day! As for next year........

This is the last Millennium News of, well - the millennium! Christmas is fast approaching and it doesn't seem like any time at all since we started on our endeavours back in August 1998 to prepare for the millennium. We have also moved on from initial thoughts of a party, which of course we are still having, but we have also achieved much, much more.

THANK YOU to everyone who has helped and contributed so much time and energy to the various millennium projects and fundraising events which have made it all possible. To date, we have raised nearly £2000. The Community Council is giving £500 towards the **Green** next to the Philips Hall and we have a 50% grant from Powys of £1400 for this project. This is well under way and the land is due to be handed over to the parish any day now. A further £1000 has been recieved from the Prince's Trust for the four **wall hangings**. The first of these has been finished, is being framed and will hopefully be on display on the 31st in the hall. This is truly spectacular and is the result of hundreds of hours of work. I am advised that the remaining three pieces will be completed by this time next year! The **seat** at Bwlch y Sarnau is almost complete, with only the Plaque to add. It is already a welcome addition to the village and will, I am sure, be well used in the warmer weather. The Millennium **book** is also well under way with over half of the contributions now received. If you have not replied yet, please let us have a short piece about your family and where you live as soon as possible. The book won't be complete without you.

HAPPY NEW YEAR TO ALL

Millenium Celebrations

Mugs continued…

One hundred correct versions were made, and Nita Morris, then Church Warden, and Elsie Antell, of Cefn Pawl, went round the parish giving the mugs out to the children. The remainder were sold at cost price, and went like hot cakes! The mugs are small and squat, a pretty shape in white with gold edging top and bottom. The design of the buildings is in black on one side and on the other side is the Prince Llewelyn coat of arms in red and white, with Millennium 2000 underneath. Above is either 'Abbey Cwmhir' or 'Parish of Abbey Cwmhir, Bwlch y Sarnau' depending on the design.

Party - 31st December 1999

A party for the whole of the parish was organised to see in the new Millennium, with food, music and dancing provided, (paid for through earlier fundraising events), and a bar available. At 7pm, all across the country, beacons were being lit to mark the new era, starting with one in Westminster being lit by Her Majesty The Queen. We duly had one in Abbeycwmhir, accompanied by fireworks and mulled wine. It was a special evening, and a grand time was had by all.

The Millennium Wall Hangings

Summer (183)

This idea developed over a series of weeks. After speaking with CARAD about the Rhayader tapestry created in 1993, and picking up a few tips, we met in the Philips Hall to decide on a size and content for our own work. Given the space available, it seemed more appropriate to do four

Millenium Celebrations

smaller' ones rather than one large one. The chronological order then arose and quickly the seasons, to give each piece a colour scheme and variation of flora and fauna.

The design has a central picture, surrounded by smaller squares and rectangles, demarcated with velvet ribbon. Each Wall Hanging represents a season, reflected in the content or colours. There is a consistency through all four Wall Hangings in terms of the content of the squares; the central one having the main subject matter of the era; the five running along the top and bottom expanding or complementing this subject; the two rectangles either side of the main picture having people (except in the Spring hanging), the four smallest pieces above and below the latter having flora or fauna appropriate to the season, and finally the two long rectangles having trees.

The eras themselves seemed to divide naturally into 1000 – 1500, 1500 – 1700, 1700 – 1900, and 1900 – 2000.

1000 – 1500, (Summer) The Abbey. Depicting the Abbey in its heyday and focussing on the activities of the monks. The Abbey forms the centre piece, with the monks undertaking various activities in the surrounding squares. Owain Glyndwr and Prince Llewelyn feature. Also Prince Llewelyn's Grave.

1500 – 1700 (Autumn) The dissolution of the Abbey. Devannor, which was built from the stones

Autumn (184)

and probably the oldest remaining house in the parish, forms the centre piece, home industry and agriculture being the focus of the other squares. Devannor was the home of the High Sheriff of Radnorshire and where the Court Leets were held. There were said to be three monks left in the Abbey after its demise.

Abbeycwmhir Community Book

1700 – 1900 (Winter) A Victorian Christmas. Many of the buildings, bridges, chapels and churches were built in this era, with the schools, Smithy, mill, Brickyard, Hall and vicarage all featuring.

1900 – 2000 (Spring) The Village Green. The arrival of electricity, post and telephone, Forestry, mechanised agriculture, The Philips Hall, Glyndwr's Way National Trail, River Conservation and the Lych Gate.

A great deal of research went into the designs of the individual squares, to ensure the content was as representative as possible, for instance the activities of the monks, the clothing styles of the figures, and the dates of the buildings.

The Wall Hanging Project took 2 years to complete, from March 1999 to June 2001, when a celebratory party was held in The Hall.

During this time, the working group met every Tuesday night without fail at 7pm in Victoria's kitchen at The Hall, a welcoming and comfortable environment which added to the enjoyment of these social gatherings.

Funding. Shortly after the idea for the Wall Hangings was formalised, we issued a press release to the local papers. As a result of this, the Prince's Trust got in touch saying this was precisely the sort of community project they supported. So we costed the project and applied to the Prince's

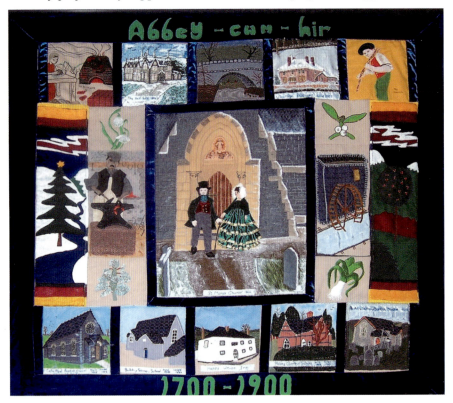

Winter (185)

Trust, initially for £650, to cover the cost of backing material, ribbons, framing and use of the Philips Hall. Match funding was from the volunteer labour to do the project. All the material for the squares was donated by the women of the parish taking part. The ribbon had to be exactly 3 inches wide for the surround, and 1 inch wide for the interior, for the pieces to all fit together, and we had not anticipated the difficulty of finding such ribbon – a task which turned out to be almost impossible; between us we looked in shops far and wide, and then Averil Williams of the Brickyard, also of Wimbledon, found VV Rouleaux in London, which had velvet ribbon of exactly the right size, in beautiful colours, but at a higher cost than we had put in our application to the Prince's Trust. However, the application had not been to the deciding panel yet, so we put in a last minute plea to increase the application to £1000, to cover the extra cost of the ribbon (£420 as opposed to our estimated £50), and were successful.

By this time, November 1999, all the squares for two Wall Hangings, 'The Abbey' and 'The Village Green' were completed. As the Prince's Trust paid half the grant to us immediately, we were able to purchase the ribbon and start putting the pieces together on the backing cloth ready for framing, not an easy task for which we employed the help of Mary Griffiths, Church Farm, Cross Gates. Gemini Antiques, Kidderminster, carried out the framing and in May 2000 we held a Wild West themed party in the Philips Hall to 'unveil' these wonderful achievements. Earlier in the year we had held a cake stall outside Llandrindod Train Station on Good Friday, for which we had made Easter crafts as well as cakes. This was very successful and boosted our funds to cover any unforeseen costs which may arise.

Spring (186)

Work continued with the next two wallhangings, the pieces for which were distributed in September 2000, and collected back in in February 2001. For these occasions we invited everyone in the

Community to the Philips Hall and laid out on tables the wallhangings, with pictures of the designs, so people could choose the piece they wanted to do. We packaged up each piece with the design (drawn either by Mary Strong or Jake Berriman) and materials, to make them as self contained as possible and convenient to complete. The ribbon was selected and purchased, pieces joined together, this time with the help of Val Webb, School House, framed by Gemini Antiques and hung on the wall. A celebratory party was held at The Hall on 22 June 2001, to which everyone who had been involved, including the framer, was invited.

With left over funds the Wall Hanging group arranged for the frame of the portrait of Colonel Philips to be repaired. This was carried out by Gemini Antiques in early 2002.

The wallhangings are in the Philips Hall, 4 very beautiful pieces of work, testament to what a community can achieve when it works together.

Millennium Seat, Bwlch y Sarnau

The seat is located on the roadside near to the chapel gate. The idea was suggested by Mr Fred Wozencraft, Bryndreanog, who cared for the bench until his death in 2004. A small amount of stone was removed from the wall of the graveyard to install the wooden seat and plaque.

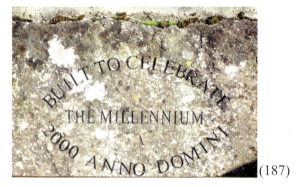 (187)

So a very productive time was seen in the parish in the lead up to the Millennium, with a whole host of community events to raise funds or celebrate our achievements. At times it was hard work, but always good fun, and the results will be with us forever.

Diana Berriman, Little Plock , 2008.

Millenium Celebrations

HYMN 2000

Lord, give me faith to trust in you
When my work is hard and drear.
Give me the strength to carry on,
And feel your presence ever near.

Lord, give me faith to trust in you
When I am lone and have no friend.
You were alone on Calvary,
So empathise and understand.

Lord, give me faith to trust in you;
Greed and envy cause such strife.
Help me to count my blessings Lord,
And make me lead a better life.

Lord, give me faith to trust in you,
You are kind and strong and meek.
Give me the courage to defend
All those despondent, sad and weak.

Lord, I have faith and trust that you
Wisdom will give to those who reign,
That they may shape a better world,
Where peace and harmony remain.

Brenda Griffiths

This hymn was specially composed for the Millennium. Words by Brenda Griffiths and music by Averil Williams

Other Celebrations

Barbecue at the Cefn after the treasure hunt. Queens Golden Jubilee 3rd June 2002.*

The Lovominable Snowman*

The Philips Hall prepared for the Gathering on the Queens Golden Jubilee 1st June 2002. (Village Photo on page 122) (188)

Celebrations

"Mens' Full Monty"
Queens Golden Jubilee
1st June 2002 (189)

The "Harry Potter"
Abbeycwmhir float for the
Rhayader Carnival 2005 (190)

The Builth Wells Historic
Pageant held in the grounds
of Llanelwedd Hall on 11th
August 1909.
Over a 1000 people took part
in the event before a
crowd of around 5000. (191)

The Cistercian Monks of Abbey-cwm-hir

137

Weeping for your lost reign - Wets your slate - Cwmhir the urn of old Wales.

This hard stone - to remember - Your military justice
Your undying death - Bleeding over captive Wales

(192)

The *Carreg Goffa* Memorial to Llywelyn ap Gruffydd

The campaign in the 1970's to place a Memorial Stone to Llywellyn ap Gruffydd in the Cwmhir Abbey ruins, where he is said to be buried, was led by Peter Barnes who negotiated with the Department of the Environment and the Radnor District Council who gave permission in 1977. He also designed the stone with the help of staff from the National Museum of Wales - the stone mason was Ben Lloyd of Rhayader. On Oct 7th 1978 the Archdruid of Wales placed the memorial stone & wrote the poem across the base of the above picture.[1]

(193)

A NATIONAL SHRINE TO LLYWELYN ap GRUFFYDD

"A National shrine to Llywelyn II has been erected over his burial place in the ruins of Abbeycwmhir. The shrine was officially unveiled by Robat ap Risiart of Garthwin, a descendant of Prince Llywelyn. Among others officiating were Geraint Bowen the Archdruid of Wales. The ceremony was followed by a Noson Lawen in the Village Hall at Abbeycwmhir."[2] *Welsh Nation* October 1978)

The date being remembered is 11th December 1282 but the Memorial Services are held on the Sunday closest - the first one was held on 10th December 1978. On the Saturday a Memorial Servie is held at Cilmery. The poem across the top of the picture above is a the second verse of a Welsh Language poem by Tom Parri-Jones from his poem "Llywelyn".[3]

IN LIVING MEMORY?

The Twentieth Century

Steam comes to Abbeycwmhir - in the form of a Steam Roller seen in the centre of the village. (left of picture.) Macadam roads came to the village centre around 1938-9 (194)

"How did road's start? Was it when the men started cultivating the land? The women would perhaps carry the stones off the land and put them in tidy rows at the side or bottom of an area being cultivated. And then in winter, they found that by waking on these stones, they would have a cleaner dryer area on which to walk. And so word went around, and they all did their bit and soon there would be a stone track from one homestead to the next." NP

Jack Griffiths of Devannor (195)

Fowler's Cave

When I was a child in the 1950s, each year the family went for a fortnight to see Grandpa (Col. Lionel Philips) at Abbeycwmhir for our holiday in August, timed for his birthday. To get the children out of the house, and to ensure some exercise and fresh air, the family legend was that there was money hidden years ago in Fowlers Cave on Great Park. By 1956 when I was twelve, I had realised that at least one parent used to come up with us each time, which was why we managed to locate pennies in the crevices of the rock. My 1956 diary records how I went up on my own to hide some money, so that later my seven year old sister could find it. However, one other time when I was up there with my older brother we actually found a penny deep in the cracks which we had some difficulty in getting out. It was very discoloured and was dated 1892! So the legend was more than just a legend!

*Flavia Swann
(Grand daughter of Colonel JL
& Nancy Philips)*

WENALLT BARN

Wenallt Barn fallen down before 1919 when it was rebuilt (below) by Bill Wozencraft of School House - his last job as a stone mason. (196) Above: A pitching or marking iron.

In 2010 (197)

In Living Memory

The rebuilt Wenallt Barn with (left) it's perfectly vertical wall of 1919 and inside (bottom right) the cosy shepherds' warming room (still there) handy for the sheeps' footbath (centre). **'Wenallt'** means 'White Wooded Hill' (cf p309)

Cefn Pawl Shearing

Sheep shearing at Cefn Pawl, around 1928. The shearers are (L-R) George Wozencraft Snr., Cefn Pawl, overseeing operations; John Williams, Estate Shepherd, the Wenallt; George Wozencraft Jnr., Cefn Pawl; Joe Williams (sporting clogs) and Tom Davies, Bailey Bog. (198)

The annual sheep shearing was probably the most important activity in the life of the hill farms. As well as being a practical necessity it was also a big social event and the skill of the farmer's wife was needed to cater for the greatly increased numbers of people working on the farm. In the past when 'shearings' were really big events, the work was done with hand shears. The bigger flocks would require 15 to 20 men shearing on benches.

Two or more men would bring in sheep to be shorn and take away those done. Others would re-mark (brand) the shorn, rolling up fleeces or fetch more as required. The 'floor-man' had to keep the floor tidy and consequently the fleeces clean and attend to any accidental injuries or cuts.

He also distributed drink, usually cider, and tobacco and cigarettes amongst the workmen. The accounts of the Abbeycwmhir Estate regularly showed purchases of cider through the summer months, 195 gallons at a time! In the outhouse the women would be busy with the preparation of the meals for almost half the population of the neighbourhood, and invited guests or relatives from other walks of life were often present.

The shearings were a kind of social and festive occasion. Some concluded with a football match in the late evening. Each farm, by ancient practice and custom, had its own day, commencing with the lower hill farms about mid-June. The shearing season continued daily until the end of July, all the time working further up into the higher hills, with their correspondingly later season. The system was of a co-operative nature and did not require much extra labour. The farmers and shepherds simply exchanged assistance, moving from one farm to another each day, as did their wives and daughters, helping with the housework.[4]

The Shearing

When my life was thrifty, thrifty,
Soon one sheep grew to fifty;
After that I lived for fun
And found my flock was back to one.

-Anonymous Welsh Verse [5]

Abe Wozencraft of Cwmyscawen (199)

In Living Memory

Clogs

The clogs being worn by Joe Williams (father of Lindsey) with his foot on the bench (opposite) echoes the recollection by the late William Lewis, Esgairwy, of a clog maker working in the area about this time.

"Alder trees grow freely along the banks of some Radnorshire streams. A clogger named Mr Orrell, from Lancashire spent a couple of years plying his craft along the banks of Clywedog and Bachell brooks. He lived in a horse-drawn caravan. The horse was used to haul trees to his tarpaulin and timber workshop and then, later, the finished product to the railway station at Penybont. His was a solitary life by the stream, felling and sawing up trees or working in his crude tent, splitting the logs skilfully shaping the cleft wood into the finished article, clogs, for some Lancashire lass. All his work was done with hand tools. It is most unlikely that a clog maker will ever be seen in Abbeycwmhir again!" [6]

Through the ditch homeward if it is homewards.
I hefted the gate-post, still doubtful,
And oh, before I reached the back-door,
The sound of building a new earth, new heaven,
Were my mother's clogs on the kitchen floor.

Waldo Wiliams [7]

Geese at The Dafan, Bwlch y Sarnau. (200)   (201 →)   Mel Hamer washing a sheeps face

Local names for local places

There are places around the Abbey that we will never hear of again. *The people who used these names, day after day, have all gone. Places like "The Dung Hill" and "The Green Door".*

*I expect **"The Abbey Pitch"** will always be called that. It was called "a pitch" in the first place because coming from Cross Gates with roads not very good – nor the bikes in those days – it was the only place where you had to get off the bike, and push.*   Continued →

Local names for local places *Continued*

*"**The Sheep Parlour**" was the Great Park.*

*"Where have you left your bike? " and you would say "**By the Green Door**". And everyone would know that your bike was at the top of the little hill as you travel out of the village, above Home Farm yard. There is an iron gate there now, an entrance on to The Hall lawn. In my day there was a very solid green door there.*

*"**The Dung Hill**" is there at the very large sycamore between the Village Hall and the school.*

*Of course "**The Tunnel**" is where the trees are between The Blacksmiths and Llwy Cottage. When I started school the trees were much thicker on the bottom side of the road and there were large fir trees growing on the top side. And yes, it was very much like a tunnel.*

*Next comes "**Six Days Math**". (?) Please don't ask me how it got it's name! It is Cefn Pawl's field that is right opposite the turn going to the farm and everyone walking from or to Devannor from the Abbey would use the footpath that went from gate at the top to the bridge at the bottom. It saved a few steps if you travelled the road.*

*And so we come to "**Cuckoo Gate**". This used to be a gate at the entrance to Llwynneuadd.. And "**Cuckoos Bridge**" is there by Keepers Cottage. There is a little coppice beside the road by the Llwynneuadd turn. On the Abbey side of those few bushes there is a space and then some oak trees just back from the road, there used to be a dwelling called "**Cuckoos Nest**". So that's where the name came from. I bet it won't ever be called that again – no-one will know it's history. (George Lewis [8] says that the Cuckoo name was given because it was here that the first cuckoo was heard in Radnorshuire each year. Ed.)*

*Between the Little Park and The Great Park is the **Deer Barn** – only the base of it is left. Someone was talking of excavating the site, but I should think all they would find is well rotted deer manure.*

- Noel Price

Photography developed rapidly from the 1830's. In the 1840's static portraiture was possible; in the 1850's the Crimean War was photographed. It wasn't until 1888 that the Eastman's Kodak camera went on the market with the slogan "You press the button, we do the rest". 1901 saw the introduction of the Kodak Brownie camera. Probably our oldest photograph is from about 1860 of Wilson's Hall. Kodachrom Colour Film was introduced in 1935. Digital photography came with the Millennium.

Dates of Arrival of Utilities at Abbeycwmhir

- 1865 Penybont Railway Station opened.
- 1870 Postal Service.
- 1904/5 Telelphone [9] (Also in Sale Doc. of 1919)
    (Home Farm telephone box is Grade II listed building)
- 1920 Jack Went's water generator near The Mill provides electricity to Home Farm & The Hall.
- 1925 Pelten wheel installed in Home Farm.
- 1924 Penybont Telephone Exchange opened.[10]
- 1938/9 Macadam Road.
- 1959 Connected to National Electricity Grid.
- 1968 Sewage for centre of village up to Piccadilly.
- 1973 Water Mains from Bwlch y Sarnau where there had been a reservoir.
- 1979 TV Connection to aerial on Llwy Hill.

London name for local place - *Piccadilly Here We Come*

The origin of the name Piccadilly is not clear. A local tradition, recorded by George Lewis in his book "Henfryn, Radnorshire hill farming life in the 1930's and 40's", suggested that the name Piccadilly was given by the old drovers who named their resting places along the route after the market to which they were heading. I doubt this, as I can find no reference to a Piccadilly market.

It has also been suggested that it was named by soldiers returning from the first world war, the name occurring in the popular song 'Tipperary'.

However, my researches suggest that Piccádilly Cottages were originally known as "School Cottages", logical since they were opposite the school and constructed at the same time. An inventory of the estate, completed in 1893 as part of a tax rebate claim in times of 'Agricultural Depression', makes no reference to Piccadilly Cottages but does refer to School Cottages, the rent at that time being one shilling a week. A gravestone in the front burial ground records Ann and Evan Owen, School Cottage, Abbeycwmhir, 1899 and 1905. The church Burial Register records both of them as living at Piccadilly, which suggests that Piccadilly and School Cottage are in fact the same place.

So why Piccadilly? It is possible, although I have yet to confirm it, that the Philips family had their London home in Piccadilly, which, in mid Victorian times, was a very fashionable residential area of London. There is an interested recording in the Baptism register which seems to confirm this.

"Mary Florence (Mabel Florence Mary - Ed. cf P 83), daughter of George Henry and Anna Theophila Philips, The Hall, Abbeycwmhir, Esq., H.M. Dalmaine, Curate, St. James, Piccadilly, London, Feb. 8th 1869. This Baptism, no, 304, was solemnised in St. James Church, Piccadilly, London, and copied into this register book by me, James J. Evans, vicar of Abbeycwmhir. Ash Wednesday 1871."

This event was very close to the time when the school and the cottages were built and may be the key to the origin of the name.

- Julian Lovell

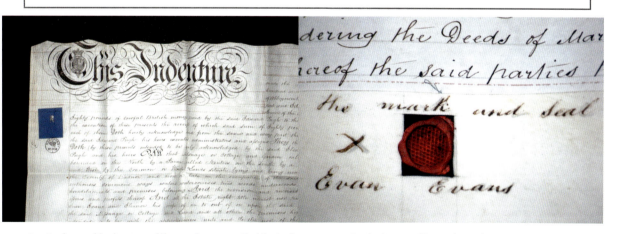

An *indented* indenture like a *denture* divided along a toothed ziz zag line where it connects to an identical duplicate representing a bond or agreement - in this case over the purchase of a property.

Ambrose Davies leading the hunt at Home Farm in 1969 including Frederick, Mel, Caroline and Carla Hamer.(203)

Lindsey Williams MBE, Forestry Commission Wildlife Ranger. (204)

MURDER AT CEFN PAWL

In February 1911 "two farm servants, William Davies, aged 22 years, and John Cecil Pugh, aged 37 years, were employed at this farm. These men shared bedrooms with one of their employers sons. Davies and Pugh were not by any means friends and it was apparent that certain incidents which had occurred between these two men had caused Davies to hate the very sight of Pugh.

At 9 pm, Pugh and his empl.oyers son went to bed and were shortly afterwards joined by Davies. Fifteen minutes later, without a word appranetly passing between them, Davies in the light of a stable lamp shot Pugh with a double barrelled shot gun, as the latter lay in bed.. This gun had been kept in a case behind a grandfather clock in the kitchen, together with a number of cartridges......after the shooting Davies left the house and eventually turned up at a farm some distance from Cefn Pawl where he was arrested by the police.......Pugh died from his wounds in the bedroom shortly after midnight......at the Radnorshire Assizes, held at Presteigne. Davies was found guilty but insane and was ordered to be detained during His Majesty's Pleasure".[11]

In Living Memory

Abbeycwmhir Shooting Club
Man Jailed - *Independent 21.2.1997*
Jason Curtis, 28 of Llandrindod Wells was jailed for 4½ years for ten fire-arm and drug possession offences and planning, in writing, a killing spree; the mass murder by shooting of shoppers and police in Middleton Street "a truly horrific piece of writing…" said the Judge.

Noel Price (NP) in 2010: *Life long resident, last at Keepers Cottage, and author of "Tales of a Welsh Postman" & much of "In Living Memory" (in italics) in this book .* (209)

Whose who on this page - on next page →

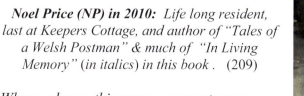

Horse Sense

(211)

Then in the 1930's more timber was going to Penybont, but this time the roads were much better and they moved it with horses. A chap by the name of Wilfred Smith was the man to get this timber to Penybont with his three horses. He was a man from Kerry and would lodge with the people at Abbey Mill going home on Saturday night and returning on Sunday night ready for work on Monday morning. He liked his ale. He would load a large oak tree on his wagon, he and his team, and would take it to the station to unload. The he would sometimes call at Crossgates Pub. Leaving the horses outside he would sometimes get quite drunk, and coming out of there he would climb up on the wagon but behind the wheels, so that if he fell off he would not get run over. And the horses would get him safely home. He used to stable his horses at Cefn Pawl, there being a large stable there. Wilfred Smith married the daughter from The Mill and she was the first cook at the Abbey School. NP

WHOSE-WHO ON PREVIOUS PAGE

183 Gwyn Griffiths, Devannor, sitting on the binder & Clarence Griffiths driving the tractor.
184 A WAR-AG [12] on a "Fordson County Crawler" at Devannor towards the end of the war.
185 Abe Wozencraft & Bill Price at Pencwm, Laithdu.
186 Abe Wozencrafton riding *Bovril* at Glanalders
188 At Knighton Fair - Doug Brown & Abe Wozencraft

ON THIS PAGE

190 Fred Hamer & Alfred Rowlands at Devannor C 1930

(212)

The first car at Beili Bog Farm Ford "Popular" saloon. C.1955.

In Living Memory

Traces of strange creatures on glaciofluvial landslide at Lower Cwmhir! (214)

> **SHOOTING:** THERE IS AT THE PRESENT TIME GOOD ROUGH SHOOTING OVER THE ESTATE CONSISTING OF PHEASANTS, PARTRIDGES, GROUSE AND ANY QUANTITY OF RABBITS AND WILD DUCK. THIS HAS, HOWEVER, NOT BEEN PROPERLY SUPERINTENDED DURING THE WAR, AND WITH VERY LITTLE EXPENSE A VERY LARGE BAG COULD BE OBTAINED IN A FEW SEASONS OWING TO THE EXCEPTIONAL FACILITIES OF THE ESTATE AND TO THE WILLINGNESS OF THE TENANTS TO CO-OPERATE IN PRESERVING GAME. **FISHING:** THERE IS GOOD TROUT FISHING IN THE THREE POOLS ON THE PROPERTY AND TROUT OF ONE AND A HALF POUNDS HAVE BEEN RECENTLY CAUGHT.
>
> — *DRIVER JONAS & CO. 1919* [13]

	Grouse	Rabbits	Pheas.	Partridge	Hares	Duck	W. cock	Snipe	Roe	Black	S.Deer	
1899-00	43	73	52	16	29	8	–	–	–	–	–	=221
1900-01		102	47	11	3	10	1	–	–	–	–	=174
1901-2	191	109	56	14	39	19	2	3	1	1	–	=446
1902-3	209	197	67	20	47	6	7	3	–	–	–	556
1903-4	117	217	79	–	28	4	11	4	–	–	–	460
1904-5	–	138	75	4	6	5	3	–	–	–	–	231
1905-6	153	83	43	12	32	3	–	3	21	–	–	350
1906-7	5	136	160	7	10	3	9	–	–	1 Chamois	–	330
1907	76	25	–	1	7	2	–	6	–	2	–	119
	88	4		87	15			1				195
				1		10		45				56

The Colonel's Shooting note book 1899 - 1907 (Age 21 - 29) (215)

An Eye-Witness Account of the opening of the Philips Hall 1937

The original variegated cedar shingle clad Philip's Hall built in 1937 by Colonel J.L and Chrystine A.Philips to celebrate the hundredth anniversary of the Philips purchase of the Abbeycwmhir Estate. "...constructed throughout by Empire wood of such durability that no repairs will be necessary for at least 40 years."[13] Presented to a committee to administer in 1958. It became a Registered Charity in 1979. A brick exterior was added in 1997. (JE). (Interior picture on page 136) (216)

William Lewis of Esgairwy wrote, "The most outstanding event of this nature that I remember was a concert given by the local mixed Chorus on the occasion of the opening of the new 'Village Hall' in 1937. This hall had been provided by the Philips family, the owners of the estate, to commemorate the centenary of their purchase of it in 1837. They engaged the late Mr. H.P. Jones of Llanddewi, a well known musician as musician and conductor. Also they engaged a twelve piece orchestra from Hereford for the concert. A few celebrated soloists from neighbouring villages also provided assistance by giving supporting items, or supporting the chorus.

The main work of the evening was a choral piece entitled "The Wreck of the Hesperus". Supporting items included "Myfanwy" and others. A short piece called "Gallia" was so beautifully rendered that I was almost spellbound. I have enjoyed much good music since then but none has given me a greater thrill than the performance of "Gallia" did that evening in 1937. Those people who had trudged their way to the village in the darkness of winter evenings, twice weekly for several weeks, for practice were to be admired and applauded, as indeed they were that evening.

Abbeycwmhir Music

In earlier times singing classes were held in the farmhouses. I have seen the account of such classes held at Llwynneuadd in the year 1879. Those participating paid 2/6 for the course of fourteen lessons. (2/6 was a considerable amount in those days) A local man named James Griffiths then living at Brickyard Cottage, was the Tutor. At Rock Chapel, 46 persons were taking lessons in singing, this is recorded in a diary of 1879. The people of Abbeycwmhir had a great love of music and neighbours gathered in the homes of others for 'sing-songs'. Hymns were very popular items on such occasions. A few homes had pianos and others had organs." [14]

The Community Council developed from the elected **Civil Parish Council** which was started at a Public Meeting on Dec 4th and began work on December 28th 1894 - a result of the Local Governemnt Act of that year. Rev Ernest Hermitage Day was the Chairman, Richard Price was Vice-Chairman, Anna Theophilia Philips was the Treasurer and Chrystine Anna was the Clerk. "Mrs Philips gives the use of Church House for meetings for free. When the School is used for Parish Meetings a small charge will be made".

Community Councils replaced Civil Parish Councils in Wales forty years ago, in 1974, but work in exactly the same way. The Community Council is a group of seven Councillors democratically elected (every four years) by the community to represent its interests and advise the County Council. It has four fixed meetings per year: January, May, September, November plus any special planning meetings. Alan Bennet at 81 is longest serving counselor – since 1967 when Jack Went was Secretary. He is Chair again at the time of this book going to print.

In Living Memory

Community of Initatives

In 1979 eleven households in Abbeycwmhir clubbed together to obtain 625 line colour TV lead by Reg Hamer of Home Farm who argued that "the winters would be long up here without television." The villagers also did much of the work cutting the ride for the cable and positioning the TV relay arial 1528 ft on the top of Llwyw Hill. A route was gouged out of the forest and down the precipitous hillside and across the road in three places. Households paid £275 each which was matched pound for pound by the Development Board for Rural Wales.Many people worked on the project as well. A Mr Reg Williams, a physicist arranged much of the official work, planned the technical side and even did much of the wiring. Abbeycwmhir had a better service than most urban areas with five channel colour television. In July 1979 A

(217a,b)

colour television was set up in the Philips Hall and a dance held when the Development Board handed over their final cheque of £2500.

§ At the Parish Council meeting held at Church House on Friday 8th February 1895, the Vice Chairman, Richard Price "proposed that the District Council be petitioned to provide a bridge at Devannor Ford. The Road Surveyors roughly estimated the cost at £100. J.P.Severn Esq. offers £50 towards it. Councillors Williams, George, Evans and Pugh thought the bridge very necessary… carried unanimously."[15]

§ 19.8.1895 "……the total cost of the bridge would be £98, towards which Mr J.P.Severn had promised £50, and timber worth £3, the neighbours would haul to the bridge to the value of £10, which with the £20 offered by the District Council, leaves £15 still to be provided. It was intended to use Bessemer steel girders with wood ties in the building of the bridge."[16]

§ 104 (4.4.1898) "Motion by the Chairman. "Whereas the existing railways are insufficient either to meet the present needs of Radnorshire or to develop its resources; resolved that the Parish Council of Abbey Cwmhir expresses its entire approval of the East and West Wales Railway scheme, and desires the Member for Radnorshire to support it in the House of Commons." Motion carried. Cslr Rich. Price did not vote.[17]

Abbeycwmhir Community Book

Making the Community tick

Womens Institute in 1973 re-started in 1960 (218) Right - WI plants a tree beside the Philips Hall in 1966. (219)

Children's Committee Christmas Grotto (220)

Children's Committee Annual Pickled Onion Competition in the Happy Union Inn. (222)

The Community Council; Philips Hall Committee; Children's Commitee; Women Instituite; Local Walks and Sports.

FOOTBALL

The Major, Francis III (1873-1932), was pass the school one day at playtime when he asked boys why they were not playing footb "Because we haven't got a football, Sir," was reply. They were told to call at The Hall following day when the Major presented th with two footballs, one for practice and the o for match-play. Thereafter the Major saw that boys had a football, even replacing one 'pinch by some visiting footballers.[18]

Abbey Sports

I remember the sports held every year on the meadow below the Abbey. Children's races: Children up to ten years, Children up to thirteen years, children up to sixteen years. There would be football matches, tug of war, men's one mile race. Men over 40 yrs, one hundred yards race! Ladies "Watch the Cockerel Race". Someone would give a cockerel. The ladies would stand in line and someone would be standing 15-20 yards away holding the cockerel. When the gun went off, the person would loose the cockerel and off would race the ladies. In those days, the pool was full of mud and reeds grew tall along the edge. You can guess the rest so it will save me ink! Yes, of course, the cockerel went in the reeds. Although everyone had their best clothes on, one lady wanted that cockerel. It was something for nothing, well almost, it would be a cockerel for the one shilling entrance fee. With no fuss or bother, one lady kicked off her shoes, up with her frock, undid her stockings and took them off. Paddelling up to her knees in mud she managed to catch her prize.

The Treasurer for the Abbey Sport was a man that liked his ale. Myself and a couple of others had won a race and were given a slip of paper and told that if we took it to The Happy Union we would find the Treasurer there and he would pay us. In those days if you won the under ten race you would get a shilling. If you won the under thirteen race your would get two shillings and if you won the under sixteen race you would get half-a-crown. There were sweetest baby competitions and glamorous grandmother competitions. There was plenty going on. There was always a large marquee where the ladies would serve tea, sandwiches and cakes. Another night to go home tired but happy! NP

Women's Institute Walk led by Lindsey Williams circa 1975.(224)
Village walks continue today - including the Christmas Cracker.

TUG-OF-WAR TEAMS

Also in the 1920's and 30's Abbeycwmhir had two very famous tug-of-war teams. The men and women teams would win trophies at the local sports in the area. Strong farming folk who spent all day and every day carrying sacks of coal, flour, feed for animals and fertilizer. Also carrying sticks for the fences. What they couldn't carry they would drag along the ground – things they needed all their strength to shift.. NP

Abbeycwmhir Community Book

The very successful Clywedog Rovers Darts Team being presented with the Crossgates Darts League Trophy in 1987 in the Philips Hall. (225)

Cricket

Not a game in which Wales has been particularly remarkable - yet it has thriven in Radnorshire. In 1869 Nantmel & Abbeycwmhir were playing matches under the leadership of their respective squires and the sons of squires.

The Shepherd

And I have not forgotten the shepherd, Mr Williams who lived out at Wennalt Cottages. During the first two years or so at school, we would often see him riding his Welsh mountain pony either up or down past the school.

I can remember his funeral day: the bearers carrying the coffin in relays from the Wennalt Cottage to the Church. And seeing the mourners and all his friends and the folk from the surrounding area coming to pay their respects. Yes he had a fine white pony that had carried him many a mile around the Abbey Hills. NP

Radnorshire.

The *Hereford Journal* can be obtained of Mr Prosser, at the Shop, Aberedw.

ABBEY-CWM-HIR.

On Saturday this quiet though pretty little village was greatly enlivened, athletic sports taking place, and, considering the rather short notice given, a great number of persons assembled on the ground. The arrangements were under the management of Masters Francis George Prescot, Charles Kenrick, and John Lion Philips, to whom great praise is due, and especially to Master Charles Kenrick, who took an extremely active part. The lower part of the village was decorated with flags, as was also the meadow, in which the sports were held. A table was elaborately laid out with tea, cake, buns, &c., to which Mrs. G. H. Philips (with her usual generosity) heartily invited everyone. Under the superintendence of Mr. R. T. Hawkins a stand was also erected, from which were suspended a quantity of small bottles, where anyone wishing to try his skill in shooting could be supplied with gun and cartridges for the purpose. This was well patronised. The ever popular "Old Aunt Sally" was also present. The athletic sports continued till the shades of evening closed in, when another invitation was given to the tea table, and, after having done ample justice to the good things provided, ringing cheers were given for Mrs. Philips and family. The results of the sports were as follow:—

50 Yards Flat Race for Men.—Five competitors: 1st, Thomas Pembridge; 2nd, John Capers.

50 Yards Flat Race for Boys.—Four Competitors: 1st, David John Bradley; 2nd, James Price.

High Jump for Men.—Four competitors: 1st, W. Wozencroft; 2nd, John Davies (smith).

Egg and Spoon Race for Women or Girls.—Five competitors: 1st, Emily Davies; 2nd, Mrs. J. Davies.

Egg and Spoon Race for Girls.—Four competitors: 1st, Sarah J. Pratley; 2nd, Edith A. Evans.

Egg and Spoon Race for Men.—Four competitors: 1st, John Davies; 2nd, Thomas D. Owen.

Egg and Spoon Race for Boys.—Five competitors: 1st, Richard Kinsey; 2nd, Charles Evans.

100 Yards Hurdle Race.—Five competitors; two heats: 1st, Thomas Pembridge; 2nd, John Davies (groom).

Three-legged Race for Men.—Three competitors: 1st, John Davies (groom) and John Capers; 2nd, Smout and T. D. Owen.

There is a photo of the three Philip's sons of George Henry on page 82. (226)

The Great Flood

It was in 1932 that the Abbey had a great flood up the road towards Bwlch y Sarnau. Just past Fishpool Farm. You will see a grassy bank and at the far side a large gap. Well, dear friends, In the summer of 1932 on a Saturday evening there was a cloud burst. The monk's had made a pool up there. This one had an earth dam amd as it had been raining all day and then having this cloud burst, it was too much to bear and it gave way. With all that extra water coming down the stream, it washed away the bridge at the blacksmiths and also Devannor bridge. Lower down at Coedtrewernau Mill, my father's uncle was getting ready for bed. His wife had gone upstairs already. He was just checking around when it got there. He was up to his waist in water. A cupboard that was in the house was caught by the flood and ended up at Larch Grove. A few miles down the river, a Mr Brown was getting ready to go to bed, his wife had gone upstairs, when he found himself waist deep in water. A cupboard that was in the flood is now safe at Larch Grove, Llandegley.

The breach of 1932 in the fishpools lake dam - in 2010 (227)

How did that dam burst after 800-900 years? It had to burst on that evening! Jack Smith, the Blacksmith was telling me that he was coming down from the pub that night. It was still thundering and lightening and raining heavily. He said he came around the corner at the bottom of the pitch and he found himself in a lot of water. (A good knee deep). As he went further round there was a flash of lightening and he saw the rails of the bridge going across the road in front of him – instead of across the river. BRIDGE IS WASHED AWAY? Only for that he would have walked right over the edge and perhaps been drowned that night. He turned around and trundled back to spend the night in the pub. NP

"The freak storm of May 1932…swept away every bridge down the Clewedog and Bachell, burst the dam holding the Fishpool near the farm of that name (this has not been re-built) and brought all the surface soil off the Horse Piece above Tyfaenor amd dumped it in the lane, thus raising the level by three or four feet. The field had not been sown with turnips, and the crop started to appear in the road. The road is still considerably higher than previously…" Teddy Bennet[19]

"In 1932, when the Fishpools dam broke and a huge flood of water tumbled through the village – the occupants of Piccadilly Cottages were right in the flood path. In those days everyone had a pig and when the water came they pulled the pig upstairs into the bedroom". (Doreen Hughes, 1 Wennalt Cottages)

In the pub, apparently, people speculated on whether the gentleman, in the dark, would be able to distinguish his wife from the pig!

A Lesser Flood

There is a story that Paddock Cottages, The Happy Union and Home Farm were flooded either by the Hall pond (whose water previously used to drive machinery in Home Farm workshops) which over-flowed or by a blockage in the culvert. Was this the Poeth overflowing at the same time as the Fishpool 1932 flood or a result of melt water from the terrible snow storms lasting all winter into 1947 - the worst winter on record? Or something else at another time?

The Ffron Farmhouse 2010 (228)

The Abbey Windows, as they are called, probably came from the Coalbrookdale Factory founded by Abraham Derby in the Ironbridge Gorge. It is said they were made especially for Abbeycwmhir.

In a rut

"In the 1920's a tremendous amount of timber from round the Abbey area (its before The Forestry? No forwarders to make deep ruts, what did?) In those days there were only stone roads – no tar and no chippings, and the roads would get very rutted, almost impassable. Two brothers, living at Llywy Cottage, worked in the Builth Quarry. They would ride their bicycles the sixteen or seventeen miles to be at work by 8am. Work until 5pm and then ride their bicycles the sixteen or so miles home 6.5 days a week, come rain or shine. And they would say about the ruts. They said each would get in a rut outside their home and they would not see each other until they reached the main road - the ruts were so deep. Someone once said he once heard them going down the Road One would shout "Be ye there boy?" and the answer came "I be here"! NP

The Saw Mill

The Carpenter lived in Cross Cottage, opposite the Happy Union, it was also known as The Laundry because in the Major's time, it was where the Hall had it's bed linen washed. The Carpenter, a Mr Evans was also a good workman and used to make all the gates for the farms on the estate as well as all the other jobs and repairs that needed doing. He had his own workshop and saw mill where he would saw very large oak trees into whatever size he needed. On every gate, on the top bar, was carved "Abbey Cwmhir Estate" and the date – and all gates were painted green.

The Saw Mill was all water powered. Up behind the church on the right hand side is another pool. The water came down a six inch pipe, it not only drove the circular saws but also the bench that these big trees sat on through the saw. What power there is in water! NP

Mill Sparks

I can remember the Mill with the water wheel and grinding stones, and all the big iron cog wheels. The water that drove the mill then went down a pipe into the river. In the early nineteen twenties when the chap who was then the blacksmith came back from the war, he asked the Major about electricity – the Major had heard of it. But how to make it work? This man, by the name of Jack Went, a very clever chap, knew his stuff. He told the Major if he would get the equipment needed, the blacksmith would do the rest. Borrowing the Carpenter to build a shed over this pipe they set to work, the carpenter making a shed and the blacksmith digging down to the pipe and then cutting a hole in it he started making a small water wheel to fit into the hole. So it was done. The shed was finished, the little home-made water wheel drove the dynamo. And so electricity came to Abbeycwmhir. Years before it came to Llandrindod Wells, we had electric light through the village and up as far as the school. NP

*I remember **Jack Went** the Blacksmith, he was Clerk to the Parish Council at the Abbey when Alan Bennet was first elected. I used to call on him every night. "Anything I can do?" "Yes please, bring me twenty cigarettes?" He would give me the money and off I would go. JP*

In First World War he served in France in the Engineers as a Blacksmith where, it is said, he supervised 200 Chinese repairing tanks and shoeing horses. He claimed to have 26 letters after his name! During the second World War he returned to military service where he was the Lieutenant of No.4 Platoon, Abbeycwmhir - Bwlch y Sarnau of the Radnor Home Guard of which Lt.Colonel JL Philips D.S.O. became the Commanding Officer.[20]

"Later Jack Went wouldn't change his clothes. He had a hump on his neck the size of a pigeon's egg but when I knew him it was all down his back from his neck as big as your head. He couldn't get his shirt over it. My mother looked after him a bit. I had to change his shirt". Albert Philips.

" In the Abbey farm-house lived many years a tenant named George Lewis, whose memory will be respected as long as good nature, a social and friendly disposition, and hospitality, are virtues esteemed by mankind; his house and table were free to all comers; his neighbours and near acquaintances never failed to meet with their kindest and most friendly reception, and the poor of the vicinity always experienced his bounty. Here the weather beaten and benighted traveller found the comfort and shelter and repose; gentlemen who came from distant parts to sport on the hills made this house their home; and respectable members of the Society of Friends have often expressed a grateful sense of the hospitality which they here receive in their annual peregrinations through the county. In short, the fame for alms and hospitality which the monastery of Cwmhir had acquired in ancient times underwent little or no diminution in the recent days of the good-natured and facetious George Lewis" "History of Radnorshire" Jonathan Williams 1905.[21]

Silver Wedding Celebration of James John and Clarice Griffths at Devanor 2nd June 1944.   (229)

Wild Flowers and Fruit of the past

*"I remember as a boy collecting over a hundred different species of flowering plants in a few weeks during one spring. The hedgerows, usually consisting of hawthorn, blackthorn and hazel, are prolific in this respect. Here, in the Spring, the first celandines, primroses and violets are to be found, and the little strawberry plants that will yield tiny delicious fruit in the early Summer. As children we used to thread these on to a stem of grass and when we had almost filled it, we could relish them by the mouthful. In the woods, too, primroses will grow in massive bosses of bright yellow a foot or more across, their flowers usually larger than the hedgerow. Red Campions and Bluebells are a glorious sight in some of the woods and wider hedge banks where the hedges have been allowed to grow high. They are quickly overtaken, however, by the ubiquitous bracken, which very soon ousts the Campion altogether. Where woods have been completely cut down, bluebells will still continue to grow and flower, even in the open...an afternoons walk can yield one quite a hearty meal of delicious blackberries. They are at their best just as the hazel nuts are beginning to brown -"brown shielers" we used to call these, because they slip so easily out of their sheathes. The kernel is sweet and succulent at this time, and mixes very well with the blackberries." **Teddy Bennett of Tynycoed**.* [22]

> Remember with love and honour
> Those who died for us in the Great War
>
> George Francis Hermitage Day RFA
> John Evans 1st Hereford Regt.
> Jason Lewis SWB
> Leonard Samuel Morgan Hereford Regt.
> Abraham Davies Wozencraft RWF
> Thomas Davies Mytton RWF
>
> Grant them O Lord Eternal Rest and
> Let light perpetual shine on them.

Abbeycwmhir Home Guard 1943 at Cwmscawen. Meredith Wozencraft 6th from right top row. Jack Wozencraft 2nd from right top row. Ted Wozencraft 4th from right top row. Edmund Vaughan 6th from left top row. (230)

"Minky (a.k.a.Domenica), a lonely evacuee from Liverpool, happy at last in the hills, able to confide her troubles to the sheepdog, Sweep, who proudly carries her gas-mask. When Minky's selfish mother arrives to reclaim her so she can avoid being called up for ATS war-work, Minky's tears on being forced to leave for Merseyside stand in for those of all war-victims". *Peter Conradi "At the Bright Hem of God - a Radnorshire Pastoral"*[23]

Potatoes and the Second World War

Sometimes in the war, farmers had to grow lots of potatoes, acres of them. Whether it was because they were a source of food when everything was rationed, I don't know. But Home Farm had to grow so much and every year the oldest kids would have to help pick them. Often, at lunch time, the Colonel would come to the school, talk quietly to the teacher, and then, after we had eaten our sandwiches, she would pick so many of us to go and report to the potato field where we would be given a bucket each; or, sometimes, if we didn't look very strong, one bucket between two. I think it may have been better than being in a class room all day. But some of us got more of the same when we got home – and it was a known fact that later we would hear of a surplus and hundred of tons would be sprayed with a purple spray and were reported to be unfit for human consumption and would be fed to animals. And it happened every year! Those in power have a lot to answer for. (There has never been so much waste as anything to do with Government.)

Great War Memorial in St. Mary's Church (Text on left page) Full details of the men and their places of burial can be obtained from the British Legion Website.[24] (231)

Second World War

The German Bombers used to fly over Abbeycwmhir on their way to bomb Liverpool. Some didn't want to and would drop their bombs anywhere. Six bombs came down near Cwm Bedw. Five of them blew holes in a field, the other went into a bog and never exploded. It's still there somewhere.

One bomb exploded in the pen of the Porth dipping bath – later they had to fill the hole in.

These bombers would go over about 7.00 -7.30 each night. Which way they went back I don't know –but it was not this way. I remember one Sunday night, my Father and I were coming from Llaithdu about 9 pm and we stopped on the top of the Bog Quarry "Look there" he said to me. I looked to the North and the sky was all red. And I remember him saying with a tremble in his voice "That is Liverpool burning". I will never forget it.

Then came the German prisoners of war chaps. There was a camp at Crossgates. From here gangs would go out to work. A lot of the younger ones would go and work on the farms. The boys that usually worked on the farms being called up for the army....This boy could speak very good English – he said it was taught in school in Germany, everybody had to learn English, they said, so they would be ready, when they won the war, to take over England. NP

They were there on Penybont Common. A lot of them in tents. We did alright out of the(American) soldiers. I can remember going home with this soldier's helmet full of onions! Big Spanish Onions! I'd go up to see them and they'd be having a meal and they'd cut me a piece of thick bread and I'd have margarine on it and then they'd put on lots of marmalade. I remember going home and I was all covered in marmalade!

- Albert Philips   2, Cwmhir Cottage

Abbeycwmhir National School

*Village School, School House and School Cottages 1947
(Photo Albert Mytton)   (232)*

1846 - 28 children attending probably in the Church.
1857 Moved to Cross Cottage.
1868 School Built [25]
1922/3 Closed - temporary move to Cefn Pawl Chapel.
1923 A Council School.
1941 Evacuees from Bootle.
1943 Canteen lunch provided
1969 Closed 18th July [26]

The dates of the National Education Acts are listed on the next page under Bwlch y Sarnau School

The Teacher at Abbeycwmhir School before 1940 was Miss Sybil Evans. She came from The Bwlch, Oakley Park, near Llanidloes, and lodged at School House with Mrs Amy Wozencraft during the week. To get there on a Monday morning, she walked two miles from her home to Dolwen Station to meet the 5.30 am mail train. She had to apply to Oswestry for permission to get on the train and for it to stop for her, as mail trains would only stop where there was a post office – Llandinam, Llanidloes and Pantydwr. At Pantydwr she would alight and walk the six miles to Abbeycwmhir, ready to start lessons. Then back again the same way on a Friday evening.

After a year or two Sybil bought a car, one of the first in the Valley. Her son, David Pugh, told me that she didn't know how to drive it so the blacksmith, Jack Went, taught her. She drove 20 miles in a big triangle to Rhayader, CrossGates and back to the Abbey, after which she knew she could drive. She never did pass a driving test, ever.

Sybil (born in 1909) taught in Oakley Park School for a short time, then went to college in Sheffield after taking a teaching post at Penrhos near Oswestry andshe became the Head of Abbeycwmhir. Her assistant here was Agnes Lewis, Esgairwy, wife of Bill Lewis.

Sybil Evans left in 1940 when she married a Huw Pugh, a policeman. They went to live in Liverpool. All through the bombing they were there, having two children, David in 1943 and Susan in 1945. Sybil died in 2002.   *Diana Berriman (Little Plock).*

About my school days – it is History, I think.

Yes, I started at the Abbey School in 1939. I remember a young lady of 11 or 12 by the name of Mary Lewis, who would look after me, take me to school and bring me home. I was living at Broad Oak and Mary lived at Brickyard Cottages. Like all cottages on the estate it was a two-up-two-down affair. There being a Mr. Morris next door. Of course it was dinner bag over one shoulder and gas mask over the other. Oh yes, she looked after me well. Then she moved, and I made a new friend from next door.... Glyn Jones from the "Happy Union". Our job was to take the one gallon can of milk to the school.NP

In Living Memory

The milkman would milk the cows then take the buckets of milk up to the back of The Hall, where a Mr Davies would get it ready for us. Mr & Mrs Davies lived in at The Hall, she being the cook and he being butler come handyman. Two maids also lived in.

Every year at the Abbey School, or at least, every Autumn we would be working hard on our Christmas Concert as well as learning the usual things. At about 5pm there would be a tea party and The Colonel and Mrs Phillips would give each child a small gift. Then we would play games until the concert started at 7pm.

Children would sing, recite poetry. Some of the bravest would sing solo, some in pairs and we had a choir of sorts. We would do sketches and all sorts of things for two hours or so. Then it would be home, happy and very sleepy. The money we made on concert night would be kept safe and then in Summer it would pay for school trips to Aberystwyth – another evening when we would go home tired and happy. I used to think tha the best part of the day was stopping for fish and chips in Rhayader – a treat we only had once a year. (Sybil's sister Elined, now in her late nineties, recalls one weekend in about 1935 when three coaches left Abbeycwmhir to visit Blackpool to see the lights, and back the following night.)

Sybil with her husband Hugh Pugh at the wheel. (233)

"Yes we had evacuees from Liverpool, lots of them, and they brought a teacher with them, a very good teacher by the name of Miss Jones. I can't remember how long they stayed but they certainly filled our school.....Then came the Italians and the one that came to work for the Colonel stayed here, Greeno Barbierato, or something like that. He worked at Home Farm until the end of the war, and some time after. They were allowed to go home. He asked if he could come back to this country and the Colonel said yes. He went to try and find his childhood sweetheart – and he found her. I can't remember if he brought her back on the next trip or not - but he brought her over soon after. And then he was made Gardener and lived in the Gardeners Cottage. NP

Mrs Smith the cook serving in the new canteen.. (234)

Abbeycwmhir Community Book

Bwlch y Sarnau Primary School

"Bwlch y Sarnau School Then and Now - by the Bwlch y Sarnau Art Group hanging in Community Hall at Bwlch y Sarnau. Key to subjects and painters on Page 295.

1870 Founded by officers and members of the Bylch y Sarnau Baptist Church. *Foster Education Act started School Boards in the same year.*
1874 First Grant from Wales & Monmouthshire Board of Education.
1880 School attendance compulsory between 5 -10. Fees payable.
1891 Free Education. School age went up in 1893 to 11yrs; in 1899 to 12yrs.
1902 Compulsory Education went up to 14 years.
1924 Building bought by Radnoshire Education Authority.
1942 Built a canteen adjoining - cooked meal provided.
1949 Laithddu School fire - whose children attended Bwlch y Sarnau.
1990 - July. Closed. Community allowed to use but fabric becomes unsafe.
2000 Community takes responsibility, raises funds and becomes Community Hall Charity.

In Living Memory

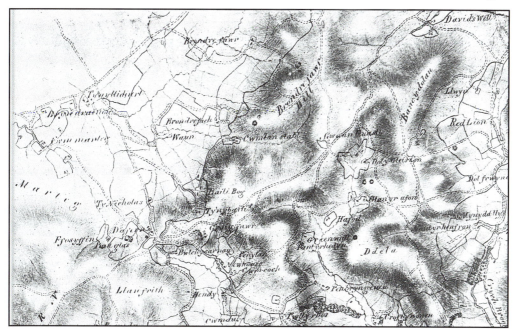

Bwlch y Sarnau C 1817 on Ordinance Survey Surveyors sketch map. (235)

Hirddywel = 'Long View'; *hir* 'long' + *dywel*, 'intensive view'. An extensive moorland region once covering parts of Llandinam, Llanbadarn Fynydd and Llanbister parishes, including the northermost parts of the present-day Abbeycwmhir Community. Some earlier maps have the eroneous spelling "Rhyddhywel" In the middle ages, Hirddywel was famous for its own breed of mountain ponies, and part of the area just north of the Abbeycwmhir community boundary is now the site of a wind-farm. One Christmas Eve in the mid 16th century the *prifardd,* 'chief poet', Hywel ap Syr Mathew almost lost his life on Hirddywel because of the foul weather. He later, in a poem full of venom, described the scene of his misfortunes as *hers Uffern* 'the arse of Hell'.[27]

Benjamin Rees, Chairman of the School Board at the Centenary in 1970. (236)

Bwlch y Sarnau School 1922 (237)

"Remember now Thy Creator in the Days of Thy Youth"

CONSUMPTION & BRONDREFACH

Grave of Jane Pugh 7 mths of Cwmderw Farm

"A pale consumption gave the final blow
The stroke was certain, but the effect was slow.
With wasting pain, death found me long oppressed,
Pitied my sighs and kindly brought me rest."
(*Gravestone at Bwlch y Sarnau Chapel*)

Grave of Thomas Rees 3yrs of Brondrefach

This poem is on the tombstone at Bwlch y Sarnau chapel of a 20yr old girl (Jane George, of Bryn-rhyg, Llananno) who died in 1864, about the same time as the children from Brondrefach. The word "Consumption" in modern language means "T.B." - Pulmonary Turberculosis. It was often referred to as the "decline" one hundred and fifty years ago.

At Brondrefach, the original external stone steps still lead up to the first floor to the old house - a mere 4.5 x 5.5 metres in area - what is now called 'The Granary', used for storage with the ground floor used to house a small tractor and gambo trailer.

However despite these small dimensions, we have learnt from gravestones at Bwlch y Sarnau Chapel that my great, great, great grandfather Jacob Rees (Senior) and his wife Jane, would have lived here with their five children, Hugh, Jacob, Richard, William and Jane. Sadly only one of these children exceeded the age of twenty nine years and the last child, a girl, died at the age of nine.

three years later the middle son, Richard (24) died, and his mother follows him in the same year (aged 56). leaving their only daughter, Jane then 7 years old, to be cared for presumably by the two remaining sons, →

Tomb of Mary 15, Edward 22, Elizabeth 15 and Bejamin Rees 19, of Brondrefach between 1855 and 1875. (238)

Jacob and William, (28 and 22). Little Jane was next to go - she died within 2 years of losing her mother. (who was actually 49 years old when she gave birth to this last child!). William was the last to succumb and died at the age of 29 leaving just Jacob, who within 10 years had seen his entire family, (parents and four siblings) wiped out! Of these six deaths, only one Certificate can be located, that of Richard, which states that the cause of his death was "Consumption" (Pulmonary Tuberculosis or TB of the Lungs), so we can perhaps assume that this was the disease that eradicated this entire family, bar the one remaining son, Jacob (Junior).

So just one son, Jacob, remained to carry on the family name, and to farm Brondrefach. However, his sorrow was not to end with the death of his parents and four siblings. Far from it! As the next generation of Rees's are raised in the old Brondrefach house, the same pattern of early death begins to emerge.

Of the five children Jacob's wife Elizabeth bore to him, their eldest daughter Mary dies at age 15, of "inflammation of the bowel", leaving two boys, Thomas and Edward (7&8). The year after Mary's death, twins are born, Elizabeth and Benjamin in 1840. When these twins reach the age of 14, their big brother Edward succumbs to, yet again, consumption (or "Phthisis" as it was then known and recorded on the Death Certificate). The following year Elizabeth at 15 succumbs to the same disease, as does her twin brother Benjamin, four years later in 1875, at the age of 19yrs.

So again, we see just one son, Thomas, remaining, to carry on the family name, and as with his father before him, by the time he was 28 years old, all his siblings had gone. He did however have his father around for another 12 years, and his mother lived on until 1901, probably witnessing the building of the new house at Brondrefach, and possibly even living there herself for a short time with her son Thomas and his family.

This Thomas Rees then, was my grandfather, and he and his wife Mary (nee Lewis Rhosgoch, Nantgwyn) went on again to have five children, Elizabeth, Jacob, Jack (mentioned ealier), his twin brother Thomas, and Benjamin, my father. These children were the first generation to be raised in the present farmhouse at Brondrefach. Of these five children, thankfully only one died young - this was my Uncle Jack's twin, Thomas, who died in 1897 of diptheria at the age of 3yrs 3months. Apparently all the children had the disease but only Thomas succumbed. (His little ornately shaped headstone can be viewed in Bwlch y Sarnau Chapel (pictured top right of previous page) immediately on the left as you enter the gate, along with ten others of the Rees family, my grandparents included.

By Julia Rees of Brondrefach
(cf p 178)

Mrs Price the Huckstress (Huck - Hip. Basket on,
Hip - Hawker or pedlar?) at Bwlch y Sarnau (239)

The Beautiful Day

Ernest Hermitage Day DD, (1866-1946) Chaplain of the Order of St John of Jerusalem and Vicar of this Parish 1891-1907. Aged 80 Years. His ashes are interred under the altar of St.Mary's, Abbeycwmhir.(240)

The Rev Ernest Hermitage Day B.A. took his first service at the Parish Church on 21st July 1891. He was 25 years old and had recentlty completed his first degree at Keble College, Oxford and had been priested in London the year before. Two years later he married Doris Elinor Philips, the youngest daughter of the late squire, George Henry. His good looks and handsome bearing earned him the soubriquet "The Beautiful Day". Mary Beatrice or Anna Theophilia Philips built Brynmoel, the very remarkable Old Vicarage for him (cf p 262).

Ernest Day was a modern young man of the 1900's - having a car, which he kept at the, still standing, garage next to The Smithy. He also used a camera and had photographs published along with an academic historical paper in Archaeologica Cambrensis.[28] He was a Fellow of the Society of Antiquaries (FSA). He also chaired the first Abbeycwmhir Parish Council in 1894 at Church House, Frogtown - close to his garage.

The Marriage of Rev Hermitage Day to Doris Philips in 1893. (241) when the children and Village wished them "Happiness". See picture on page 120

He remained in the parish for sixteen years. When he left Abbeycwmhir in 1907 he was presented with an oak ink stand by the staff and pupils of the School with whom he was very popular. He had recently completed his Doctorate in Divinity and was next promoted to be a Rector at All Saints, Pickwell, Leicester. However he soon returned to this area living at Belmont, Herefordshire where he wrote several books 'Some London Churches' in 1911, 'The Ministry of the Church' in 1913, 'St. Francis and the Greyfriars' in 1926 and then, between 1915-1924, become the editor of the important Church Times a weekly national newspaper still published today. He then became the Examing Chaplain of new priests for the Bishop of Hereford [29] and eventually the Chaplain of the Knights of St John of Jerusalem - the Order from which the St John's Ambulance Brigade emerged.

He died in South Africa in 1946 at the age of 80 years. His ashes were brought to Abbeycwmhir, where he started his career, by his wife Doris née Philips and are interred under the altar of St. Mary's Church.

In Living Memory

Ascension Day Tea at the Vicarage (1950's)

Back Row	1,	2,	3,	4,	5,	6,	7,	8,	9,	10..	(242)
Middle Back		1,	2,	3,	4,	5,	6,	7.			
Middle Front			1,	2,	3,	4,	5,	6,	7,	8.	
Front Row			1,	2,	3,	4,	5,	6.			Key on page 293

St. Mary's with the Philips' Enclosure started and with Llwy Hill before it was planted - and as it has largely come back to be in 2014 (243).

The Beautiful Day & Doris some years later. "Just because you don't smoke in this world doesn't mean you won't smoke in the next" my father, a smoking Reverend, told me.
- Ed. (244)

Abbeycwmhir Community Book

Pre-Amble
to
HOMES & PEOPLE

The richness of any community is in the variety of people living and working in it and in the concrete forms – the houses, buildings and permanent structures they leave behind to tell their story.

There was a wonderful response to the request for photographs and information - *home-brewed, homely homework* - bringing *home* to us, how important the *home stretch* to *home* is for all of us *home-steaders*. Indeed this is the *home-ward home-thrust* of this book and includes the original material which was collected for the Millennium 2000 by Willie Griffiths of Devannor and the working group. At least we'll know each other better as a result of it!

The information about the home and family in the following section is as it was provided although some lists of names have been smoothed into continuous prose. If obtained by interview, it was checked by the home-owners. Some people responded to the request for an "Update to 2008" but not everybody - and some continued to send contributions right into 2010 - which would be the latest date of information.

Dwellings are listed in aproximate alphabetical order by the main name of the house not inlcuding "Upper" & "Lower" and "New","Old", or "Little" for example. However these are included in the name on the home's page. Names in bold italics are those of the owners at the time and their children.

By the time of publication all of this section is also history - right up to the *contemporary period* of the twenty first century. A chance to notice, without criticism, how we got from there to where we are now and to see local history unfolding. Dates are given when known.

Most photographs which are not labelled were *supplied* by the home owners for the original Millennium Book in 1999/2000 or later. Those that Roger Coward took after 2008 have a date and an asterisk*.

Inevitably contributions came in different lengths so there has been space available to insert photographs and texts of general interest (indicated by a grey background and external frame). Mostly this has no direct bearing on the property on the same page but in a few cases they have been taken from the relevant page of the 1919 Estate Sale Prospectus's either for Abbeycwmhir or Penybont. It's the auctioneers' names which have been acknowledged underneath.*

The editor takes no responsibility for the historical accuracy or completeness of residents' contributions.

NB Short continuations are normally at the bottom of the next page.

Painting on opposite page is by Angela Lewis of Cwmffwrn.

The auctioneers for Abbeycwmhir were Driver, Jonas & Co "at The Metropole Hotel, Llandrindod Wells, on Tuesday the 21st Day of October 1919 at 3 0'Clock precisely as a whole – unless an Acceptable Offer is made in the meantime"[1] The The Penybont Estate was prepared for auction by Messrs R.A.Campbell (F.A.I.) & Hamer "at The Iron Room, Penybont on Wednesday, the 24th day of September 1919 at 1.30 o'clock precisely (Subject to Conditions)"[2].

HOMES

& PEOPLE

Ashdale

2009*

In 2002, **Harold** and **Ceridwen Rees** built a bungalow on Brondrefach Farm called Ashdale –which we live in after retiring from farming Brondrefach since 1961 - when we were given the opportunity to return to my father's old home, having farmed for five years since our marriage, at Pentre, Newbridge-on-Wye. We came with our three children, Roger, Hugh and Julia but it is our youngest son, Gareth, born after we came here, who is taking over the running of the farm.
(cf Brondrefach p 178)

Avalon Bungalow

was built in 1968 on the Upper Esgair Farm, Abbeycwmhir where Shirley Stephens was brought up. The bungalow is owned and occupied by **Gwynne & Shirley Stephens**. Gwynne ran his own Animal Health Product Business until his retirement in 2005. Shirley works for the Local Authority. Glyn and Ken Davies and his wife Rose continue to farm Upper Esgair Farm to this day with other family members assisting at peak times.(cf Upper Esgair Farm p 209).

Bachel Brook Caravan

Marjorie Sermukslis (English) and *Elmars Sermukslis* (native of Latvia in the Baltic States) were married on 31st May 1952 and first came to Wales in 1961. They bought the caravan in 1968.

They had four children—three girls and one boy. All are married. We now have nine grandchildren and all visit the caravan from time to time.

(Could this caravan site have been where the Clog Maker stayed mentioned on page 143 -Ed.) *

Abbey Mill

Harriet Preller and her family have given the property it's old name - it had been known as Mill House for many years. Harriet was born in St.Albans, but grew up in Cornwall, where her parents farmed, as did she with her young family.

She now works as a Shepherdess for Robert and Violet Lewis at Tynpistyl, Cwmdeuddwr, and for Ian and Angela Lewis at Cwmffwrn. She trains her own working dogs and shepherds both hill and lowland flocks. The traditional shepherding on the hills is of particular interest to her.

Mill ruin with house in background 2008*

She came to the area as a result of working on the YHA at Clun. Enjoying the rural life, and the friendly locals, she and her parents, **Pat** and **Michael,** found Abbey Mill for sale, which they duly bought, though it needed a lot of work to make it a home. They did the majority of the work themselves as Michael is a Structural Engineer and Architect. Her parents often stay as they enjoy working on the Mill ruins preserving it and preventing it from deteriorating any further. Pat has become a very adept stone mason. At first Harriet helped with the lambing at Tynpistyl, and is now working there full time. She is also an alternative to kennels host for "Barking Mad". She loves the rural life.

Harriet has three children, **Sarah** (24), who lives in Canada with her Canadian boyfriend, working for the Marriott Hotels there, **David** (22), who is studying a Mechanics course in Newtown, and **Sam** (12) lives with his father in Sussex, coming to Abbeycwmhir for his school holidays.

Previous to her farm work, Harriet also worked locally for the Elan Hotel in Rhayader, and "Fingers and Forks" catering in Landewi. She helps out at the Royal Welsh Show in the Sponsorship Pavillion. One of the old Mill buildings has been converted to kennels by her Mother, doing the stone work, and Father, doing the roof. Next door is the old stable which provides a bedroom for the children, but has been built in a way to preserve the history of the buildings.

For Mill History see page 97

"A WATER DRIVEN **CORN MILL** WITH TWO PAIRS OF PEAK STONES, STONE BUILT AND SLATED, IN GOOD REPAIR, WITH INTERIOR FITTINGS, SHAFTING AND MACHINERY, AND CONSIDERED THE BEST MILL IN THE COUNTY OF RADNORSHIRE." *DRIVER, JONAS & CO.1919.*[3]

Beili Bog

Owen & Medina Davies outside Beili Bog

Beili Bog has been in our family for ten generations and is situated near the village of Bwlch y Sarnau. Beili Bog is a stock rearing farm and is run with Fishpool Farm. Beili Bog is owned and farmed by the Davies family.

The farm is well sheltered from the east by a hill which rapidly rises to 1,500 ft, but is exposed to the west by a wide open valley which is the widest in Wales. The house is made of stone and has five bedrooms and is about one hundred and fifty years old. The old house is where the cow shed is now! In January 1971 on a very snowy night the building caught fire and the smoke killed some cows so the surviving cows and calves had burns on them for years to come.

Owen thinks the name "Bog" comes from an old ruin below the old house, where it was very wet and boggy. We went to bury a horse and dug down to find a pitch floor indicating that there had been old round huts there. We also found three mill stones.

In the year 2000 we had a new wall built with a water spout and tank. In the wall we put one of the mill stones and had it engraved with the year 2000.

Through all the generations of the Davieses at the Bog, farming had progressed and it was time for change. So in the year 2001, The Bog had officially achieved organic status for all beef and lamb from the farm. Rhydian and Owen now do the farming. Owen - the cattle and ponies and Rhydian looks after the Baltix sheep which he breeds and shows.

Owen and **Medina** both went to Bwlch y Sarnau Primary School and afterwards to Brynterion Secondary School in Rhayader. They are both members of the Bwlch y Sarnau Baptist Chapel and were baptized in the River Marteg.

Owen enjoys bowls at Pant-y-dwr and Art Classes at Bwlch y Sarnau Community Centre.
Medina is a member of Bwlch y Sarnau Womens Institute, the Art Club, Gardening Club and Library Coffee Morning Club and The Flower Arranging Club.

Owen and Medina have two children: **Rhydian Thomas Owen Davies**, born September 1968, who works on the farm at Beili Bog and **Teresa Valerie Davies,** born April 1973, who is a teacher in the College at Newtown.

Austen Pryce Vaughan Davies, Owen's brother, born in November 1939, spent all his life at The Bog and always worked very hard. He loved animals and even risked his life in 1971 when the cow shed was ablaze. His dedication proved invaluable to the farm when he saved the lives of many cattle outside in his night attire and bare feet resulting in hospital treatment. Austen was sadly missed on the farm after his death in 1994 after a short illness. He never married.

Homes and People

Thomas Davies (Owen's father) was widely known as a breeder of Hereford Cattle and Kerry Hill sheep and always took a special interest in the breeding of ponies. He had been a successful exhibitor at local shows over many years. Mr Davies was a school manager of Bwlch y Sarnay Primary School and had been the Chairman over many years. He was also a member and Deacon of Bwlch y Sarnau Baptist Church.

Mary Davies (Owen's Mum) was like the Queen because she had two birthdays because she was not registered in time. Her registered birthday was on 22nd July 1912 but her proper birthday was on the 15th July. Mary was noted in the area for her beautiful Welsh Cakes. Mary cut the cake in the year 2000 at the Abbeycwmhir Party as she was the oldest person in Bwlch y Sarnau.

Owen's Father Thomas Davies

John Davies (Owen's grandfather) was a great pony man. He went up to Colwyn Bay and bought a stallion but could not find any transport to bring him home so he walked him home. He always had shire stallions and mares were brought to him from miles around.

Edward Meredith (Owen's Great Grandfather) was known as "Boss of the Bog". He use to go round the farms complaining that he had one cold foot – so he could go in for a warm.

Josiah Pugh, of The Bog, was a deacon and provided the land for the site of the first Bwlch y Sarnau Chapel commenced in 1828.

Winford Vaughan Thomas and Toby, the Welsh Cob. When Winford Vaughan Thomas was doing a trek across Wales on horse back to record a programme for the Radio, Tom and Mary rode with him over the hills, passing our land at Banc Gwyn, Llaithddu. Tom got the dog to gather the sheep by whistling and this was recorded. Then we rode on showing him the way to Llandinam. When we listen to the programme on the radio, the dog was with us and when we heard Tom whistling, he was jumping all around trying to find Tom.

John Davies & Talkie Bonfire Station

2, Brickyard Cottages

No.2 Brickyard Cottages 2008

The present occupants are **John** & **Pippa Adams**.

2, Brickyard Cottages is a semi-detached cottage, built about the 1870's out of the surrounding clay as a labourers' cottage on Cefn Pawl Farm. We have water from own spring. Previous residents were Tommy Jones, brother of Vi Nichols of next door - before that 'Old Man Powell' (retired farmer) when it was part of the Abbeycwmhir Estate.

John was born in Putney, London and has lived previously in Privet Hants, Londonderry, West Meon (Hants), Singapore, Malta, Malvern, Tarland (Scotland), Aldershot, Brighton, Brabourne (Kent), Norwich. He has worked at the Cwm Bedw Barns Foundation, and the Old Stores Writing Group, Rhayader.

Pippa was born in Aylesbury, Bucks and previously lived in Kingsnorth and Brabourne (Kent) the Philippines, Brighton, London, Garve (Scotland), and Norwich. She worked as an administrator for Powys Mental Health Development Project, & Amnesty.

We moved here 27 years ago, wanting an affordable house in a rural environment. We were attracted by the beauty and the relative remoteness and emptiness of the area and in particular the feel of this house. There is a sense of contact with nature and continuity with the past - the kitchen flagstones directly on the earth, the appreciation of water coming directly out of the hill and many small things like the rag rugs and underfelting of old coats and trouser legs on the stairs. We were surprised and at many times disappointed by the shortness of the growing season and the lack of sun but feel maybe this is the trade-off for the absence of the traffic and congestion in much of England.

Special Comments: John: I hope that in the coming century, things like Genetic Engineering do not turn into the nightmare we fear.

Update to 2008

Since writing about our reasons for living here in 1999, things have changed and our options for movement have been dramatically reduced. This lack of choice, though frustrating, has made me more relaxed about living here. I am always looking at the hills, old trackways, ruins etc and they remind me that our presence here in itself is a small fleeting phenomena. While we haven't put down any lasting roots I do feel that in the course of the last 36 years we have setttled a bit, to the point of resembling moss or lichen. That's what I like to think anyway.

1, Brickyard Cottages

Averil Williams, the present occupant, was born in Oxford, and is now also resident in Wimbledon. Previously she has been resident in Putney, Iceland, Ilford and Upton-by-Chester (beside the zoo).

This is one of a pair of cottages, semi-detached, built presumably for those working at The Brickyard which existed then circa 1830. There is no trace of the kiln now but the field in which the cottages stand is full of pits and hollows where the clay pits remain as evidence of the workings. Many dwellings in the Abbey are built with these bricks. The cottage itself does not cover a large area but has two upper storeys, and a garden of 0.20 acres. In 1994 when I bought the cottage, a cattle grid (built by Robert Antell and Brian Parfitt) was installed at the foot of the track onto the road, and a bore hole and septic tank sunk in the garden. Another project has been to make the upper floor into a studio with a hoist (of which I am rather proud!) for bringing up wood and coal. There is a spring for the two properties which is very depleted but which still serves the cottage for drinking water. The bore hole picked up the sulphurous spar water of Llandrindod Wells and it doesn't taste good. Unsurprisingly the cottages are built of Brickyard bricks which are quite an orangy-red,

Averil outside No.1, Brickyard Cottages in 2000.*

but because they can become a bit crumbly and porous much of the brickwork has been rendered over. This cottage had previously been occupied for about 40 years by Sam and Violet Nichols who brought up their family here. Sadly Sam died and the cottage became vacant. Two years ago the Vaughan family called here, and I met May Vaughan who had been born in the cottage 90 years ago.

My work is music (Flautist. Professor at the Guildhall School of Music and Drama) and also as a Psychotherapist (private practice in Wimbledon).

Reasons for buying a property in Abbeycwmhir? I have always loved the country and animals ever since living in Cheshire as a child, and my original plan for years had been to study agriculture so that I could return to the country, farming and cows. For some reason I suddenly decided to study music, aged 16. Now things have come full circle and I enjoy nothing more than to get away from it all and be in the valley with sheep and cows outside the gate. The valley is so beautiful and unspoilt. It's a pity about the drive to get here. Originally I came to Abbeycwmhir via Turkey (!) in 1988 when I met Roger Coward whilst on holiday and just before he bought Cwm Bedw. From the moment of my first visit I felt very at home in the valley, and it was fortuitous that eventually I could get my own place. It does take time to become part of the community, especially as a 'part time' resident, which means it is less easy to contribute. On Sundays I usually attend the services at Devannor across the valley and this has been a very important part of my life. As a contribution to mark the Millennium I am planning to write a hymn for Devannor for which Brenda Griffiths of Devannor has agreed to write the words.

Broad Oak

Broad Oak 2008

Broad Oak was built around the end of the nineteenth century. Originally a Baptist manse with an adjacent servants' quarters, the two buildings are now one. We bought the house from Tom and Freda Coleman who moved on to Herefordshire. Sadly Tom has since died.

Tom and Freda must have spent every waking minute working on the house - extensions have been built, windows, staircases, doors, flooring replaced, a central heating system installed and a borehole sunk. The garden has a well, which provided the water before the borehole. Judging by the ages of former Broad Oak occupants buried in Cefn Pawl chapel grounds, it is a source of health and longevity.

Andrew and ***Mary Strong*** and their children ***Jacob*** (born in 1994) and ***Elinor*** (born in 1996) moved into broad Oak in August 1997. We moved when Andrew was appointed head of the primary school at Llanbister. Neither of us had been to the Abbey before we came to look at the house but we knew Broad Oak was the place for us as soon as we stepped through the door. Both of us feel privileged to live here, and never want to leave.

Tom and Freda changed the name of the house - from Broad Oak - to Dove Tree Cottage. We had been here only a few days when Andrew realised that many inhabitants of the Abbey are known by their house names. Thinking 'Mr Dove Tree Cottage' a little long winded we looked at an O.S. map and rediscovered Broad Oak.

Mary and Andrew met whilst working in London, Andrew had been there for nearly twelve years, Mary for two. We tried settling down there, but eventually decided to move back to Andrew's place of birth, Newport, Gwent where we still have many friends. Mary was born and brought up in North Yorkshire where her parents still live. Mary's parents originate from south west Wales and she always had a secret longing to return to the principality.

In the short time we have lived here we have got to know more of our neighbours than we did in five years of living in Newport and ten in London. We are regulars at the Happy Union, although not as regular as we'd like.

Broad Oak has always felt like a ship, and has needed constant, loving attention to keep it afloat. It's a house we've grown to love, and could never imagine leaving. Mary has decorated the house from top to bottom at least twice since we've been here, and the garden, despite being overrun with cattle on two occasions, is looking good, with its apple trees, blackcurrant bushes, pear and plum trees and manageable vegetable garden.

Homes and People

We're all musicians: Ellie passed her grade 8 drum exam aged 10, and has taken up the piano. Jake and Mary both play cello and piano, and Andrew is a jack of all trades, master of none. We have a house full of instruments, and love making noise. If we lived anywhere else we would have been marched out of town by now.

Another luxury of this big house is our table tennis room. We play almost every night, and most of our arguments centre on Jake's interpretation of the international table tennis laws (e.g. the height of the ball on service must be at least sixteen centimetres). Otherwise life is slow. We still haven't quite got used to how quiet it can be here, often remembering the days when we lived in a small terraced house in the centre of Newport, and can't quite believe our luck.

Andrew enjoys his visits to the Happy Union in the village, and is looking forward to the time when, like Dave Worgan, he can sit at the bar night after night, and yet look healthier for it. It is the friendliest pub in the country and John and Karen paly a key role in binding a community spread out over so many hills.

The last ten years have flown, and despite a few ups and downs, Abbeycwmhir has become our home. We're looking forward to the next ten years, knowing that whatever happens in the rest of the world, nothing much will change in the Abbey.

Additional info from Mary: There is a Broad Oak tree. ***Additional info from Noel Price***: who used to live there, Broad Oak was closer to the road when he was a boy.

Update to 2008

Jake and Ellie, their children, are now 14 and 12; they attend and enjoy Llandrindod High School.

Andrew is still headteacher at Llanbister Primary and Mary teaches four days a week at the primary school in Dolau.

Cwm Aran Castle (with farm in the upper bailey) likely Court of Cadwallon ap Madog (d 1179) founder of the Abbey of Cwmhir (Castle 3 on Map p 40 & Appendix p 290)   (245)

Brondrefach

Brondrefach Farm House with Monkey Puzzle Tree 2008*

The meaning of "Brondrefach" is 'a small farm on the breast of a hill'. "Brondrefach has been farmed by the **Rees** family for six generations or possibly more as existing records only date as far back as the late 1700's.

The present house at Brondrefach was built at the turn of the last century and belonged to the Philips estate of Abbeycwmhir. There are in the parish two other farm houses built of identical design (though probably altered somewhat today) namely, Bwlch y Sarnau farm and Cwmyscawen. The bricks for the present house were obtained from the farm itself! The clay for them was found on a field adjoining Beili Bog property (our neighbours). It was my father's generation who would have been raised in the present house, and on my grandfather's death my Uncle Jack farmed Brondrefach until his retirement in 1961.

It was my (Harold Rees's) father Benjamin's generation that was raised in the present house, by their parents Thomas and Mary Rees. In 1925, five years before my grandfather Thomas's death, his second son, my Uncle Jack took over the running of the farm, by which time he was no longer a tenant farmer to Colonel Philips of Abbeywmhir Estate but had now become the owner. So the second generation to live at Brondrefach was my Uncle Jack, Auntie Gertie and their only daughter Janet, (who married John Williams of Cefngwylgy Fawr, Llanidloes). Compared to the old farmhouse, this new one had 6 bedrooms, the smallest of which was made into a bathroom in 1952. A distinguishing feature in the front garden at Brondrefach is the monkey puzzle tree, which Uncle Jack planted soon after he took over the farm, (tho' several severe winters since have taken their toll on it!) We are fortunate to have always had our own water supply from a spring up on the hillside, so have never been connected to the Mains. (Those who have tasted nothing other than Mainswater, have been known to comment on the pure taste of our tap water!) The old pump outside the front door at Brondrefach, still stands there today! Uncle Jack farmed Brondrefach until his retirement in the Autumn of 1960, at which time my wife Ceridwen (nee Lewis eldest daughter of Maesygwaelod) and I were given the opportunity to return to what had been my father's old home. Previous to this we had farmed at Pentre, Newbridge-on-Wye for the first five years of our married life.

The original House now "The Granary" 2008*

So we came to Brondrefach in 1961 with our three children, Roger, Hugh and Julia. Sadly, in July 2009, Roger was taken from us. It is our youngest son, **Gareth**, born after we came here, who is taking

Homes and People

over the running of the farm. He got married in 2002 to **Sian** (Née Williams of Rhayader) and have two children, a daughter, **Kaitlyn**, born in 2006 and a son, **Jayden**, born in 2008.

We also have two other grandchildren: Roger's son, Ben, born in 1990 and Hugh's Daughter, Carly, born in 1994.

In 2002, we built a bungalow on the farm called Ashdale –which we live in. Gareth and his family live in the main farm house.

Up to 1971, the only access to the farm was through our neighbours' Beili Bog farmyard. It was then we decided to approach the Forestry Comission about making an alternative route via their ground. The road was built and we continue to use this route to the present day.

From Ashdale to Brondrefach Farm House

Brondrefach, like most farms in this area, is a beef and sheep farm comprising 400 acres. There are two old derelect dwellings to be found on the farm. One, aptly named "Cwm-Nant-Ystable" – a stable by the stream in the dingle, purported to have housed a large family (ancestors of the late Fred Wozencraft of Bryndraenog, formerly Penbwlch). All that remains of the actual house is a few foundation stones, but the stable nearby still stands intact today and has recently undergone restoration work done by Mostyn Griffiths, a local builder. So "The Cwm", as we call it, is now in good order.

The other "Old Waen" also has just a small part of its walls remaining. The Powell family of the present Waen Farm (less than a mile away) had ancestors living there.

The original house at Brondrefach, (pre 1900) still stands. These days the ground floor is used to house a small tractor and gambo trailer and is a mere 4.5 x 5.5 metres in area. The original old stone steps to the first floor are external and lead up to what is now called 'The Granary' (today used for storage).

However despite these small dimensions, we have learnt from gravestones at Bwlch

Photo c.1904   On far left Jack Rees 1897 – 1989 who later bought the Monkey Puzzle Tree and 2nd left his father Thomas Rees who survived the deaths of all the siblings like his father.

Brondrefach continued

y Sarnau Chapel that my great, great grandfather Jacob Rees (Senior) and his wife Jane, would have lived here with their five children, Hugh, Jacob, Richard, William and Jane. Sadly only one of these children exceeded the age of twenty nine years and the last child, a girl, died at the age of nine.

Hugh, the eldest, died at the age of 28, in 1835, just months after his father Jacob (aged 63). Then 3 years later the middle son, Richard (24) died, and his mother follows him in the same year, (aged 56) leaving their only daughter Jane, then 7 years old, to be cared for presumably by the two remaining sons, Jacob and William, (28 and 22). Little Jane was next to go - she died within 2 years of losing her mother. (who was actually 49 years old when she gave birth to this last child!). William was the last to succumb and died at the age of 29 leaving just Jacob, who within 10 years had seen his entire family, (parents and four siblings) wiped out! Of these six deaths, only one Certificate can be located, that of Richard, which states that the cause of his death was "Consumption" (Pulmonary Tuberculosis or TB of the Lungs), so we can perhaps assume that this was the disease that eradicated this entire family, bar the one remaining son, Jacob (Junior).

So just one son remained to carry on the family name, and to farm Brondrefach. However, his sorrow was not to end with the death of his parents and four siblings. Far from it! As the next generation of Rees's are raised in the old Brondrefach house, the same pattern of early death begins to emerge.

Of the five children Jacob (Junior's) wife Elizabeth bore to him, their eldest daughter Mary dies at age 15, ("inflammation of the bowel"), leaving two boys, Thomas and Edward (7 and 8). The year after Mary's death, twins are born, Elizabeth and Benjamin in 1840. When these twins reach the age of 14, their big brother Edward succumbs to, yet again, consumption (or "Phthisis" as it was then known and recorded on the Death Certificate). The following year Elizabeth at 15 succumbs to the same disease, as does her twin brother Benjamin, four years later in 1875, at the age of 19.

So again, we see just one son, Thomas, remaining, to carry on the family name, and as with his father before him, by the time he was 28 years old, all his siblings had gone. He did however have his father around for another 12 years, and his mother lived on until 1901, probably witnessing the building of the new house at Brondrefach, and possibly even living there herself for a short time with her son Thomas and his family.

This Thomas Rees then, was my grandfather, and he and his wife Mary (nee Lewis Rhosgoch, Nantgwyn) went on again to have five children, Elizabeth, Jacob, Jack (mentioned earlier), his twin brother Thomas, and Benjamin, my father. These children were the first generation to be raised in the the present farmhouse at Brondrefach. Of these five children, thankfully only one died young - this was my Uncle Jack's twin, Thomas, who died in 1897, of diptheria at the age of 3yrs 3months. Apparently all the children had the disease but only Thomas succumbed. His little ornately shaped headstone can be viewed in Bwlch y Sarnau Chapel, immediately on the left as you enter the gate, along with ten others of the Rees family, my parents included.

And so to the present day, and to the most recent death in our immediate family. Sadly, the last Rees to be raised at Brondrefach, and buried at Bwlch y Sarnau Chapel has been our eldest son Roger, (known to most as "Yogi'). On the 28th July 2009, we received with great shock and sadness the news of Roger's sudden death at the age of 52 , due to a massive heart attack. Roger's body was laid to rest on the 7th August in a plot at the back of the Chapel, from where, just a mile across →

Bryncamlo

In 1919 F.G.Philips sold it to a J.L.Greenaway whose sister, Louisa Livingstone Layborn, owned it from 1936. In 1941 his tenant David John George bought it from him.

Dennis and ***Lucy Froggat*** bought it from the George family in 1980 and connected to the telephone in 1981.

Lucy was born in Burton on Trent in 1935 of farming parents.

Dennis came from Hamstall Ridware, near Rugely in Staffordshire between Lichfield and Burton. He farmed with

his grand father and then had his own farm. They were married in 1959 and lived on his farm.

Their daughter, ***Patricia,*** came to work at Troedrhiwfelin which belonged to a Mrs Lewis who was the daughter of Mr George of Bryncamlo - and that's how Lucy got to know the area and fell in love with the place. In 1984 Patricia married Philip Harley from Hundred House. They have three children.

Their son, ***Henry*** married Sarah Lawrence from Brynllygoed and they farmed there after her father died**.** They separated and divorced. Henry is now married to Donna and lives in Kent. They have a daughter called Olivia. Henry is an animal health officer for DEFRA.

Update to 2008

In October 2000 Dennis sadly died. In April 2006 Lucy's ageing aunt Catherine Mansell from Wolverhampton came to convalesce at Bryn Camlo and ***Fred Hall*** came to stay and help as he had encouraged Lucy to have her. Fred was in the same class as Lucy at junior school and had to walk to school across the fields of Lucy's parents' farm. Needless to say they became firm friends and both know each other's families.

Lucy started the WI stall in Llandrindod Wells and was its treasurer for many years. She was a Church Warden at St.Mary's, Abbeycwmhir and Church Treasurer for nine years. She has held a barbecue at Bryncamlo in aid of the Church for three years.

A FINE SHEEP FARM - *DRIVER, JONAS & CO.1919.*[4]

→ the valley, across the green fields and meadows, can be seen, nestling against the hillside, Roger's old homestead and place of his childhood haunts, Brondrefach, where so many Rees's have come and gone before him; Brondrefach, affording a beautiful view of the expansive valley beyond; Brondrefach, where the seventh generation of Rees's are now being raised.

I can but conclude by saying that I am happy to have lived and farmed most of my adult life at this beautiful old homestead of Brondrefach.

Brondrefawr

Graham & Ivy Jones outside the new house

It was first built by the monks of Abbeycwmhir when the Abbey was dissolved in 1536. It was a large house made of stone, with big high rooms and oak beams and there was a very large cellar which was approached from outside by a flight of steps. The cellar had a huge fire grate with a washing boiler and oven. Brondrefawr was built at the same time as Devannor by the monks. It had the same style chimney. It is said that there is a tunnel leading from Brondrefawr to the monastery in Abbeycwmhir or to Fowlers Arm Chair on Cruchel Hill by Tyn-y-Berth Hill.

Vavasour Powell preached there in 1650 and his pulpit which he left behind whilst fleeing from arrest is in Bwlch y Sarnau Baptist Chapel. The Rev Stephen Pugh farmed it in 1817 and also preached there before Bwlch y Sarnau Chapel was built. It was once 1000 acres. The old part of the house made of stone was demolished in 1986 to make way for a new extension which was built by a local builder Edward Wood of Pant-y-dwr.

Brondrefawr was part of the Fowler Estate. There were two houses that were known to have been built on the farm which have now gone: Cwt and Cwm Defaid. Brondrefawr then came into the hands of the Pugh family and it was this family that built the brick end of the house; Margaret Ivy Jones who now lives here is a descendant of these Pughs.

Then Edward Joseph Lewis and his wife came to live there when they married. They had five children, three boys and two girls who were all born there. The Forestry then owned the farm for a time renting it out to Ivy's parents, Mr & Mrs Sims. They then moved to Tynfron in Mochdre with their youngest daughter Ruth. Ivy and her brothers, Cliff & Pugh stayed to farm Brondrefawr. Then Mr & Mrs Sims returned to Brondrefawr and Pugh went to Tynfron and Cliff to Penlan, Pant-y-dwr. When Mrs Sims died, Mr Sims went to live with his son, Cliff at Penlan, Pant-y-dwr.

Brondrefawr is now occupied by **Joseph Graham Jones** and **Margaret Ivy Jones**. They took over the tenancy of the farm and eventually bought it from the Forestry in 1976. They are

Barn with 1986 house behind

now retired. Ivy came to live at Brondrefawr in 1939 having been born at Penlan, Pant-y-dwr. She married Graham of Garthfawr, Beulah who was born in Laindon, Essex. He had previously lived at Moat House, Bridge Street, Chepstow, then to a farm called Ty Newydd, Machynlleth. He then came to Garthfawr in 1948 and to Brondrefawr when he married in 1951. Their son, **Jason**, now owns and farms the family farm with the help of his two nephews. He lives in a bungalow not far from the farmhouse.

Back elevation of old Brondrefawr house

Ivy's Thoughts

There's always remained a good sense of comradeship between neighbours and everyone in the locality. I have always remained here after leaving with my parents from Penlan and I am happy here. I would find it difficult to live anywhere else. Our children are farming quite close. I'm quite busy and attend Bwlch y Sarnau Baptist Chapel. Really my complaint is that the days are not long enough.

Margaret *Ivy* Sims Jones is the author of the book "*The Forgotten Composer Edward Meredith Price of Penlan. A brief history of the Pugh's of Radnorshire 1712 to the Fifties. Farming with the Sims Family 1889 - 1950*" - Ed.

"A MOST INTERESTING RELIC OF MEDIEVAL TIMES AND ONE OF THE HOMES OF THE FOWLERS OF ABBEYCWMHIR"

- R. A. CAMPBELL & HAMER [5]

Left: stone shed still in existence

Brondrefawr Bungalow

Jason Jones with Moss outside Brondrefawr Bungalow 2004*

Jason was born in the old brick house of Brondrefawr where his granny and grandfather also lived with his parents Ivy and Joseph ***Jones***. He left school at fifteen "when the weights a measures changed" and farmed Brynhesglwyn, with his brother, Vincent Jones, for a time. When their father had a heart attack Vincent moved to Brynhesglwyn, Llydiatywaun, and Jason took over Brondrefawr. Their sister lives on a farm at Mochdre.

Farming is his life and he wouldn't change it for anything. Recently he was breaking new ground on a hill side for a neighbour. He remembers 1974 when there was very heavy snow and they had to walk out to feed and rescue cattle and sheep. Today there is too much red tape.

The dog in the photograph is called "Moss". Jason says, "He is the best in the world – he could read your mind. He knew how many sheep to bring in. It would be difficult to find another. You only find one like him in a life time."

Bwlch y Sarnau Farm

The farm was purchased from the Abbeycwmhir estate in 1925 for the sum of £1300. The current occupiers are ***Archie Thomas Rees*** and his wife ***Gertrude May.*** Archie and May have formally retired but are still active on the farm.

The farmhouse is about 100 years old, replacing the original house, which is still standing nearby and was used as a stable and granary.

The replacement house was originally divided into two separate dwellings, Archie's mother and father living in one half, Archie and May living in the other. In later years the house was extended to create two larger downstairs rooms and a kitchen.

In the 1930's the farm employed a waggoner, a cowman and a maid all for £12 per year plus board and lodging. In the past Bwlch y Sarnau Farm supplied the milk to the local school, the milk being delivered each day at about 10.30 in the morning, the rest of the milk being collected by a creamery in Llandeilo.

Bryneithin

Bryneithin, (Gorse Hill) Bwlch y Sarnau is a smallholding of just under four acres, purchased by the Woolley family in 1996. The original date of the house is uncertain but a date of 1839 has been scratched on the front wall of the house, about the date when all the dwellings on the Philips estate were renovated. Informed opinion suggests that the cottage is much older than that but much research would need to be done to find out exactly how old. The initials LL are scratched in above the date, but who LL is can only be surmised.

The current owners, **Stephen** and **Margaret Woolley** have an original lease document dated 4 December 1837, written in the usual copperplate writing of the time. The lease is between Thomas and Edward Rowland and John Lewis then of Upper Esgair, Abbey Cwm Hir, enigmatically suggesting that it may not have been part of the Philips estate after all. The terms of the lease were £13 sterling and a peppercorn rent for a term of Nine hundred and ninety nine years. The document refers to a cottage and land known as Bryneithin in the parish of Llanbister, in the county of Radnorshire and is signed with an X. From other documents the holding has variously been in the parishes of Llanbister, Pant-y-dwr and finally in Abbeycwmhir.

By about 1915, again the date is uncertain, the cottage had been turned into a shop and was known locally simply as the shop. Many of the older residents have told that when it was a shop there was a sign on the front door saying "Knock and Enter". As the door was a bit stiff to open it became known as "Kick and Enter".

Although the date once again is not clear, Bryneithin passed into the ownership of a local female entrepreneur, Annie Jones of Pant-y-dwr. It then became part of the Annie Jones Trust until the early seventies when it was sold on. Up to the present time it has passed through many hands becoming derelict and then heavily rebuilt, sadly with many of the original features, including the bread oven, fire places and range being taken out.

The house and building that comprise Bryneithin have been extended at various periods throughout the nineteenth and twentieth centuries and now consists of the house, a coach house/garage, an attached barn, a block of two loose boxes and an open fronted shed. As well as the fields, known from the top rather unimaginatively as the Top Field, Bank, Middle Field and Bottom Field, there is now a kitchen garden with a polytunnel and a small orchard. Before the current owners changed the field configuration, there were just two fields known as the Upper Bryn and the Lower Common.

Bryneithin was bought to keep horses, but has reverted to agricultural use in breeding a flock of rare breed coloured Ryeland sheep. Also to fatten a few pigs and for poultry rearing.

Abbeycwmhir Community Book

Bryneithin continued

Stephen was born in Abergavenny, the son of a farm labourer and a childrens' nanny. When he was a very small boy in the early fifties, the family was forced to move to North Warwickshire where he was brought up, to search for work. He retired from the West Midlands Police after serving for thirty years and returned to live in Wales.

Margaret was a city girl born and bred in the city of Leicester, the daughter of an engineer and a shop assistant. After leaving grammar school she worked in a bank and then went on to work in business administration.

Stephen and Margaret are, like many villagers of Bwlch y Sarnau, from the Midlands although Stephen, like his father, was actually born in Wales. They have two sons, the oldest living in nearby Llandrindod Wells; the youngest is a businessman in Tapworth, Staffordshire.

Cefn View Bungalow

Cefn View Bungalow was built on the boundary of Upper Esgair Farm in 1996 and is owned and occupied by **Michael** and **Jacqueline Davies** (daughter and son-in-law of Ken & Rose of Upper & Lower Esgair).

Michael is a Machine Operator at Brynpostig Landfill and his wife Jacky is a cook at Elan Valley Lodge, Elan Valley.

cf Upper & Lower Esgair and Avalon.

A Hymn

Composed by Rev Stephen Pugh the first Minister of the Bwlch y Sarnau chapel in 1833 [6]

May God in rich abundance send	Here may the mountain Pilgrims find
His Word to every country,	Refreshment on their journey
While fruitful showers of grace attend	And not a soul be left behind
The Gospel of Bylch y Sarnau.	Belonging to Bylch y Sarnau

May Zion's King his grace display,
Through all this hilly Country,
While hundreds meet each Sabbath Day,
To praise him, at Bylch y Sarnau.

Bwlch y Sarnau Manse

The Manse is a pre 1900 red-bricked house built originally for the Baptist minister. In its time it was considered sophisticated with such details as sash windows and the yellow brick details. Each room had an open fire and this was the main source of heat until the house was modernised in the 1960's.

Lindsey and *Carol Williams* currently reside here along with their youngest daughter *Lorraine*. They have been occupying 'The Manse' for the last 28 years from 31st January 1971. Previous occupants included Mr and Mrs Raymond Rees, and Mrs Bevan who taught Lindsey Williams in Abbeycwmhir Primary School.

This was the second marital home for Lindsey and Carol, which proved to be an ideal location for work purposes. Carol Williams is an active member of Bwlch-y-Sarnau Women's Institute and a loyal member of the Philips Hall Committee whilst Lindsey partakes in the sport of darts playing for the 'Bantams' of the 'Bear Inn' Rhayader for the last 41 years. His interests also lie with the Rhayader Motor cycle and light car club.

Lorraine who is a keen musician also holds a passion for rugby, gaining a place, as one of 30, to represent Wales in the University of Wales Women's Rugby team.

When first built, 'The Manse' neighboured a stone cottage situated 4ft to the North. This dwelling was called 'Foesfeen' and it has been strongly suggested that the final occupants of this cottage were the great grand parents of Lindsey Williams - Mr and Mrs Thomas Williams.

Lindsey Williams was born and brought up at no.2 Wenallt Cottages. Carol Williams was born in 'Newtown County Infirmary' and was brought up at 'Lower Cwmharry' in Tregynon, Newtown.

Lindsey Williams on leaving school at Easter in 1955 began his employment in forest management, following in his father's footsteps. 44 years on he is now the leading wildlife ranger with the Forest Enterprise. He was honoured with an MBE in the 2000 New Years Honours.

Carol Williams is currently employed by the Royal British Legion Residential Home for the elderly, as a domestic. Previously, she was the caretaker (for 17 years) at Bwlch y Sarnau Primary School from 1973 until its closure in 1990.

Lorraine is reaching the end of her higher education and is hoping to graduate from the University of Wales College, Newport in September 1999 with a Bachelor of Education Honours Degree.

Update to 2008 After 50 years with Forest Enterprise, Lindsey has now retired and in 2005 became Church Warden at St.Mary's Church, Abbeycwmhir. Lorraine has graduated and is now teaching at Cross Gates C.P. School and has recently purchased No.2. Paddock Cottages, Abbeycwmhir.

Cefn Pawl

Talford Price and his Mother at Cefn Pawl 1920.
(The section left of the left chimney was demolished in 1983.)

The house and farm go back a long way being an old "township" in its own right which used to include The Brickyard, a mill, Broad Oak and the Baptist Chapel. Cefn Pawl is mentioned in *The History of Radnorshire* by Rev Jonathon Williams(1754-1829), "The authenticated history of Abbeycwnhir may be traced to so early a period as the reign of Henry II, King of England, and his contemporaries, Rhys, Prince of South Wales, and cousin of Cadwallon, the founder of Abbeycwmhir. Hence it may justly be inferred that the lordship of Golon, with the dependent manors of Cwmhir and Dolelfeu, were the most extensive manorial properties in the county of Radnor, including in its wide circuit the township of Cefn Pawl...."

George Herbert Wozencraft and his wife Annie moved to Cefn Pawl in 1923/3 from the Porth. Cefn Pawl was part of the Abbey Estate owned by the Philips family who were renowned for being fair landlords. George and Annie had fifteen children, thirteen of which survived, Meredith was the youngest child and stayed at Cefn Pawl to farm, he was ten years old when the family moved.

Robert's mother, Elsie Antell had lived in the mining town of Ebbw Vale and was a widow. She came to Abbeycwmhir to visit her sister, Ivy, who was working and living-in at The Hall. They went to a dance where she met Meredith Wozencraft whom she married in 1953. Elsie was a widow and brought her young son Robert to live with them. Lesley was born in 1954 and Christine in 1956.

Being a big family nearly every Sunday in the summer relatives would come for Sunday tea or we would go to visit them. Summers were beautiful at Cefn Pawl but winters were cold and draughty. Mr Jack Went (The Blacksmith) came every Christmas day for dinner. He was Meredith's accountant and Meredith was his Barber! Robert, Christine and Lesley went to the Abbey school and if we got fed up of walking up the road we would cut across the Blacksmith side, coming out at 'Frogtown' (The Blacksmiths, mill and houses). Coming home, we would go up past the vicarage and out opposite Llewy cottage, it probably took longer but was more fun. We always met up with friends along the way.

Miss Nora Lewis was the school teacher and Mr Price would drive her in a A40 car from Llandrindod every morning and collect her every afternoon, until she learned to drive and brought herself a A35 car. She was a lovely person, who was quite strict but fair. Mrs Conner was school cook and lived at Piccadilly. We always had good tasty meals and she made the best roast potatoes I have ever tasted! She was always kind to all of the children. Every morning Uncle Fred Hamer (Home Farm) brought fresh milk for the day as there was then a dairy at Home Farm, where villagers collected their milk. Nearly all of the school pupils were from local farms or their fathers worked on the forestry and lived in the cottages.

The highlights of our year were the children's Christmas party in school, church Christmas party in the hall and Sunday school outings. Reverend Lee started a church choir, where we could meet and sing with our friends. When we got older we could go to youth club on Thursday nights at the Village Hall but walking home in the dark could be a bit scary. We looked forward to whist drives starting in the winter and they would be packed out with a dance after.

There was always a weekly routine at Cefn Pawl. Monday was wash day and Builth auction if you needed a calf. Tuesday was ironing, cleaning and cooking. Wednesday was Pant-y-dwr van day, where the grocery van came and we could have 6d worth of sweets each. Rhayader auction was also on a Wednesday. Thursday was when we would collect bread from the Union. Friday was bedroom cleaning day. Saturday we would go to Llandod shopping and had another 6d of sweets. Sunday was church and visitors or visiting for tea.

Robert Antell met **Elsie Hughes,** who lived at Cecethin, Pant-y-dwr, at a dance in Llandrindod Wells. They were married on September 2nd 1978 and she moved into Cefn Pawl, where he had been brought up straight away and found Abbeycwmhir a nice friendly place to live.

Robert worked the farm with sheep and cattle and for many years supplied the Christmas Geese for the village. Stories of a murder at the farm are confirmed by Elsie who saw blood on the walls at the end of the building. There was also a fire in the stone barn which was destroyed so they replaced it with a metal barn. Elsie now works as a night carer in the Hafran old people's home in Rhayader and at Brynhafryd in Llandrindod wells. They now live at Rock Road, Fron.

*Cefn Pawl in 2009**

They have two children: **Anthony**, born in 1980 who works as an agricultural labourer and **Lisa**, born in 1982 who works with horses and pigs.

Abbeycwmhir Community Book

Coedglasson

Coedglasson stands on a levelled site on a hillock and was originally built with timber framed walls which are now enclosed in stone and brick. The one and a half storey house is of an L shaped three unit plan of the early 17th century. Coedglasson is first recorded as the house of a John Davies in 1623. A John Davies of the same abode was High Sheriff of Radnorshire in 1684. While in 1705 when David Morgan held the same office, he is also listed as being from Coedglasson, and in 1724 was followed by his son Hugh Morgan.

Then in the early 1900s the Hamers came to Coedglasson and their son John was born on the farm. In 1975 **Janet Sale** came to work for John (RH picture below) till his death in 1997 and I inherited the farm from him. In 1998 I married **Kenward Price** and we have a daughter called **Sally** in 1998 and a son, **Kris,** in 2002.

Millennium Tapestry Presented to the Baptist Chapel by Bwlch y Sarnau WI March 2000
(246)

Homes and People

Clewedog Bungalow

Our house is named after the local darts team "The Clewedog Rovers" – no, seriously, after the little brook that runs through the village.

David Evans – past carpenter and now farmer; ***Julie Evans*** – Maintenance Assistant, Housing Department, Powys County Council; ***Gayle Evans*** (18yrs), working at Knills, Crosssgates; ***Marc Hamer-Evans*** (15yrs) at school; Rover - old black Hunterway who belonged to Reg Hamer and moved here after Reg passed away; Ricky – 3 year old Hunterway.

Clewedog Bungalow 1983

On September 26th 1981, Julie Hamer (School House, Abbeycwmhir) married David Evans (Bailey Heulwen, Pant-y-dwr) and for the first two years of married life lived in David's grandmother's home, Gorswysfa, Bwlch y Sarnau. We had our first child, Gayle on 20th October 1982. we decided that the only way we could afford a home of our own was to build it ourselves.

Work started on Clewedog Bungalow in the Spring of 1982 and was finished some eighteen months later. After a struggle financially and tons of hard work our home was built without the aid of a mortgage. David was a carpenter by trade back then, so he was able to do all the carpentry side of the project himself. We also had lots of help from Julie's father, Reg Hamer. He fitted all the plumbing and wiring and spent many, many hours helping us out including tiling the roof. (cf photo?) The actual brickwork of the house was done by Julie's Uncle Neville. One particular memory sticks out was when the Electricity Board informed us at extremely short notice that they were coming to connect the electricity the next day. This was a problem because its was actually snowing (well blizzard conditions really) and the trench had not been dug for the cable. This was when Uncle Mel in his trusty digger – *with no cab* - came to the rescue braving the conditions. Mel finished digging the trench, despite the dreadful cold, ready for the electricity board the next day – many thanks to him! After the main works were completed, Julie and her Mum, the late Ellen Hamer, spend many hours priming wood and painting every room in the house. We moved in in1983 and Marc was born two years later on December 3rd 1985.

Abbeycwmhir is a very special place. We have a super friendly community who all get along great and share an extremely good social life in our local pub The Happy Union.

Update to 2008

David Evans - Farmer, local darts player; vice-chair of the Village Hall Committee; very keen football supporter (Up Man.U!) Julie Evans – Housing Officer, County Council; Secretary to the Village Hall Committee, Community Councillor, Very keen Grand Prix fan – to the point of boring everybody to death! Gayle Evans – has moved away and is a cook in a boarding school, loves every minute of it but still enjoys coming home for a drink in the Happy Union with her old

Clewedog Bungalow continued

friends. Likes very expensive holidays abroad! Marc Hamer-Evans – after three years in Swansea University studying motor sport engineering works part time for a local motor bike garage, E.T.James of Rhayader. The rest of his time is spent at home on the farm. He is also a very keen enduro and motorcross rider and takes part in lots of events. He is also responsible for maintaining the Millennium Village Green.

Rover, sadly no longer with us is buried back home in the garden of School House. Ricky – very elderly black Hunterway sheepdog likes to sleep in the middle of the road making all vehicles go round him. He is known as "The Village's Sleeping Policeman" or "Roundabout"! Rhys – the young pup! Also a black Hunterway who is now nearly two but is still very naughty and chews everything he can find. He can also open the kitchen door all by himself (hence the scratch marks down the front of the house door). If no one catches him going in he will be found sitting on the sofa whether he is covered in mud or not! He also likes to lie in the middle of the road as does Ricky!

We have been granted planning permission for an extension to our original home. Again we intend to do most of the work ourselves. Perhaps a sign of the tough times that may lurk ahead, this two room extension will cost far more to build than the whole of the original bungalow cost to build back in 1982. It is amazing how times do change!

Cross Cottage "The Laundry"

Cross Cottage stands on the roadside in the centre of the settlement of Abbeycwmhir in front of and adjacent to St Mary's Church and opposite the 'Happy Union' public house.

2010 *

Built in 1857 in local hand made brick under a decorative Welsh slate roof, Cross Cottage is the former school masters dwelling serving the 'original village school which is attached to and now forms part of the present dwelling'.

The school, one of the first in the old County of Radnorshire, lasted for only 7 years before, it is said, the lady of The Hall, the squire's residence, found the noise of the children at play in front of the present lych gate intolerable. The school was closed and a new one built a quarter of a mile down the road opposite Piccadilly Cottages and the former school became the village laundry. Although the mangle has long since gone the pulleys used to lift drying washing into place remain in situ.

In recent times Cross Cottage was inhabited by Mr and Mrs Evans, he was the village carpenter and it is often told by those who remember how, for many years, he used to ride his motorbike and side car along these lanes. He kept his pride in the wooden garage on the detached garden soon to become the village green for the millennium celebrations.

The house and the school were sold by the Estate in the mid 1970s to a London architect and his family. Cross Cottage became the Gibberd's summer and holiday home until they sold it in 1989 to a Peter Eley who soon moved on. The Gibberds knocked through into the school to make a larger house and converted the roof space in the two-bedroomed cottage to a studio; otherwise the property remains largely as built.

Portman Market, Paddington, London 1833. His investment in this project which was unsuccessful required Thomas Wilson to sell the Abbeycwmhir Estate. (247)

In 1990 **Jake Berriman**, a town and country planner, having moved from central Bristol to work in Llandrindod for Radnor District Council spent a year looking for a place to settle before he was drawn to the village for its remoteness and apparent closeness of community. The house, Jake says, 'just seemed to fit'. Married to **Diana Griffiths** from Devannor in July 1998, the couple are determined to stay in Abbeycwmhir despite the fact that Jake now works in Kidderminster and Diana worked as a housing manager in Leominster for a Housing Association until the birth of **Abraham** in April 1999. Their second child is due in February 2001.

Jake and Diana enjoy hill walking and mountain biking. Jake spends most of his spare time 'playing' at farming at Diana's parents' family farm. Diana enjoys wine making and handicrafts, especially, at present, co-ordinating the millennium wallhangings project. Diana is also clerk to the Community Council (since 1995).

Update to 2008

A lot has changed at Cross Cottage since 2000. Most notable is the birth of **Reuben** in February 2001. Diana, Jake and the boys moved back from Leek (where they had moved to in 2002 from Kidderminster, but still returning to the Abbey every weekend) in 2005 and the family are now firmly settled in the village – not at Cross Cottage however – they moved from there one mile up the road to Little Plock at Devannor in the Autumn of 2005 to be nearer Diana's mother Brenda Griffiths and to help out on the family farm. In the meantime Cross Cottage has been let out a couple of times before undergoing substantial redecoration by Ann, Jake's mum, in 2008 and is now occupied by Bill and Gloria Mans, and thus life at Cross Cottage and in the village goes on in a timeless way.

Cwm Bedw

Roger and Cwm Bedw Cross 1999

Originally, Cwm Bedw was probably part of an ancient Celtic settlement since there is a Standing Stone exactly due west of the house, at the head of the valley, called Llyn Dwr Stone from the Bronze Age and several ancient monuments from the same period all along the top of the hill from Camlo Hill Cairn and Standing Stone, past Black Bank to 'The Devil's Apronful of Stones' Cairn.

By 1919, when it was offered for sale as one of the farms on the Abbeycwmhir Hall estate, its lands still extended to Camlo Hill and Llyn Dwr and reached right along to Rhiw Gam.

There is also evidence of medieval field patterns from before 1530, according to the Clwyd Powys Archaeological Trust, so it goes back a long way. Before the Nineteenth Century, the house was not where it is now but at a right angled bend in the bridle path from Rhiw Gam to Cwm Bedw. There was an ancient trackway to the present site, where there were a couple of small barns, with much used branches off to Llwynneuadd and Esgairwy via a lost farm called Cwm y Hebog at the bottom of the valley.

The oldest of the original leases in the County Archive Office, dated 1817, shows it leased to Thomas Lewis and in 1841 to Daniel Lewis. One of the best preserved head-stones in the Parish Churchyard refers to the death of Edward Lewis of Cwm Bedw, Age 56 in 1761, with the humorous but somewhat sceptical rhyme: 'Life is a jest,
All things show it.
Once I thought so
Now I know it.'

As the existing stone barns are quite large their present form may be Mid-Nineteenth Century. However, when Roger bought Cwm Bedw in 1988, nothing had changed since 1919 as in the estate sale document the property is all mapped and described. In the house the present sitting room with its ceiling meat hooks was the main kitchen, the present dining area was a back kitchen and the existing kitchen workstation was a dairy. Outside, the 'Beast House' is unchanged with tyings for 22 cattle, calf pens and a 2-stall hackney stable. The pigsty is now called The Gazebo and I keep my trailer in the cart shed! But the Threshing Barn and Corn Bay have been developed into what we call the Big Barn. At the time of the estate sale Cwm Bedw was considered 'A Very Useful Sheep Farm' of 222 acres, and was being rented to a John Lewis for £57 per annum!

The farm was bought by the Ministry of Agriculture and Fisheries in 1946 from James Arthur William Davies, the fields were planted with various kinds of fir tree, mainly sitka spruce, and the buildings rented out until 1988 when I bought the freehold from the Forestry Commission. Ray Cadwallader, currently Mayor of Llandrindod Wells again, who works for the Royal Mail, lived here for a time and Alan and Rita Gayse of Rhayader rented Cwm Bedw as a weekend cottage for the previous twenty years. They were a great help to me when I moved in as was my friend Averil Williams, of the Brickyard, whom I'd met on holiday in Turkey.

Roger Coward was born nearby in Great Malvern in Worcestershire and has worked in the Film Industry, was a University Lecturer until 1997 and since 1982 has worked as a Psychotherapist both in London and increasingly in Powys.

Cwm Bedw is situated nearly two miles along a forestry track and has wonderful views of the Radnor Forest. It has its own water collection point but had no electricity at the time of purchase. I have installed a diesel generator - bought from and installed with John Ford and Patrick Owen of Pant-y-dwr and a telephone whose armoured cable was laid from a drum on a silage spit all the way around Llywy Hill by the whole Antell family of Cefn Pawl, Robert, Elsie, Lisa and Anthony – an amazing task. They had also supplied my two cats named and sized Mini and Maxi employed to keep the rabbits from the garden.

Major blowdowns have twice seriously blocked the forestry track in the past eleven years. I cut my way through 22 trees on my way to London one Sunday afternoon, but when 25 trees trapped my car I left it to the Forestry Commission to clear and took a taxi! Another massive blow down led to the clearing of the valley in front of the house and the opening of the view. Many times kind neighbours have towed me up the snow-bound track and once from a ditch with the whole of the Christmas shopping on board!

Meditations were held in the barn once a month for seven years. Just after purchasing Cwm Bedw I was inspired to make a Circle-Cross in the lawn. The trenches were dug immediately by Keith Powell of Esgairwy, but – probably because I was feeling a bit embarrassed – the brickwork wasn't started until 1993. The equal armed Cross within a circle is nearly 20ft across and about 3ft deep. Brian Parfitt, of Mill Cottage, did an excellent job with the unusual brickwork which I designed. It is known as 'The Foundations'. I guess my main reason for living here is to look after this.

Roger and Sandy with new pond and land 2003

Update to 2008

Roger and **Sandy Underhill** met in the year of the Millennium and Sandy moved into Cwm Bedw in September 2001. Sandy was born and was brought up in what is now Birmingham where she trained as a floral designer and developed her interest in horses, achieving British Horse Society Assistant Instructor and Stage 4 Stable Management qualifications. In 1973 she married a farmer

Cwm Bedw continued

in Pumpsaint, Carmathenshire and in 1977 they emigrated to Canada where Sandy followed her equestrian career and was a member of the Alberta Province team which won the Gold Medal for the Three Day Event at the Western Canada Summer Games at Spruce Meadows in 1983.

They returned to Wales in 1987 and bought Caebalciog in St.Harmon where she ran an organic market garden. In 1995 she started to train as a Homoeopath and graduated in 1999. She divorced in 2000 and moved to Newbridge on Wye.

After moving into Cwm Bedw, Roger and Sandy completed the purchase of extra land for pasture, a manage and a large pond for Roger to swim in. We have continued to improve the house including installing a heavy duty battery bank and inverter/charger so that we have continuous electricity without running the generator and building stables in the Long Barn for Sandy's horses.

They were married in 2006 just before Sandy's father died. Sandy has a Homoeopathy Practice and has run the Charity Horse Fun Ride in aid of St. Mary's church in Abbeycwmhir. Roger has prepared this book.

Cwmcringlyn

Wendy Madeley with Ellen & Kirsty 2009*

Timothy and ***Wendy Madeley*** have rented and farmed here since May 2002 and moved in, after adding a kitchen and making other improvements, in January 2003.

Prior to this they had lived and farmed a rented property for 3-4 years at Pontesbury in Shropshire which was close to Tim's parents farm in Pulverbatch which they continue to work together with Cwmcringlyn as a sheep and cattle farm. Cwmcringlyn Bank above the farm is 423 metres (or 1388 feet) high.

Wendy was originally from Llanwen Farm near Knighton and helps with the farm work and does the paperwork.

They believe that Cwmcringlyn is at least 200 years old. It is built of stone and has its own spring. Jean Hughes, of Neuadd Fach, bought it from somebody in Llanbister instead of the Forestry Commission. Her son, David, still owns it. They have heard that it used to be possible to drive directly to Llanbister along a right of way through Llanerchffraith.

In 2002 their daughter ***Ellen*** was born and in 2004, ***Kirsty.*** They both attend the school at Llanbister.

The black and white photo is of Cwmcringlyn circa 1954.→

Cwmdu Cottages

Cwmdu Cottages, comprising of Higher and Lower Cwmdu, two separate dwellings, stand on the Bwlch y Sarnau to Castle Vale road between Bwlch y Sarnau Farm and Hendy Farm. Set in a dip in the road hence the name Cwmdu (dark valley) is well known for its mild climate and sheltered position from the winds that sweep across the Bwlch y Sarnau forest. The stream and spring that run near the cottages were once the winter habitat of those characters of the road, the tramp. We remember some 15 years ago Paddy an Irishman who made Abbeycwmhir and

Upper Cwmdu Cottage 1985

district his regular route, often being accommodated in barns by local farmers, calling at Cwmdu for a bottle of warm tea. On one occasion Sara our daughter, who was five at the time wanted to hand him the bottle, a redundant lemonade variety, and dropped it on the floor to the dismay of Paddy. The offer of a replacement couldn't capture the same quality of his favourite travelling companion, still Paddy was sent on his way with a new bottle and a pack of jam sandwiches.

Lower Cwmdu

Presently occupied by **Stephen Dexter**, has changed little with its basic construction retaining original Abbey windows and low doorways. From the 1960s he rented Cwmdu from Hendy Farm for holidays moving permanently from Bootle in 1980 following the passing away of his wife. He takes great pride in his five daughters, fourteen grandchildren and six great-grandchildren. Stephen Dexter is one of those special tradesmen who can put his hand to any kind of building work though his interest is rearing and keeping poultry, which he would tell you is in his blood. He is well known for his preaching in local chapels, which he considers a privilege to the glory of God.

Previously Lower Cwmdu was occupied by Elwen and Van Hughes between 1953 and 1965. Before that were Fred Wozencraft and Tom and Miriam Bennett. Tom was known for rabbit catching with ferrets, pig killing and farm labouring, "A man with hands like shovels". Going further back Cwmdu cottages and the adjoining farms were part of the Philips Estate.

Cwmdu Cottages continued

Higher Cwmdu 2000

Higher Cwmdu

Presently occupied by Stephen Dexter's daughter and son in law, **John** and **Sandra Petch** and their three children **Matthew, Jonathan** and **Sara**, has undergone major changes since 1985 when we moved in. Before this time it had a similar look to Lower Cwmdu. The need to modernise and extend as family requirements increased became a necessity with the design and building entirely completed by the owners and Steve Dexter.

We moved from Liverpool in 1983 when I took up a teaching post with Powys as an area Learning Support Teacher working mainly in the Newtown area. This continued until 1997 when I started working independently, following restructuring, as a learning consultant and authored a computer learning program now used by most Powys schools. Sandra works as a Housing Officer covering most of Mid-Wales on her travels. Our eldest son Matthew is a Senior House Doctor working at a hospital in Liverpool, he is on the road to specialising in surgery. Jonathan is in his final year studying for a degree in Archaeology at Liverpool University. He recently spent two months in Israel working with the University of Jerusalem on a dig at Hazor in Northern Israel. Sarah is working towards a career in business finishing her course at Coleg Powys, Newtown. Finally Josh the retriever who keeps us fit with his favourite walk to the quarry and back and Harry the cat his companion complete the Petch household.

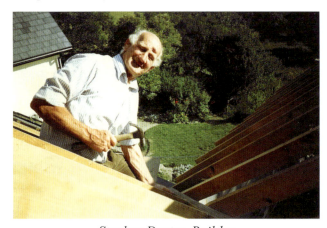

Stephen Dexter, Builder

Ernie and Alice Price, the mother and father of Sandra's brother in law, occupied Higher Cwmdu prior to the Petch family. They happened to be passing by during a heavy rainstorm and sheltered in the building, which had fallen in to disrepair. Seeing its potential they bought it and set about putting it right. Further back it was owned by Mrs Davies. Mrs Davies had a small sweet shop at Higher Cwmdu and was known for making coffee a favourite with local children coming down from the village. During the 1930's it was occupied by a family named Jones, they used to collect skins and sheep tails to sell on.

Sometime around the turn of the century Cwmdu was the home of Emma whose grave is found in Bwlch y Sarnau Chapel and according to some people is still believed to frequent the lane.

Cwmfaerdy

Cwmfaerdy is a mixed beef and sheep farm, which dates back to the 17th Century.

The Old Cwmfaerdy house was reputed to have been built by the Cistercian monks who had occupied the Abbey of Cwmhir.

In 1660 Cwmfaerdy was owned by Mr Peter Gregory. At this time the house was the meeting place for the baptist worship, the pastor for the dissenting worshippers was Mr Henry Gregory, both men were farmers and suffered at the hands of persecutors and had livestock taken off them.

In 1689 the owner of Cwmfaerdy was Nathan Davies after the death of Henry Gregory, Mr Nathan Davies was ordained to the pastorate and was the preacher at the association meetings which were held at Cwmfaerdy in 1721 was Mr Davies. Later that year the worshippers of Cwmfaerdy moved to the Rock after the premises were given to the Baptist denomination. Rev N Davies was the minister at the rock until his death in 1726.

A new house was built at Cwmfaerdy in 1873, some of the past owners have been the Edwards family and the Thomas family. In February 1966 Mr and Mrs Jim Powell and family moved to Cwmfaerdy.

The present owners **Graham Powell** (son) and **Diane** (nee Hardwick) moved to Cwmfaerdy in May 1994. They had four children: **Hayley** born 5.12.94 who sadly passed away in May 99; **Jack** who was born on 26th April 1996; **Harry** who was born on 20th September 2000 and **Nia,** who was born on 2nd August 2002.

Tinboeth Castle above Llananno on the A483.

(248)   (cf p 15)

Cwmffwrn

Cwmffwrn in 2009

Cwmffwrn means "Valley of the Furnace" of a blacksmith – or an oven, used for drying oats. The present farm comprises of four former small holdings: Upper Cwmhir (formerly Glan yr afon - below), Gelynen which means "Holly" and was a long house, Llanerch Dirion which means "Fair Patch" and Cwmffwrn. The new house is built above the ruin of the old house whose stones are still just visible. The farm used to include the site of the old small holding at the top of the Rhayader road, Cwm y Rog which is thought to have been a drovers inn. The new Cwmffwrn house is at 390 mtrs (1280 feet) above sea level and the highest point of the farm is at 443mtrs (1450 feet).

The present occupants are **Ian** and **Angela Lewis** and family. Ian was born at TynPistyll Farm, Cwmdauddwr, his parents being Gerald and Violet Lewis. Violet was born at Fronrhydnewydd, Abbeycwmhir daughter to Stanley and Hilda Williams and moved to Rhayader when she married – and later inherited Cwmhir. It is known that the Williams family were farming Cwmffwrn in 1841. Ian is a farmer and an engineer.

Angela was born at "New House", Leighton, near Welshpool and is a farmer's wife and artist.

They have four children: **Donna** (21yrs) who is in Glamorgan University training to be a chiropractor; **Rosie** (17yrs) who is doing her "A" Levels; **Elinor** (14yrs); and **Ben** (7yrs).

Upper Cwmhir (formerly Glan yr Afon)   (249)

1 Cwmhir Cottage

The present occupants of 1 Cwm Hir Cottage are **Shaun Payne** and his wife of 5 years **Kerry** and Shaun's eldest son **Tom** who is 15 years old and attends Llandrindod High School.

The cottage dates back to the mid 1800s and previous occupants include Mr and Mrs Ivor Evans who sold the cottage in 1964 to Mr Harry Hitchcock. Mr Hitchcock used the cottage as a holiday home until his death in the late 1980s. The cottage then passed on to Mr Hitchcock's sister and husband Mr and Mrs Davis of Solihull. They continued to use the cottage as a holiday home until 1998 when they sold it to the present occupiers.

Shaun and Kerry purchased the house in September 1998 after living in Penybont for 12 months. There was no mains water or sewerage connected and their first task was to install a bathroom and have water pumped into the house from a natural spring in the garden. We believe it to be the last house in the Abbey to have water connected. A telephone line was also connected for the first time. Other plans for the cottage include replacing the old coal fire with a wood-burner and running central heating to the upstairs of the cottage which at present has no form of heating. Also new windows will be installed to replace the draughty sash windows. This work is due to take place in June 1999.

Shaun and Kerry are of Irish parentage and were born and raised in Leicester, where Kerry's parents (Liam and Dolores) and Shaun's father (Patrick) had settled after moving from the Irish Republic. Tom was also born in Leicester in February 1984, as was Shaun's youngest son Jack. Shaun and Kerry met in 1990 in Leicester after Shaun had returned to full time education and 6 months later they moved to Bedford where Shaun attended De Montfort University. In the final year of Shaun's degree an opportunity arose for them to buy a share in a business in Llandrindod Wells with Kerry's cousin Pauline who lived in Builth Wells. In March 1997 Kerry moved to Penybont to take an active role in running the business and Shaun followed in July after completing his degree. Kerry and her cousin control the day to day running of the business whilst Shaun has worked for the Post Office before securing a temporary teaching post at Llandrindod High School. At present Shaun spends his time between the business and supply teaching at the school.

Shaun and Kerry have always wanted to live in the country and were contemplating moving to Ireland before the business opportunity arose. When they saw the cottage they knew instantly they had found the dream home for themselves, the five cats, dog and fishtank they had accumulated on their travels. They have all settled in very well and have been made to feel part of the Abbey by the friendly nature of the residents. A special mention to our neighbours the 'Phillips' whose unconditional helpfulness and friendliness rekindles your faith in the human race especially after spending so many years in the city.

2 Cwmhir Cottage

*May 2008**

Albert Phillips was born at 'Swydd Villa', Penybont having previously lived in various houses in the Llanbadan Fawr area.

We purchased 2 Cwmhir Cottage in the Autumn of 1960 and moved in on the 14th January 1961.

Albert was a Forestry commission worker from July 1961 to 1997 when he retired.

Mary Phillips place of birth was Wenallt Cottage, Abbeycwmhir and had previously lived at Cwmdu Cottage, Bwlch y Samau.

She began her working life at the age of 15 as Cook in Charge at Glanwye belonging to Mrs Bronley-Martin and then as Head Cook at the Beaufort Hotel, Llandrindod Wells before getting married and becoming a housewife.

Their daughter **Mandy Phillips** was born in Llandrindod Wells Hospital and has lived at Cwmhir Cottage all her life. She now works as an Administrative Officer for Powys Association of Voluntary Organisations in Llandrindod Wells.

Previously Mr and Mrs Alan Bennett and their son John had lived here.

The age of Cwmhir Cottage is pre 1877 and is built of bricks made at the brickworks at Brickyard, Abbeycwmhir and stone. The exact date of building is not known but we know it is before 1877 because an additional window was made on the East side of the house in 1877 and the date was inscribed above the window. This was put in for the then resident Gamekeeper so he could look out at the kennels across the field, which are now just a few bricks.

Mains electricity was installed in 1977 and telephone connected in 1987, the property had its own water supply in the late 1960s.

In the grounds of 2 Cwmhir Cottage is the remains of the original Cwmhir Cottage, which was lived in until the mid 1800s and is now used as a utility building.

You see it advertised about Llandegley Airport. Well, I've got on and got off an aeroplane in Llandegley! I'm the only one whose done it. The (American) soldiers round the common had two little planes come over and they landed in a field down LLandegley. I lived up there, Llandegley wasn't far from home- we cut a path down across and out at Leitho Bridge down the road. I only had to go across two fields and I was there in the big field where the planes came down. This soldier he took me in the plane, set me in the cockpit.[7]

- Albert Philips *(cf page 159)*

Homes and People

Cwmpoeth

Cwmpoeth was originally a pair of estate workers cottages - two up two down plus kitchen. It was converted into a single dwelling during 1960's.

It is approximately 200 years old and had mains electricity connected in 1960 and telephone in 1979. It has a private water supply and drainage.

Cwmpoeth was previously occupied by the Griffiths family and Jones family at a rental of two shillings per week.

It has been occupied by **Tom** and **Hazel Griffiths** and family since 1954

when the rent was four shillings per week. They had previously lived at the Ventic for three and a half years. In 1958 there were able to purchased it. They have brought up five children who are all now living elsewhere, namely **Pauline, Susan, Heather, Geoffrey** and **Joanne**. We have six grand children.

Leonard Thomas Griffiths was born at Cwmpoeth in 1923, and Margaret Hazel (nee Lewis) was bom at Caecethin, Pantydwr in 1927, later moving with her parents to Penlan, Dolau. Whilst in the RAF from 1943 to 1947 LT Griffiths served in Europe and North Africa.

Tom previously worked on farms and then the Forestry - initially on tree planting. In his last twenty years he worked with road construction plant, and Hazel worked at the Social Services Hafan Home as a cook.

We live here because of work and family ties. We just like living here and have many memories - good and not so good - and too lazy to make a move!! Cousin Gus Williams said his grandfather lived here in 1820.

Castle Collen Roman Fort at Llanyre - a model reconstruction in the Radnorshire Museum, Llandrindod Wells (250)

Abbeycwmhir Community Book

Cwmtelma

2000

The present farmhouse was built around 1800. The old house is now used as part of the farm buildings.

Elizabeth Anne (Nancy) Lewis moved to Cwmtelma in 1944 together with my husband, ***Howell,*** and 2 of our 4 children. When we came to Cwmtelma we were tenants of the Greenway Manor Estate. Cwmtelma was 161 acres. Rent £85.00 a year to be paid half yearly.

Mr Robert Greenway Gilbert sold the Greenway Estate in 1967. We bought Cwmtelma for £6,500. In 1969 we bought Pentwyn (joining Cwm Telma on the south side) from Captain E P Carlisle. In 1982 we added part of Bryncamlo which we bought from Mr D J Froggatt who had recently moved into the area, 46 acres adjoining Cwm Telma for £73,000.

My husband died in 1988 and now my daughter *Aelwen* helps me manage the farm. I was born at Coedglasson also adjoining Cwmtelma and also on the Greenway Manor Estate. I was the only surviving daughter of Susannah and Stanley Hamer. (My father died in 1921). My brother John Alfred Hamer lived at Coedglasson until his death in 1997. My sister Olwen died aged 3 years.

I married Howell Vivian Lewis of Argoed, Doldowlod and lived with my mother and brother at Coedglasson before moving to Cwmtelma.

My fathers grandparents lived at Bryncamlo in the 1800's and are buried at Abbeycwmhir. The inscription on the tombstone "Edward Price Bryncamlo died 1897 and his wife Bridget Price died 1906". Their daughter Sarah married Evan Joseph Hamer of BwIchmawr, Nantmel (my grandparents).

My husband and I had 4 children: ***Idris John*** worked in various branches of Barclays Bank. He has 2 daughters Alison Joy and Hilary Joanne. ***Ellis Lynn*** has always worked in farming and has 4 children, Amanda Elizabeth, Max Hamer, Adam Hamer and Samantha Ruth.

Aelwen Hamer married Austin Pugh of Bwlchmawr, Nantmel and have no children. Bwlchmawr was the home of the Hamer family from 1750 to 1900.

Vivienne Hamer married John Hughes Dolswydd, Penybont. They have 2 children Suzanne Mary who is married to Jason Protheroe of School Farm, Kington and James Edward who is finishing High school this year. So ends our family history to date. I wonder what the next 1000 years holds in store.

> *"Abbeycwmhir where the ducks fly backwards"*
> Comment by a gentleman from Knighton after attending a windy shooting party.

Homes and People

Cwmydea

The name means south facing and deep in the valley. **Glyn Edwards** lives with his mother **Mrs Doris Violet Edwards** (nee Lewis). Glyn is not married but his nephew, **Mark**, has been living there for the last twenty years. Glyn's parents moved here from Fishpools Farm in 1944 just before he was born in 1945. He has lived there all his life. The farm has actually been in the family, on his father's side for three generations since 1850. It is around 200 acres with mixed cattle and sheep.

Cwmydea in 1904. Seated is David Lewis Great Grandfather of Glyn Edwards

The farmhouse, which is of stone, was built around 1840 and has four bedrooms. We were connected to the mains electricity in 1960.

As a boy I went to school in Bwlch y Sarnau and then to Bryn Tirion in Rhayader. I have two sisters, who are married and have moved away. Doris Edwards died 28th December 2009 Age 93.

Left: Mark & Caroline Bound, grandchildren of Doris Edwards (right) in 1994.

Beili Hill, Bwlch y Sarmau (251)

The Dafan

The Dafan is situated in the Village of Bwlch y Sarnau; it attained its name from its previous purpose - a public house. The building is over 200 years old but has undergone several alterations during its existence. It was discovered in 1966 when the house was renovated and extended that the roof had already been raised twice before. The extension involved the adding of what are now the kitchen and the bedroom above. The Dafan is a small holding with two fields; these fields join with and are used by Beili Bog.

In the days when the Dafan was used as a Public House, it was a stopping place for farmers taking their stock to market. The buildings outside were used to shoe the animals; cattle and geese were shod with a tar and sand mixture.

The old Roman Road passes behind the house. An 18th Century map indicates that there was once a shop in part of the garden. It is not known when it existed as the map itself bears only the mark 'Old Shop'.

David and Miriam Pugh and stepdaughter Mary Pugh now Mary Davies Beili Bog purchased the property on the 26th July 1932 from Josiah Pugh of Llwydiarth.

The current residents at the Dafan are of local origin. **Owen Meredith Davies** is the youngest son from Beili Bog and was indeed born there. **Valerie Medina** was previously a Watkins from Pantglas and was born at Penguelan, Pant-y-dwr. Owen and Medina moved to the Dafan in 1966 after their marriage, and have stayed there until present day. Owen is a farmer and works at Beili Bog. Medina is a farmer's wife, and is the organist at Bwlch y Sarnau Baptist Chapel. They have two children, **Rhydian Thomas Owen** and **Teresa Valerie** who were both born at Llanidloes Hospital.

Rhydian and Teresa both attended Bwlch y Sarnau primary school before it closed down and then went on to Llanidloes High School. Rhydian studied agriculture at Newtown Tec. and then went on to do a year at Llysfasi College. He now works with his father at Beili Bog. Teresa studied Travel and Tourism in Newtown and then went on to Bangor University to study Leisure and Tourism Resource Management (BA 2.1) Teresa is now looking to pursue a career in the tourism industry.

With both families being part of the local farming community our roots are too deep to want to live anywhere else, our friends and family are living all around us.

We feel sorry that although we are Welsh, our great grandparents did not pass down the use of the language to us.

> The Abbey "also possessed five mountains, viz: Clog Arthur now denominated the Great Park; Clog Withan; Clog Bervath, now called the Little Park; Allt Monarchlog and another". Rev Jonathan Williams [8]

Homes and People

Devannor

Devannor was originally called Ty Faenor but has been anglicised over the years to Devannor. It is thought to have been built sometime during the reign of King James I (1566-1625).

The land was purchased by Richard Fowler, who was High Sheriff of Radnorshire in 1600 and again in 1615. His son, also named Richard, was High Sheriff in 1626 and 1655.

Tyfaenor is one of the oldest houses in the parish and remained the property of the Fowler family for six generations until 1760.

Devannor is owned by **Dr David William Griffiths** (known as Willie) and his wife **Brenda**.

Willie was born at Devannor in 1940. His ancestor Thomas Griffiths and his wife, Sarah Griffiths and their three children moved to Devannor in 1818. They were staunch Methodists and as there was no Methodist Church in Abbeycwmhir they started holding services in Devannor house. The practice was maintained all through the years and services were held at Devannor every Sunday.

When the Griffiths family moved to Devannor in 1818 they farmed Devannor, Tyn y Coed, Cwmcringlyn and part of Brondre Fawr Hill.

Willie is the youngest of the eight children of James John Griffiths and Clarice (nee Lewis, Troedrhiwfelen). He went to Abbeycwmhir Primary School, and Llandrindod Grammar School. He was the first Head Boy of the present Llandrindod High school when it was newly built and opened in 1958. He went to Manchester University and from there he was awarded a Commonwealth Scholarship to Canada, to study for a masters degree at the University of Saskatchewan. He studied for a PhD at Cardiff University, in Civil and Structural Engineering. He is currently a vice principal of Coleg Powys. He also originated this Community Book at the time of the Millennium.

Brenda and Willie were married in 1962 and have three children, **Jonathon** who is an anaesthetist living in Cardiff. **Evan** who is a biologist living in Glasgow. **Diana** is a housing officer, married to Jake Berriman and living at Cross Cottage.

Update to 2008

Methodist services were held at Devannor every Sunday until 2003.

Willie very sadly died in 2004.

The present occupants of Devannor are Brenda Griffiths, her son Evan and his partner **Patrizia Scheeder,** who are farming the land for sheep.

Happy is he who knows the origin of things.

Erw Fair

Erw Fair, Abbeycwmhir was built in 1995 by Mr Reginald Williams who, at that time, lived at The Hall, Abbeycwmhir. Mr Williams lived at Erw Fair until March 1997 when he sadly passed away. Erw Fair translated means "Mary's Acre" and Mr Williams named the property apparently after Mary Chamberlain who owned the land on which it was built.

The property then remained empty for some 3 years until it was purchased by Meryl Wozencraft and her daughter Rebecca in the millennium year 2000 and who moved from The Gardens to Erw Fair in May 2000. The property was modified in 2003 from a three bedroomed bungalow and garage into a four bedroomed property with an extra bathroom.

Meryl and Rebecca were both born in Llandrindod Wells. Meryl's first home in Abbeycwmhir was The Vicarage and then moved to the Happy Union Inn in 1965 and thereafter to The Gardens Cottage, Abbeycwmhir on her marriage to Byron Wozencraft who sadly passed away in December 1998 before moving to Erw Fair in 2000. My partner, Chris Smout, is a mechanic and lives and works in Caersws.

Rebecca was born in August 1997 and attends Crossgates CP School and in September 2008 will be attending Llandrindod Wells High School.

Erw Fair provides bed and breakfast to walkers and tourists who visit Abbeycwmhir and you can also order a hanging basket if you wish.

As well as the main occupants a Jack Russell called Smith and a very fat cat called Tommy live at Erw Fair along with about 20 chickens and 15 goldfish and don't forget the hamster.

Lower Esgair Farm continued

Glyn, Ken & Muriel took over the farm and carried on farming until Muriel's marriage in 1966.

Glyn, Ken and his wife **Rosebury** continued to farm with other members of the family assisting at peak times, and the milking herd taking early retirement with a change over to beef and sheep farming, to the present day.

AVALON BUNGALOW Was built in 1968 on the farm and is owned/occupied by Gwynne and Shirley Stephens. (cf page 170)

CEFN VIEW BUNGALOW Built on the boundary of the farm in 1996, and is owned/ occupied by Mike and Jacqueline Davies (daughter of Ken and Rosebury Davies) (cf page 186)

Homes and People

Upper and Lower Esgair

Upper and Lower Esgair farms were purchased by Mr. John Powell and family from the Abbeycwmhir Estate. They later retired from farming in 1950 to live at the Brickyard Cottage, Abbeycwmhir.

Albert Davies and his wife purchased the farms and moved from Penglanionon, Elan Valley in 1950, along with the family Austin, Leslie, Muriel, Tommy, Glyn, Ken, Shirley and Glenys, to live at Upper Esgair, at this time there was no tapped water, electricity or a road to the farm.

Upper Esgair

The farm was run as a milk farm plus sheep. All the milking was carried out manually mostly by the lady folk as the older sons were employed on other farms. Muriel spent much of her time working out on the farm, including delivering the milk chums to the main road with the horse and cart for collection; carrying the eggs over the mountain to the shop in Bwlch y Sarnau, which only opened on a Tuesday evening, and carrying grocery back home with a helping hand from Glyn/Ken who were getting off the school bus in Bwlch y Sarnau. An annual event was Mr. Davies, Glyn and Ken walking the sale ewes over the mountain to the annual sheep sale held in Pantydwr.

Lower Esgair Farm

The farmhouse at Lower Esgair was inhabitable when the farms were first purchased; but was first used as a farm machinery store and accommodation for the hens. During 1955 renovations were carried out and the house was occupied by Austin, his wife and family until he moved to Llandewi to his own farm. Lower Esgair underwent a number of 'facelifts' over the years, the second was for Ken, following his marriage to Rosebury, and again after the windstorm in 1975 when it suffered severe damage from falling trees. Lastly in 1991 when fire spread from the adjoining barn fire the house was virtually rebuilt in September 1964.

Albert Davies and his wife retired from farming and moved to live at Mayfield, East Street, Rhayader.

Lower Esgair

←

Esgairwy

The Old House demolished in 2000.

Purchased by Mr Jim Powell in 1971 after the death of the previous occupant Mr William Lewis. At that time it consisted of 253 acres and was amalgamated with his home farm Cwmfaerdy. Since his retirement it has returned to a self contained unit of 390 acres comprising: 253 acres originally Esgairwy; 92 acres part of Bryn-camlo; 45 acres part of Llwynneuadd top hill. It runs from the Abbeycwmhir road to the boundaries of Nantmel Parish.

It has a council road to the farm gate as well as telephone and electricity. Esgairwy boasts its own excellent water supply – which supplies both house and buildings adequately being piped over a mile from the top hill.

During recent years some of the older buildings have been replaced due to deterioration or storm damage. A new dwelling has also been built because of structural damage on the old one. This will be ready during 1999 for habitation.

The occupants since 1986 have been **Keith** and **Angela Powell** along with their three children, **Martha-Jane, Edwyn** and **Morien.** Keith was born in 1961 second son to Jim & Dora Powell previously living at Poyning Farm in the parish of Llandewi and then at Cwmfaerdy, with his family. He has farmed alongside his father and brothers since leaving school. He also attended agricultural courses run by Coleg Powys. Another generation is now working in the family business as his son Edwyn attends a part-time agricultural course in Coleg Powys along with working at home.

Angela was born in 1956 the only daughter and youngest of four children to Trevor and Lilian Pugh of Upper Rhymney, Nantmel. On leaving school she attended a Teacher training course at Caerleon College in Gwent. She was a full time primary school teacher until the birth of her children.

Martha-Jane was born in 1987, the eldest child and only daughter of Keith and Angela, at Aberystwyth Bronglais Hospital.

Edwyn was born in 1989 and has started at Llandrindod High School.

Morien was born in 1995, the third child and second son at the County Hospital in Hereford.

We live here because we farm the land.

The history of Esgairwy can be traced a long way back:

On 6 April 1580 it was recorded that "David ap Meredith ap Ieuan David Lloid of Llanddewy Ystradenny bequeathed on his death to Hugh ap David and John ap David of Llanddewy a lease of

Homes and People

2 tenements called Saio Vaynor and Esker Wydd in Llandewy so that if they do fall out Hugh shall have the house where I dwell called Saffren Mywo and a close of arable called Kay yr Gywallen and a half meadow called Y Wryghloth Vawr which are part of Esker Wydd, provided that Katherine Verch Rhees during life shall have a third part of said 2 tenements." (Transactions of the Radnorshire Society 1987)

On the 1839 Tithe map Esgair Wy consisted of 192 acres 2 rods 24 perch. The annual tithe was £9-9-0. The 1891 census states that Esgairwy, under James Price, had three Farm Servants and one Domestic Servant.

Jim Powell writes,
"My parents were farming at Grafteronen when they were offered the rent of Esgairwy in 1919. It was owned at the time by Major Philips, The Hall, Abbeycwmhir. The Griffiths family that had been there up to a couple of years before had moved to a farm at Abergavenny and some of the family are still there. It was formed in 1918 by the estate. Major Philips rode on a journey up to Grafteronen to offer the tenancy to my parents. They moved there in 1918. In 1922 they had to buy it as several farms were put up for sale. He gave £2500 for it. In 1925 he died at the age of 47 and left my mother with four children and a mortgage. My oldest brother William farmed it till he lost his wife and was sold to Mr J Powell."

Update to 2008

Martha Jane is currently pursuing a degree course in psychology in Cardiff and Morien is still attending the local high school. Edin is at Agricultural College and working at home on the farm.

Angela has continued with supply and temporary teaching work.

Ffynongarreg

The current stone Ffynnongarreg farmhouse was built in the late 1860s as a replacement for the original house which was located further up the hill. At this time the house and surrounding farmland was part of the Abbeycwmhir estate.

Since 1992 the owners have been **John** and **Vera Morris** whose daughter **Sandra** *lives with them.*

The acreage now is about 93 but in 1871 the census shows a Richard Humphries - a farmer of 60 acres. After he died the farmhouse was subsequently occupied by a branch of the Wozencroft family until the turn of the century.

The farm was advertised for sale in 1919 when the Abbeycwmhir estate was sold up. The particulars of sale list the annual rental for Ffynnongarreg as £30. 15 shillings.

211

Ffynongarreg continued

The farm was sold in 1927 to William and Sarah Davies and in 1936 they were joined by their grandson William (Billy) Manual. Over the years the family added further parcels of land as it became available until the farm reached the size it is today. William and Sarah Davies died in the 1950s leaving Billy to farm on his own for many years. As well as farming, Billy was a prominent member of the Bwlch y Sarnau Baptist Chapel, being their treasurer for many years.

Billy married late in life to Dorothy Hamer, when they were both in their mid fifties. They continued to live at Ffynnongarreg for another ten years, when in 1991, Billy decided to reduce his farming activities and the farm was put up for sale. Billy and Dorothy moved to her smallholding at Cantal where Billy continued to farm until his death. Billy remained a member of the Bwlch y Sarnau Chapel all his life and is buried there.

When Ffynnongarreg was built there were another three occupied properties on the current acreage — Tan Ffynnon, Gwar-y-cae and Garregllwyd. Today little remains of Garregllwyd and it is hard to imagine that Gwar-y-cae was ever lived in. It is thought that Tan Ffynnon was located in part of the stone barns adjacent to the farmhouse. As these are of 17th Century origin, clearly the land has been in occupation for a very long time.

Although some of the land has been used for arable crops in the past, today the land is all down to permanent pasture and is home to a small flock of Llanwenog and Black Welsh Mountain sheep.

Fishpools

The fish pool from which the farm gets its name was the Cwmhir Abbey's monks' fishpool which is just up the valley from the farmhouse which just escaped being submerged when the bank holding the pool broke during a remarkable storm in 1932 and which caused havoc further down in the village.

The farm is now owned by **Evelyn** and **Joyce Davies** who have lived here since November 18th 1958. They met at Bwlch y Sarnau Baptist Chapel. Evelyn is one of four children and was brought up at Beili Bog. Joyce is one of seven and was brought up at Pengeulan. They met at the Bwlch y Sarnau Baptist Chapel.

Homes and People

They have four children, all girls: **Anne** who lives in Pant-y-dwr and works at Boots. **Gwen** who lives in Rhayader and works at Hafron Vet Surgery, Crossgates. **Ceinwen** who is a missionary in Latvia and **Fiona** who lives in Solihul and has two children. Altogether Evelyn and Joyce have ten grandchildren.

Cwmyscawen (above), which is now not lived in, is also part of their farm. The name means "Elderberry Valley" The other part of the Davies family lives at Beili Bog.

Fishpool Farm Sale 1958

A 21 yr old man was killed during a shooting party on Fishpools land around 1979.

Flying Gate

Llidiartywaun means "Gate to the meadows" and "flying gate" it is said, was, the gate on the old drovers road between Rhayader and Llanidloes outside the house which used to flap open all the time. The property was previously known as "New Farm" and had 69 acres. When **Susan Lowe** and her husband bought it on 1st March 1985 it had 4 acres but now has 8 on which, today, she keeps ten Swale Dale sheep.. The ridge in the road outside the house is exactly

where streams leading to the Wye and the Severn go in opposite directions. Glyndwr's Way also passes here.

In about 1888 it was part of the estate of a Henry Radcliffe Linden and in 1910 a Mrs Powel paid £30-4s -6d rent per annum. In 1976 the present house was built on the old site of New Farm – the old barn from which still stands outside the house.

Susan moved here because her husband had taken voluntary severance and wanted to live in Wales – his family was from South Wales. She remembers being made very welcome by friendly →

Foresters House

The photos show the house from the field behind it. Evelyn Davies, of Fishpool farm is very kindly, cutting our overgrown hedge, in about 1993.

The house was built in 1953 when the Forestry Commission bought several farms, I think it was when the Philips estate was sold. The single storey part was the Forestry office until the depot next door was built. This is now closed and is to be sold.

As far as I know, the Manager of the forestry lived in the house up to about 1982, it was then unoccupied for some time, as apparently no one in the Forestry wanted it. Then it was sold and within a year sold again in 1983 - which was when we came here.

My wife *Susan* (nee Lucas) and I live here and our four children often visit sometimes with us and sometimes with friends. Susan was born in Merthyr Tydfil, so were her parents, and her grandfather was born in St.Harmon in the 1880s. His family farmed at Pencraig.

I, *Jim Hardiman,* was born in Slough. We met at the Royal Free Hospital School of Medicine in London and spent most of our working lives in London. Susan has lived in Merthyr Tydfil, Basingstoke and now London and here. I have lived in Slough, Romsey, Shefford, London, then in about 90 places when I was in the RAF, then on a farm in Cookstown, Ontario in Canada, then Montreal in Quebec then Mont Joli also in Quebec, then London again, Basingstoke, London and here.

Flying Gate continued

neighbours who gave them eggs amongst other things to help out. She was born in Kent but was living in Gosport, Hants with her two children *Gorran* (b.1976) and *Joseph* (b.1981). Later *Sara* (b.1988) and *Peter* (b.1990) were born at Flying Gate. In 1994 she married *David* who works as a Maintenance Engineer for the Forestry Commission in Newtown. He is from Portsmouth.

In 1996 mains electricity replaced the generator and in 1994 a new well replaced an unreliable spring.

Update to 2008

Gorran works in security systems in Brighton. Joseph runs PCQ computer shop in Llanidloes. Sara works for Somerfield in Llanidloes and Peter lives with his grandmother in Gosport and works in retail.

Susan, who is now a widow, is interested in history and photography especially of stone circles and Celtic sites. She is pleased to live close to Fowlers Arm Chair with its remains of a stone circle and burial mound probably of Vortican the post Roman leader.

Homes and People

My wife, Susan, had so many happy memories on her grandfather's farm on the Epynt and we had spent many family holidays when our children were small on a farm we rented at Bailey Bedw, near Painscastle. So we naturally looked to this area when we decided to buy a house – and found Foresters House at Abbey just the place we wanted.

Update to 2008

We retired from full time work in 1995. We have grown older and our four children have grown up: two now live in London, one in Sheffield and one in Sydney, Australia. Our first grandchild was born in 1999 and four more have arrived since. The grandchildren and their parents love visiting Foresters House despite being unable to use their mobile phones and there being no television.

A few years ago a medical colleague gave us some photographs taken by his uncle who was vicar of the parish church here about 1916. we gave copies of some of these – including one of the vicar himself – to the Happy Union Pub.

Jim Hardiman climbing a gate and Susan and our daughter Sophie.

Forest Lodge

Forest Lodge was built by the Forestry Commission in 1960 as a supervisor's house for the then Coed Sarnau forest. In those days all supervisory staff were 'mobile' and could be posted, often at very short notice to any part of the country. So each forest had sufficient houses for its staff, the larger forests even having small villages, housing supervisors and forest workers.

In the first 14 years of its life the house had three families, the Browns, the Websters, and the Humphreys. The house was empty from 1974 to 1976 when the **Richards** family moved in, two adults, two girls, and two dogs. This was our sixth house in twenty years, and at long last we could walk to a pub. Then came Mrs Thatcher's reign, and the decision was made to sell off all the Commission's domestic properties. Sitting tenants were given first option, prices varied according to the length of service of the tenant, ours cost just £16,000, about one third of it's resale value. →

Forest View

2010*

Forest View is a 3-bedroomed bungalow, situated exactly 1 mile from Bwlch y Sarnau on the road to Pant-y dwr.

The present bungalow is built on an old farmhouse site originally known as Nant y Ffin. This translates in English to "boundary stream" and a stream runs just to the south of the bungalow down from Pant Glas Farm to join the Afon Marteg less than half a mile below us. The boundary in question is that marking the parishes of Abbeycwmhir and St Harmons.

Originally, the bungalow was built as a small prefabricated dwelling by a local family. Since then it has been added to with conventional cavity-walled extension to its present size of 3 bedrooms with dining kitchen area and sitting room. It has mains electric and water supply, but has a septic tank, no mains drainage and no gas supply. The house is centrally heated from solar panels and a wood burner stove which is also the main cooker and oven. There is also a wood burner in the sitting room. The central heating is also linked to an oil-fired boiler, which we are not using at the moment.

The family currently living in Forest View are **Adrian Jones, Jane Jones**, both middle aged and Jane's son, **Jamie Edwards**, who's in his late teens. Adrian was born in Pontypool in Gwent, Jane in Slough and Jamie at Upper Ferley near Llangunllo in the Radnorshire Marches. Our family first got together in Pembrokeshire and moved here in 2003 via Llanwrtyd Wells to breed ponies. Both Jane and Adrian have lived in many different places in England and Wales. Jane's family is from Aberdeenshire in Scotland and Scotland is where her heart lies.

Adrian works for Powys County Council, where, according to Jane, he has developed his expertise for leaning on shovels. Jane works for a local charitable agency that provides housing and support to people with learning disabilities and to homeless people. Jamie is training to be a farrier, working weekdays in Cheshire, where he is soon to be taking up an apprenticeship for the next four years.

The bungalow has changed hands several times and the smallholding around it been enlarged. Previous smallholders living here have kept pigs, goats, geese, horses and sheep over the years, in

---

→ *Forest Lodge continued*

We've made several alterations since then, extended the lounge, gas fired central heating, double-glazing, and bathroom, kitchen and dining room have all been knocked about a bit. The latest project is the landscaping of the front garden, including a stone wall alongside the road. This should be finished by the millennium, or the next.

large quantities. It has seen more than its share of tragedy, but its existence has been enhanced by its occupation for a few years by a knight of the realm. He was locally known as Dick Pig, a name gained from the Oxford Sandybacks he kept, rather than what people thought of him, or so I am led to understand! Rumour has it that he paid for his knighthood, although having met him, he didn't appear as a rich person and I didn't like to ask. Other circumstantial evidence is that his family name is also the name of a family who came over with William the Conqueror and I believe "settled" or whatever euphemism passes for the bloody land-grabbing of the time, in the Welsh Marches around Flintshire.

Wenallt Hill early morning (252)

Now, in 2010, Forest View is a 4-acre small holding with garages and outbuildings, including portable stables. We breed Welsh ponies of cob type here and also have a small flock of Wiltshire Horn sheep and a rather larger flock, as I write this, of Norwegian Forest Cats. All these breeds are tremendous loss-makers and so we work full time to keep them in the lifestyle they expect. Oh yes, and there is also a hive of bees which we've kept for 18 months, which true to the traditions of Forest View, have produced no honey whatsoever to date. To be fair, the Wiltshire Horn sheep produce lovely lamb to eat, a view supported by the friends and colleagues we've given and sold lamb to. To rear all these otherwise useless animals, we rent several acres from local farmers for grazing – a couple of acres across the road and a few more acres on the banks of the Afon Marteg, just below its confluence with the Nant y Ffin stream.

But it is the animals who provide the stories here. There was our Irish Wolf Hound, now very sadly for us, dead, who used to chase the school bus and the salt gritting lorry down the road. She burst out of the entrance, once, to greet a couple of shocked cyclists out for a peaceful ride. She was only being friendly, mind, a gentle giant. She also, once, chased after one of our lambs, picked it up in her mouth and bounded back to us to drop it at our feet. The lamb, as shocked as the cyclists, ran off to join its mother. The dog just stood looking at us, expecting a reward. There must have been retriever in her genes, somewhere!

And then there was our lovely old Section C pony who'd won at the Royal of England and then had been ill-treated and starved by a later owner. Her back was sunk and she was a shadow of her former self, but when she wanted to, she didn't half move and just floated over the ground. She was with us for three years, had 3 foals and eventually died in the paddock across the road a few days after her final foaling. We'd gone away thinking everything was okay, only to have to break off our holiday in Portugal to come back and feed the foal every 3 hours night and day. The foal survived and grew up and is now living in Buckinghamshire. We like going on holiday to places like France, Spain and Greece, but we didn't risk going away again like that for a long while after.

Garden Cottage

2008*

Garden Cottage was built to provide a home for the gardener who worked at The Hall Abbeycwmhir. The exact date when it was built I do not know but obviously sometime after The Hall itself was built. The main occupiers of garden Cottage have been gardeners employed at The Hall but there have been short periods of tenancy when the residents have been employed elsewhere.

The occupiers before us were Mr and Mrs Barbierato and their family who originated from Italy. Mr Barbierato came to this country as a Prisoner of War and brought his wife here in 1948 after the war finished. He was employed at The Hall as a gardener and lived in Gardens Cottage from the 1950s till 1976. Previous to that there were several occupiers going back to the beginning of the century.

Mr and Mrs Byron Wozencraft and their two daughters Donna and Michelle moved to the house in 1976. Byron Wozencraft was employed as the gardener/caretaker at the Hall from that time until 1998. Byron was brought up and lived in Nantmel before he moved to Abbeycwmhir in 1974.

At the present time the Cottage is occupied by Mrs Meryl Wozencraft (Mr B Wozencraft's second wife) and their daughter Rebecca Wozencraft who were both born in Llandrindod Wells. Meryl Wozencraft lived at the Happy Union Inn, Abbeycwmhir from 1964 to 1991 when she married and moved to Garden Cottage. Previous to that she lived at Brynmoel (The Old Vicarage), Abbeycwmhir from 1960 to 1964. She is employed by Powys County Council as a Personal Secretary. Rebecca Wozencraft is two this year (1999).

Update to 2008

In the year 2000, Garden Cottage (as called in deeds dated 1994), was sold to Mr Barry and Mrs Jackie Leggatt. During the following years they extended the property adding three more rooms including a Garden Room with lovely views over the village and valley beyond.

One of the large buildings on the property, known locally as 'The Squash Court' was sold and subsequently modelled into living accommodation. The gardens immediately surrounding the cottage were landscaped incorporating some woodland originally owned by The Hall.

At the end of 2007, the house was again sold – this time to a Mr ***Malcolm*** and Mrs ***Julie Hughes*** who wanted to move to the area on a permanent basis from West Sussex. Mr and Mrs Hughes are both pharmaceutical chemists and currently have their own consultancy business which is operated from Garden Cottage.

Glan yr Afon

Glan yr Afon was built in the late 18th Century and although the only house now standing, judging by the amount of ruins nearby, it was quite possibly part of a community of dwellings.

We came to Glan yr Afon in 1989 and have, over the years, renovated and extended the house and added outbuildings. However, we have left the land in its natural state, enjoying its natural beauty and enhancing some areas with small plants and seats. We hope to build a pond and plant some more trees. Despite having come across Glan yr Afon mentioned with reference to pagan worship we have found it to be a place where one can feel one's feet firmly on the ground whilst being aware of a closeness to God.

1999

Wendie and ***Peter Kozek***; ***William*** age 9; ***Lillie*** age 4; 5 dogs (4 collies and 1 molesmute) + 1 cat – Tizzie; Chickens Odette "7". In Memory of Buddie our Collie, died Oct '99 Age 14yrs.

Gorffwsfa

The property was built in 1959 for Mr and Mrs O.P. Davies in their retirement. Initially one room was used as the village Post Office. Mrs Davies continued to live here alone after her husband died until the early 1980s when she went to stay with her daughter Annie.

The Jones family came from Coventry and rented the bungalow while they finished building their bungalow 'Pen Pentre' up the road.

David, Mrs Davies' grandson and Julie Evans and children followed them staying here while they built their bungalow in Abbeycwmhir, Clewedog.

Then in 1984 the ***North*** family; ***Phil, Gail, James*** and ***David*** came to Gorffwysfa also from Coventry while they looked for somewhere to live..... Still here after almost 16 years and couldn't find anywhere better?!! We have made many changes to the original building and garden and still have no plans to move.

The Hall

The original house was built c.1834, by Thomas Wilson; an unusual chap. He bought the valley as a London-based solicitor. He landscaped - particularly the trees which he brought in from Regents Park. He moved to Adelaide in Australia and became Mayor.

The Philips family then owned it until the 1950s. The Hall knew much joy and happiness. They were all quite different. Mary Beatrice, one of the second generation of them had built the church. Colonel Phillips' Canadian wife was crippled in a riding accident.

Mr. Fenner, a wig-maker from Lincolnshire owned it briefly since the Philips had no heirs and gradually sold off their land. Mrs. Chamberlain came here in the early 1950s. She was really a reclusive and employed Byron as a young man. She improved the house, maintained its distinctiveness, loved and cherished it. Mr. Williams followed her and Mr. and Mrs. Reynolds had it briefly.

We now own it and want to return it to its former glory. The least wealthy but the house will prosper. On my 50th birthday we stopped at Llangoed Hall. We fell in love with the area – that's why we are here. We called in at McCartney's estate agents in Kington. We were told that properties of size rarely came up for sale. This was January 1997. That summer we almost bought a castle near Granada in Spain, but the owners had a previous tax position. Details of the Hall came through as this happened. We phoned to make an appointment on Friday, saw it on Saturday and made an accepted offer on Sunday. We are here because it is the most beautiful place on earth, and the thought and feeling of it fills the senses. We love the house, the village and the people.

Homes and People

The occupants of The Hall are **Paul** and **Victoria Humpherston**, **Tor, Adam** and **Melissa.**

Paul was born in Kingsby, Warwickshire and has previously lived in Stanton, Gloucestershire; London, and in five other places: Henley on Arden, Warwicks; Burford, Oxfordshire; Harpenden, Herts; Thurlaston, Warwicks; Milcombe, Oxfordshire. He worked as a Personnel Director.

Victoria was born in Rugby, Warwicks and has previously lived in Dunchurch, Warwicks; Killsby, Northants; Sherton, Wiltshire; Milcombe, Oxfordshire. She has been a housewife and an interior decorator.

Melissa was born in Rugby, Warwickshire and works as a lecturer and writer.

Adam was also born in Rugby, Warwickshire and works as a Sales Representative.

Tor was born in Banbury, Oxforshire and is a student.

Best memories

Byron in his felt hat and hobnail boots at The Happy Union at 8pm on a Thursday evening - Red kites in the field - budgies in the field - the Drawing Room and the Snooker Room of the Hall that take the breath away - my wife by the front door for the first time - Maldwyn Wozencraft and the men- the most talented group we have met - the last walk to Rhayader with Byron - Tor meeting Francesca - the first game of dominoes with Meredith - meeting Dennis and Cath - the two weddings and the one funeral that will never be seen again - Llanidloes fancy dress - every Saturday night in the pub - our first party, December 1997- people being unable to stand up and communicate - all developed friendships - Meryl and Albert thought that I was from the local nursery when we first visited the hall - Brian restoring the wall - walking in Thomas Wilson's wood.

Cenedl, tref, cantref, brenin - kindred, hamlet, tribe, chief

"The *cenedl* was the basis of society, for the Welsh were, and long to be, in that stage in which the tie of kinship is paramount, overshadowing all other relations. "They are above all things," wrote the keen observer, Geraldus Cambrensis, in the twelfth century, "devoted to their clan, and will fiercely avenge any injury or dishonor suffered by those of their blood." The *tref* was the economic unit, the area of co-operation for the production of food, both by tillage of the soil and otherwise. The *cantref* was the political and judicial unit, the district within which men acted together for peace or war, for the trial of causes, both criminal and for the maintenance of the chieftain and his court. In the *brenin* appears the monarchial element, binding together the community under one authority - a costly burden from the economic point of view, but able to offer in return, not only guarantees for the preservation of order within the state, but also - what was no less prized - satisfaction to the spirit of tribal pride and security from the inroads of detested rivals".

Caeth - slave, absolute property of his owner and tradeable in Chester and Bristol.
Alltud - "other country man", foreigner, lacking attachment to the soil. All who held land were reckoned proprietors, inheritors or Cymry.
Aillt or taeog - villain holder of land but subject to a lord, forbidden to hunt, unable to leave.
Uchelwr (high man) *gwrda* (goodman). Freeman & landowner. Once free, by death, from father.

(Selected from the chapter on "Early Welsh Institutions" in "A History of Wales" - JE Lloyd 1912 who drew from the traditional Welsh Laws written down by Hywel Dda - the Good in the 10th C.) [9]

Abbeycwmhir Community Book

The Happy Union

The Happy Union Inn is the local and only inn for the Village, with differing stories to how it got its name and also the reason for the unusual painting of a man riding a goat with a leek in his hat, a jug of beer in one hand and bread and cheese in the other, dated 1858.

The date of the building is to my knowledge unknown, but is obviously fairly old.

The earliest inhabitants known to me also ran the village stores and held a small parcel of land under tenancy.

Billy Price arrived between 1915 and 1920 after keeping the Crystal Palace Hotel in Aberystwyth and was apparently fond of a drink.

George Bevan was a groom for the Philips family of The Hall before becoming the next landlord. According to local folklore George Bevan was in debt to Billy Price (the previous tenant) and became landlord by marrying his daughter to stabilise his finances.

In 1937 John Thomas Jones took over the business moving from Crossgates where he had a tailoring shop. He continued his tailoring above the present shop for a number of years together with the grocery business and pub also at one stage was delivering the post.

The next landlord David John Jones was son of John Thomas Jones and took over on his death in 1963. David Jones continued the business expanding into veterinary products and increasing the mobile shop business, which lasted for 45 years. The shop incorporated the Post Office in the 70s. He had three children with his wife (Violet, postmistress) who were Yvonne, Meryl and John.

The youngest being a son became landlord on his father's death in 1995 and became the third generation of Joneses and the second John Thomas Jones. At present I, *John Jones*, continue to →

Homes and People

Hazeldene

Detached bungalow built in 1973 for Gwyn Rees and family, his parents residing in the main house on Bwlch y Sarnau farm some 50 yards down the private farm lane. Gwyn had a larger house built to accommodate his family and sold the bungalow in October 1994 to the present owners.

Richard and **Janice Newton** married in August 1968 and started married life off in Sutton, Surrey. After 8 years in Sutton, a new job for Richard meant a civil Service in 1994 and a new job involving travelling enabled Richard and Janice free to look for the retirement location they dreamed of, their son being independent and staying on in Telford.

1999

Richard is a Health and Safety Auditor with the National Training Partnership. Richard's job entails travelling around the country vetting companies involved in the Government sponsored training programmes, also spending time at the company's head office in Sheffield. Janice 'retired' in January 1999 to enjoy the surrounding countryside and be a 'lady of leisure'. Prior to 'retirement' she travelled the country training and verifying candidates undertaking National Qualifications (NVQs). Janice is now busy with the Bwlch y Sarnau Women's Institute. Richard enjoys travelling the lanes and highways on his motor cycles with or without his wife!

We found Bwlch y Sarnau by accident even though we had estate agents' directions and decided it was the ideal location to spend the rest of their lives. All that was needed was the ideal property!!
As 'townies' friends and family thought they were mad to move into the wild Welsh countryside with a name half of them didn't even attempt to pronounce. Their own son even said that it was OK to visit but not to live. Well after nearly 5 years they are happier than they could ever have imagined thanks to all the local residents of the parish.

'YAMHWA' Roger Coward 1975

→ run the pub, shop and Post Office together with my partner **Karen Jones** and our son **Luke** and also with help from my mother Violet Jones.

Lauren, a daughter, was the first baby to be born in the New Millennium at Llandrindod Wells Hospital.

Hendy View

Hendy View was built in 1987 and we came to live here in 1988.

I was 22 when I came with my mother and father (who was Welsh speaking) to live and work at the Hendy farm, in 1948. They rented the farm, but bought it from Colonel Philips in 1958. Previous to that the farm had been worked by the Meredith family for five generations. My parents had moved to this area two years before I was born, so I've been around here all of my life. I was born in Llananno parish, and although I was offered a place at grammar school, I decided not to go, and eventually left school to start work at 14.

Myfanwy and I married in 1952. We had two sons, though sadly we lost **Dennis** when he was twelve years old, but our other son **David** and his wife Hazel now live in the farmhouse and I have turned the farm over to him. Now I am helping David on the farm although I have been ill, but I like to be active and do what I have always enjoyed.

The millennium is for me of religious importance, and I have strong feelings about some of the Government money being spent on celebrations which could rather go into, say, the NHS.

Myfanwy was born in Howey but later moved to Newbridge on Wye where she met **Elwyn Hughes.** Her parents had worked in service around that area on various estates. Things were very different then. We had to do everything by hand, washing blankets, digging potatoes, bundling up the hay etc. Nowadays I help with the grandchildren who are very nearby on the farm. Hugh is 9 and Megan 11. Megan is very good at Welsh.

Homes and People

Henfryn

Is a stone built farmhouse built probably in the mid Nineteenth Century and previously owned by the Lewises who also owned Llanerffraith where the Bennetts now live.

Jim Powell bought Henfryn in 1969 and his son, **David J. Powell**, who was living with his family at Cwm Faerdy since 1966, moved there with Trisha his wife who works as a nurse.

Their daughter **Carys** was born on 30th May 2000. The house was renovated and extended with stone in 2005.

Henfryn is a beef and sheep farm with 27 chickens.

Henfryn 2008

Henfryn at the end of 18th C. (253)

225

Home Farm

Home Farm is an 18th century farm house, standing close to ruin of the Cistercian Abbey, belonged to the Hamer family since 1955. It previously being the Home Farm to the Philip's Estate. In the garden of Home Farm there is a typanium from over a door (cf page 38) depicting the Assumption of the Blessed Virgin Mary dating back to the 13th Century.

The occupants of Home Farm are **Melwyn, Anita** and **Rhiannon Hamer**

Melwyn (below right) was born at Neuadd Fach, Abbeycwmhr and lived at Brynrhyg, Bwlch y Samau from1939 to1955 and then at Paddock Cottage, Abbeycwmhir from 1974 to 1976. Home Farm is his place of work and his home.

Anita was born in Llanidloes, Montgomeryshire where she lived from 1942 until 1964 when she married and came to live here.

Rhiannon was born and brought up here, now her place of employment .

Surrounding the farmyard at Home Farm are a collection of buildings. These are made up of a cart shed, a saw mill, a coach house, a stable and a boiler house. The coach house was made into a dwelling in 1949 and occupied by the Barbierato family. Mr Barbiereto was a Prisoner of War (cf In Living Memory page 161).

Homes and People

Keepers Lodge

Keepers Lodge is situated about one mile down the road from the Abbey Village at the bend where the road crosses the Clewedog River for the second time. This has always been known as Cuckoo Bridge.

The Lodge was built in 1861 to serve as a game keepers cottage for the Abbeycwmhir Estate. In the 1851 census Thomas Davies was game keeper and he lived at Cwmpoeth, next door to Mr Benjamin Price who was the school master.

Noel Price writes: " *I lived there myself for twenty six years. No, no, don't get me wrong, I am no gamekeeper myself, nor have I any notion of being one. We were turfed out of our home at Broad Oak because the owner wanted to retire there. And with no-where to go, at the eleventh hour, our prayers were answered, and we moved to Keepers Cottage. It was a nice shady spot to live, well shaded from the North and East winds – unlike Broad Oak. It was then owned by Flossy Wozencraft of Cwmyscawen who later moved to Cascob.*

Water was a little on the scarce side. In a dry, hot summer, clean drinking water had to be carried 400-500 yards. Of course water for washing and washing clothes was carried from the river. My Mother had to carry two buckets of drinking water everyday – it became my job when I as old enough. "

Keepers Lodge is a Grade II Listed Building. The present owner is Andrew Evans of Rhayader.

Mel Hamer of Home Farm in the Abbey Field

> HOME FARM IS SITUATE CLOSE TO THE MANSION AND VERY CONVENIENT FOR THE OWNER'S OCCUPATION, AND IS A SUPERIOR STOCK REARING AND HILL SHEEP FARM PRINCIPALLY LYING VERY SHELTERED IN THE CLYWEDOG VALLEY, DIVIDED INTO HANDY ENCLOSURES AND CONTAINING AN AREA OF 552.800 ACRES. (POND AND BOAT HOUSE: 1.779 ACRES; SAW MILL POND: 338 ACRES).
> - DRIVER, JONAS & CO 1919 [10]

Llanerchffraith

The **Bennetts** have lived and farmed at Llanerchfraith since 1931 when they bought it from the Lewis Family. First Jack and Alice brought up five children here: Ivor, Olwen, Alan, Sylvia & Ida. Jack & Alice moved to Crossgates in 1977 and **John** and I, **Megan,** moved here in 1978 and brought up our three boys here: **Ian**, **Andrew** and **Martin**.

Previous occupants here were John Brown 1841, Samuel Brown 1851, John Price 1861 & 1871 and James Price 1901.

The present house was re-erected in 1837 – there is a stone on the corner that says so! I have been told that another house (Cwmysgawen Ed.) was built at the same time in the Abbey Parish with the same layout by the then owner Mr. Wilson who bought the estate in 1821.

According to Mr George Lewis, in his book "Haber Nant Llan Nerch Freit" (Logaston 1998 (Ed.) Llanerchfraith was mentioned in a Charter to the Cistercian Monks at the Abbey in the 12th Century. He also says that there was once a tunnel from here to the Old Abbey. John was once told that if the name, Llanerchfraith, was spoken in a certain way it would translate to mean "a place where the monks would prepare to go to the Abbey".

If you stand where the previous house had been built you can see Wennallt's Barn at the top end of Abbeycwmhir. When I stand at the clothes line I can see the farms of Cwmgringlyn, Tyncoed, Devannor, Cefn Pawl, Esgairwy, and the buldings at Troedrhiwfelin. We can also see the TV mast at Llanyre – so we never needed a TV aerial on the chimney! . Although we don't get the early morning sun we do get the most beautiful sunsets.

Ian, Andrew and Martin are the seventh generation of Bennetts to live in the Abbey Parish.

Update to 2008

Ian is a lorry driver and has experience working on combine harvesters on the plains of the USA, Andrew is married to Menna and works at home on the farm, Martin has moved to live in Cardiff and works in a bank.

Llywy Cottage

Although we and our family cannot count ourselves 'full time residents' of Abbeycwmhir, my wife Christel and myself at the end of the 1960s became the first Marsh's to own Llywy cottage. We later transferred the ownership, to our four children (**Brigit**, **Elisabeth**, **Laurence** and **Henry**) while we have continued to visit the cottage as far as our age and disabilities allow. All regard Llywy Cottage as our 'second home' and would much like to be included in the Millennium Project.

Llywy Cottage was probably built in the first half of the 19th century as two semi-detached cottages with a tapering strip of garden stretching up the slope towards the Llywy. At some later date the building was converted into one cottage, although two porches, one off each side of the building remain. We in our time converted the surplus front door into a window and made a small study of the entrance lobby.

The property was first 'discovered' empty and in a totally derelict state with an overgrown garden, of which the outstanding feature was a huge crop of outsize rhubarb, on September 2nd, 1968. The 'discoverers' were ourselves and our son Laurence, who were then on holiday in a cottage of Mr Pugh's at Llandewi. We had celebrated Lawrence's 21st birthday by a walk over the hill from Llandewi, and it was he who encouraged us to make enquiries about acquiring the property. Its ownership, however, was a mystery, which no one in the village could explain, beyond saying that from time to time the cottage had been occupied, especially by gatherers of sphagnum moss, hence its nickname of 'Mossmen's Cottage'. At the end of their holiday the Marshes left instructions with a Llandrindod Wells solicitor to try and discover the ownership of the cottage. After six weeks all he had been able to discover was that about ten years before it had been the subject of an unspecified legal transaction in which an unnamed firm of solicitors in Hereford were involved. A circular letter to the twenty-two solicitors in Hereford eventually led to a lady who was in fact able to dispose of the property and left us free, with the help of Mr Bywater, then at Crossgates, supplemented by the collective efforts of our family, gradually to restore Llywy Cottage to habitable condition.

In the course of nearly forty years, with the help of Mr Parfitt of Mill Cottage, the main changes have been a new roof and a flight of steps leading to the front door from a car port cut into the slope on which the cottage stands. Our son Henry has improved accessibility to the steep incline of the garden behind the cottage by constructing flights of wooden and stone steps. He has also made more or less level the tilting tool shed beside the cottage.

The Occupants of Llywy Cottage are:

Norman Stayner Marsh CBE, QC. Born: 26 July 1913 at Bath, Somerset. Barrister, Fellow and Bursar of University College, Oxford, Secretary General of International Commission of Jurists,

Continued →

Abbeycwmhir Community Book

Llwy Cottage Continued

Director of the British Institute of International and Comparative Law, Member of the Law commission, now retired.

Christiane Christinnecke, now Marsh. Born 28 July 1917 in Magdeburg, Germany. They married in 1939 in London.

Bridget Cherry, née Marsh, born 17 May 1941 in London. Architectural Historian, married to *John Cherry*, Keeper of the Medieval and Later Department in the British Museum, Archaeologist.

Elisabeth Ramsay, née Marsh, born 10 May 1944, in Pinner, SRN, married to the Revd Canon *Alan Ramsay*, Vicar of St. Mark's, Mitcham.

Laurence Marsh, born 2 September 1947 in Oxford. Barrister married to Sophia, née Roder, born in Germany, head of science in a prep school in Clapham, London.

Henry Marsh, born 5 March 1950, in Oxford. Neuro-Surgeon in London, Married *Hilary,* née *Allen.*

Norman and Christel Marsh have at present (1999) ten grandchildren and one great-grandchild who were all born in or near London. All have visited the cottage, except (as yet - in 2000) the great-grandchild.

Norman & Christiane Marsh (Easter 1999)

Llwynneuadd

Homes and People

Llwynneuadd continued

Llwynneuadd means 'Grove Hall' from Llwyn - Grove; Neuadd - Hall.

Llwynneuadd is a farm of some 500 acres approximately 1.5 miles south of Abbeycwmhir where we farm mainly sheep. We had moved as a family from Llandewi to Cwmfaerdy in 1966 when I was three and it was in 1981 that my father, Jim Powell, bought Llwynneuadd from the then owner Richard Peel. The old house wasn't in a very good state when father bought it so it remained empty for most of the time up to the late eighties when it had to be demolished. The photographs show the old house in the early eighties and our new bungalow in the early nineties. I, **Aubrey Powell,** built the bungalow in 1988 and **Sandra** and I have brought up our family of four here in the new house since then. Our children are **Paul** the eldest, **Kay, Joy** and **Cara.**

I am not sure of the history of the property or when it was originally built as Llwynneuadd but it was certainly occupied in 1860 by the Ingram family. I was contacted in 2008 by a John Ingram of Shrewsbury who in researching his own family had found reference to the birth of his great grandfather, Edward Ingram, here at Llwynneuadd m 1860. Edward's mother had been Jane Price before her marriage which is interesting in that Richard Peel bought the farm in the 1960's from Jack Price who then moved into the new Sunnydale Bungalow.

Llwynonn

The name means, in Welsh, Grove (Llwyn). As there is an Ash (Onnen in Welsh) behind the house, Llwynonn is understood to mean Ashgrove.

All the farmland at Llwynonn falls within the area of the medieval deer park associated with the monastery of Abbeycwmhir and was established by Edmund Mortimer in 1241. This site is one of only a few surviving areas of monastic parkland in Wales. The suspected eastern boundary of the park is thought to be the stream that forms the eastern boundary of the farm. The park would have been an unenclosed area largely wooded with open areas where deer were bred and hunted. The valley area was later an area of peripheral parkland related to a more formal post- medieval park associated with the later gentry house at The Hall. About 1818 the parkland was seven miles in circumference and was stocked with upwards of 200 deer. The farm house is a late 18th/early 19th century rubble stone house with a single range of buildings forming a 19th century brick cart shed. The granary is typical of 19th century traditional agricultural buildings in the area. The house plan is the

Abbeycwmhir Community Book

Llwynonn continued

Llwynonn *

same as the Vron, Esgairwy, Old House and Fishpool Farm.

Dai's family have occupied Llwynonn for over 95 years. His mother, Dorothy, was born there and used to work for The Hall. Dai was mainly brought up by his Grandmother, Ethel and David Prosser from Troedrhiwfelin where, now, Bernard Pugh, his second cousin, lives.

In the Philip's days the farm was 385 acres. In 1956 the Forestry Commission bought about two thirds of the acreage so that by 1973 it was some 148 acres.

Dai has always lived at Llwynonn, **Mandy Herbert** joined him in 1996 and they were married in 2007. Mandy previously lived at Cefn Hengroed in Mid Glamorgan. She does part time care work and works on the farm.

They both have children from previous relationships: Dai**: Rachel, Deiniol** *and* **Graham Jones**, and Mandy: **Nigel Herbert** (Mandy's maiden surname) **Brett Price** (Mandy's married surname)

Dai is a farmer, contractor and Chairman of Abbeycwmhir Community Council (2008).

Update to 2008

All the children have left home except Brett who is doing Army Preparation and hopes to soon. Rachel is married and works for The Welsh Office. Deiniol works re-furbishing pubs and has a house in Knighton. Nigel is a Practitioner in Liverpool and Graham lives and works in Rhayader.

Good Counsel

Good for good is only fair;
Bad for bad soon brings despair;
Bad for good is vile and base;
Good for bad shows forth
God's Grace.

- Anonymous Welsh Verse [11]

The 19th Century 'Old Granary' at Llwynon.

Maesgwaelod

The Brunts family came to live at Maesygwaelod from The Park, St. Harmon in the Nineteenth Century. There were four generations with the same name, Edward Brunt.

It is recorded that the first Edward Brunt was a weaver. The second, his son, was ordained as a Baptist Minister. Mary Jane Brunt was the daughter of the fourth Edward Brunt and his wife Eliza and married Thomas Edward Lewis from Pantydwr. They had eight children.

Joan, Robert and Clive Lewis in 2000

Their eldest son, also called Thomas Edward, and his brother Edwin came from The Vron each day when they left school to farm Maesygwaelod because their grandparents had died. Also Mrs Hope from St.Harmon and her four sons had rented Maesygwaelod house and the boys had helped on the farm for a time.

Thomas Edward Lewis eventually married Margaret Elizabeth Jane Price, Cefnllech, Pantydwr, and came to live and farm at Maesygwaelod. They, too, had eight children: Ceridwen, Gaynor, Sylvia, Maureen, Maglona, Evan – nicknamed Meurig –Sheila and Susan.

Evan Thomas (Meurig) Lewis took over Maesygwaelod in 1965 and married **Joan Elizabeth Price Thomas** in 1967.

Joan is the daughter of *Mary Elizabeth Thomas (nee Price)* of Hafod Fraith, Lidiartywaen, but her former home was Upper Penrhyddian, Llandinam. Mary, her Mother, was born at Penbwlch, Bwlch y Sarnau in 1927 to *David Thomas Price* and his wife *Dilys*. David Thomas Price's home was Middle Marteg. After they married they lived at lived at Bwlch y Sarnau Farm for a short time.

Meurig and Joan had five boys: **Philip** (b 1968) who is now a Baptist Minister in South Wales. **Stephen** (b1969) who is a carpenter and lives in Llandrindod Wells. **Robert** (b 1970) who is a care worker. **Brian** (b 1972) is a mechanic and lives in St.Harmon and along with his wife farms the thirty eight acres of Maesygwaelod, and **Clive** (b 1977) is one of the caretakers at Builth Wells High School.

Joan attends Bwlch y Sarnau Community Centre where she has learned to operate a computer and do first aid as well as being in the Gardening Club and Womens Institute. She also attends Nantgwyn Baptist Chapel where Meurig, aged 57, and his parents Thomas Edward, aged 71, and Margaret Jane, aged 100 are buried.

In 2000, Joan and Clive, along with local church members, marched with a banner from Nantgwyn to St.Harmon and back, stopping to sing at both St.Harmon and Pantydwr.

Outside Maesgwaelod Farm, in the field, is a Bronze Age Round Barrow sometimes known as "The Mount" or as "Beth Garmon".

Abbeycwmhir Community Book

Maesgwyn

We plan to occupy Maesgwyn in August 2009 – myself, **Helen Hughes**, my husband **Dilwyn** and **Owen** (10*)* **Ewan** (8) and **Rhian** (6)

Dilwyn was born in Laithddu and lived at School House until we married. I was born in Llandrindod Wells and lived at Felindre and then Clun until we married. All the children were born in Kington.

Dilwyn is currently building Maesgwyn and I work in the care industry for Cwmryd Rhan.

Nanteos

Nanteos was part of the Penlanole Estate and was sold as Lot 14 on 21st September 1910. It was described as a compact freehold farm with 130 acres, 3 roods and 3 perches. The farm house is stone and brick built and had a parlour, kitchen, back kitchen, dairy and three bedrooms.

It also appears in the 1841 census when a Richard Powell Age 25 lived with his wife Elizabeth (nee Bennett) also aged 25. They had eight children.

The present residents are **John Raymond Evans**, born Pengeulan, who lived here before he married **Rosemary Olwen Morris** who was born at Gorsty, Llaithddu, a shop assistant. They have always lived and farmed at Nanteos.

John had been a pupil at Bwlch y Sarnau Primary School. Rose went to Llaithddu School and they both went on to Brynterion Secondary School. John likes playing bowls at Pantydwr.

They had two sons: **Andrew,** born February 21st 1972 who sadly died in 1989 and **Julian James**, born 21st July 1977. He went to Bwlch y Sarnau CP School and then to Llanidloes High School.

> *Col JL Philips was a very distinguished oarsman. He began by rowing for Eton, then New College Oxford, and was in the Oxford and Cambridge boat race. He was the oldest surviving member of the Leander Club in the late 60s and was much fêted at Henley .*[12]

Mill Cottage

Mill Cottage was built in 1826 to house a pauper by Thomas Wilson who also moved the forge to next door but one. Mill Cottage was not built well and was then called "Step Aside". Before this there was a Church House next door since about 1750 possibly to house a vicar or curate.

The present house is made up of these two houses each of which paid rates (of £14 p.a.) in 1976. One was Mill Cottage owned by a Miss Davies and the other, Churchhouse owned by a Miss Helen Marion Wodehouse who was Principal of Girton College, Cambridge. She died 20.10.1964 at a nursing home in Llandrindod Wells. They had bought them for £50 each from the Abbeycwmhir Estate but Miss Wodehouse died and left Church House to Miss Davies who ended up owning both including the joint electricity meter. When she died she left them both to her nephew in Seaton, Devon, who sold them to a Mr Day. **Brian Parfitt** bought the two in 1976 and knocked them together making one door instead of two and adding bigger back windows, a bathroom and a kitchen – but didn't have to change the stand pipe at the end of the row because it was communal!

The whole area was called "Frogtown" – because of the toads! Both frogs and toads are still quite prolific there - also "Frog Street" and "Tradesmans Row". The Council called the old forge next door "Vulcan Hall". When Brian bought Mill Cottage, the Old Mill building was still standing.

Brian was born in Sevenoaks, Kent and won a scholarship to Sevenoaks School. He wanted to move to Wales and to live in a village with a stream running through. Mill cottage was then very overgrown with ivy and still with whitewash on the walls. When he first moved to Abbeycwmhir he stayed at Cwm Bedw and then in a mobile home outside Mill Cottage with his wife and three children. He has worked as a builder and carpenter a great deal in Abbeycwmhir where his work includes the bar of the Happy Union, St.Mary's Church, the Village noticeboards etc.. He is now retired.

His son, **Isambard** went to Llandewi School and is now in his twentieth year in the army as a Warrant Officer in the PT Core and is the Colonel's Bodyguard. His two daughters, **Della** and **Maxine,** went to Llandrindod Primary and High Schools and still live there. 'Old Pritchard's' green and cream school bus always came to pick them up even in heavy snow.

Brian and **Nita Morris** have been together for 27yrs.

The Druids wore white undied sheeps wool robes like the Cistercian Monks - as did Mayan priests.

Neuaddfach

Harold and Thoa at Neuadd Fach 2009 *

Harold Hughes bought Neuadd Fach in 1951 when he was lecturing in mathematics at Norwood Technical College in London as somewhere to bring the family in the school holidays – and to get away from the nuclear threats of the Cold War! In those days you had to collect the water from the spring and they had a generator that ran on TVO (Tractor Vaporising Oil). The house was then in Llananno Parish and had been built in 1909 from wood and corrugated iron brought from Penybont Station on horses and carts for a Mrs Millward whose daughter convalesced there from TB. There is a similar house next to Tyn-y-Berth. The house has some 35 acres beneath the "magical" landmark of Ysgwd Ffordd or Scorfa Hill as it is known locally.

Harold's wife, Jean also bought Cwmcringlyn and planted some 40,000 conifers on the other side of Cwmcringlyn Bank to prevent the Forestry Commission doing it on their side and thus spoiling the view! There was an oak wood on Neuadd Fach which had been felled in the first world war but the stumps sprouted shoots and became a new oak wood which is still standing. Harold planted additional conifers around it and some Lawson Cypress around the house. His son, David, now owns Cwmcringlyn.

Harold has lived and worked in West Africa (2 years), Nigeria (1 year), Grimsby (3 years) and Newport College of Technology in South Wales. In 1968 he obtained a lectureship in Canada. which led to a separation from his wife, Jean, who stayed at Neuadd Fach for a time and attended the WI in Abbeycwmhir which was sponsored by Colonel Philips' wife. Their son **David** was born in 1950 and **Martin** in 1953. Martin is now a grandfather. Both sons now live on the northern outskirts of London.

Harold was born in Carshalton, Sutton, near Croydon in 1924. He worked in Canada from 1968 to 1988 in Sarnia at the southern end of Lake Huron in South West Ontario where he met **Thoa**. They part own a house in Brampton, Ontario and they live there for part of each year and in Abbeycwmhir for the other part. Thoa and her sister were South Vietnamese boat people who were the first out of a family of eight to successfully escape from the regime there.

> *"A nursery on an extensive scale is recommended to be forthwith planted by the proprietor in a central and sheltered situation, with a cottage for the resident superintendant or woodreeve...... The woodreeve is recommended to number every timber-like-tree, describing it in his book...and to mark every teller with red paint and to register the number of tellers......this would be a check upon the tenants and others...from committing any further depredation.... for being aware... that with a moderate degree of attention by the woodreeve detection would be certain." ('Nursery planted behind Mount Pleasant '- Wilson) Layton Cooke Report 1822* [13]

Homes and People

New House

The occupants of New House are **Glyn Evans, Lil** and **Andrew.** Glyn says: "I was born in this house so I have always lived here. My mother, Lucy Evans, came as a housekeeper here when she was 19yrs old. She lived and worked here for Richard Price and when he died he left it to her as long as she wanted it. I was her only child and eventually bought it off the owner. My mother came from between Llandewii and Penybont, and went to school in Llanbaddarn Fawr. I went to school in Blwch y Sarnau, then Laithdu, and then Bryn Tirion. At 15 I left to start helping on the farm. I was brought up

Glyn Evans at Newhouse 1999

in peace and quiet. There was a little community here in a small block of dwellings but most of them have gone now. However I do know everyone for about 20 miles around and they are all very good neighbours.

Lilly Micheson comes from Newcastle upon Tyne and describes herself as a Rolling Stone having worked all over the country including Saunders Foot. Glyn and Lil met at Llwyneuadd. She considers she is owed the Gold Medal for shoveling muck and making cups of tea. Andrew, their son, is 17 and is now working on the farm as well as doing contract farming.

The farmhouse itself was built in 1797, but we had big alterations about 2yrs ago. The farm is 70 acres and at 1200 feet. Electricity came in 1953. Farming is very different now from when I was younger. Then we were almost self- sufficient, and could sell eggs for instance to buy the few things we needed from outside, like tea. Nowadays we buy almost everything. Of course, we used horses then. Shires for work and hunters to ride and we had a cross breed for general purpose tractor work.

I enjoy farming and being my own boss. It is a wonderful life, and there are some lovely experiences, like when you see a new-born calf, or hear the cuckoo sing, but equally of course its hard when animals die. Farming is more difficult now and has become a rat-race like a lot of other things. I enjoy hobbies like clay-pigeon shooting and darts and have cups for them, and also for showing sheep and fat lambs too. Lil does a bit to help. One of the hardest times here was in the winter of 1947. We were blocked in by snow, which came up to the roof of the house, for three months. After the snow it froze. There was little to eat, and there wasn't anything available within four or five miles if you could get there – the only way was to carry the groceries on foot. We lost lots of sheep and cattle because we had no fodder – there had been a poor summer before."

Glyn is a member of the Rhayader Hunt. Andrew was winner of the Simon Reece Memorial Trophy for motor-cycle scrambling.   *Pictures on the next page →*

The Oaks

The house was built in 2004 and is so called because of some oak trees in the field nearby. **Angela** & **Michael Winterton** moved here in December 2007 and are the first people to live there. They had been living in Lyonshall near Kington in Herefordshire where they kept a Swiss "Toggenburg" goat herd and were looking for a house in St.Harmon when they discovered the house in Abbeycwmhir.

Angela was born in Innsbruck in Austria and met Michael whilst he was working there. Michael had his own film and video company in 1979-80. Angela says "she could ski before she could walk" and trained in the 'Austrian Junior Ski Team'. They moved to the UK in 1988. Angela is now a Psychotherapist, Hypnotherapist and Counsellor working in local towns.

Michael was born in Lichfield and had worked as a land agent and agricultural auctioneer. He had also been a Captain in the 13th Hussars where he rode horses in competition for England – in Germany. He says he was "born on a horse" because his father had horses and owned the winner of the 1976 Welsh Grand National at Chepstow. Michael used to ride National Hunt Races.

They have two sons **Patric,** born in 1985 in Austria, and is now a landscape gardener in Cornwall. **Tomas**, born in 1989 in Lincoln, is at Kingston University in Surrey, reading pharmaceutical science.

Before they moved in, Angela and Michael knew the area well as walkers and used to come here every week. They love the beauty and quiet of the valley.

← *Newhouse: Glyn, Lil & Andrew*   ← *Glyn's Trophies and some of Andrew's**

Homes and People

1 Paddock Cottages—White Paddock

1 Paddock Cottage is one of a pair of cottages built in locally made bricks cir. 1868. The cottages were part of the original estate of 1919 of The Hall. The cottage was the local Post Office up until 1971, the year the money went decimal from pounds, shillings and pence. Mrs Wilcox, the postmistress, decided to retire at this point. The Post Office was housed in a small building at the back of the cottage, it is fitted with 'Abbey' windows like those in the Happy Union and buildings at Home Farm. The Post Box was housed in the thick stone wall next to the 'red' phone box. It was tastefully extended over the last 12 years by local builder Brian Parfitt of Mill Cottage Abbeycwmhir.

Suzanne and **Peter Dummer** have lived at Paddock cottage (known locally as White Paddock) since 1997; prior to this they owned and ran Rhydfelin Farm Guest House and Restaurant at Cwmbach on the A470 between Newbridge on Wye and Builth Wells.

Suzanne works as Support Team Manager running houses in Powys, supporting people with learning difficulties. Peter works for Social Services in Brecon.

As a younger man Peter 'took the Queens Shilling' for twelve years in the Parachute Regiment. Early in our married life Peter was stationed in Brecon. Our Son **Andrew** came to Brecon when he was a month old, our daughter **Claire** was born in Brecon.

We vowed that when Peter was posted back to his Battalion we would one day return to Wales, hence our venture at Rhydfelin and finally Abbeycwmhir. We had a very hectic and interrupted life living at Rhydfelin. We came to Abbeycwmhir for the peace, beauty and tranquillity it offered and have not believed our good fortune in finding our new home.

2 Paddock Cottages

This semi-detached cottage was built in around 1860 in the paddock where the Hall's horses were kept, hence it's name. It is now occupied by Lorraine Williams, who bought it from Richard Bryan in October 2007, as a result of word of mouth.

Before Anita and Mel Hamer lived here, Lorraine's great uncle George resided here. In those days, there were low, neatly trimmed box hedges running down both sides of the

→

2 Paddock Cottages continued

Path. A plumber by the name of Dick Rowlands also lived in this cottage. At a mighty six foot two inches, he travelled to work daily in Llandrindod Wells on a little BSA Bantam. On his way home, he would switch off the petrol tap somewhere near the Blacksmith, and the fuel in the carburetor would be enough to carry him to the Paddock. As he reached the gate, the bike would conk out and he would roll it down the path to the back of the house to store it in the shed.

Lorraine Williams was born in Aberystwyth hospital after a couple of false starts! She has resided at The Manse, Bwlch y Sarnau for most of her life. She attended Bwlch y Sarnau Primary School where Mrs Stanton was head teacher. (Mrs Stanton had lived in Llywy Cottage as a girl). After attending Llanidloes High School and Coleg Powys, Newtown, Lorraine went on to University Wales College Newport in Caerleon, and was the last cohort to complete the four year B.Ed. Honours degree. She specialised in Music. She achieved Grade 8 standard on the piano and Grade 5 standard in Singing whilst there. She now teaches at Crossgates Primary School.

Her hobbies include music, painting and antiques. She helped with the making of the Millennium Tapestries. She plays darts for the Happy Union Ladies darts team (though she is nowhere near her Dad's standards!) She also goes to evening classes to learn Welsh. A self confessed petrol head, Lorraine enjoys going to car shows and racing events.

Pantglas

In the year 1770 a Baptist named John Williams and his sister Mary came from Dolau, Nantmel to live at Pantglas. He was renowned for his hospitality to travelling Baptist ministers, and became affectionately known as the 'Bishop of Pantglas'.

Pantglas has been in the **Watkins** family for 3 generations 2 of which have made Pantglas their home.

The house has been enlarged during the last 25 years. Glenys and It(h)ol Watkins lived here for 50 years between 1946 and 1996. Their children were Medina born on 7th October 1945 and Nigel on 19th November 1958.

Nigel married **Gwen Eirwen Price,** from Alltgoch, St Harmon in 1992 and took the farm over. It's mixed cattle and sheep.

Their children are: **Elinor Heifena** born 9th September 1993, **Alwyn Itol** born 29th December 1994 and **Bronwen Glenys** born on 22nd May 1996.

Update to 2008
Myfanwy Megan born on 6th December 2002.

Pant-y-Rhedyn

Pant y Rhedyn appears on the 1841 census occupied by Evan George, an agricultural labourer, aged 65 years and Mary George aged 70 years. Early maps, pre-ordnance survey, show the outline of the buildings almost identical with the present, together with an area of enclosed land of approximately 7 acres. The original dwelling was a rough stone built cottage containing two ground floor rooms and two upper rooms. Probably contemporary with the cottage - an attached stone barn/stable was built butting on to the eastern gable. There does not appear to have been an original internal connecting doorway between the house and the barn. A small annexe – possibly a dairy or scullery, to the rear (north) of the cottage is shown on the early maps. This appears to have been added after the initial construction of the cottage. A free standing stone barn was built to the south of the attached barn, forming an open yard.

Census records show that the property was occupied by a succession of tenant agricultural labourers during the 19th and early 20th centuries until it was sold to become an owner/occupied private dwelling in 1950. After this sale, the living accommodation was extended to include the adjoining barn/stable. What was then believed to have been "the largest garage in Radnorshire" was added to the property in the 1970s. Electricity and telephone are the only services connected. Water is supplied from a bore-hole and from wells on land to the north.

The present owners are **Neil** and **Margaret Nuttall** who moved here from Gloucestershire in 1988 with their three children – **Jenni, Ruth** and **Thomas**. Neil and Margaret originate from Lancashire where they spent the first ten years of their married life before moving to Gloucestershire in 1978. Until his retirement in 2003 Neil was Head Teacher at Radnor Valley Primary School. Margaret taught Physical Education at Llanidloes High School before becoming a part-time Netball Development Officer for Powys County Council.

Both Neil and Margaret are active members of the Bwlch y Sarnau Community Centre committee, working to refurbish the old school building for the benefit of the local community.

Pant y Rhedyn sits on the 1400ft/430m contour above Penbryncenna Farm looking south east across to Red Lion Hill and down the Ffrydd Wen valley to Porth Farm and beyond. Close by are the ruins of numerous contemporary dwellings such as Green Well and Garreg Llywd. In the years since 2000 Pant y Rhedyn has had a new roof (timbers and slates) built by local craftsman, Robert Evans and his sons. Hopefully this will ensure its occupation well into the next millennium!

Genius Loci
- the spirit of the place -

Abbeycwmhir Community Book

Penbryncenna

The large imposing Yew tree that stands on the edge of our garden has been growing there since the house was built!

My great-grandmother moved to Penbryncennau as a widow with two sons during the 1800s. They lived in the old house situated north of the present house, little is known about it except that it had a thatched roof. Despite our efforts we have found little remains but there are four holly trees and a box tree that surrounded that dwelling.

The present house at Penbryncennau was built between 1898 and 1900. It was built by a local builder from Llanbadarn Fynydd and his total labour charge for the work was £152.00. The timber in the house is Canadian pitch pine and came by train to Pantydwr station and then by horse and cart. My grandparents George Thomas Rees and Charlotte Annie Frances Hamer (born at the neighbouring farm of Esgairfawr) married on Tuesday 24th October 1911 at Bwlch y Sarnau Baptist Church. My father was born on 23rd August 1912 followed by Annie May 16th June 1914, Winifred Doris 4th October 1916 and Sidney Hamer 13th September 1925.

My grandfather was a busy man not only farming but well known as a farrier often called in to attend sick animals at other farms (we still have some of his old tools and reference books) and also in his role as a Justice of the Peace. My aunt often told me that they saw very little of him at home!

My father George Thomas met my mother Mary Elizabeth Powell who was born and lived at the Waun Farm, Pantydwr. They were lifelong staunch members of Bwlch y Sarnau Baptist Church, dad was Deacon and Treasurer and mum was organist. My father played football for the Abbey and served in the Home Guard. My mum was a very active member of the WI. My brother Raymond Thomas was born on 24th March 1944 and I was born on 22nd March 1948 - incidentally my mother's birthday. I was very close to my maternal grandmother Mrs E A Powell, Waun Farm, she lived to be 99! Sadly my mother died on 3rd October 1974 age 63 years and so my mother and my wife were never to meet.

I, **Brian Rees** had been a keen singer for many years since Sunday School and supplemented my finances by singing in the pubs and clubs, in a country and western duo 'High Noon' during the 80s. My wife and I married on 5th August 1978 having met through the Young farmers Club when we represented our respective countries of England and Wales in Norway at the European rally of YFC in 1975. **Janet** is a Yorkshire girl from farming stock and has taught in primary schools in Powys since we married apart from 6 years at home when the children were born. She was born at Howden East Yorkshire on December 4th 1956. I took over the farm in the late 70s and changed the landscape by erecting a large stock building and silo. We have three children - **James Kinsey** born 1st June 1981, **Katie Elizabeth Mary** born 14th November 1982 and **Adam Mark** born 17th

October 1987. When the children were small Janet did a rural tourism course and we had Bed and Breakfast guests! We met a lot of interesting people including the head of Joddrell bank who spent an hour or so trying to convince Janet that it was perfectly safe to have a microwave oven but it didn't stop her keeping it out in the utility room for several years!

I joined YFC movement at the age of 19 after been dragged from the streets of Llanidloes by Martin Pugh. I owe much of my education to YFC and was very proud to gain my double gold proficiency test award after gaining 22 badges. I became involved at European level and visited many countries and had regular trips to London to meetings. In 1982 I was Chairman of England and Wales and we were fortunate to go to Buckingham Palace to a Garden Party.

Although I enjoyed farming I had a lot of problems with my back and when given the opportunity to work for the Agricultural Training Board I undertook the training with enthusiasm. From there I built up my Health and Safety Training business and grass let the farm. In the year 2000 James was living and working away from home, Katie was doing 'A' levels and Adam was in High School. Both our sons attended 2 year courses at Llysfasi Agricultural College Ruthin and now in 2008 our youngest Adam is now involved in farming Penbryncannau. We have also in 2007 built a motorcycle practise track as diversification to bring in extra income. Our daughter is a paediatric nurse and has worked at Kings College Hospital, London; Sydney Children's Hospital Australia and is at present at the Princess Elisabeth Hospital Guernsey. Our eldest son is a chef and in addition to his regular job is the proud owner of a burger van! Another change from 2008 is that Janet is now an Advisory teacher for the Foundation Phase (3 – 7 year olds) and works all around the county of Powys.

We celebrated the Millennium by having a new year party at the farm and lighting a huge bonfire on top of our hill at the back of the house – we had to make the perilous journey around the hill in trucks and cars and walk the last bit through the trees. It was well worth the effort!

Update to 2008

The change in 2008 is that most of the forestry trees have been felled and the hill stands bare.

Penbwlch

I, **Sarah Lewis,** came to Bwlch y Sarnau in May 88 from Wiltshire (although originally from London) to work at Brynhyfryd Hospital as a Sister.

My sons **Sam, Joe** and **Dylan** aged 9, 7 and nearly 2 respectively were all born in Wales.

My husband **Chris** originates from Pembrokeshire, and works on a few of the local farms.

Penpentre

Penpentre, Bwlch y Sarnau was built in 1980. It is occupied by **Edward J Harwood Jones,** now retired, who built the bungalow, and his wife ***Joanna Woodroffe.*** Edward came here in 1978 to work at a pottery in Llanidloes called Cambrian Stoneware. Joanna works from home for a National Children's Charitable Trust (thanks to modern computer technology).

It is a traditional bungalow. It was built at a time when house prices were going sky high. Unable to afford to buy a property locally even though Edward had sold a house in the Midlands, to build was the only option, as the renting of Gorffwysfa, in the village, was relatively short term. This meant he could stay in the area and support his family and continue working at Cambrian Stoneware.

The bungalow stands on a pass and has views to the Cambrian Range and on a good day to Cader Idris 50 miles away,

The existence of Castell-y-Garn, the 'domen' at the top of the hill behind the bungalow, and of many more on the hills around and the valley below is an indication that this area has been well populated since prehistoric times.

Much later came the Celts (Britons & Gaels), Romans. Normans, French and Flemish (during Henry 1st's Reign) Huguenots (persecuted by Louis XIV).

According to Richard Williams, 1871 Powys-Land Club collections, some local names reflect the Norman and French origins in such surnames as :- Brunt, Corbett, Cound, Hamer, Hibbot, Ingram, Jarman, Jervis, Jordan, Mytton, Savage, Tibbott, Woosnam to name a few. Wosencroft/Wosencraft appear to be of Anglo-Saxon origin.

The continuous swinging back and forth of the 'border" helped also with people moving in and out. Cromwells troops were also purported to have been stationed near here at one point.

The road from Bwlch y Sarnau towards Llaithddu is named on some maps as Llwybr y Gath. It appears to be the only 'named' road out of the village. The word *Gath* is Welsh for '*cat*', but in some

---

Penbwlch continued

→ Penbwlch is a Welsh long cottage - each generation/family who have lived here have added to it. The kitchen, built on by Moslyn Griffiths who grew up here, was where the geese lived when it was owned by the Griffiths family. Mr and Mrs Hall the previous occupants built on the hall and bathroom, and we have added a few rooms to it also.

In fact many local people seem to have lived here and sometime or another, it was originally a part of Bwlch y Sarnau Farm.

Homes and People

places the name may be the Irish word *Cath* meaning '*battle*'. So this may be '*The Path of the Battle*'. Only our predecessors know the answer.

It was and still is a unique area with an eclectic mix of people.

Global warming has certainly had its effect on the weather here. Winters have been much gentler now if unpredictable. We are being spoiled at present. In the winter of 1978/1979 I went back to the Midlands for Christmas. I had a telephone call on New Years day early (not a good time to get a call after a good nights celebration). It was my neighbour.

"If you want to get back you had better leave now. You might make it. They've just ploughed the road out. The snow is piled 8 feet high at the roadside! "

We left pretty quickly. We did make it back, just. The pipes were frozen in the roof, the end walls were glistening white with frost - inside the bungalow! The snow was as deep as he had said. For most of January, February, March and into April the snow came and the roads were dug out and more snow came. I lost a day a week's money for most of the time because it was impossible to get to Llanidloes through the drifts. Several days I walked and thumbed my way there and back. Thanks to some kindly neighbours I did get lifts some of the way in Land Rovers going to tend sheep.

When the snow went it rained, in fact it was a wet and dismal summer most of the time. I was wondering why on earth I had come. Its a hard country up here.

One year the Llaithddu road was closed for weeks. Snow blew off Pen y Lan Hill for hours and filled the pass below. It was twenty feet or more across the road. No one even attempted to try and dig that out. People came to see it and some friends walked across the top of the hill to visit us. It was left until the thaw. Now we grumble if we get a few inches that might disrupt traffic for an hour or so!

There is an old Radnorshire saying :- "Nine months winter three months looking for the summer"

It may have been true in the 80s but thankfully the 90s saw a change.

Specification for a Private Road (15 ft wide) and Bridleway in Inclosure Act of 1857 for Abbeycwmhir/Cefn Pawl Township. (254)

1 Piccadilly Cottages

It is said that the Cottage acquired it's unusual un-local name shortly after it was built in the 1860s when George Henry Philips was standing outside trying to think of a name when somebody walked by singing the song "Goodbye Piccadilly, Farewell Leicester Square, It's a long way to Tipperary, but my heart's just there." Out of the selection he chose "Piccadilly". (cf page 145)

Mercy Griffiths bought both numbers 1 and 2 Piccadilly Cottages (the other one is now Ty'r Ehedydd) in 1959 when the Philips estate was sold off, but only moved in finally, herself, much later in 1973. She found her way to Abbeycwmhir via Cypress.

She was born in 1924 in the small village of Limington, near Yeovil in Somerset. Her father had been a school teacher but was "knocked about", she said, in the First World War. When she was eight they moved to Cyprus where they owned and worked an olive and orange orchard. They were Quakers.

About 1947 a fellow Quaker came to stay with them who had been working in Palestine. This was Jean Hughes – to be - of Neuadd Fach. Later, when Mercy was 29, she returned to the UK and came to Neuadd Fach as a mother's help for Mrs Jean Hughes. That is how she came to Abbeycwmhir.

She soon met *Gwyn Griffiths* of Devannor and they were married on 6th June 1956 at Cefn Paul Chapel and she moved across the valley. Gwyn farmed Tyn-y-Coed and Devvnnor with Jack Griffiths and had a particularly good and favourite sheep dog called "Turk" (cf photo below.) They had five children: *John* who now lives in Oswestry, *David* who lives in Runcorn, *Clarice* who has dog kennels in Cemaes Road near Machynlleth, and the twins: *Douglas* who works in the saw mills at Newbridge and *Mary* who lives in Australia and now owns 1, Piccadily Cottages. Her sister-in-law, Ruby, lives at Crossgates.

Alas, Gwyn died very young at 46 in 1973. Later Mercy worked at the carpet factory in Llandrindod Wells as a spinner or twister, as they were called. When she retired she worked for Oxfam and delivered milk to Abbeycwmhir in her mini-car.

Mercy remembers running the youth club and dances in the Philips Hall. Also spending time with Auntie Polly sometime of Devannor and Auntie Ethel of Llwynonn. Walking from Tyn-y-Coed and doing the geese for Christmas.

Gwyn Griffiths of Tyn-y-Coed with "Turk".

NB *for 2 Piccadilly Cottages cf Ty'r Ehedydd page 260*

Homes and People

Little Plock

Jake Berriman, ***Diana Griffiths, Abe*** and ***Reuben*** moved from Cross Cottage to Little Plock at Devannor in the Autumn of 2005. The house is a modern conversion of the old French Barn which used to stand on the site and which was originally located in Devannor farmyard, and moved into the Little Plock field in the 1960s to make way for a new and larger barn. It was during this move that the old stone head was found, thought to be from the Abbey (and is now in Llandrindod Museum) A 'Plock' is, as far as we know, a Radnorshire term for a field near the *(Continued on next page →)*

Rhiw Gam

Rhiw - Gam was built in 1976 when Mr & Mrs Hamer retired from Home Farm. In 1978 Mr Hamer passed away and Mrs Hamer my Grandmother in 1995. ***Caroline Lewis*** (nee Hamer) moved here in 1996 with her two children, ***Matthew Hughes*** aged 11 and ***Janna Hughes*** aged 10. Matthew was born in Shrewsbury in 1985 and Janna was born in Llandrindod Wells in 1987. Matthew went to university in Leicester and after graduating remained there before moving to Manchester to work for Barclays Bank. Janna studied in Swansea and after graduating went on to qualify as a staff nurse and has since moved to London to work in Kings College Hospital in ITU.

In 2008 the present residents are myself who works at Llandrindod Wells Post Office and my fiancé ***Alan Lewis*** who is a Post Man in Llandrindod Wells.

I, Caroline, was born in Hereford and grew up in Abbeycwmhir until leaving for College at the age of 17 when I lodged in Hereford. Alan was born in London in 1962, moved to Cornwall in 1974, joined the RAF at the age of 17 and came to Llandrindod Wells at the age of 22. *(2009)*

Abbeycwmhir Community Book

Rose Villa

Rose Villa, a three-bedroom stone built cottage has remained virtually unchanged in character since it was built c1960 with the exception of large bar/workshop which was built by a previous occupant c 1975.

However, in 1983, renovation work was carried out - whereby new roofing timbers and tiles were replaced and new windows were fitted. Internal improvements were also made.

The earliest known occupant residing at Rose Villa we understand was a Mr Lewis Jones and wife (buried in the Baptist Churchyard, Bwlch y Samau) who died on 20 November 1885 and reputed to have been a 'tailor' by trade. Over the remaining years up until present time, Rose Villa has had many owners and was previously used as a small holding and other business ventures.

Andy and **Jane Thornicroft** bought the cottage set in almost two acres of land, including two ponds, a spinney and stream in June 1997, for the purpose of starting a wholesale nursery and decided to call it 'Rose Villa Nurseries'.

The wholesale nursery supplies plants to the local retail shops and garden centres in Llanidloes, Newtown, Llandrindod Wells and surrounding areas.

Jane was born in Coventry and lived and worked in Coventry until moving to Bwlch y Samau in June 1997. She was previously employed at the University of Warwick as a Secretary.

Andy, was born in Leamington Spar, Warwickshire and lived in a village called 'Harbury' which is situated close to Leamington Spa and Warwick, later moved to Coventry before moving to Bwlch y Samau in June 1997.

Andy and I had spent over a year looking in many parts of the country travelling down to Cornwall and Devon then back to Lincolnshire before looking in Shropshire but to no avail. Then one day, whilst visiting friends in Shropshire we travelled over the border into mid-Wales and loved it so much we decided to purchase 'Rose Villa'.

→ *Little Plock continued*

homestead – there is a field named 'Big Plock' also. So the house is named after the field in which it stands. In 2008 we installed solar panels generating hot water, and in 2010 solar photo-voltaic panels generating electricity. All our hot water from April to October is generated by the sun, and the peak capacity of the PV panels exceeds our annual electricity consumption. This is an attempt to reduce our dependency on fossil fuels and lower our carbon footprint and save money on fuel bills. Jake works in Shrewsbury for Shropshire Council and Diana in Llanidloes for an Environmental Charity. Reuben attends Cross Gates Primary School and Abe is about to start Llandrindod High School. (2010)

The Old School

As the name suggests, this building used to be the village school, built by the Philips' family in 1868. It ceased being a school in 1970 and in 1972, Mr Knox, a retired headmaster from Leominster purchased it with the intention of using it as a holiday retreat for underprivileged boys. His plans didn't come to fruition though as he later suffered a severe stroke.

We moved into the valley in 1995 after buying 2, Piccadilly Cottage which is opposite the School. We'd always admired the building and thought it would make a great home and wrote to Mr Knox asking if he would consider selling it. We were delighted when he said he would and it became ours in 2001.

It was in a sorry state after being empty and neglected for so long. It took us two years to renovate and convert it. We spend those two years in a caravan in the school yard alternately freezing or roasting. It was worth it though as we have created a lovely home. Peter did most of the work here himself working long into the night to get things finished. I, **Sandra,** did all the planning and made sure Peter's stomach was kept fuelled with 'tough guy's grub'! Renovating has been a big part of our lives. We've bought many wrecks of houses over the years and transformed them into lovely homes. It was a dirty, tiring and frustrating job, especially as we had to leave them just as they became fit to live in – and then start all over again. We both agree, though, that the School was our most challenging and fulfilling, and we are very proud of it.

Peter Bowen and I were both born in Worcestershire, Peter in 1950 and me in 1952. We met in 1969, were married in 1971 and had our first daughter **Emma** in 1974 and our second, **Charlotte** in 1977. Emma is an occupational therapist, is married to Kevin, an American and lives in Indiana.

Charlotte is a graduate consultant and lives and works in Manchester.

Peter has worked in agriculture most of his life, mainly as a herdsman, but after moving to Wales in 1987 to a smallholding we had bought in Llanyre. He worked at Mid-Wales Yarns and later at Forest Fencing .

I worked as a laboratory assistant and clerk until becoming a full time Mum. We were also foster parents for a while.

Peter has now taken on the mammoth task of being my carer due to my having a

The Old School continued

debilitating disease. That and gardening are his main occupations at this time. Mine are threatening to sack him on a nearly daily basis and also finding lots of things to moan about. Our lives are mostly spiced up by having dozens of rows a day, mainly due to us both being diabetics and one or other of us having either high or low blood sugars which tend to make us tired and cranky. Miraculously though we haven't killed each other yet and remain two big happy puddings most of the time. We find plenty of things to laugh and smile about and love living in this valley in all it's glorious seasons. Winter is the best. We go into hibernation in late October, cosying down and snuggling up to the fire keeping our "nuts and berries" warm and emerge around April when Peter starts the garden again – and I usually turn around and go back to the fire!

Hobbies: We love studying wildlife which we have plenty of here and we go to the Pembrokeshire Coast to watch the sea life there too. My family and ancestors are from Neyland so we know the area well. Peter sea fishes but prefers to fish rivers. The fish tease Peter for hours but occasionally they feel sorry for him and throw themselves on to the hook – but not as often as he'd like. He's very good at gardening though and grows a mean onion.

I like drawing, painting and reading but I'm best at being a couch potato. I would like to try something exciting though, like sky diving but I fear that at my size that could start off an earth extinction level shockwave on impact which could make the New Mexico event which wiped out the Dinosaurs, look like a tiny blip.

Memorable Moments here: Mine would be watching Mel from Home Farm crash rolling his tractor down the hill at the side of Piccadilly Cottage like an ace stunt man and then walking away with all his body bits still attached. Also, one Autumn morning watching a horse galloping along the top of the hill at the back of the school, when suddenly she skidded onto her backside and then tobogganed down the hill with her hind legs up around her ears. At the bottom she got up, shook herself and, I swear, walked off looking extremely embarrassed.

And talking of swearing, Peter's memories are of working in the garden over the years listening to the sound of the sheep or cattle being rounded up and moved. He's come to the conclusion that all the farm dogs around here have exactly the same name. It's an amazing co-incidence, but it is true. They all seemed to be called "**cking Bastard". No boring old names like Rex or Rover round here. Peter's considering calling our next dog "**cking Bitch" so that she fits in with the rest, but I've told him not to whilst I'm still on the planet.

As to our aspirations for the future?

We're too boring, we haven't got any! But if we had any wishes we'd wish that all children were taught that evil, cruelty, selfishness and greed were wrong and that tolerance and a love of this planet and the plants and trees and creatures they shared it with was right. Then the earth would be in capable hands.

And on a less serious note, we'd wish that the earth would never run out of chocolate.

(2008)

Homes and People

School House - Cwmlliw

The first people we know of who lived here were Mill and Amy Wozencraft. They were followed by Reg and Ellen Hamer who came here in 1957. We came in 1997.

Clinton Webb was born in Barhrain and has lived in Dubai, London and Milton Keynes

Valerie Webb was born in Llandrindod Wells and has lived in Llanidloes, London and Milton Keynes where ***Yvonne*** and ***Jamie*** were born and were brought up for a while. Both Clinton and Valerie work at Mid Wales Yarns Ltd.

Valerie's reason for living here is "that it has been my home all my life and we love it, it's a great place to bring up children."

Her special memory is of when she was a little girl, "Meryl and I would go out on the horses for hours on end without anyone worrying about us at all."

Home Farm pond in Colonel Philips' time (255)

Abbeycwmhir Community Book

The Smithy

The Smithy was the village Blacksmith's shop. Many people who lived and worked here remember Jack Went, the last working blacksmith, who lived and worked here from about 1918 until his death in 1972. In that time the building consisted of a 1 bedroom cottage and blacksmiths workshop but was subsequently converted to its present form.

The Smithy, or Vulcan Hall as it was originally known, is the home of **Tony, Anne, Katy** and **James Stock** (in 2000). We have lived in Abbeycwmhir, at The Smithy, since Dec 18th 1987, but we are not strangers to the area as we have family living in Llandrindod Wells.

Katy, 23 years old, and James 21 years old, both attended Crossgates Primary School and Llandrindod High School. Katy went on to The University of Derby and she now works in Derby. James is a third year student at the University of Leeds. Tony is well known as the carpet man and Anne works for Powys County Council in the Education Department.

Update to 2008

The Smithy, is now home to **Kerrie Harries** & **Matty, (Neil Matheson)** and their 2 cats Molly and Oska.

We moved into the Smithy at the end of May 2007, after living in Knighton and Norton. We have family in Knighton and Llandrindod Wells so we haven't ventured too far.

Matty was born in Llandrindod in 1968 and Kerrie was born in Birmingham in 1974. Matty is a plasterer, well known round the Knighton area, and Kerrie works in the fraud department at M & M Direct in Leominster.

We came to live in the area after failing to settle in Canada and having had our dreams shattered we decided to return to Wales. We decided on Abbeycwmhir after taking my Mum to the big house as a birthday treat and fell in love with the area. After a trip to the beach on bank holiday we drove through the village and spotted the Smithy was for sale, the rest is history.

According to the previous occupants the Smithy was the old Blacksmiths, which consisted of a one bedroom cottage belonging to a man called Jack Went, but has since been considerably renovated into what it is today. (cf p 99 & 101)

Homes and People

Stonesthrow

The reason it is called 'Stonesthrow' is because it is a stone's throw away from our former home Hazeldene.

Gwyn Rees was born in Llanidloes and originally lived at Bwlch y Sarnau Farm where he farmed along with his father and when alive his grandfather. Hazeldene was built in 1974. Stonesthrow was built in 1992 and Gwyn and ***Ceri*** still live there.

Gwyn and Ceri have lived in the area all their lives. Ceri was born in Llandrindod Wells and except for a short spell during her formative years lived elsewhere. Eventually along with her family she moved to Yronen Farm in Nantmel. This was the original family farm where her father had grown up. She resided there until 1974 until she married Gwyn in the same year and moved to Hazeldene.

May and Archie Rees (Gwyn's parents) moved to Rhayader Christmas 2007. The reason we live at Bwlch y Sarnau is because Gwyn farms there.

Bwlch y Sarnau Farm was sold on 31st March 2009. At present it is unoccupied but the land is being farmed. Gwyn has retained some of the original land and it is still used for agricultural purposes.

Marc married Rachel on July 29th 2009 presently he lives in Newtown – eventually he intends to build a house and live in Bwlch y Sarnau. My eldest daughter ***Cherie*** is married to Will and lives in Pantydwr with her young son Jacob. ***Emma*** and ***Nichole*** still live at home. Emma works at the Gwalia in Llandrindod Wells. Nichole works for the NHS.

Sunnydale

Rob, myself and our daughter Amy came to Sunnydale Bungalow when she was just 8 months old, in July 1992. Sunnydale had stood empty for some years after the death of the previous owner Violet Price, who lies in the cemetery of the nearby Cefn Pawl chapel, itself now a memory of those left who once worshiped there.

For us Sunnydale and the valley where we now spend our lives has become home. We love the changing pattern of

Sunnydale continued

the seasons here. The wonderful landscape-scape with its rich tapestry of woodland, farmland and its history, which in many ways you can still feel as you live and work in the countryside around you.

It is this echo of the past and landscape that my husband Rob finds inspiring and daunting in his work as a landscape artist, with images for his paintings at every turn. I have a passion for growing plants and from humble beginnings (one small greenhouse) the nursery has blossomed and evolved. Sunnydale is an apt name for the nursery and plants grow well in this sheltered acre. Working with plants you work with the seasons, as with farming, which I find brings me closer to nature.

Our daughter Amy shares our life and wonder for where we live, and in a changing world she feels a warmth and security at home in the valley.

For us the spirit of Violet Price is still at Sunnydale and as time passes by the Parkin family know that they are sharing just a tiny moment of the valley's long history.

Robert Parkin Born 1955 Ilkeston, Derbyshire, Qualified in horticulture, conservation and art married, in 1977, **Angela Clare Parkin**, Born 1955 in Edgeware, Middlesex, Qualified in horticulture & conservation. **Amy Claire Parkin,** Born 1991 in Hereford. Pupil at Crossgates Primary School.

Update to 2008

Peter Kirk Born 1945 Warsop, Notts. Retired Building Surveyor
Wendy Kirk Born 1945 Ebbw Vale Retired Civil Servant, Artist & Plantswomen

We moved here in 2006 so are very much newcomers to the valley, but feel accepted and at home here in Abbeycwmhir. We both fell in love with Sunnydale the moment we saw it and whilst the once used nursery was a possibility for us, sense took over soon after we settled in with the pleasure of working on the house and garden being enough for us.

The place is peaceful, the location is beautiful and the people great, do we need more……...........?

Tri Mynydd

Tri Mynydd was built in 1984 by **Colin Wozencraft**, an Agricultural Contractor who was born at Cefn Pawl, Abbeycwmhir. It is situated on Glyndwr's Way, overlooking St Mary's Church and approximately 100 yards from the Village Square.

Mr Don Richards, a friend of the family, who took a great interest in the history of Abbeycwmhir and had spent many holidays in the village visited the bungalow whilst in the building stage and suggested the name Tri Mynydd. Tri Mynydd means three mountains and from the back door you look out on Sugar Loaf, Little Park and Great Park.

On 13 October 1984, Colin married **Anne**, (a Radnorshire girl and the daughter of Doug Evans, Fronwen, Dolau,) at Gravel Baptist Chapel and following that, moved into Tri Mynydd. Anne worked in the Education Department of Powys County Council in Llandrindod Wells.

Sandy was the first addition to the family in May 1987 – a Pembrokeshire Corgi with a tail, who looked more like a fox than a dog and had to be shut in every time there was a fox hunt in the area. Sandy was vehicle mad and would spend all day every day with Colin in the tractor. In hot weather Colin took the windows out of the tractor and Sandy would sit on the back mudguard much to the amusement of people who could not believe that he never fell off.

At 03.24 a m on Friday, 20 December 1991, with snow falling, **Ellen Louise** was born in Hereford County Hospital and came home on 23 December 1991, to spend her first Christmas at Tri Mynydd.

In October 1994 Colin was diagnosed with a very rare illness and despite undergoing treatment lost his battle for life on Sunday 21 January 1996. On Saturday, 27 January 1996, when the ground was frozen solid and deep snow lay everywhere, Colin was buried in St Mary's Churchyard and from the yard of Tri Mynydd you can look down on his grave.

At the time of the millennium Anne and Ellen still live at Tri Mynydd, Anne working for Powys County Council and Ellen attending Llandrindod Wells C P School – Cefnllys.

In August 2001 Sandy died of old age and is buried in the front garden at Tri Mynydd,

In October 2004 Ellen had two kittens, a ginger and white one with a kinky tail,
which she named Oscar and a jet black one named Charlie.

Update to 2008

The Wozencraft's are still at Tri Mynydd, Anne continues to work for Powys County Council and currently Ellen is sitting her GCSEs at Llandrindod High School. Ellen will attend the 6th Form in Llandrindod High School in September 2008 and eventually hopes to fulfil her lifelong ambition to become a primary school teacher.

Trinnant

Near Lizdart–y-Waen*, Tylwch, Llanidloes, (*for convenience of the Post Office!)

The farm is now 240 acres, Lower land adjoining Prysgduon bought plus part of new house (Flying Gate).

David is the fourth generation of Hamers to live here. The house is a basic two up two down with one large fireplace. In recent years the adjoining stable has been made into a bathroom, bedroom and sitting room.

Vernwyn Thomas Hamer, born in Llanidloes always lived here.

Sarah Anne Edwards (partner) was born in Llandrindod Wells from a farm called Foesidoes, Cascob, Presteigne, Powys. (Grandmother is a Pugh from Brondre Fawr.)

We both work at home on the farm.

David Thomas Hamer, Age 7 was born in Aberystwyth.

The Welsh Section 'C' Ponies here are registered with the prefix "Cwmhir".

Trinnant circa 1955

Trinnant circa 1964 with Dorothy Blodwen, Rose Hamer and Eileen Davies.

Trinnant Prysdwen   *Trinnant circa 2008*

Troedrhiwfelin

Troedrhiwfelen means "at the foot of the "yellow" hill"

Troedrhiwfelen is actually formed from three original buildings with the land possibly forming part of the estate belonging to the Cistercian Abbey in the village. The lower and middle sections of the house formed the original residential parts with the upper section being a granary dating from around the 1700s. Old army maps of Radnorshire surveyed in the early 1800s show Troedrhiwfelen existed in its current form then.

The old granary is now the main living area with the other sections having been former servants quarters and stables. These lower sections were re-bricked in 1904 and 1934 respectively. We are currently extending the accommodation into these lower sections once more.

I believe there is some evidence of roman occupation of the site with, I understand, remains of a roman road running above the property to the east. Whilst clearing old pools to the south of the house, we found quern stones which have been described by the local museum as being of roman origin with later mill stones found in other excavations on the site. The pools themselves also had a considerable ash deposit layer which may have come from a smithy or forge. Indeed, recent visitors to Troedrhiwfelen who were tracing their own ancestry (Griffiths) and who were, they believed, early forge-masters in South Wales, are understood to originally have come from here. It would appear they moved to South Wales in the 1680's and are purported to have built the first iron bridge there.

Since 1983 **Bernie** and **Karen Pugh** have been the occupants of Troedrhiwfelin. Bernie was born at Cwmglascwm in Nantmel parish and took over Troedrhiwfelen from his grandfather who, although born here, only bought the property off the Hall estate in 1933.

We run an off-road driving school and also host bike events and shows.

This is the family home with my great grandfather (Lewis) having moved into Troedrhiwfelen around 1889 from Tynyberth. My paternal grandfather (Lewis) was born at Troedrhiwfelen, in 1901, as was my mother in 1926. She went on to marry John Pugh of Cwmglascwm. Grandfather Lewis was one of eleven children living at Troedrhiwfelen, eight girls and three boys, with a number of the girls marrying into local families in this and neighbouring valleys.

Ty Cartreff

Ty-Cartreff was built in 1977 for my parents Elsie and Meredith Wozencraft to spend their retirement years. It was built on the edge of the farm Cefn Pawl where my father lived and farmed for most of his life. I was born at Llandrindod Wells hospital, I lived at Cefn Pawl with my family until 1977, then moved into Ty-Cartreff until I married in 1978 in St Mary's church, Abbeycwmhir. My parents lived at Ty-Cartreff until Mr Wozencraft died in 2004 at the age of 90. Now it is owned by myself **Christine Powel** and husband **Eithyl**. Currently our daughter and her son live at Ty-Cartreff.

Ty Nant

Is a new house built on Mel's field and finished in 2008. It was built largely by **Darren Peel** for himself and **Maria** his wife and family.

Darren comes from Llandrindod Wells and Rhayader and works as an agricultural builder and steel fabricator.

Maria has lived in Llanidloes and Rhayader and works as a mother and secretary.

They hacve three children: **Eloise** (6yrs) born in June 2002; **Kieran** (3yrs) born in February 2006 and **Ethan** born in Abbeycwmhir in February 2009.

They like Abbeycwmhir for its peace and quiet.

Looking west from Camlo Hill

Homes and People

Tynyberth

John, Lynne, Jack and ***Danny Lydiate.*** We took over Tynyberth family farm in September 1994 from Lynne's parents Doug and Joan Price. We moved here from Llandewi in April 1995.

Lynne's family home for 4 generations. John's home is in Salford England. John is one of 7 children his father, grandfather and great grandfather all worked on the docks in Salford, John used to until it closed down. His great grandmother came from Newtown so there is Welsh blood in him yet!! John is also a qualified swimming instructor. Jack is 14 and Danny is 12, both play rugby for Llandrindod High School and also play for Powys and Builth Wells Club. Lynne is a S.R.H (State registered hairdresser) she enjoys competing in local cookery shows.

Update to 2008

Jack (23) played rugby for Welsh Colleges and was picked to represent Great Britain and won four out of five games. He was the signed for Ebbw Vale and went on to Llandovery for a season and then Pontypool. Unfortunately he dislocated his ankle and broke his leg playing for them and had three major ops and pins inserted to plate his leg together and was out for the rest of the season.

Danny (21) Had five Welsh caps for the under 20s and played against Ireland, Scotland, England, France and Italy. He went to the Gwent Academy and is now professional for the Gwent Dragons, Newport. He broke his neck at Pepereian in France playing for the Gwent Dragons, had major surgery and was out for a season. He is now back playing for the Gwent Dragons.

Lynne's still busy having joined the Bwlch y Sarnau flower arranging club. She has many inspirations at competitions and enjoys arranging the pedestal of flowers at Rock Baptist Chapel once a month and provides the flowers for wedding and funerals. She also helps at "The Hall" in the Abbey for floral decorations.

Left*: Abbeycwmhir from west of the Clywedog. On the right is School House, once called Cwm Lliw meaning colourful valley (257).*

Tyn y Coed

Tom Griffiths was born and brought up at Devannor farm.

Brenda's father, William Hardwick, took the tenancy of Cwmcringlyn in 1957. Tom & **Brenda** got married in 1966 and purchased a small dairy farm in Carmarthenshire.

In 1975 when Brenda's father retired they took over the tenancy of Cwmcringlyn and bought Tyn y Coed off the Griffiths family.

They finally came to live at Tyn y Coed in 2001 where a new house was built in 1995 and are supposed to be semi-retired!!

Ty'r Eherdydd

I, *Julian Lovell,* came to live in Abbeycwmhir in April 2007. My house was formerly called 2 Piccadilly Cottage but I changed the name to Ty'r Ehedydd which means the Lark House. Piccadilly, although the traditional estate name, sounded too English for me! (cf page 145.)

To the best of my knowledge the house was built in 1868 as part of the rebuilding and expansion which took place on the estate at that time, when the present church was built and the school relocated to the site opposite me. In the early 1990's the house was renovated and 'updated', the kitchen and the porch extensions were added and the windows replaced, although by then, as 1 recently learnt from an aerial photograph, the original windows had already gone (circa 1960-64). The weather side walls were also slate hung at that time. Peter Bowen Old School, has a copy of the photograph. As part of the renovation the roof space was converted to make additional attic bedrooms, so the cottage now has four bedrooms, as well as a large dining room and sitting room, kitchen, utility and upstairs bathroom. It has mains water, electricity and a BT connection.

Previous Owners were: 2000-2007- Rachel and Gary Haggety; 1994-2000 - Peter and Sandra Owen; 1990-1994 - Douglas Griffiths; 1959-1990 - Mercy Griffiths.

Prior to 1959 the house was owned by the Abbeycwmhir estate and saw a number of tenants. I am the only person living here now. I am not from Radnorshire. My family came in part from Pembrokeshire and Montgomeryshire but like many Welsh families became very dispersed during the first half of the 20th Century. I have relatives near Narberth, Pembrokeshire, Aberaeron, Ceridigion and Abersychan in S.Wales. Before coming to live here I was away working in Gloucestershire. I am a teacher by profession and have just completed 39 years working in a variety of schools. My main teaching subjects are Geography and History.

I came to live here because I wanted to be within a ten mile radius of Rhaedr. It is an area I have known and loved since my youngest days and the way of life suits my temperament. It is a welcoming community and I feel as though I have never lived anywhere else. The

Homes and People

associations of Abbeycwmhir with Welsh history has a great appeal for me. I am involved with quite a few things in the local area. As a lay preacher, regularly taking services, I have made a lot of contacts with the local chapels and churches and made many new friends. I am a member of the Rhaeadr Male Voice choir and the Voices in Unity choir which is also based in Rhaeadr. I am a member of the mid-Wales Geology Club and enjoy researching local and family history. I have always been a keen walker and mountain climber and there are lots of opportunities in this part of Wales. I am also able to indulge my love of mountain biking. I am a member of the BTO and the Radnorshire Wildlife Trust.

Ty'r Eherdydd drawn by Mercy Griffiths

I found everybody here to be most welcoming and friendly. It is a great privilege to live in such a beautiful village and to be able to make a contribution to the way of life which we enjoy. I hope that in the long term the valley and surrounding areas will not become spoilt by developments which are out of character with the high quality of the landscape of Radnorshire. It would be nice to see some official protections put in place.

Ventic

The Ventic (or Fanteg) was, we understand, built by a woodsman working for the Penybont estate, who obtained the piece of land on which it stands from the Abbeycwmhir estate. Ventic means, we think, "a pleasant place".

The earliest date confirmed by the census is 1841, when the Ventic was inhabited by John and Elizabeth Edwards together with their four children, John, Richard, Thomas and Elizabeth. Also mentioned was Sarah Jones, perhaps a member of the family or mother's help. Miss Elizabeth Davies who left it to Dorothy Prosser. It was then sold to Geoffrey Barnsley and finally on the 3rd August 1961 to our grandpa Mr A J McDonagh. Upon his death in November 1961 the Ventic passed through the family and the cottage now belongs to **Jean** and **Catherine** and is used as a holiday home.

The Old Vicarage (Brynmoel)

The current owners of the Old Vicarage in Abbeycwmhir, **Barry** and **Jenny Williams,** are led to understand that the house was completed in 1893 in time for the wedding in September of the vicar to one of George Henry Philips' daughters from The Hall. It is further understood that the Philips injected money into the construction of Brynmoel, as it was known then, because it was the intended eventual place of residence for one of them. Changes to death duty laws and other peripheral financial difficulties meant that these intentions had to be put to one side. So the property, following its extravagant build with hand cast JCE bricks from Lancashire and bevel cut Westmoreland green slates, would you believe in the middle of Wales, became a home and work place for a succession of vicars who conducted matters at St Mary's Church in Abbeycwmhir. The Church was delighted with the Philips' financial input during the construction of Brynmoel, which boasts masonry reveals to all windows and an abundance of stained glass throughout the ground floor. Vicarages were traditionally fine houses but Brynmoel with its two dozen plus rooms was a little extraordinary even by Church of Wales standards because, as already noted, one of the Philips wished to eventually vacate the Hall and live there.

It was sited facing south in a perfect position in the middle of the original road to Newtown which used to pass the Fanteg and Dyfanor. Allegedly, the Philips in agreement with the church acquired the services of the architect Stephen William Williams to design Brynmoel and records in the National Library of Wales confirm this fact and it was a rare excursion for the architect whose work centred on public buildings as opposed to private dwellings. His initial work as a land and civil engineer meant that he spent many years preparing plans for the rapidly growing railway network. He was posted to Rhayader 1862 to work on the proposed railway to Aberystwyth. Although this line was never built he must have seen opportunities for a man with his skills, for shortly after arriving he left his employer and set up in the town in private practice. He travelled all over mid Wales surveying for the new railway network and within a few months had married Maria James of Penralley House in Rhayader.

Coming back to the Old Vicarage known then as Brynmoel, to the current owner's knowledge, the nearest example of other work by the celebrated Stephen William Williams is the beautifully

Ventic continued

Update to 2008

Madge Sinnock, my Mum, sadly passed away in 2003 .Jean and Alan live in Great Malvern, and their daughter Tracey lives in Witney, Oxfordshire, with Stefan. Catherine and Robin live in Kibworth Beauchamp, Leicester, with their daughter Rosemary.

elaborate Police Station and Court Rooms in the nearby market town of Rhayader. As County surveyor he built the delightful Erwood Bridge, rebuilt many others and was then asked to rebuild the above mentioned Police Station and Court Rooms. His eye catching design was duly noted by the local gentry and as his private work became very much in the ascendancy by the late 1870s/1880s it must have been at this time that he was brought to the attention of Colonel Philips, hence their coming together on the creation of Brynmoel.

An additional factor here would be Stephen Williams' interest in Cistercian architecture and his visits to the ruins in Abbeycwmhir must have been a further opportunity for their getting together. Amongst his more public work was the churches he completely rebuilt at Llanyre, Llanbadarn Fawr and Llanddewi Ystradenni parish churches in Radnorshire. He restored parish churches at Llanhamlach, Llanfigan and Llanafan Fawr in Breconshire and he was also responsible for the completely new All Saints church in the Decorated style at Newbridge on Wye, for which he built his only lofty spire. Williams also built the small chapel of ease at Nantgwyllt in the Elan Valley, which was needed to replace the older building lost under the waters of the newly developed reservoir. When the Elan Valley reservoir system was first conceived it was inevitable that someone of Williams' ability would be utilised and so he also assisted in the planning and building of the workers' village.

Basrry, Charlotte, Jenny., James and Rosanna at Christmas 1999 just before The Millennium.

So that completes the story of how the Old Vicarage of Abbeycwmhir, then known as Brynmoel, came about. Brynmoel meaning "bare hill" in Welsh certainly applied at the time of construction when Abbeycwmhir was bedecked with rich hills of indigenous heather and whimberries as opposed to the imported forestry which has completely changed the local landscape in some cases to people's liking in others maybe not.

It must have been following the sale of Brynmoel by the Church into public ownership in 1952 when the house took on the name by which it is known today as it had become, definitively, The Old Vicarage. The original name lingers on in some official correspondence and Ordinance Survey maps but the house has enjoyed being known by its new name for nearly 60 years now. In all that time the property has been in domestic use as opposed to its former days with a vicar in residence offering parishioners afternoon tea and advice and occasionally in fine weather allowing Sunday School to take place in the garden.

At one time sadly the house was quite crudely divided to create two dwellings. There was of course ample space for this but it was most alien to the original design of this property. Tasteless plumbing and electricity was run across surfaces and down walls destroying, in some cases, elegant

The Old Vicarage continued

coving in order to create a kitchen at the opposite end to the original; thankfully this period came to an end and the property once again returned to single ownership.

When the current owners took possession in 1986 the extra kitchen and disastrous partitioning in the house had thankfully been removed. It was, "a can of worms" when we first took control of the house and at the time we were confronted with continuous headaches due to some of the astonishing work carried out by the previous owner, or to be accurate, on his behalf.

Looking back we often dine out on some of the recollections, the worst of which was prior to the house being repossessed. The previous owner, who allegedly indulged in a drink from time to time, came home the worst for wear, loaded a huge multi-fuel boiler to the brim with dry kindling, not appreciating that the central heating system had not been completed with the safety feature of an expansion tank in the roof, left the bottom of the boiler open in order to catch light. He omitted to close it down and instead just fell sound asleep on his bed. This was a home made bomb scenario and in hind sight, thank heavens, he was sound asleep elsewhere in such a solidly built house. Meanwhile the boiler packed with dry timber was developing enormous heat and therefore the explosion that eventually took place was immense. In a smaller less sturdy modern property for example, somebody could have been killed. As it was we don't even know if it woke him up!!"

"He", being the person in question will remain nameless in this article, but he was allegedly removed from the house when it was repossessed by the bank because none of the due mortgage instalments had been paid over several years - and he was a solicitor!!! Allegedly the solicitor in town handling the repossession of the property for the Bank decided to enter into an exchange race and try and buy the property themselves for speculative reasons. Scurrilous behaviour by someone who thought himself a large fish in a small pond; what he didn't know is that our solicitor was a large shark in the ocean and we ate him for supper!

What we do know is that, as we took possession, the legacy of the work attempted by the above mentioned previous owner, particularly in his final months at the property, turned into a catastrophe that was there for all to see. Cupboards and doors had been obliterated and crudely replaced, but the long term damage was weeks of work for local builder Brian Parfitt rectifying the huge cracks and shakes in all the rooms and ceilings on the first floor, not to

The Old Vicarage (Brynmoel) in 1955.

Homes and People

mention the renovation of the main leaded stained glass windows on the middle landing that were bellowed outwards like the sails of an old fashioned galleon, making attempts to heat the property, apart from some individual rooms, a fruitless exercise.

Despite all those hurdles in those early years, it has been a labour of love at the Old Vicarage and a generation of hard work with the skills of many local craftsmen returning the property to its former Victorian elegance. It has been a fantastic family home and our three children, **Charlotte**, **James** and

The Vicarage at the Millennium.

Rosanna all thoroughly enjoyed growing up here and although they have all flown the nest, as they say, they all get back to the Vicarage on every occasion they can. In particular, Christmas has always been rather special and for some 15 years or more now the village is invited for drinks, food and festivities to enjoy the traditional fare on offer. My favourite recollections are however, the time, when as a surprise, I had arranged for the Rhayader Male Voice Choir to entertain us with a concert standing four abreast up the stairs, all 32 of them! The villagers not only loved that evening but as you would expect from the land of song all as one heartily joined in. So many faces have gone since that memorable night. Although there have been others that we have lost I particularly remember Byron and Colin Wozencraft and Dai the Union thoroughly enjoying proceedings and the ambience of it all."

The Old Vicarage (Brynmoel) in 2005.

To conclude, as you can now see, the Old Vicarage, formerly Brynmoel, has had a very full existence to date and for the last 22 years it has, especially for us, been a wonderful family home. It is our sincere wish, whoever the new owners will be one day, that they are part of a large family, as we once were, giving The Old Vicarage the opportunity to continue, what we consider to be the best part of its history, by simply being just a family home.

Waun Pistyll

A stone built, white-washed small house (two-up, two-down) with an adjoining farmer's barn-cow-house, situated on the roadside just within the Parish Boundary of Abbeycwmhir by about 400 metres. Bwlch y Sarnau being the nearest village, the road leading to Llidiart-y-Waun.

Waun Pistyll once had approximately 12.5 acres of adjoining fields between the road and the River Marteg. These fields are now farmed by a neighbouring farmer. Waun Pistyll would then, perhaps, be described as a small holding; the owner needing to have other full time work. Waun Pistyll is now lived in by myself, **Bryn Stonebridge** who is not a native of this area and being resident here for only the last sixteen years – living here permanently, that is.

The first known deeds of the house record a transaction of ownership in 1854 for the sum of £80. The house being named Waen Pistyll and having eight acres of ground. The present Forestry Commission plantation opposite the house being described as waste, common ground. At about 100 metres into the forestry there is a spring which, perhaps, gives an explanation of the name of the house. The deeds for 1925, 1933, 1980 give the property being named "New House". This name reverting to "Waun Pistyll" before I came to live here.

I was born and bred in Croydon, Surry. The family connection that I have with Rhayader is that my grandparents lived there, though my grandfather, a carpenter, was a native of Blithfield, Staffordhire and came to this area to work on the construction of the Birmingham Corporation dams in the Elan Valley in the late 1890s. My father was born and bred in Rhayader but left in his teens to join the RAF as an apprentice carpenter and subsequently always worked away. His retirement back to Rhayader brought myself likewise and then myself to Waun Pistyll.

In January 1974 I was employed by Birmingham Corporation to work on the Elan Dams Estate. In April of that year, Severn Trent Water took over the pipe line and Bryn was then employed by Welsh Water and its Trust to work on the watershed's forestry and land. When he started there were fourteen men working and when he finished just himself and another.

Update to 2008

Bryn retired in 2005 at 65 years.

1 Wenallt Cottages

The Philips family built and owned the two cottages. Doreen Hughes now lives in number one, but her grandparents and parents had lived in number two. Her grandfather was shepherd to the Hall. Her mother bought number one for £225 in the 1950s after living at Nanteos and Cwmydea where her father died when he was 50 years old. She remembers having to put out the lights and the fire because of German bombers overhead during the First World War. They also moved out for a while to Garden Cottage whilst the extensions on the side of the cottages were built. 1,Wennalt Cottage has a spring half way up Wennalt Hill but number two is on the village mains.

Doreen Hughes, born in 1937 as Doreen Owens, is first cousin to Lyndsey Williams of Bwlch y Sarnau Manse and her sister, Mary is married to Albert Phillips of 2,Cwmhir Cottages. Her son, **Gwyn** was married to Brian Parfitt's daughter, Maxine, of Mill Cottage and is the Parking Attendant in Llandrindod Wells. Doreen had two older brothers both of whom died, Idris at 51 and Dennis at 58 years old.

Doreen attended Bwlch y Sarnau Primary School where the teacher was Miss Ingram. She remembers when the Llaithddu School was burned down and all the children came to Bwlch y Sarnau making it very crowded indeed. Doreen went on to attend Brynterion School in Rhayader.

From the age of sixteen she worked for Colonel Philips at The Hall, cleaning and cooking, and helped to pack up The Hall when the Philips moved out to Ivy Lodge in Hereford. She went on to work in the "Welsh Arms" public house in Llandewi and, for six and a half years, at The Happy Union and shop with Dai and Violet Jones.

She married **Jim Hughes** in 1957. He was one of twelve children from "Old House" Llaithddu all of whom were singers. Jim also had a good voice but sometimes sang out of tune! He worked for the Forestry Commission for 38 years as a planter. He could often be heard singing in the woods. He died in 2006 from a heart attack whilst loading a trailer in the yard – singing away!

They have five grandchildren - four boys and a girl. The eldest, Ieuan, (20yrs) is studying music at Hereford College and, Cheyenne (7 yrs) sang in the Llandrindod Wells Eisteddfod – the singing tradition goes on in the third generation.

Doreen cleaned St.Mary's Church for forty four years and remembers the autumn colours of the oaks on Sugar Loaf Hill opposite the house before the forestry came.

Blessed is the eye
Betwixt the Severn and Wye.

2 Wenallt Cottages

I believe that 2 Wenallt Cottage was built by the Philips Estate to house the Estate Shepherd. I do not know when the Cottage was built. The Cottage has two bedrooms, a bathroom, a living room and a back kitchen with a pantry. There were the usual out buildings including toilet and wash house. There is also a large garden.

Before the water was piped to the house from the well in the spring near the top of the Wenallt Hill in 1934, we used to have to carry water from the well on the edge of the 'Planting' which is situated at the far side of the field next to number 1 Wenallt Cottage. In 1959 the house was wired for electricity and in 1968 the Cottage was further modernised with the installation of a hot water system and a septic tank. These improvements made life so much easier. Lindsey piped water mains.

The cottage is presently owned by **Elsie May Williams**. After my parents, John Williams (native of Philander) and Margaret Jane George (native of Abbeycwmhir) got married they came to live at 2 Wenallt Cottage and my father got the shepherd's job on the Estate. My father kept his job for 40 years. His wages were £3.8 shillings a fortnight and out of that he had to pay 2 shillings a week rent.

My parents spent all their married life at 2 Wenallt and both died there. I was born in 1914, the youngest of four children (George, Margaret and Richard) born and reared at the Wenallt. One of my nephews (Sidney) was also brought up at the Cottage. I can remember my Granny used to live next door at Number 1.

In 1937, I got married to **Joe (Idris Owen Williams,** who came from Tylwch near Llanidloes) and we carried on living at the Wenallt. Jo worked on the Forestry for 37 years. Sadly, my husband died some 11 years age, but I am very lucky to have my three children, **Reg, Lindsey** and **Eirlys** (all of whom were born at the Wenallt and lived there until they got married) living close by.

For many years I was a member of the Mothers' Union and regularly attend church.

I have many memories and can clearly remember the late Mrs Prosser and her brothers bringing my Granny a ton of coal with the horse and cart. I can also remember Mrs Edwards from the Fishpool going to Llandrindod Wells every week with her pony and trap. Times have changed since I was a child, but there is one thing that has not and still brings me great joy every year - the arrival of the swallow. I remember Mr Evans from Cross Cottage coming to do some repairs and he knocked down the swallows' nests and Granny was so cross. My grand children also tell me that they have happy childhood memories of staying at the Wenallt and waking up on gloriously sunny mornings to hear the swallows chattering and screaming outside.

I hope that future generations of the family will have as many happy years living at the Wenallt as I have (some 85 all told!).

Wenallt Cottages (258)

Waun Farm

Built in the 1880s by the Powell Family, the house has six bedrooms and is currently occupied by *Mr & Mrs Glyn Powell.*

Glyn is the fourth generation to live here and farm the land. Glyn has lived here all his life, Eileen (née Davies) moved in when they married in 1965.

Glyn and Eileen took over the farm in 1977 when Kinsey Powell (Glyn's father) retired.

(259)

> "In collecting materials for the tract, the author had to regret much their being so few, and he was obliged to use no small diligence in searching for, and gathering together from various sources, what is herein contained. He however hopes that a perusal will not prove wearisome and distasteful, but on the contrary, although the little work is far from what the author wished it to be, it will, as far as it goes, be found interesting and satisfactory."
>
> - from *The Preface* to the first publication about Cwmhir in 1850 "An Historical & Descriptive account of the Ruinated Abbey of Cwmhir" by Rev WJ Rees, Rector of Cascob and Rural Dean of Lower Melenith. [14]

CHURCH NEXT TO A PUBLIC HOUSE

When the Inn stands close to the church it strongly suggests that it was the successor of the Church House where the Churchwardens brewed beer and baked bread for the village feast and other local events. Church Ale was the churchwardens most universal means of raising money from the parish - a perennial problem! The Ale was held in the Church House, a building close to the Church. Millers might also be involved as they would be handling grain and barley and might have a cauldron available for hops. In Abbeycwmhir, Church House was next to the Corn Mill although it is doubtful it was ever a public house. Today it is half of Mill Cottage.

Churches brewed their own beer to keep the people sober! The logic behind this was that Welsh people at that time used to brew home-made mead, and this particular drink was apparently extremely intoxicating "... *getting drunk on mead meant a dreadful drunkenness, damaging to the body, people getting so drunk that they could not sober up for many days. In addition to this, its effect on the body's equilibrium was very different from the effect of getting drunk on beer. A man who gets drunk drinking beer leans forward, and such a drunkard moves forward, but mead would make one lean backwards, and a drunkard drunk on mead would be impelled 'backwards' despite all efforts to move forwards.*

(Evan Roberts, Llandderfel. (*Yr Haul* the 'Church in Wales' magazine, July 1932)[15]

INDEX TO APPENDICES

- 272 - Picture Acknowledgements
- 278 - Sources of information - Citations
- 288 - Abbeycwmhir & General Bibliographies. *Early History sites locations*.
- 290 - *Granges Map* **Key** *& OS References**
- 291 - *Castles Map* **Key** *& OS References**
- 292 - Ruins Excavation Dates; More Castles
- 292 - High Sherrifs from Abbeycwmhir
- 293 - Mabli Explained. **Key** to Ascension Day Photograph
- 294 - Tapestries Subjects & Makers - **Key**
- 295 - "Bwlch y Sarnau School Then & Now" painting & Back Cover - **Key**
- 296 - **Key**: Queens Jubilee Village Photo & Community Research
- 298 - 1993 Village Photo **Key**
- 299 - Full text of GH Philips letter to tenants
- 300 - Abbots & what we know about them
- 301 - Layton Cooke's other publications
- 302 - *Ordnance Survey Bench Marks**
- 303 - Names index for *Homes and People*
- 310 - Local Welsh Place Names - translated

* Places for possible exploration, excursions and walks.

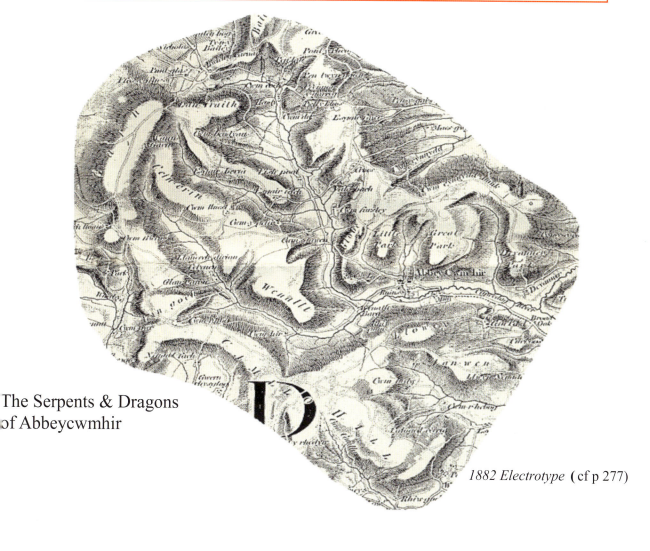

The Serpents & Dragons of Abbeycwmhir

1882 Electrotype (cf p 277)

Abbeycwmhir Community Book Appendices

Picture Acknowledgements

We thank those below for giving us permission to use their images

Abbreviations for main sources: CARAD: Community Arts Rhayader and District; CPAT - Clywed Powys Archaeological Trust; NLW National Library of Wales *Llyfrgell Genedlaethol Cymru;* NMW: National Museum of Wales *Amgueddfa Cymru*; RC: Roger Coward; RCAMHW - Royal Commission for Ancient Monuments and Houses in Wales*;* TRS: Transactions of the Radnorshire Society.

The Abbey *pages 13 - 44*

1 After page 10 on pages 13, 14, 15, 41, 54, 65, 128-131, 161, 295, 302, 313. Key p 294
2 Tapestry photographed by Diana Berriman, Devannor. Illustrated p 128-131. cf key p 294
3 Map drawn by Roger Bennett based maps in the "*Historical Atlas of Wales*" - by William Rees (Faber & Faber 1959) from information provided by John Davies & assembled by Roger Coward.
4 Drawings of ruins from Jones, N.W. *Abbeycwmhir: Survey of the Ruins* (CPAT- 2000), report no. 225.2
5 Drawn by Worthington Smith for Stephen Williams - (Trans.Hon.Soc. Cymmrodorion 1894-5)
6 Photo RC
7 University College, London Archive
8 Extra calligraphy by Alan Quincy of Howey, Honoured Fellow of the Calligraphy and Lettering Arts Soc.
9 Typanum from the Abbey now in Home Farm photographed in 1952 RCAMHW
10 Brian Timms Heraldy Data Base (cf note 29 p 279)
11 Abbey Ruins & Home Farm Circa 1994-5. Radnorshire Museum, Llandrindod Wells
12 RC
13 RC
14 William Bruges Garter Book c. 1430- c. 1440 (British Library Stowe 594 ff. 15)
15 RC
16 Parker Library, Corpus Christi College, Cambridge
17 National Museum Wales, Amgueddfa Cymru
18 Nattydreadful (Natalie Lancaster)
19 Royal Collection Trust © Her Majesty Queen Elizabeth II 2013
20 Wrexham Heritage Service (Bark Illustration)
21 Brian Timms Heraldy Data Base (cf note 29 p 277).
22 The Royal Collection © 2011 Her Majesty Queen Elizabeth II
23 "The Head of Llewellyn the last reigning Prince of Wales, publicly exposed on a pole in Cheap-side, London." Engraved in copper by Rennoldson after a picture by Wale, published in Russel's *New and Authentic History of England ...*, 1781. National Library of Wales *Llyfrgell Genedlaethol Cymru*
24 RC
25 National Library of Wales *Llyfrgell Genedlaethol Cymru*
26 Cadw, Welsh Government (Crown Copyright)
27 Cadw, Welsh Government (Crown Copyright)
28 National Museum Wales, Amgueddfa Cymru.
29 National Archives, Kew
30   "   "   "
31   "   "   "
32 National Museum Wales, Amgueddfa Cymru.
33a National Museum Wales, Amgueddfa Cymru.
33b Wikimedia Commons
33c Wikimedia Commons

Picture Acknowledgements

34a National Museum Wales, Amgueddfa Cymru.
34b Wikimedia Commons
35a Portable Antiquities Scheme IOW-AFE665
35b Notre-Dame de Paris, GNU Free Documentation License
35c Pope 190 from "Pope by Pope" sketches (2007) by designer matt@mattkirkland.com
36a Denier of Henry II or III. Edward Besl, National Museum Wales, Amgueddfa Cymru.
36b National Museum Wales, Amgueddfa Cymru
37 RC
38 *From a plan produced by Pete Lawrence for* Cadw, Welsh Government (Crown Copyright)
39 David Bennett *[sketchy_bennett@hotmail.com]*
40 RC photographed in the Radnorshire Museum, Llandrindod Wells
41 Typanum from the Abbey now in Home Farm photographed in 1952 RCAMHW
42 RC
43 From "Abbeycwmhir a Geographical Study" by Edward (Teddy) Bennet 1953, Devannor
44 All pictures on page by RC
45 Map drawn by Roger Bennett from information provided by Julian Lovell, Paul Remfry, DH Williams, John Davies. Assembled by Roger Coward
46 Millennium Tapestry "Summer". Image by Anita Hamer
47 Provided by the current owners of Nant-y-Arian
48 RC
49 RC
50 DH Williams
51 RC
52 CUCAP - Cambridge University Collection of Aerial Photography 1949. SO239686
53 RC
54 RCAMHW

Early Settlemements *pages 48 - 49*

55 Sheelah na Gig, Radnorshire Museum, Llandrindod Wells
56 All pictures on pages 48-49 RC except following:
57 Photo by Ian Hulm, Rhayader.
58 Photo by Ian Hulm, Rhayader
59 Map drawn by Roger Bennett. Information Clywed-Powys Archaeological Trust. Assembled by RC

After the Abbey *pages 50 - 58*

60 RC
61 National Library of Wales *Llyfrgell Genedlaethol Cymru*
62 After Hans Holbein. Gallerie D'Antiquities, Rome.
63 "Seven Views Illustrating the County of Radnorshire" Lithograph of drawing made at the location by Joseph Murray Ince from Presteigne (1806 - 1858). National Library of Wales *Llyfrgell Gened-laethol Cymru*. Ref. book by Margaret Newman Turner - (Logaston 2013)
64 Bishop William Morgan Bible, NLW. On display at Tŷ Mawr Wybrnant, Penmachno
65 Julian Lovell, Ty'r Eherdydd
66 RC
67 RC

St Mary's Church & Chapels *pages 58 - 67*

68 Collection of St Mary's Church, Abbeycwmhir, where it is displayed
69 "The Church built in 1680" painted by Mary Leighton 1856. Collection of Mr & Mrs Davis"
70 Collection of CARAD

Abbeycwmhir Community Book Appendices

71 Radnorshire Museum, Llandrindod Wells
72 St.Mary's Church, Abbeycwmhir
73 Windows of St.Mary's Church photographed by Roger Coward
74 RC.
75 Collection of Owen & Medina Davies, Beilibog
76 Collection of the Baptist Chapel, Bwlch y Sarnau
77 Collection of the Baptist Chapel, Bwlch y Sarnau
78 Trowel above and Cefn Pawl gravestone - RC
79 Collection of the Griffiths of Devannor
80 Collection of the Griffiths of Devannor
81 RC.
82 Averil Williams, 1 Brickyard Cottages
83 RC
84 Patrizia Scheeder, Devannor

The Hall *pages 68 - 79*

85 George Heriot, watercolour, National Library of Wales *Llyfrgell Genedlaethol Cymru*
86 RC 2010
87 Surveyors sketch for the Ordnance Survey 1817 NLW
88 Radnorhire Society Library. Thanks to Geoff Ridyard.
89 Collection of Dr Peter Cameron Wilson, Adelaide
90 Collection of Ken & Shirley Stephens, Upper Esgair
91 Collection of Owen & Medina Davies, Beilibog
92 Collection of Owen & Medina Davies, Beilibog
93 JJ Halls - Collection of Dr John G.Wilson, North Adelaide, South Australia
94 BRA/1862?27-28 Powys County Archives
95 Frank Howard - Collection of Dr Peter Cameron Wilson, Adelaide, South Australia
96 Photo C 1900. Collection of Dr Peter Cameron Wilson , Adelaide, South Australia
97 The Radnorshire Society Library. Thanks to Geoff Ridyard
98 "Report on Abbey Cwm Hir Estate 1822" - Layton Cooke, The Radnorshire Society Library
99 Plans A,B,C, "Report on Abbey Cwm Hir Estate 1822" - Layton Cooke, The Radnorshire Society Library
100 RC
101 Collection of Prof. Flavia Swann, Grandaughter of Colonel Lionel Philips
102 Photograph probably taken by Rev E.Hermitage Day and given to members of the Wilson family who he and his new wife, Doris Philips, entertained at the Hall.in 1901. Collection of Prof. Flavia Swann, Grandaughter of Colonel Lionel Philips
103 Powys County Archives
104 Engraving made on GH Philip's death in 1886 from an original Painting by J.Graham Gilbert RSA in 1834; Collection of Prof. Flavia Swann, Grandaughter of Colonel John Lionel Philips
105 Augusts Henry Fox was painting between 1841 -1855. Radnorshire Museum, Llandrindod Wells
106 Philips family private collection
107 Anna Thoephilia Close-up from Wedding Photo 1892 *on p 84 by Mr T.Roberts of Llandrindod Wells*
108 Mary Beatrice Close-up from Wedding Photo 1892 *on p 84 by Mr T.Roberts of Llandrindod Wells*
109 St Mary's Churchyard, Abbeycwmhir - RC
110 Branding Tools thanks to Mel & Anita Hamer, Home Farm; impression & photo - RC
111 Photograph in the Collection of Shropshire Regimental Museum of a painting owned by Mr M. Drein.
112 Collection of St Mary's Church, Abbeycwmhir
113 Collection of Abbeycwmhir Philips Hall. Painted by Dorothea Selous RBA (Royal Society of British Artists) in 1927

Picture Acknowledgements

The Hall continued P 79 - 88

114 West Window St Mary's Church, Abbeycwmhir
115 Collection of Julie Evans, Clywedog Bungalow
116 RC
117 Collection of Paul & Victoria Humpherston
118 Collection of Paul & Victoria Humpherston
119 Collection of Professor Flavia Swan, Grandaughter of Col. JL Philips
120 Collection of Barry Williams, The Old Vicarage, Brynmoel). Photo by Mr T.Roberts of Llandrindod
121 Photo by Mr T.Roberts of Llandrindod.Collection of Flavia Swann, Grandaughter of Col JL Philips
122 Collection of Professor Flavia Swan, Grandaughter of Col. JL Philips
123 Collection of Professor Flavia Swan, Grandaughter of Col. JL Philips
124 Collection of Paul & Victoria Humpherston
125 RC
126 Radnorshire Society Library. Thanks to Librarian Geoff Ridyard
127 Collection of the Griffiths of Devannor c/o CARAD
128 Collection of Julie Evans, Clywedog Bungalow

The Happy Union *pages 89 - 96*

129 Top left: Father & Son by the Sign: Father John Thomas Jones with son David Jones (Dai the Union) Photo: Geoff Charles (1909-1002) Radnor Times 31.01.53. National Library of Wales *Llyfrgell Genedlaethol Cymru.*
Top centre: By Stephen Dexter of Laithdu painted in the 1980's. Photo 1991
Top right: Close up of sign from lower picture
Below: Man leaning on wall with unmade road 1850 -1939 (before road ashfelted) Note two roofs.
Photo Geoff Charles (1909-1002) Radnor Times 31.01.53 Courtesy of Radnorshire Museum
130 RC 2008
131 Published by Bowles, London 1781. National Library of Wales *Llyfrgell Genedlaethol Cymru*
132 Intaglio Cartoons Published by William Dicey, London c 1747 NLW
133 Ditto
134 Published by Fores, London 1786. National Library of Wales *Llyfrgell Genedlaethol Cymru*
135 Courtesy The Welsh Guards, Wellington Barracks, Knightsgbridge
136 The Regimental Museum of The Royal Welsh (Brecon)
137 Royal Welsch Fusiliers Museum, Caernarvon
138 Courtesy The Welsh Guards, Wellington Barracks, Knightsgbridge
139 The Regimental Museum of The Royal Welsh, Brecon
140 1894 Painting by unknown artist. Collection of Ian & Angela Lewis, Cwmffwrn.
141 Cluster of images thanks to Wikimedia Commons
142 www.freemasonywatch
143 RC
144 Jack Black the Rat Catcher to Queen Victoria 1851. "Occupational Costume in England" - Philis Cunningham & Catherine Lucas (Black, London 1967)
145 Wilsons handwritten note on the 1837 Sales Prospectus. "Advowson" means the right to appoint to a benefice or job.Shirley Cameron Wilson Bequest, State Library of South Australia.SLSA/PRG 1399/75
146 Courtesy Mel & Anita Hamer, Home Farm

The Mill pages 97 - 101

147 Radnorshire Museum, Llandrindod Wells
148 Collection of Brian Parfitt.

Abbeycwmhir Community Book Appendices

The Mill continued pages 97 - 101

149 Prof G.W.Tucker "Water Mills of Radnorshire" 1989 Melin 5 Plate IX
150 Radnorshire Museum, Llandrindod wells.
151 Line drawings from an 18th Century Encyclopaedia
152 Background plan by Michael Preller, information: Brian Parfitt & others, assembled by RC.
153 Collection of Brian Parfitt
154 Both photographs on this page by RC
155 Powys County Archives
156 Mills along the Clywedog map from "Henfryn" by George F.Lewis (Logaston 2002) p133.
157 George F Lewis Ibid p 134. Mill is left hand part.
158 RC with thanks to Tim & Mel Haines-Walters of Coedtrewernau
159 All pictures on this page by Roger Coward
160 Map and front cover of the "London County Council Report on Available sources of Water for London" (1894) from the collection of Richard Rhys Rees of Llanwrda.

Homes No More pages *105 - 113*

161 Radnorshire Society Library
162 Radnorshire Society Library
163 Map drawn by Roger Bennet, information by Julian Lovell. Assembled by Roger Coward
164 Background from Buddugre Hill Inclosure Map, Powys County Archives
165 "A Radnorshire Farm Diary 1879-1883" (David & Sheila Leitch, Glasbury 1999) p21
166 Painting by Augustus Henry Fox 1822-1895, Radnorshire Museum, Llandrindod Wells
167 Painting by Augustus Henry Fox 1822-1895, Radnorshire Museum, Llandrindod Wells.
168 Radnorshire Museum, Llandrindod Wells
169 All maps on this page permission of Powys County Archives R/QS/DE/2/1-3

The Forestry *pages 114 - 119*

170 RC
171 Bibliothèque Municipale, Dijon
172 RC
173 Bibliothèque Municipale, Dijon
174 Bibliothèque Municipale, Dijon
175 RC
176 Newspaper Photograph. Collection of CARAD, Rhayader
177 Alan Gayse. Collection of Roger Coward
178 Collection of Albert Philips

Village Photographs, Millennium and Celebrations *pages 120 - 136*

179 Collection of Barry Williams, Old Vicarage
180 Ray Carpenter of Penybont
181 Paul Humpherston, The Hall, Abbeycwmhir
182 RC - Mugs loaned by the Berrimans, Little Plock
*   Pages 125 - 7. Thanks to all photographers and owners who placed their pictures on the notice board in the Philips Hall
**   Page 129 hotographs from the collections of Paul & Victoria Humpherston, The Hall & Julie Evans of Clywedog Bungalow
183 - 186 Diana Berriman, Little Plock
187 RC
188 -190 Collection of Julie Evans, Clywedog Bungalow
191 From Builth Wells Historical Pageant Photograph Album 1909. The photograph is by P B Abery (1877-1948) and Wallace Jones

Picture Acknowledgements

IN LIVING MEMORY *pages 138 - 167*

192 John Davies 2005
193 John Davies 2008
194 Collection of John Jones, The Happy Union
195 Collection of the Griffitrhs of Devannor (c/o CARAD).
196 Collection of Julie Evans, Clywedog Bungalow
197 All other pictures on pages 140-141 by RC
198 Collection of Abe Wozencraft, Rhayader
199 Collection of Abe Wozencraft, Rhayader
200 Collection of Owen Davies, Beili Bog
201 Collection of Mel Hamer, Home Farm
202 Thanks to Bryn Stonebridge of Waun Pistyll
203 Collection of E.Hamer (c/o CARAD)
204 Collection of Tudor Ingram (c/o CARAD)
205 Collection of the Griffiths of Devannor
206 Collection of the Griffiths of Devannor
207 Collection of Abe Wozencraft, Rhayader
208 Collection of Abe Wozencraft, Rhayader
209 RC
210 Collection of Abe Wozencraft, Rhayader
211 Collection of Mel Hamer (c/o CARAD)
212 Collection of The Griffiths of Devannor
213 Collection of Owen Davies, Beili Bog
214 RC
215 Collection of Prof.Flavia Swann/Philips
216 Collection of Julie Evans, Clywedog Bungalow
217a Mid Wales Journal 13.07.1979 from the
217b Collection of Julie Evans, Clywedog Bungalow
218 Collection of Mel Hamer, Home Farm (CARAD)
219 Collection of Julie Evans, Clywedog Bungalow
220 Collection of Julie Evans, Clywedog Bungalow.
221 Collection of Mel Hamer, Home Farm.
222 Collection of Mel Hamer, Home Farm
223 Collection of Mel Hamer, Home Farm (CARAD)
224 Collection of Mel Hamer, Home Farm (CARAD)
225 Collection of Julie Evans, Clywedog Bungalow
226 Collection of Prof.Flavia Swann
227 RC
228 The Vron Farmhouse - RC
229 Collection of the Griffiths of Devannor (CARAD)
230 CARAD. Newspaper photo and caption
231 RC
232 Collection of Albert Mytton, Rhayader
233 Collection of David Pugh son of Sybil Pugh

234 Collection of the Griffiths of Devannor.(CARAD)
235 NLW
236 Collection of William Manuel (c/o CARAD)
237 Collection of the Bwlch y Sarnau Community Hall Committee
238 All pictures on this page by Roger Coward
239 Collection of William Manuel (c/o CARAD)
240 RC
241 Collection of Barry Williams, The Old Vicarage
242 Collection of Barry Williams, The Old Vicarage
243 Radnorshire Museum, Llandrindod Wells
244 Collection of Professor Flavia Swann, Grandaughter of Colonel JL Philips.

Homes & People Inserts *pages 168 - 270*

245 RC (p 177)
246 Collection, Bwlch y Sarnau Baptist Church(p 190)
247 Portman Market - a contemporary painting.(p193)
248 Wiki-Media Commons - Jasper Fforde (p 199)
249 RC (p 200)
250 Radnorshire Museum, Llandrindod Wells.(p 201)
251 RC (p 205)
252 RC (p 217)
253 "Henfryn" George Lewis (Logaston 2002) (p 225)
254 Powys County Archive R/QS/DE/2/1-3 (p 245)
255 Collection of Prof. Flavia Swann/Philips (p 249)
256 RC (p 258)
257 RC (p 259)
258 CMAHW (p 269)
259 RC (p 270)

Celebration pages *1- 7 & 314-320*

Pages 1-5 & pages 314 -320 Roger Coward;
Pages 7-8 RCAMHW

Appendix *page 271*

Electrotype map developed from surveyors map of 1817. Republished by Redwood press, Melksham Wilts in 1970

We have attempted to contact all picture owners to obtain their permission and apologise if any errors have been made.

Abbeycwmhir Community Book Appendices

Sources of Information

Each section of the book has its own notes starting from number 1

Abbreviations for main sources: AC - Archaeologica Cambrensis; CPAT - Clywed Powys Archaeological Trust; **NLW** - National Library of Wales *Llyfrgell Genedlaethol Cymru;* PCA - Powys County Archives; RCAMHW - Royal Commission for Ancient Monuments and Houses in Wales; TRS - The Transactions of the Radnorshire Society; UWP - University of Wales Press.

Celebration *and Introduction pages 1 - 9*

1 Williams, Jonathan & Davies, Edwin *History of the County of Radnor* (Brecon 1905). *p* 135
2 Leland, John *Itinerary 1539 to 1541* (Centaur Press 1964). Father of local history and a poet
3 Reason for authorising public sacraments in 1232. Calendar of Papal Registers i 131

The Abbey *pages 10 - 16*

1. From the song *As Time Goes By* by Herman Hupfeld played in the movie *Casablanca* (1942) by Sam (Dooley Wilson) for Ilsa (Ingrid Bergman) who said "Play it, Sam. Play 'As Time Goes By'." Later he plays it for (Rick Blaine) Humphrey Bogart
2. And by the Norweigian Leif Ericsson circa 1000 AD (described in the *Saga of Eric the Red* (1387) and the Welsh Madoc circa 1130
3 In a Lecture to the Cambrian Archaeological Society 1848, Published in *Archaeologica Cambrensis IV* 1849. And as a separate monograph in 1850 *An Historical and Descriptive Account of the Ruinated Abbey of Cwmhir in the County of Radnor*. Rev Jonathan Williams had already used it in his *History of Radnorshire* before he died in 1829 but it wasn't published until 1859. "dingle" was repeated by the the Rev Hermitage Day DD FSA of the Old Vicarage (Brynmoel), Abbeycwmhir in a lecture to the Cambrian Archaeological Society.(AC - Vol 11, 1911).
4 Devannor = *de faenor* = maenor = main; *Geriadur Prifysgol Cymru* (UWP 1987-98). Earliest record in writing is 12thC before the English Manorial system came to Wales in the 14th C.
5 "1644. The Parliament tooke and burned the Abby of Nant-cwm-hir", Wynnstay Library Document quoted in AC I: 1846
6 Published by Samuel Lewis & Co, London 1833
7 *Flores Historiarum* (Flowers of History) St Albans. Bodleian Library (Douce Man. 207)
8 Robinson, David M *Cistercian Abbeys of Britain* (English Heritage 1998) p 96
9 Rule of Cistercian Order, Statute 1.13. 1134 "Our houses shall not be built near cities, castles or villages, but in places far removed from the conversations of men"
10 Janauschek, L.*Originum Cisterciensium (1877)*
11 Calendar of Papal Registers i 131. Reason for authorising public sacraments in 1232
12 Jones, N.W. - 2000, *Abbeycwmhir: Survey of the Ruins* CPAT report no. 225.2
13 Remfry, Paul *Cadwallon ap Madog Rex Delvain, 1140-79 and the re-establishment of local autonomy in Cynllibwg*. TRS, 1995 p 11
14 Remfry Ibid
15 Translated in Lloyd, JYW *History of Powys Fadog* (1885) p 309-15
16 Two later documents state that Cwmhir was the foundation of Cadwallon ap Madog. (1) *Calendar of Petitions relating to Wales,* ed. W. Rees [Cardiff, 1975], no. 1972, of c.1322-3. "The abbot claimed that they were the 'foundation of Cadwallan ap Madauk and other lords, formerly of Mallenyth', (2) Leland,John *The Itinerary in Wales in or about 1536-9 Ed LT Smith (1906)*
17 1215 Charter of Confirmation by King John of England Rot. Chart., 206i Cited by Remfry, Paul *A Political History of Abbeycwmhir* (Castle Studies 2004).P 31

Sources of Information

The Abbey continued pages 17 - 25

18 There is a Church Dedicated to St Mabli there. Peter Bartram *Dictionary of Welsh Saints* Vol III, 1993 based on Welsh Classical Dictionary Baring-Gould & John Fisher (Cwmarodorion 1911). The first child of the Abbeycwmhir Philips was also christened Mabel (cf p 83)

19 Wilson may have caused the confusion by hand writing in 1833 in the Layton Cooke Report that, "The stone coffin of one of the Abbots was found". However by circa 1855 he had read and been inspired by *Ruinated Abbey*, which we know he had in Australia, and changed his mind writing in the Prefatory to his poem *The Abbot of Coombe* Here "the author ...discovered in the nave a lid of a stone coffin, the burial place of a female with a very ancient abbreviated Latin inscription, recommending her soul to God." thus acknowledging it was the tomb of a female. State Library of South Australia) Shirley Cameron Wilson Bequest (PRG/1399/78/5)

20 Williams, DHW *Cistercians in Wales* (Gracewing 2001) p295

21 Rees *An Historical and Descriptive Account of the Ruinated Abbey of Cwmhir in the County of Radnor*. (Monograph 1850) p23

22 Rees Ibid P 6

23 The story of the opening of a tomb in 1836 - amongst the flower beds in the ruins - in which there was an abbot's skeleton which turned to dust on opening - except for the teeth one of which was borrowed and worn by Francis Philips - must be a conflation of several incidents and probably fantasy written down in a letter to the South Wales Daily Newspaper 59 years after the event by someone who was either not born or was a young child at the time.The matter was reported in TRS Vol.4 - 1934 pp 60-61. Only DNA testing will establish whether the tooth was from a man or woman and if its in the jaw of Frances Philips then an exhumation and post mortem will have to be arranged

24 *Grifini* was Gruffudd ap Cynan (d1200) cf p 45

25 Charles, B. G. *An Early Charter of Cwmhir"* includes a translation of the Charter (TRS 1970).

26 Stephenson, David *Llywelyn Fawr, The Mortimers and Cwmhir Abbey: The Politics of Monastic Rebuilding* TRS 2010. p 29ff

27 Charles, BG *An Early Charter of Cwmhir"* TRS 1970 p 68

28 Charles Ibid

29 Note on Coats of Arms:- Coats of Arms were not worn until the Thirteenth Century so for earlier rulers and knights the heraldry has been ascribed posthumously. So the Arms illustrated for Cadwallon ap Madog are the arms of the family of Elystan Glodrydd – his great grandfather. His personal Arms are not known and he may not have had any. It was only just becoming normal for knights to pass their shield designs on to eldest sons - previously they used any kind of design. The Llewelyn and Owain Glendower and English King's Arms are known. The Mortimer Arms are correct for the family but may not be right for the person. The Oliver Cromwell Arms are actually those of the Parliamentary Common - wealth as the government he led was called at that time. Several Coats of Arms were advised & provided by Brian Timms personally and from his Data Base, thanks

30 Davies, John *Abaty'r Cwm Hir* (NLW Manuscript 1993) p 1 "Abaty'r" is the correct Welsh for "Abbey" of" Cwm-hir"

31 Conradi, Peter J *At the Bright Hem of God* (Seren 2009) p 22

32 Leland, John *Itinerary 1539 to 1541* (Centaur Press 1964)

33 Roger of Wendover in 1231. *Flores Historiarum* (*Flowers of History*) III 11-12 . Cited by David M Robinson The Cistercian Abbeys in Wales (Society of Antiquaries 2001) note 225

34 Ibid

35 Beauchamp Cartulary 216-7 Nos 382,383. Cited by Remfry, PM *Political History of Abbeycwmhir* (Castle Books 2004) p23

36 *Chronica Majora* Matthew Paris. Parker Library, Corpus Christi College, Cambridge

37 Papal i.131 Cited by Williams, DH "*White Monks of Powys*" in *Cistercian Studies Quarterly* (1976) p75.

38 Brut y Tywysogion *Peniarth 20 Version* MS. Jones ,Thomas, ed. (Cardiff: University of Wales Press, 1952) Cited by *Davies, John Abaty'r Cwm Hir* (NLW Manuscript 2003). P27

Abbeycwmhir Community Book Appendices

The Abbey continued pages 25 - 31

39   "For with lance and shield did he tame his fows; he kept peace for the men of religion; to the needy he gave food and raiment."Ab Ithel, Cistercian Annalist (Ann.C.MS.B), Lloydd JE *History of Wales* p 693

40   "gold" was a term used for the satisfaction of an insult "paid only to the King at Aberffraw" - the court of Princes of Gwynedd

41   Translated by Loydd JE *History of Wales* (1912) p 691 Note: Myv.Arch I 301(213)

42   The Remembrance Ceremony is held during the weekend closest to the 11th Dec (cf p 138). The title *Ein Llyw Olaf*, Our Last Leader, Prince or rudder was ascribed in the 1950's in the title of a poem by Gwennallt in a volume called Gwreiddiau" (1959). It is ascribed to Llywelyn rather than the later Owain Glyndwr because the former was acknowledged by the English King Henry whereas the latter was a rebellious baron and a self proclaimed Prince whose ascendency lasted just 14 years.

43   Gruffydd ap Llywelyn (Fawr), eldest but illegitimate son by Tangwystl. He died in 1244

44   Remfry, Paul *A PoliticalHisory of Abbeycwmhir 1176 - 1282* (Castle Studeis 2004) P 26

45   Peter de Montfort Letters i, Lloyd Ibid P 731

46   Loydd JE *History of Wales* (Longmans 1912) p 739

47   Davies, John *A History of Wales* (Penguin 1993) p 157

48   Reece, Williams *Callendar of Ancient Correspondences & petitions*(UW Board of Celtic Studies, History & Law series No 28 1975)

49   "Cyfraeth Howell" or "Leges Howelda Wallici" - Laws of Hywel (Dda - The Good) AD 945

50   Lloyd, JE *A History of Wales* p761 note 234. "Brillioant Assemblage" Lloyd JE Ibid p 761

51   We know the South Wales Valleys supported him from the *"Callendar of Ancient Petitions for Wales?"* - Williams Reece UW Board of Celtic Studies, History & Law series no 28 1975

52   The Black Book of Peterborough - Society of Antiquaries MS 60. Translated by Thomâ Stapleton, Camden Society xlviii (1849) p 57

53   Brut y Tywysogion Peniarth MS 20. 291a-9-292b. NLW. The Red Book of Hergest & Brenhinedd y Saeffon. All agree on this

54   Chronicle of Florence of Worcester AC (1911) p 35

55   Peckham Register AC 1911 P 36

56   Davies, *John Chronology of the story of Llanrhymny Hall & Llywelyn* (National Eisteddfod of Wales, Newport 2000)

57   Day,Hermitage *The Burial of Llywelyn ap Gruffyd* AC 1911

58   So prevalent was the practice that in 1299, Pope Boniface VIII made a decree *Detestande feritatus* against it although the practice continued amongst the aristocracy until the late Eighteenth Century. Bynum, CW *Fragmentation and Redemption: Essays in Gender and the Human Body in Medieval Religion* (Zone Books, New York 1991) pp 265-96

59   Owens, Margaret *The Stages of Dismemberment: The Fragmented Body in Late Medieval and Early Modern Drama* (Delaware 2005) p35

60   *"Llywelyn Ein Llyw Olaf"* (Our Last Prince) from *Gwreiddiau* (1959) by Gwennallt the bardic name of David James Jones, 1899 – 1968 translated & quoted by Llywelyn,Dorian in *Sacred Place, Chosen People* (University of Wales Press 1999) to whom thanks for permission to quote. P 240

61   Hailes Abbey (Cistercian) Chronicle, Gloucestershire. Quoted in Remfry, Paul *The Final Campaign of Prince Llywelyn* (Castle Books 1998)

62   Just as he removed the Stone of Scone from Scotland in 1296. After being transfered to the Tower of London the coronet was "lost" at the time of Cromwell. Davies, RR *The Age of Conquest: Wales 1063-1415* - (OUP 2000) p 544

63   Taylor, Arnold J *"A fragment of a Dona account of 1284". Bulletin of the Board of Celtic Studies, vol 27, part 2 (1977),* pp 253-262.)

64   Ibid p 257

65   Ibid. cf Note 3 p 257 The name on its base reads "Nicol'us me fecit de *Herfordie*" which is often mistakenly translated as *Hereford*. As late as the 17thC it was the spelling of Hartford, near Chester where his family came from

66   Red Book of Hergest 180-1. Cited by Robinson,David *Cistercians in Wales* p 345 Note 5

Pages 32 - 44

67 Davies, RR *The Revolt of Owain Glyndwr's* OUP 1995
68 Shakespeare Henry IV Part I Davies RR Ibid p335
69 Leland,John *Itinerary 1539 to 1541* (Centaur Press 1964).
70 Davies, John *Abaty'r Cwmhir a Chronicle 1143-1992* - (NLW Manuscript 2003) p64
71 Davies, John Ibid p57
72 Davies, RR *The Revolt of Owain Glyndwr's* (OUP 1995) p 339
73 Davies RR Ibid p 336
74 Williman DH *"Catalogue of Welsh Ecclesiastical Seals Part IV"* P147 (AC 1987)
75 National Archives Kew (Reference E 329/244)
76 Williams DH *Catalogue of Seals in the National Museum of Wales Vol 1* (Cardiff 1993) p 4
77 Williams, DH *The Welsh Cistercians* (Gracewing 2001) p221
78 William of Leicester. Davies, John *Abaty'r Cwmhir a Chronicle 1143-1992* (NLW Manuscript 2003) p 86
79 Williams,DH *Cistercians in the Early Middle Ages* (Gracewing 1998) p7
80 Prefatory to the poem *"The Abbot of Coombe Here"* by Thomas Wilson written Circa 1855 Shirley Cameron Wilson Bequest, State Library of South Australia.(PRG/1399/78/5)
81 Brand, John *Bulletin de la Societé française de Numismatique* 1978, p 372-3. The deniere's given by Colonel JL Philips in 1986 to the National Museum of Wales, Cardiff, (Accession no 86.76H).
82 Robinson,David *The Cistercians in Wales* (Society of Antiquaries 2006) p 110
83 CPAT is Clywd-Powys Archaeological Trust, 41, Broad St., Welshpool, SY21 7RR 01938 553670 www.cpat.org.uk
84 Williams, Stephen, W. "The Cistercian Abbey of Cwmhir, Radnorshire", *Transactions of the Honourable Society of Cymmrodorion* (1894-5)
85 In the Welsh Stone Forum Newsletter Number 11 March 2014. A report using petrologists research noted that large creamy yellow mica chrystals occur in the Abbey stone but not at Grinshill whose quartz veins do not appear in the Abbey stone suggesting it is from the Younger Silurian period. This is a similar mineralogy to the "Tilestones" of Epynt but the exact outcrop of this lithology has yet to be located
86 Williams, DH *Welsh Cistercians* p 244
87 Willaims, DH Ibid p 212
88 Remfry , Paul *Castles & History of Wales* (Castle Studies & Research 2008) p 169
90 Lloyd, JE *A History of Wales* p 255 & Y Geririadur Mawr (Gomer/Davies 1968)
91 Remfry, Paul *Castles & History of Wales* (Castle Studies & Research 2008)
92 Williams, DH "White Monks in Powys".(Cistercian Studies Quarterly 1976) p 96
93 Williams, DH, Ibid p78

Before the Abbey - Bumps on Hills *pages 46 - 49*

1 Now in the Alan Foxall Collection in Brecon Museum
2 Flint Find sometime before 1895 and now in the Shrewsbury Museum.
3 Now part of the Alan Foxall Collection in Brecon Museum
4 Williams 1858 records it as a most perfect cairn accompanied with a stone chest, human bones, black earth and other corresponding appendages'. CPAT No 240
5 CPAT No 3464. In 1911 in the collection of Mr SW Williams, Penrally, Rhayader. Now - unknown.
6 Jerman, H.Noel *"The Bronze Age in Radnorshire"*(TRS 1936) p 377

After the Abbey *pages 50 - 53*

1 Williams, DH *The Cistercians in Wales* (Gracewing 2001) p77
2 Williams, DH Ibid P78
3 Williams, Jonathan & Davies, Edwin and others *History of Radnorshire* (Brecon 1905) p 136.
4 Williams, DH "White Monks in Powys". (Cistercian Studies Quarterly 1976) p 92.
5 Williams, DH Ibid p 89

The Fowlers *pages 54 - 57*

1. Shropshire County Archives, Fowler Family of Harnage Grange (2089/1-10, 1514/534/4-9)
2. Powys County Archives BRA/1862
3. Shropshire County Archives The Fowler estate Sales Particulars 1783-1790 (2089/1-10, 1514/534/4-9)
4. Williams, Jonathan *History of Radnorshire (1859)* p 233
5. Sugget, Richard *Houses & History in the March of Wales—Radnorshire 1400—1800* - ((RCAHMW 2005) where it is described as a retreat because it had no large hall for business and was very like Robert Smythesons Elizabethan designs for Lodges. N.Cooper in "Houses of the Gentry 1480-1680) (Newhaven & London 1999) describes it as "a good platte for little houses"!
6. However it should be noted that the documentation for High Sheriff was filed in the preceding year, so that would mean that Devannor was in existence in 1655 when Richard Fowler applied for the job.
7. Sugget, Richard *Houses & History in the March of Wales—Radnorshire 1400—1800*" (RCAHMW 2005)
8. Rowse, AH *Radnorshire* (Hereford 1949) p 49
9. Coe, Andrew *Perfect Occurences of Parliament, and chief collections of letters 1644*-1646. (National Archives) Letter from Colonel Mytton from Powys Castle 9th Dec 1644.
10. Parker, Keith. *Radnorshire from Civil War to Restoration* (Logaston 2000)
11. "*Roll of High Sheriffs for Radnorshire*". TRS 1955 pp 40-45
12. Shropshire County Archives - .Parish Records of St.Peter's Cound, Shropshire.
13. Ionides, Julia *Thomas Farnolls Pritchard - Architect* (Dog Rose press 1999)
14. His date of birth as recorded in Llanbister church register is 1734 so he was 26. cf Note 15.
15. TRS 1977 p 35
16. Also in the *Complete Baronetcy Vol IV 1665-1707*. (William Pollard & Co. Exeter 1904) NLW.

St Mary's Church and Chapels *pages 58 - 60*

1. Williams , DH *Welsh Cistercians* (Gracewing 2001) p88
2. Corregio *"Agony in the Garden"* (1494-1534) Aspley House.Hyde Park Corner, London
3. Wilson,Shirley Cameron & Borrow, KTY Bridge over the Ocean (Adelaide, South Australia 1973) p49
4. Williams, DH *"White Monks in Powys"*. *Cistercian Studies Quarterly* (1976) p 87
5. "*A Most Extraordinary Will*" N.M.Owens. M*ontgomery Collection Vol 47 1941-42 p 103*
6. Mary Leighton has an *entry on page 357 in the "Dictionary of British Watercolour Artists up to 1920"- by H.L.Mallalieu (Antique Collectors Club 1998/2002)*
7. His handwritten notes in the Leighton Cooke Report 1822 (TRS 1981) p55.
8. PCA. Case and opinions re. Evans v. George for Dilapidations to Abbeycwmhir; legal costs of Green and Peters re. Dilapidations of living of Abbeycwmhir 1848-51. (BRA/1862/61-64).
9. *Maddox,Wilfred Charles "Abbey- cwm-hir - The Story of a Radnorshire Village"* (Manuscript 1971*) November 1971) P 49 and in the poem* written by Mercy M. Griffiths (1968) for the commemoration of the centennial anniversary of the rebuilding of the Church

> "Poudly it rose from the ashes of History
> To stand as a symbol of days long gone by
> When Christians came forth to expound the Great Mystery
> In the wilderness where flocks of wild curlews cry…..
> See in the Vestry her portrait who built it:
> Miss Beatrice M. Philips, who lived in the Hall.

Source: Prof Flavia Swann/Philips

Sources of Information

St Mary's Church and Chapels continued pages 60-67

10 Window and architectural information from Pevsner's "Buildings of Wales - Radnorshire" Richard Haslam (Penguin 1979) p 215 confirmed in a letter from Lawrence & Co., Canterbury and Hereford, stained glass specialists, in reply to an enquiry from the Rev. Mark Griffiths, Abbeycwmhir, March 1998
11 Crockford's Clerical Directory 1918-1919. 1930 pp 77 - 80.
12 from *Buchedd Garmon* by Saunders Lewis transalted by Harri Pritchard Jones and quoted by by Dorian Llywelyn in "Sacred Place, Chosen People" . University of Wales Press 1999 to whom thanks for permission to quote

- **Chapels: Baptists** - Batley, Alwyn *Cefn Pawl Baptist Church Centenary (*Booklet1985); William Manuel, *Bwlch y Sarnau Baptist Church Ter-Jubilee (*Booklet 1979); Lovell, Julien (Editor) *Portrait of a Radnorshire Valley; The reminiscences and recollections of William Lewis, Esgairy "1907 - 1971"*

- **Chapels: Methodism -** Griffiths, Diana Sarah *175 Years of Methodism at Devannor,1818 to 1993* (1993)

13 Williams, Waldo "*Y Twr a'r Graig"* by translated & quoted by Dorian Llywelyn in *Sacred Place, Chosen People* (UWP 1999) to whom thanks for permission to quote

The Hall *pages 69 - 72*

1 Cooke, Layton *Report on the Abbey Cwm Hir estate 1822* Original in Radnorshire Society Library; Transcription in TRS for 1965, 1966, 1981
2 Wilson, Shirley Cameron & Borrow, KT *The Bridge over the Ocean* - (Adelaide, Sth Australia, 1973).
3 Thomas Wilson's first purchase of 5-6th April 1824 was of Cwm Cynydd, Gwar Cae, Bron Rhyd Newydd, Cwm Scawen, Cwm Varsley, Cwm Fforn, Gilfach, Fishpool, Penyllan, Groes, Llanerch Fraidd, Cwm Bedw for £6000. *Powys County Archives - Researched & Summarized by Julian Lovell.)*
4 Reece, Rev WJ . *An Historical and Descriptive Account of the Ruinated Abbey of Cwmhir in the County of Radnor.* (1850) repinted from AC 1849 p 16
5 Thomas Wilson's second purchase from the Fowler Estate of 15-16th October 1828 was of Site of Monastery The Abbey, The Great Park, Wenallt, Cwm Hir, Gilfach, Cefn y Pawl, Cwm Hir, Gelenin, Cwm Giver, Escair Ucha, Escair Fach, Troedrhiwfelin, Hen Kefn, Cwm Quarrel, Vale Fach, Cwm Lyest, Abbey Mill, Mount Pleasant, Blacksmith's Shop. *Powys County Archives - Researched & Summarized by Julian Lovell 03/11/10*
6 It was not until 1860 that The Young Haymakers was sent to South Australia. Wilson, Shirley Cameron & Borrow, KT *The Bridge over the Ocean* (Adelaide, Sth Australia, 1973) p50 Ibid note 2
7 Introduction p xvii to "The Bridge over the Ocean" by Ursula Hoff, O.B.E., Ph.D., Assistant Director, National Gallery of Victoria (Wilson & Borrow Ibid)
8 2 Rembrandts (F,4.75; F,7.79;) and 5 other makers' prints that he donated are in the British Museum collection in 2014 but in the Appendix (p291) of his Biography (Ibid) 65 are listed. Wilson published a *Catalogue Raisonnée* of his private collection in 1828 and *A Descriptive Catalogue of the Prints of Rembrandt in 1836*
9 Wilson, Thomas *The Abbot of Coombe Heere* (August 1857) is about Mabli, whose tomb he found, and Abbot Rhyrid. "Wilson contrives Sir Everard and the Abbot of Cwmhir to be one and the same person. The abbot was young when he was appointed to his post at the abbey, but wanted to be married so left it secretly and went to Antwerp where he met Orpah, married her while claiming to be a knight and had two sons with her. As their lives together went on, he was consumed by the fact of his forsaking his sacred vows and leaving the Abbey long before, so that he left Orpah in Antwerp and went to Rome to beg forgiveness from Pope Honorius. Orpah, broken hearted because Sir Everard seemed to have deserted her, died of grief. Everard / the abbot (Ririd?) came back to the abbey with the Pope's blessing

The Hall continued pp 72 - 88

bringing Orpah's (Mabli's) body which he had buried there. Later, their two sons, both at the Crusades, died while fighting there and their bodies were brought to the Abbey for burial. What Wilson has done in the poem is to construct a story which gathers together all the relics which Wilson had found on the Abbey site (Mabli's tomb, papal bulls, skeletons etc -Ed.) and makes them characters in his narrative. ." - Neil Thomas, State Library of South Australia (PRG 1399/78/5)

10   Cooke, Layton *Report on the Abbey Cwm Hir estate 1822* Transcription in TRS for 1965, 1966, 1981
11   Ibid TRS 1965 p 44
12   Ibid TRS 1965 p 46
13   Ibid TRS 1981 p 55
14   NLW. Crosswood Manuscripts. Letter to a Reverend John Jenkins, the Vicar of Kerry
15   Rees, Rev WJ *An Historical and Descriptive Account of the Ruinated Abbey of Cwmhir in the County of Radnor* (1850) repinted from Archaeologica Cambrensis IV 1849 p 27
16   Cooke, Layton Ibid RST 1981 p 55
17   Sales Document 1837, Shirley Cameron Wilson Bequest, State Library of South Australia(PRG 1399/75)
18   cf note 5
19   Rees, Rev WJ *An Historical and Descriptive Account of the Ruinated Abbey of Cwmhir in the County of Radnor* (1850) p 16
20   Layton Cooke, had already advertised the sale of the Abbeycwmhir Estate for Auction in November 1820 at the Garraway Coffee House, Cornhill (in the *Hereford Journal* Oct 1820 - RST 1981 P45). Presumably the estate was not sold but perhaps Cooke had attracted Wilson's interest so instead they had coffee together. A handwritten note on his 1837 sale document.(cf Note 15) indicates that Wilson was already interested in Abbeycwmhir in 1821 and was perhaps committed enough to commission Layton Cooke to make his report by the next year.
21   Wilson, Shirley Cameron & Borrow, KT *The Bridge over the Ocean* (Adelaide, Sth Australia, 1973).
22   Cooke, Layton Ibid TRS 1981 p46
23   Wilson, Shirley Cameron & Borrow, KT Ibid p50 ; also TRS 1934 p 60.
24   Sales Document 1837, Shirley Cameron Wilson Bequest, State Library of South Australia. PRG 1399/75
25   CADW /ICOMOS Register of Landscapes, Parks and Gardens of Special Historic Interest
26   Messrs. Driver, Jonas & Co. *The Charming Freehold, Historical, Residential and Sporting Estate known as Abbey Cwmhir 1919.* (Powys County Archives R/D/CL/2/2)
27   Most of the information on this page can be found in Burke's *Landed Gentry* (1952) confirmed from family records by Prof Flavia Swann, Grandaughter of Col.JL Philips
28   *The London Gazette* Supplement No 566693 - Vol. 189, 1850 "Published by Authority"- an official journal of record of the British government
29   Maddox, WC *Abbey-Cwm-Hir. The story of a Radnorshire Village'*(Manuscript 1971) p 73 .
30   Maddox, WC Ibid p 75
31   Williams, Jonathan & Davies, Edwin *History of Radnorshire* (Brecon 1905) note on page 266.
32   Maddox, WC Ibid p 73
33   All wedding information from *Hereford Journal* October 29th 1982.
34   They made a Claim for Compensation recorded in the *Legacies of British Slave Ownership.*
35   PCA (RD/BRS/2489/1-18)
36   Maddox, WC Ibid p 69
37   Radnorshire Society Library
38   Noel Price hand written document "This is all before 1950" commissioned by the Editor.
39   *Express & Times* (Stockport?) April 2nd 1960
40   Description & info from a Welsh Newspaper printed in colour - bar code 9 770964 076205. Circa 1995.
41   Maddox, WC Ibid p78

Sources of Information

The Happy Union *pages 89 - 95*

1. The National Library of Wales has a programme called *Gathering the Jewels* concerned with Welsh cultural history
2. An article in the Western Mail of 1935 by John Kyrle Fletcher recorded "The story of the inn sign, as told me by the innkeeper, was that about eighty years ago...." (*aprox. 1858 Ed.*) in 'Radnorshire Inns' by Rev.D.Stedman Davies MA .TRS 1941 p7
3. Two Rembrandts (F,4.75; F,7.79;) and 5 other makers prints that he donated are in the British Museum collection in 2014 but in the Appendix (p 291) of his Biography (Hall note 2) 65 are listed. Wilson published a *Catalogue Raisonnée* of his private collection in 1828 and *A Descriptive Catalogue of the Prints of Rembrandt in 1836.*
4. Lord, Peter, *Words with Pictures: Welsh Images and Images of Wales in the Popular Press, 1640-1860* (Planet 2009)
5. Lord, Peter Ibid.
6. Hughes, Arthur *The Welsh National Emblem: Leek or Daffodil?* - Y Cymroder 1916 p 147
7. Conradi, Peter J "At the Bright Hem of God" (Seren 2009)
8. Hughes, Arthur Ibid
9. Hughes, Arthur Ibid
10. Plawiuk, Eugene W. - Master Mason -*Liber Capricornus The Symbolism of the Goat.* Presented to Norwood Lodge No.90 A.F.& A.M. G.R.A. September 3 1991 C.
11. Sales Document 1837, Shirley Cameron Wilson Bequest, State Library of South Australia. SLSA/PRG 1399/75
12. Kilvert's Diary 22nd April 1870 quoted by WC Maddox Ibid p 73
13. *Liber Capricornus* The Symbolism of the Goat by Eugene W. Plawiuk, Master Mason. cf Note 10
14. Cooke, Layton *Report on the Abbeycwmhir Estate 1822* (TRS 1981) p 52
15. Cooke, Layton Ibid p 52 - 53
16. Davies MA, Rev.D.Stedman p6 "*Radnorshire Inns*" (TRS 1941) p 7

The Mill *pages 97 - 101*

1. The Welsh word *gylanennaidd/gylanennog* – means soft and flannelly and indeed a *gwlanennwr* means a Flannel Merchant so it could have been a flannel mill. Or possibly a corruption of *Felin isa'* meaning Lower Mill
2. Williams, DH "*The White Monks of Powys*" Cistercian Studies Quarterly (1976) p 89
3. Williams, DH *The Welsh Cistercians* (Gracewing 2001) p 242
4. Williams, DH "*The White Monks of Powys*" Cistercian Studies Quarterly (1976) p 97
5. Tucker, D G, "*The water mills of Radnorshire*", (Melin 5, 1989) p 3-45
6. The Old Welsh Laws, codified by Hywel Dda (Hywel the Good) in the tenth century, contain what is believed to be the earliest known reference to milling. 'Soke' was the obligation placed upon tenants to grind their corn at a specific mill"."*Welsh corn mills - the past, present, and future?*" by Gerallt D Nash 1992 in *Industrial Review Papers*. CBA/Cadw
7. Cooke, Layton report 1822 TRS 1981 p 49
8. Ridyard, Geof - WWW "Powys: *A Day in the Life of....Water Corn Mills in Radnorshire.*" A *Radnor shire Society Contribution.* Also the 1840 Tithe Awards refer to a Kiln Room
9. Layton Cooke Report 1822 (TRS 1981) p 55
10. Lewis, George F *Henfryn* (Logaston 2002) p 135
11. Layton Cooke Report 1822 (RST 1981) in p 52
12. PCA (R/D/BRA/1862/34).

Water for London *page 104*

1. Rees, Richard Rhys (RST 2012) p 25

Abbeycwmhir Community Book Appendices

Homes No More *Pages 105 - 113*

1. CPAT Regional Sites & Monuments Nos 16261 (SO 03407112); 70187 (SO 05667110) ; 21792 (SO 0560969862); 21794 (SO 0353072425)
2. Layton Cooke 1822 (TRS 1966) p 58
3. Layton Cooke Ibid p 57
4. Layton Cooke Ibid p 57
5. Layton Cooke Ibid p 57
6. Layton Cooke Ibid (TRS 1965) p 44
7. Layton Cooke Ibid (TRS 1966) p 56
8. Wiliam, Eurwyn *The Welsh Cottage 1750 - 1900*
9. Census of England & Wales 1841-1911
10. Sugget, Richard *Houses & History in the March of Wales—Radnorshire 1400 -1800* (RCAHMW 2005)
11. Quoted by Peter J.Conradi in his *"At the Bright Hem of God - A Radnorshire Pastoral"* (Seren 2009)
12. Government Web Site *uk.gov.com* (2014)
13. The Abbeycwmhir Inclosure was started by Francis Philips in 1846 and completed by Francis Aspinal Philips in 1857. *A Guide to the Parliamentary Enclosures of Wales* - John Chapman (UWP 1992). John Cheesement Severn and Jonathon Field were co-signatories. The Awards are based on former manors, rather than on the civil parishes. As a result of this, the Llanbadarn Fynydd Enclosure Award also includes some of Abbeycwmhir. (Powys County archive & NLW 3A 36P) . The spelling of enclosure with an "I" is on the original maps, is used by Layton Cooke - and is expressive.
14. Young, Arthur *Annals of Agriculture* (1793)
15. Instead of by a locally negotiated inclosure with meetings between those affected.
16. Asserted by J L and Barbara Hammond in *The Village Labourer*, in 1911
17. "Commoners: Common Right, Enclosure and Social Change in England 1700-1820" - JM Neeson (Cambridge 1993) page 44-5
18. *The Tickler Magazine* 1 February 1821.
19. Parker, Keith *Parliamentary Enclosure in Radnorshire* (TRS 2003)
20. Text - Radnorshire Muesum, Llandrindod Wells
21. From *"To a Fallen Elm"* by John Clare" in *John Clare* by John Lucas (Northcote House & British Council, Plymouth, 1994)

Forestry *pages 114-119*

1. Williams, Jonathan & Davies, Edwin and others *History of Radnorshire* (Brecon 1905) p 266 . "Embosomed with Wood" page 135
2. Williams,Jonathan *History of Radnorshire* (The Red Shop 1859) Williams died in 1829 and his book was published posthumously. (The original was re-printed in 2010 by Stephen Collard, 2, South Street, Rhayader LD6 5BH). In 1905 the original was re-edited and often reworded by Edwin Davies of Brecon " and others" including the Rev WJ Rees of Cascob with excerpts from his "The Ruinated Abbey of Abbeycwmhir" included
3. Layton Cooke Report (TRS 1965) p 48
4. Known documents show that Wilson bought the lands which made up his estate in 1824 & 1837 but the Layton Cooke report is dated 1822 and Wilson wrote in 1833 of planting in 1823 - did he make a mistake or are there facts we don't know?
5. Cooke, Layton Ibid p 49
6. Cooke, Layton Ibid P48
7. The Mabinogion translated by G & T Jones (Everyman 1966) p 113 ix) cited by Linnard, William '*Welsh Woods and Forests*" (Gomer 2000) p 17
8. Caesar, De Bello Galico V P12 cited in Linnard, William Ibid page 14.
9. Williams, DH "The Welsh Cistercians" (Gracewing 2001) p 225

Sources of Information

10. Williams DH *White Monks in Gwent and the Borders* (Pontypool 1976)
11. Williams, DH *The Welsh Cistercians* (Gracewing 2001) p 226
12. Williams, DH Ibid p 226
13. *Statuta 1, 69 1158/5*; Williams, DH *The Cistercians in the Early Middle Ages* (Gracewing 1998) p 317 note 92
14. Williams, DH "The White Monks of Powys" Cistercian Studies Quarterly (1976) p 98
15. 'History of the Forestry Commission' - internal document provided by previous local manager Jim Ralph
16. Caption to photograph in a newspaper from the period 1919 - 1927. Collection of CARAD
17. Jones, D. Gwennallt from *Ysgubau'r Awen* (JD Lewis & Sons Ltd - Gwasg Gomer -1938)

Village Group Picture *page 120*

1. Hobbs, Tony *Pubs of Radnorshire* (Logaston 2006) p 299
2. Maddox, WC *Abbey-Cwm-Hir. The story of a Radnorshire Village* (Manuscript 1971).p 77

In Living Memory *pages 138 - 167*

1. Davies, John *Abaty'r Cwmhir - a chronicle 1143-1992* (Manuscript NLW '93) p 245
2. *Welsh Nation* October 1978 cited in Ibid p 247
3. Jones, Tom Parri "Anthology" (1978) cited in Davies, John Ibid p 248
4. Ithon Valley Trumpet. Article by Julian Lovell from notes by William Lewis of Esgairwy
5. Oxford Book of Welsh Verse in English (OUP 1977) p 92
6. Ithon Valley Trumpet. Article byJulian Lovell from notes by William Lewis of Esgairwy
7. Williams, Waldo from "Cwmwl Haf "(A Summer Cloud) by Translated by Joseph P. Clancy. Oxford Book of Welsh Verse in English (OUP 1977) p 218
8. Lewis, George F *Henfryn* (Logaston 2002) p 133
9. *Potrait of a Radnorshire Valley: the Reminiscences of William Lewis, Esgairwy* - Ed. Julian Lovell (Manuscript) p15.
10. British Telecom Archives
11. Maddox,WC *A history of the Radnorshire Constabulary* (Radnorshire Society (1959) 1981 p 56
12. The WAR-AG's job was to convert common and high lands to useful fields especially potatoes during the Second World War. They had the best equipment some of which is still in use today. There was a hostel in Talgarth for forty men working as WAR-AGs
13. PCA R/D/CL/2/2
14. Ithon Valley Trumpet & Julian Lovell, (Editor of "*Potrait of a Radnorshire Valley: the reminiscences of William Lewis, Esgairwy*" (Manuscripr) p 16
15. Abbecycwmhir Parish Council Minutes Friday 8th February 1895
16. Abbecycwmhir Parish Council Minutes 19th August 1895
17. Abbeycwmhir Parish Council Minutes 4th April 1898
18. Maddox, WC '*Abbey-Cwm-Hir. The story of a Radnorshire Village*' (Manuscript 1971) p 109
19. Bennet, Edward (Teddy) of Tyn y Coed *Abbeycwmhir a Geographical Study*, (Manuscript 1953)
20. Parfitt, Arthur G "*Military History*" (TRS 1958) p 38
21. Williams, Jonathan & Davies, Edwin and others *History of Radnorshire* (Brecon 1905) p 268
22. Bennet, Edward (Teddy) of Tyn y Coed *Abbeycwmhir a Geographical Study*, (Manuscript 1953)
23. Conradi, Peter *At the Bright Hem of God - a Radnorshuire Pastoral* - (Seren 2009) p162 quoting from Elizabeth Clarke's "The Valley" (1969)
24. Full details of men on the plaque from:http://www.roll-of-honour.com/Radnorshire/index.html
25. Maddox, WC *Abbeycwmhir School* (TRS 1979) p 69
26. Abbey Cwmhir National School Log Book, Digital History, Powys County Archives R/E/PS/1/L1
27. Hawkins, Dai cf page 310ff
28. He lectured to the Cambrian Archaeological Society.(*Archaeologia Cambrensis* -Vol 11, 1911).
29. *Crockford's Clerical Directory* 1918-1919, 1930

Abbeycwmhir Community Book Appendices

Homes and People Inserts *pages 168 - 270*

1. Powys County Archives (R/B/JGW/18/1) Abbeycwmhir Estate (p 168)
2. Powys County Archives (R/B/JGW/20/1) Penybont Estate (p 168)
3. Powys County Archives (R/B/JGW/18/1) - Abbeycwmhir Estate - The Mill (p171)
4. Powys County Archives (R/B/JGW/18/1) - Abbeycwmhir Estate - Bryncamlo (p 179)
5. Powys County Archives (R/B/JGW/20/1 - Abbeycwmhir Estate - Brondrefawr (181)
6. 'Bwlch y Sarnau Baptist Church Ter-Jubilee' (St Idloes Press1979) p 14 (p 186)
7. Interview with Albert Philips for this book (cf pages 118 & 159) (p 204)
8. Williams, Jonathan & Davies, Edwin and others *History of Radnorshire* (Brecon 1905) p 136 (p 207)
9. Lloyd,JE "A History of Wales" (Longmans, Green, and Co.1912) p 283ff (p218)
10. Powys County Archives (R/B/JGW/18/1) Abbeycwmhir Estate - Home Farm (p 227)
11. Oxford Book of Welsh Verse in English (OUP 1971) Poem 62, p 92 (p 230)
12. Email from Prof Flavia Swann 25th September 2014 (p 206)
13. Cooke, Layton . *Report on the Abbeycwmhir Estate 1822* (TRS 1965) pp 48-49.
14. From The Preface of '*An Historical & Descriptive account of the Ruinated Abbey of Cwmhir*' by Rev WJ Rees, Rector of Cascob and Rural Dean of Lower Melenith
15. Roberts, Evan, Llandderfel, *Yr Haul - The Church in Wales* magazine, July 1932

We have attempted to contact all to obtain necessary permissions - we apologise if any errors have been made.

Many thanks go to the excellent and indispensable proof readers of this book who were Diana Berriman of Little Plock, Julian Lovall of Ty'r Ehedydd and Prof Flavia Swann, Grandaughter of Colonel JL Philips.

Abbeycwmhir Bibliography
For more detailed information

- *Abbaty'r Cwm Hir - A Chronicle 1143 - 1992* - Dr John Davies (ABC Trust) (1993) Manuscript - available in Llandrindod Library Local History Shelf and in National Library of Wales
- *Political History of Abbeycwmhir* - Paul Remfry (Castle Studies 2004).
- "*The White Monks of Powys I*" DH Williams. *Cistercian Studies Quarterly* (1976) in Llandrindod Library
- *Abbey-cwm-hir -The Story of a Radnorshire Village* - Wilfred Charles Maddox (Manuscript, November 1971, Crossgates) Maddox also wrote an early version of the Guide to St.Mary's Church and an article for RST on *Abbeycwmhir School* (TRS 1979). He worked as a Police Seargaent and later an Inspector and wrote *A history of the Radnorshire Constabulary* (Radnorshire Society (1959) published in 1981
- *Report on Abbey Cwm Hir Estate 1822* - Layton Cooke. Report used by Thomas Wilson. Reprinted in TRS 1965 ,1966 & 1981. Original in Radnorshire Society Library
- *Portrait of a Radnorshire Valley; The Reminiscences and Recollections of William Lewis, Esgairy "1907 - 1971* - Julian Lovell, (Editor)
- *The Bridge over the Ocean* - Shirley Cameron Wilson, & KT Borrow (Adelaide, South Australia 1973)
- *A Radnorshire Farm Diary 1879-1883* - David & Sheila Leitch (1999)
- *Henfryn - Radnorshire hill farming in the 1930's & 40's*-George F.Lewis (Logaston 2002)
- *Haber Nant Llan Nerch Freit - an upbriniging on a Radnorshire Hill Farm* - Georg F.Lewis (Logaston 1998).
- *Cefn Pawl Baptist Church Centenary* - Alwyn Batley (Booklet1985)
- *Bwlch y Sarnau Baptist Church Ter-Jubilee* - William Manuel (Booklet St Idloes Press1979)
- *175 Years of Methodism at Devannor 1818 to 1993* (1993) - Diana Sarah Griffiths

The Cistercians - Bibliography

- *The Welsh Cistercians* - David H. Williams (Gracewing 2001)
- *Cistercians in Wales - Architecture & Archaeology* - Jonathan Robinson (The Society of Antiquaries 2006)
- *The Cistercian Abbeys of Britain* - David Robinson (Editor) (Batsford 1998)
- *The Cistercians in the Early Middle Ages* - DH Williams (Gracewing 1998)

NB There is a *Cistercian Abbey Trail* - http://cistercian-way.newport.ac.uk/

Wales in General Bibliography

- *An Historical Atlas of Wales* - William Rees (Faber 1951)
- *A History of Wales* - JE Lloydd Vols 1 & 2 (Longmans Green & Co 1912)
- *A History of Wales* - John Davies (Penguin 1993)
- *Llywelyb ap Gruffudd* - J.Beverley Smith (UW Press 1998)
- *The Revolt of Owain Glyndwr's* R.R.Davies (OUP 1995)
- *Castles of Radnorshire* - Paul Martin Remfry (Logaston Press 1996)
- *Welsh Pub Names* - Myrddin ap Dafyddd (Welsh Heritage series No 1, 1991)
- *Words with Pictures: Welsh Images an Images of Wales in the Popular Press, 1640-1860* - by Peter Lord (Planet 1995)
- *Roads & Trackways of Wales* - Richard Colyer (Morland Publishing 1984)
- *Oxford Companion to the Literature of Wales* - Meic Stephens (OUP 1986)
- *Oxford Book of Welsh Verse in English* (OUP 1971)
- *The Welsh and their Religion. Historical Essays* - Glanmor Williams (Cardiff UWP 1991)
- *Sacred Place, Chosen People* - Dorian Llywelyn (UWP 1999)

Early History Sites - *Page 49*
Ordnance Survey Map References and Public Record Numbers (PRN)

Listed according to site numbers on map on page 49

1 Cwmtelma Farm (13206) SO 075678
2 A flint axe head Abbeycwmhir village centre (4460) - in Shrewsbury Museum.
3 Hide or woodworking thumb scraper at Devannor (13205) SO 071371 - in Brecon Museum.
4 Enclosure from the same period near Cwm Pistyll (4161) SO 0103076840
5 Domen Ddu (553 mtrs) cairn (959) SO 01697826 and round barrow (960) SO 01697829)
6 Banc Du's Fowlers Armchair stone circle (957) SO 0416279177 and cairn (958) SO 04167916
7 Crugyn Llwyd (571 mtrs) cairn (961) SO 0240879619
8.Fuallt settlement: hut, stones and enclosure (4163) SO 02547927
9 Castell y Garn by Cefn Crin (240) SO 0187473578
10 Creigiau, the Hynod Cairn built on rocks (242) SO 0368570042
11 Llwn Dwr standing stone (1154) SO 04776960 and barrow (1153) SO 0467069620
12 The Devils Apronful of Stones cairn (1635) SO 053688
13 Bronze Age field system at Blaen Trinnant (6678) SO 018789
14. The Mount" behind Maes y Gwaelod. (RD 073) SO 012756
15 **Iron Age** (1100BC – 700AD) Camp Wood (2072) SO 08357019

Source: Clwyd-Powys Archaeological Trust Regional Sites and Monuments Record.

Abbeycwmhir Community Book Appendices

Key to map on page 40 - Granges circa 1500
With Ordnance Survey Reference Numbers

Initials and names are of donors recorded in the 1215 Confirmation of the Charter by King John.

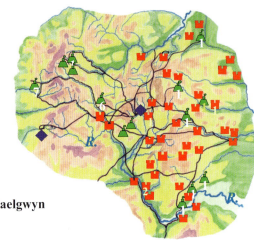

Numbers from map:

In Abbeycwmhir (not on map) -
1) **Golon Manor** abbey site (SO 055711) **MM = Maradudd ap Maelgwyn**
2), **Tý Faenor** (SO 071711) **MM**
3) **Cefn Pawl** (SO 066706) **MM**

Closest to Abbeycwmhir - Nantmel area -
4) **Nantymynach** (SO 014662),
5) **Rhymney** (SO 049680)

North West Area -
6) **Dolhelfa Grange**: (SN 927738) barn is oldest feature;
7) **Nant-yr-arian** Grange (SN 715813; important pastoral more extensive than present farm.
8) **Esgair-maen** (SN 860840).
9) **Mynachlog** SN 860840.
10) **Cwmbiga Grange** (SN 859892), important for transhumance

North East Area -
11) **Gwern-y-go Grange** SO 222919; held with lands in Brompton, Churchstoke and Foxton.

Teme & Lugg -
12) **Cwmbugail** (SO 182796)
13) **Mynachdy-poeth Grange** (SO 255747), and Ysgubor (SO 268744) two ponds on tributary of Teme.
14) **Mynachdy-Treburvaugh Grange** :Mynachty (SO 229697), tradition of burials at more southerly 'mynachdy' (SO 235694), 'Coed-y-mynach' (SO 250672). "Thlayan-vvyddan' and 'Blakenhavoe' Granges (noted in 1297) perhaps in this area.

Hay-on-Wye Area -
15) **Lands in Brilley:** uncertain location, stretched towards Michaelchurch;. **EP = Prince Einion o'r Porth**
16) **Gabalfa Grange** (c.SO 236460); **EP**
17) **Carnaf Grange**: 'tir-y-mynach' (SO 225434). Did Court Farm relate ? (SO 213433).

from "The Welsh Cistercians" by DH Williams Page 301 (Gracewing 2001).

Other Lands recorded in 1215

18) Llwyngwyn SO 901793
19) Dolygarn (SO 087785) **MM**
20) Laithddu (SO 068801) **MM**
21) Cwm Nant-du (SO 097807) **MM**
22) Old Neuadd Bank (SO 095842) **MM**
23) Hopton (SO 365782) **MM**
24) Bachaethlon (SO 211904) **MM**
25) Caelber Isaf (SO214928) **MM**
26) Gwenthriw (SO 195904) **MM**
27) Duthlas/Cwmbugail (SO 209778) **MM**
28) Skyberry (SO 266744) **William Fitz Allan**
29) Monaughty (SO 239686) **MM**
30) Dol-llugan (SO 215680) Rog.Mortimer 1200
31) Crug (SO 192723) **MM**
32) Foesidoes (SO 225653) **MM**
33) Llechrydd (SO 025539) **MM**
34) Cilgwynfydd (SO 035544) **MM**
35) Buddugre (SO 100691) **MM**
36) Pilleth (SO 258678) **Rog.Mortimer 1200**
37) Waen Wenn (SO 217546) **Einion o'r Porth**
38) Cefnhir (SO 210558) **Llywelyn ab Arnarawd.**

From "A Political History of Abbey Cwmhir" - Paul M.Remfry P 31-2. (Castle Studies Research & Publishing 2004).

Granges & Castles

Key to map on page 40 - Castles
With Ordnance Survey Reference Numbers

Numbers from Map

1) Buddugre SO 102697
2) Tinboeth SO 091754
3) Cwmaran SO153273
4) Cefn Lys SO 089614
5) Dinieithon SO 091632

6) Rhayader (a) SN 966681 (b) SN 971681
7) Builth Wells SO 046509
8) Crugerydd SO 157593
9) Tomen SO 173589
10) Bleddfa SO 268212
11) New Radnor SO 2066612

12) Knucklas SO249746
13) Llanfair Waterdine SO 245764
14) Beguildy SO 188805
15) Knighton SO 292722
16) Ceri SO 147895
17) Mochdre SO 077878
18) Montgomery SO 220968
19) Bishops Castle SO 323892

20) Presteigne SO 309646
21) Norton SO 303673

22) City SO 206896

23) Painscastle SO 168462
24) Clyro SO 216437
25) Hay SO 225422
26) Aberedw (a) SO 078472 (b) SO 076474
27) Three Cocks SO 175376
28) Penarth SO 124526
29) Colwyn SO 103532
30) Gwernceste SO 163 537
31) Stapleton, Presteigne, SO 324656
32) Clun SO 298809
33) Newcastle SO 244821
34) Ruthin today Bryn Amllwg SO167849
35) Pilleth SO 258678

In alphabetical order

Aberedw (**26a/b**) (SE of Builth) a) SO 078472
　　　　　　　　　　　　　　 (b) SO 076474
Beguildy (**14**) SO 188805 (R.Teme N. of Knighton)
Bishops Castle (**19**) SO 323892
Bleddfa (**10**) SO 212682
Builth Wells (**7**) SO 046509
Buddugre (**1**) SO 102697
Cefnllys (**4**) SO 089614 (W.of Llandrindod Wells)
Ceri (**16**) SO 147895
City (**22**) SO 206896 (South of Montgomery)
Clun (**32**) SO 298809
Clyro (**24**) SO 216437 (North of Hay on Wye)
Colwyn (**29**) SO 103532
Crugerydd (**8**) SO 157593
Cwmaran (**3**) SO 153273 (SW of Llanbister Rd. Stn.)
Dinieithon (**5**) (Llandrindod Wells)
Gwernceste (**30**) SO 163537
Hay on Wye (**25**) SO 225422
Knighton (**15**)SO 292722
Knucklas (**12**) SO 249746 (NW of Knighton)
Llanfair Waterdine (**13**) SO245764
Mochdre (**17**) SO 079878
Montgomery (**18**) SO 220968
Newcastle (**33**) SO 244821
New Radnor (**11**) SO 206612
Norton (**21**) SO303673 (North of Presteigne)
Painscastle (**23**) SO 168462
Penarth, (**28**) SO 124526 (Cregrina)
Pilleth (**35**) SO 258678
Presteigne (**20**)SO 309646
Rhayader (**6a/b**) SO O971681 & SO 971681
Ruthin (**34**) today Bryn Amllwg SO167849
Stapleton (**31**) SO 324656 (Presteigne)
Three Cocks (**27**) SO 175376
Tinboeth (**2**) SO 091754 (North of Llanbister)
Tomen (**9**) 173589 (Opp.Forest Inn across A44)

Further castles known to be in the area but not on the map are listed on the next page →

Further castles known but not on map on page 40

Boughrood (SO 134394 (Between Builth Wells & Hay on Wye)
Caemardy SO 035531 (Builth Road)
Clifford SO 242456
Crickadarn SO 088421 (South of Builth Wells)
Crug SO 190723 (West of Llangunllo)
Fforest SO 101529 (East of Builth Wells)
Glasbury SO 172381 (West of Hay)
Hen Domen SO 214980 (Just North of Montgomery)
Hopton SO 780365 (South of Montgomery)
Hundred House SO 116544 (East of Builth Wells)
Llandewi SO 126449 (Between Builth Wells & Hay on Wye (Ex PMR *Trewern*)
Llanstephan SO 108438 (Between Builth Wells & Hay on Wye North of town at Twyn y Garth)
Stanage SO 332730 (East of Knighton)

- there may be many others.

Dates of Excavations & Investigations at Cwmhir Abbey

1824 Thomas Wilson's *"clearance"*. (cf Page 70ff).
1848 Written up by Rev W.Jenkin Rees "An Historical Account of the Ruinated Abbey of Cwmhir in The County of Radnor". 1848 2nd Meeting of the Cambrian Archaeolgical Association; printed in Archaeologia Cambrensis No 16; Reprinted as monogram 1850. 2/- Hard Back.
1894-5 Stephen.W.Williams "The Cistercian Abbey of Cwmhir, Radnorshire" - Transactions of the Honourable Society of Cwmmrodorion (1894-5). (cf illustrations at top of pages 14-17).
1933 Made an Ancient Monument (1913 & 1931).
1988 CPAT Survey, Drawing & Photographing the site.
1993 CPAT Assessment of deterioration using drawings from 1988.
1994 Repair & Recording. Non-intrusive excavation only within walling. Archaeological survey.
1997-2000 Re-Survey.
1998 Geophysical Survey - unpublished report by GeoQuest Associates.

Radnorshire High Sherrifs from Abbeycwmhir

The office of High Sheriff is over 1000 years old being established before the Norman Conquest. The job was to be the Sovereign's senior representative in the County for all matters relating to the Judiciary and the maintenance of law and order and so its importance varied with the importance of the monarch. In 1908, in the reign of Edward VII, the Lord-Lieutenant became the senior post and since local government re-organisation in 1974 there is both a Lord-Lieutenant and a High Sherriff of Powys - only a one year position arranged the year before. (Cf also pages 56 & 84). (From an article by WH Howse in TRS 1955 p39-45)

1597 Richard Fowler, Abbeycwmhir.
1613 Richard Fowler, Abbeycwmhir
1656 Richard Fowler "Tyfaenor" Abbeycwmhir
1684 John Davies, Coedglasson, (Nantmel)*
1690 John Fowler, Brondrefawr, Abbeycwmhir
(1695 William Fowler, Harnage Grange, Salop)
1705 David Morgan, Coedglasson (Nantmel)*
1714 Walter price, Cefnpawl, Abbeycwmhir

1715 Edward Fowler, Tyfaenor, Abbeycwmhir
1724 Hugh Morgan, Coedglasson, (Nantmel)*
1765 Sir Hans Fowler'Tyfaenor' Abbeycwmhir
1771 Charles Gore, 'Tyfaenor' Abbeycwmhir
1851 Francis Aspinal Philips, The Hall, ACH
1860 George Henry Philips, The Hall, ACH
1906 Francis George Prescot Philips (The Major)
1935 Lt-Col John Lionel Philips, DSO
   (The Colonel) of Abbeycwmhir.

* Coedglasson is now in Abbeycwmhir cf page 181.

Mabli & Others

How historians have interpreted Mabel's Tomb Lid

English: Here   lies   M a -

Latin: h I   C   I   A   C   E   T   M   A-

- B L I   c A I e   P P I C I E T   D E O

Contractions: (ujus)   (ro)   (ur)

Follow the black arrows (n)(ma)

Notes: 2 in 1   double 'P'

tin:- **B L I**   **cujus Animae**   **Propi c i e - tur**   **D E O**

glish:-bel   on whose Soul,   merciful,   may God be

The thirteenth Century stone mason may have run out of space after carving the Lombardic letters above the floriated Cross - although shortening and contraction were common. Above the letter "C" a squiggle stands in for the rest of the latin word "cujus" meaning "on whose". The small box above the "I" stands for two sets of letters "n" and "ma" part of the word "animae" meaning soul - feminine. Above the "T" the other squiggle stands for "ur" part of the word "propicietur" meaning "merciful". Final Translation: Here lies Mabel, on whose female soul may God be Merciful." (Thanks to Paul Martin Remfry).

Ascension Day Tea Party at the Vicarage page 167 - Key to photo

Back Row: 1 Mrs Vaughan (Piccadilly), 2 Mrs Wozencraft (Broad Oak), 3 Mrs Prosser (Llwynonn), 4 Lucy Williams (Cwmhir Farm), 5 Mrs Evans (Piccadilly), 6 Mervyn & Mrs Wozencraft Cwmyscawen), 7 Mrs Margaret Jones (Happy Union), 8 Mrs Ellinor Lewis (Troedrhiwfelin), 9 Alice Rowlands (Paddock Cottage), 10 Margaret Jones (Happy Union).

Middle Back (Standing): 1 Dorothy Wozencraft, 2 George Wozencraft (Frog Town), 3 Eddie Wozencraft, 4 David Jones (Happy Union), 5 John Wozencraft (Frog Town), 6 Baden Vaughan (Cwmhir Cottage), 7 Dilwyn Jones (Happy Union).

Middle Front (Sitting): 1 Winnie Wozencraft, 2 Evangeline Vaughan, 3 Muriel Evans (Piccadilly), 4 Phyllis Griffiths (Cwmpoeth) , 5 Tilly Wozencraft, 6 Enid Pugh (Troedrhiwfelin), 7 Freda Wozencraft, 8 Iris Williams (Ffron Farm)

Front Row: 1 Jean Bennet, 2 Phyllis Griffiths (Cwmpoeth), 3 Dorothy Prosser (Llwynon), 4 Violet Williams (Ffron Farm), 5 John Wozencraft (Frog Town), 6 Gordon Lewis (Troedrhiwfelin)

Abbeycwmhir Community Book Appendices

KEY TO TAPESTRY SUBJECTS & MAKERS

Photographs of the Tapestries are on pages 130 -133

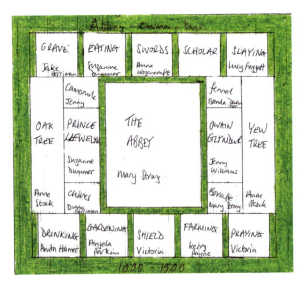

Summer 1000 - 1500

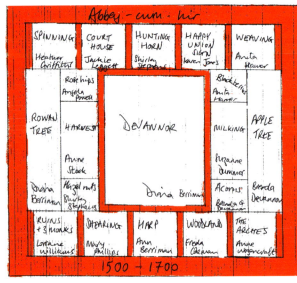

Autumn 1500 -1700

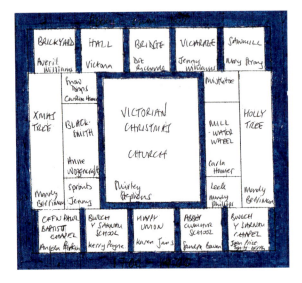

Winter 1700 - 1900

Spring 1900 - 2000

We apologise if any names have been incorrectly ascribed or missed out—it was made over a decade ago. The selection from the tapestries on the back cover are listed opposite.

Key to *"Bwlch y Sarnau School Then and Now"*

Flower Arranging	Pony Show	Dog Show	Football	W.I.
Teresa Davies	Jane Jones	Lucy Davies	Jake Berriman	Angela Lewis
Glyndwrs Way				Celebrations
Michael Wilson		The School through the years. Angela Lewis		Karen Smith
Snooker				Ballroom Dancing
Evelyn Davies				Owen Davies
Gardening Group	Yoga	Signposts	Art Group	Mobile Library
Katherine Loads	Medina Davies	Dot Smith	Stephanie Adams	Mike Smith

by the Bwlch y Sarnau Art Group 2012.

The Back Cover

Is a montage of images selected from the four Millennium Tapestries on display in the Philips Hall. They were made by the women of the Community around 2000AD.

Top Left: Electricity by Averil Williams (Spring 1900 - 2000)
Top Centre Left: Glyndwrs Way by Anita Hamer (Spring 1900 - 2000)
Top Centre Right: Shield by Victoria Humpherston (Summer 1000 - 1500)
Top Right: Sawmill by Mary Strong (Winter 1700 - 1900)
Centre Left: Hawthorn Tree by Shirley Stephens (Spring 1900 - 2000)
Centre: The Abbey by Mary Strong (Summer 1000 - 1500)
Centre Right: Hazel Tree by Shirely Stephens (Spring 1900 - 2000)
Bottom Left: Blacksmith by Anne Wozencraft (Winter 1700 - 1900)
Bottom Centre: Grave by Jake Berriman (Summer 1000-1500)
Bottom Right: Village Green by Mary Strong and Diana Berriman (Spring 1900 - 2000).

Abbeycwmhir Community Book Appendices

Key to the photo of th[e]

What does community mean to you?

Where we live. A place of belonging and dissonance. A group of kindred spirits and diverse minds. A memory or sense of a feeling for which I had no words. Responsible citizens living in harmony and working towards common goals. Connections. A place where people come together, feel like they belong, and draw common strength and identity. A sense of place and belonging. A place where things are pleasantly familiar, safe and a welcoming circle larger than self. People living together creatively and humanely in all their similarities and differences. People relying on one another. A safe space and a space you feel connected to. Friends, enemies, engagement. Belonging. Escape from isolation. I can count on someone. A group of individuals brought together by a common geography, cultural background or belonging. A place where I belong/fit and am accepted and respected by others - home. Old fashioned neighbourliness in which we look out for each other and the village raises the child. Realising that you are not your own person but somebody elses as well. All ages and backgrounds together. Community is a sense of pride in a region or area that results in a high level of volunteerism, and means that people co-operate meaningfully to attain goals for the benefit of all. Community is an old quilt: patchwork at times; fraying in a few parts; warm in times of need; forgotten often when times are good; virtual in the parts that are missing.

Excerpts from research by Tamarack - An Institute for Community Engagement.

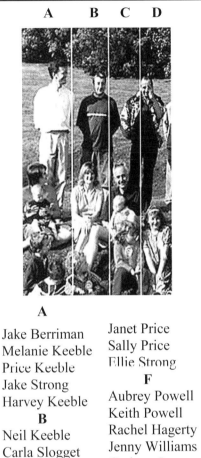

A
Jake Berriman
Melanie Keeble
Price Keeble
Jake Strong
Harvey Keeble
B
Neil Keeble
Carla Slogget
George Sloggett
C
Paul Sloggett
Siobhan Sloggett
Bronwyn Watkins
D
Mark Edwards
Elinor Watkins
E
Sandra Powell
Victoria - Humpherston
Leslie Lewis

Janet Price
Sally Price
Ellie Strong
F
Aubrey Powell
Keith Powell
Rachel Hagerty
Jenny Williams
Graham Jones
Nigel Watkins
Alwyn Watkins
G
Mandy Jones
Brenda Griffithis
Owen Davies
Angela Powell
Morion Powell
?
H
David Jones
John Bennett

Community Group Pictures

Village at The Hall for the Queen's Golden Jubilee 2003 *pages 120-121*

E F G H I J K L M N O P Q R S T U V W X Y Z

Danny Lydiat
Edna Brian
Paul Powell

T
Bryn Worgan
Medina Davies
Janet Rees

U
Julie Evans
Lyndsey Williams
?
Kenwood Price
Dot Brian
Jack Powell

V
Josie Worgan
Evan Griffiths
Deiniol Jones
Kay Powell
Yvonne Webb

W
Dave Worgan
Richard Brian
Rachel Jones

X
Archie Rees
Aelwyn Pugh
Janna Hughes

Y
Brian Rees
Alan Bennett
Jean Bennett
Martha Powell

Z
Matthew Hughes

Megan Bennett
Willie Griffiths
Teresa Davies
Andrew Strong
Gwen Watkins

I
Baby Gibberd
Mrs G. Gibberd
Mel Hamer
Averil Williams
Mary Strong
Ellen Wozencraft
Abraham Berriman

J
Vernon Gibberd
George Gibberd
Glyn Evans
Anita Hamer
Caroline Hamer
Meryl Wozencraft
Diana Berriman

Reuben Berriman
Cara Powell

K
Barry Legget
Andrew Evans
Rhiannon Hamer
Clinton Webb
Gayle Evans
Rebecca Wozencraft
Joy Powell

L
Gary Hagerty
Will Hagerty
Anthony Antell
Jackie Legget
Rosie Williams
Mrs Davies
Karen Jones
Brett Price

M
James Stock
Tony Stock
Anne Wozen-
craft
Luke Jones
Jamie Webb

N
?
Anne Stock
Nicola Edwards
Nancy Lewis

O
Harry Powell
?
Shirley Stevens
Val Webb
John Jones
Liam McKay

P
Graham Powell
Gwynne Stephens

Ivy Jones
Lauren Jones

Q
Gary Edwards
Mercy Griffiths
Rev Mark
     Griffiths
John Lydiat
?

R
David Evans
Clarice Griffiths
Suzanne Dummer
Lynne Lydiat
Doris Edwards
Edwin Powell

S
Andrew Worgan
Diane Powell
Peter Dummer
Jack Lydiat

With apologies to those whose names we couldn't find.

Photo by Paul Humperston, The Hall
Identifications by Diana Berriman

Key to 1993 Village Photograph by Ray Carpenter - *page 121*

1 Tom Griffiths Cwmporth	2 Mel Hamer Home Farm	3 Tom Griffths Cwmgringlyn	4 John Jones Happy Union	5 Dr Willi Griffiths Devannor
6 Graham Powell Cwmferdy	7 Dave Worgan Esgairwy Cottage	8 Mark Warwick Home Farm	9 Reg Hamer School House	
10 Andrew Worgan Esgairwy Cottage	11 Brenda Griffiths Devannor	12 Pippa Adams 2 Brickyard Cottage	13 Daisy Evans Fron Farm	14 John Adams 2 Brickyard Cottage
15 Doug Pryce Tynyberth	16 Dr Jonathan Griffiths, Devannor	17 Ted Wozencraft Mynyddlys	18 Jack Griffiths The Croft	
19 Byron Wozencraft, Gardenners Cottage	20 Meryl Wozencraft Gardenners Cottage	21 Dianne Powell Cwmferdy	22 Charlotte Williams Old Vicarage	23 Nathan Jones Llwynon
24 Colin Wozencraft Trimynydd	25 Bernard Pugh Troedrhiwfelen	26 Abe Wozencraft Mynyddlys	27 Tom Coalman Broad Oak	
28 Rob Csöndör Cross Cottage	29 Albert Philips Cwm Hir Cottage	30 Jake Berriman Cross Cottage	31 Lew Richards Forrest Lodge	32 Gwyn Stevens Avalon
33 Josie Worgan Esgairwy Cottage	34 Anita Hamer Home Farm	35 Fabrizio Faraldi Home Farm	36 Dot Richards Forrest Lodge	
37 Rob Parkin Sunnydale	38 Aubry Powell Llwyn Neuadd	39 Melanie Hamer Home Farm	40 Robert Antell Cefn Pawl	41 Carla Williams Home Farm
42 Roger Powell Esgairwy	43 Hazel Griffiths Cwmpoeth	44 Jane Ellwood Peterborough	45 Nita Morris Mill Cottage	
46 Keith Powell Esgairwy	47 David Evans Clywedog Bungalow	48 David Jones Happy Union	49 Julie Evans Clywedog Bungalow	50 Jenny Williams Old Vicarage
51 Michelle Wozencraft, Gardenners Cottage	52 Jamie Williams Old Vicarage	53 Joan Price Tynyberth	54 David Jones Llwynon	
55 Karen Jones Happy Union	56 Rachel Jones Llwynon	57 Karen Pugh Troedrhiwfelin	58 Shirley Stevens Avalon	59 Jodie Faraldi Forrest Lodge
60 Jan Faraldi Forrest Lodge	61 Brenda Griffths Cwmcringlyn	62 Angela Parkin Sunnydale	63 Amy Parkin Sunnydale	
64 Angela Powell Esgairwy	65 Kaley Stock The Smithy	66 Rhiannon Hamer Home Farm	67 Philip Wood Paddock Cottage	68 Tony Stock The Smithy
69 Tina Jones Llwynon	70 Anne Stock The Smithy	71 James Stock The Smithy	72 Freda Coleman Broad Oak	
73 Mrs Lewis Cwmferdy	74 SandraPowell Llwyn Neuadd	75 Joy Powell Llwyn Neuadd	76 Tonia Charles Cross Cottage	77 Anne Wozencraft Trimynydd
78 Ellen Wozencraft Trimynydd	79 Elsie Worgan Ceribach	80 Meredith Wozencraft Ty Cartref	81 Violet Jones Happy Union	
82 Jim Powell Cwmfaerdy	83 Doris Edwards Cwmydea	84 Ellen Hamer School House	85 Mrs Lewis Troedrhiwfelen	86 John Connor Piccadilly Cottages
87 Mrs Williams Wennallt	88 Mrs Hamer Rhiwgam	89 Eirys Bywater Nant-y-Ffin	90 Rosie Williams Old Vicarage	
91 Mark Evans Clywedog Byngalow	92 Matthew Hughes Home Farm	93 Janna Hughes Home Farm	94 Edwin Powell Esgairwy	95 Paul Powell Llwyneuadd
96 Kay Powell Llwyneuadd	97 Martha Jane Powell Esgairwy	98 Kate Wood Paddock Cottage	99 Lisa Antel Cefn Pawl	
100 Gail Evans Clywedog Bungalow	101 Anthony Antel Cefn Pawl	102 Graham Jones Llwynon	103 Deiniol Jones Llwynon	

Full text from excerpts on page 86

TO THE TENANTS AND LABOURERS OF THE ABBEYCWMHIR ESTATE

Having by my Father's lamented death succeeded to the Abbey Cwmhir property, I take this opportunity of addressing you in a few words.

It was always your late Landlords desire and ambition to see around him an industrious and prosperous Tenantry, an intelligent and honest set of Labourers; and the means he took to secure his object was to act the part of an encouraging and Liberal Landlord, a kind and indulgent master - to follow his example in this respect, will ever be my wish and earnest endeavour.

Within the last fifteen years very considerable sums have been expended in the formation and improvement of roads, in planting, fencing, &c, which you must allow have greatly tended to increase the value of your Farms; still the rents have remained the same, with the exception, that when Stock, Wool, and other Farming Produce were selling at reduced prices, you had an allowance of ten per cent. made you.

Bearing in mind these and other liberal acts of your two former Landlords, I beg each of you ask himself the questions—Have I done all I can to improve my farm, my Cattle and my Sheep? Have I tried by increased exertion to show that I appreciate the many acts of kindness that have been offered me? Or have I been content to farm in the same way as my ancestors did for the last hundred years or more, without taking advantage of modern experience? I am very thankful to say that with the last few years there has been a great advance made among many of you; your farms look neater, your crops cleaner and more prolific; and rest assured it is by your increased energy, your skill and perseverance in improving your Farms that you can alone expect to retain possession of them for any length of time, owing to the gradual approach of railways, the easier access to the great manufacturing districts of England as your markets, and the consequntly enhanced value and demand for the larger class of your Farms.

I shall expect each of you on your parts to adhere strictly to the various clauses of your Agreements, and I hope, personally, to inspect each Farm once a year, when I trust you will point out everything required to be done on my part as your Landlord. I shall be willing to build, drain, and carry out other improvements, charging a moderate percentage on the outlay; and as the cost of draining is now reduced by the manufacture of pipes on the Property, I hope to see a great spirit of improvement going on in this most necessary of all agricultural undertakings.

You have had a School provided for you, affording the advantages of a good education for your children, but I much regret the lukewarmness there is among some of you in sending your children to it. If you have received a good education yourselves, you surely must know the benefits derived from it - if, on the contrary, you have not been well-educated yourselves why deprive your children of the opportunity now offered you? I hope it cannot be the few pence you have to pay, for then you surely are not in a fit position to hold your Farms. Let me beg of you to send your children to School, and above all let me impress on you the necessity to send them regularly.

And now a few words to the LABOURERS:- Having for the last two or three years taken considerable interest in the Home Farm and general management of the Estate, it is with great pleasure I can say I have always found you intelligent and anxious to give satisfaction in following out any instructions. You have comfortable cottages, and have always received, perhaps, rather more than the full wages of the country; many of you have proved that you are contented with the treatment you have received, in that you have now been employed a great number of years on the Property. I have always observed with great satisfaction that you send your children to School very regularly, and I wish some of the Tenants would follow your example in his respect.

In conclusion, I have only to say to both TENANTS and Labourers, that I believe I shall best consult my own interests by promoting your comfort and welfare, by acting liberally,and assisting those who are desirous of improvement, and at the same time, if there are any opposed to progress, unwilling to take advantage of modern experience, you will soon find that I am by no means inclined to encourage idleness.

Trusting you will accept these remarks in the same kind of feeling in which they are given.
I remain,

Your affectionate friend,
GH Philips July 1st 1859

Abbeycwmhir Community Book - Appendices

Abbots of Cwmhir - what we know about them.

c. 1176 - 1184 Meurig probably first Abbot.(Welsh) died 1184 - probably succeeded by:

c. 1190 Canawg - Canog - (Welsh). Supported St.David's. Archdeacon of Brecon, Giraldus Cambrensis visited Abbeycwmhir at least once (1199) during his Abbacy possibly because he hoped for his nomination to the vacant see. Geraldus also describes a vision by a monk of Cwmhir in which Geraldus and the King were seen sitting together in dispute over the succession to St Davids. He later wrote to Canawg lamenting their loss of contact.

c. 1200 Rhiryd. Welsh but probably a Mortimer appointment as he resigned on the death or Roger Mortimer in 1215. He was Pro-Canterbury to whom he complained that St.David's was putting unfair pressure on the Cistercian Order "amounting to bribery" He also gave land - according to the 1215 charter. "The Abbot of Cwmhir" poem written about him by Thomas Wilson suggesting that he wanted to get married and eloped with a nun to France. Pope Honorious III (1216-27) intervened and persuaded him to return to Abbeycwmhir - the poem imagines.

c.1215-1122 Gwrgenau (Welsh). Took over promptly after death of Roger Mortimer. He was recorded as Prior in 1206.

1217 Monks who had been sent to the Abbey - probably Anglo-Normans - were returned. One was a lay brother from Margam Abbey outside Norman Cardiff.

c.1224 Granted "Royal Letter of Protection" by King Henry III till 1228.

1226 "A" - all we know of his name but an important time. In **1229** Henry III confirmed previous grants and added others, including a Mill at "Biscuant" in Ceredigion as "legit". Then in **1231** a monk apparently deceived the Royal Army to the advantage of Llewelyn Fawr so Henry III came to the gate intending to burn the Abbey down but the Abbot paid him off with 300 Marks - the money available to finish the Abbey building! As a reward Henry III confirmed previous grants and gave a writ of protection in **1232** "to be exempt from the payment of toll and custom throughout his territories, with respect to what they bought and sold of their property, provided that they took good care that what they bought and sold did not get into the hands of the king's enemies"

c. 1241 Philip. After Death of Llywelyn Fawr, Ralph Mortimer was ready and waiting. A new Abbot with an English sounding name in support *"Philip, Abbot of Cwmhir and the monks thereof granted Sir Ralph the right to make hedges for the hunting of animals in the chase of the Abbey's wood of Cwmhir, and to have wood for that purpose".*

1260-1276 Gruffydd (Welsh) 1274 Abbot of Cwmhir wrote, with others, to the Pope asking him to order the Archbishop of Canterbury not to excommunicate Llywelyn ap Gruffydd because *"the prince, has shown himself protector, not only of the Order (Cistercians), but of each and every order in Wales".*

1276 - 80 Cadwgan became Abbot by standing surety of £40 to Llywelyn *"pledging the prince all the land held in Ceri and Gwrtheyrnion for the release of John ap Hywel ap Maurig from the prince's prison"* DHW

1281- 97 Cadwgan ab Ieva (perhaps the same as above) was abbot at the time Llywelyn ap Gruffudd's body was brought here. Or was he a new Cadwgan since the abbots of Cymer, Aberconwy & Strata Florida were changed after 1282 becaue they were not considered acceptable to Edward I's new regime in Wales

- **1475 - 90   Owain ap David**
- **1490 - 91   Owain Ellis** (possibly the same)
- **1491 - 94   Humphrey** - *Names are more English after Owain Glwndwr*
- **1499 -1508 Thomas**
- **1516   William Jones** (or Johns)
- **1516 - 30   Richard Vayn**
- **1532 - 34   Geoffrey Davis**
- **1535 - 37   John Glyn**   Had been deposed at two other houses for "misguiding & decaying them". Rode to London on 2nd Feb and rerturned on 15th, 1537 probably on dissolution business.

(Based on Williams, DH "White Monks in Powys". (Cistercian Studies Quarterly 1976)

Layton Cooke's other publications:

One can tell from the amount of detail, analysis and practical advice in the Layton Cooke Report (cf pp 70 - 74) that he knows what he is talking about. From his 69 Great Russell Street, Bloomsbury Square office he also advised on the Estate of a William Leake, Esq. in the parishes of Welham and Weston, Northants[1] and had a cash account with Lord Sheffield. A list of his general writings which show him to be very much in touch with his times in which the population of the UK sextupled from 5 to 30 million, there was food shortage, the Corn Laws kept prices high and the Napoleonic Wars prevented imports from France. Agriculture needed reform and Layton Cooke was ahead of the game. Here's what he wrote:-

- *Practical Observations on the importation of foreign corn* - 15 editions published between 1826 and 2005.

- *Tables adapted to the use of farmers and graziers calculated to ascertain the quantity of land which may be worked with agricultural implements of various dimensions, in a given space of time* - 15 editions published in 1813.

- *The value of landed property demonstrated by practical deductions and illustrations, tending especially to facilitate the valuation of estates as applicable to the purposes of agriculture.* 10 editions published in 1844.

- *Observations upon the construction and operation of duties on the importation of foreign corn and suggestions for lessening fluctuations in the price of wheat : addressed to the Right Honourable Sir Robert Peel Bart.*- 11 editions published between 1842 and 2005.

- *To Charles Shaw Lefevre, Esq.M.P* - 4 editions published in 1838.

- *The grazier's manual being tables, showing, on new principles, the nett profitable weight of neat cattle, calves, etc. and for assimilating ... the provincial weights used in estimating live stock"* 2 editions published in 1819.

- *Observations on renting and rating railways, on the depreciation of the moveable stock, and the mode of computing the tenant's profit in a letter, addressed to David Waddington, Esq., M.P., deputy chairman of the directors of the Eastern Counties Railway Company* - 6 editions published in 1848.

- *Bread for the people! - secured by the skilful cultivation and efficient supervision of estates - 2* editions published in 1855.

- *A series of statistical charts shewing the fluctuations in quantity and value of the products of the soil with various ascertainments obviously influential on the husbandry of the British Empire founded on official and other authentic documents* - Book 2 editions published between 1828 and 1832.

- *The Grazier's Manual: being tables showing, on new principles, the nett profitable weight of neat cattle, calves, sheep, and swine; and for assimilating to each other the provincial weights used in estimating live s stock. Second edition, etc* - (Book) 2nd Edition (1819) Dedicated, with permission, to the Right Honorable John Lord Somerville *Printed for the Author. Sold by Longman & Co Paternoster Row.*

- *A Series of statistical charts shewing the fluctuations in quantity and value of the products of the soil with various ascertainments obviously influential on the husbandry of the British Empire founded on official and other authentic documents"* - Published 1827 with 15 hand-coloured engraved charts; early pencil annotations to the first two charts. [2]

1. Leicester County Archives DE3214/4623;
2. Senate House Library, University of London and 286 WWW.WorldCat member libraries worldwide.

Abbeycwmhir Community Book Appendices

Hunt the Bench Marks
There are over 30 in the Community area either in the form of a cut mark as on the Cwmhir Bridge (page 75) or as a steel rivet head. *NBM.**

Height is above *mean sea level. All references are in map square "SO".*

East.	Nrth.	Mark type	Description (All verified in 1977)	Height	Mtrs abov grnd
0028	7842	RIVET	BR PARA E SIDE RD C STR	300.4	0
0057	7564	CUT MARK	NEWHOUSE S ANG SE FACE	302.4	0
0087	7570	RIVET	CUL N SIDE RD 3.0M E PRODN HEDGE OPP	305.9	0
0332	7483	RIVET	ROCK N SIDE RD 97.5M E HEDGE JUNC	415.1	0.3
0353	7462	RIVET	DRAIN NE SIDE RD 29.0M E PRODN HEDGE OPP	360.5	0
0353	7462	RIVET	DRAIN NE SIDE RD 29.0M E PRODN HEDGE OPP	360.5	0
0376	7454	CUT MARK	HO UPPER CWM DU E ANG NE FACE	341.7	0.5
0376	7454	CUT MARK	HO UPPER CWM DU E ANG NE FACE	341.7	0.5
0405	7052	RIVET	BR N SIDE RD C STR	280.0	0
0414	7422	RIVET	STO NE SIDE RD PRODN HEDGE OPP	361.8	0
0440	7137	CUT MARK	COTT W SIDE RD NE ANG N FACE	286.6	0.4
0441	7195	CUT MARK	COTT W SIDE RD NE ANG N FACE	283.6	0.4
0447	7161	CUT MARK	ROCK W SIDE RD 6.5M SW FENCE JUNC S FACE	282.7	0.4
0462	7429	CUT MARK	HO FFYNNON GARREG 2.2M SE ANG E FACE	383.5	0
0485	7087	CUT MARK	BLDG **WENALLT BARN** S ANG SW FACE	263.2	0
0499	7099	CUT MARK	BR NW SIDE RD C CLYWEDOG BROOK *(Clywedog Bridge)*	256.5	0
0538	7131	CUT MARK	**ST MARYS CH** JUT 3.6M NW ANG W FACE	262.8	0.3
0547	7404	RIVET	STO S SIDE RD 8.4M W ANG FENCE	348.9	0
0558	7120	CUT MARK	WALL N SIDE RD 15.5M E GATEWAY **THE HALL**	265.1	0.6
0596	7112	RIVET	**MILL BRIDGE** E SIDE RD S END WALL	245.2	1
0688	7090	RIVET	STO S SIDE RD PRODN STRAIGHT FENCE OPP 2.8M W HEDGE ANG	242.3	0
0710	7108	RIVET	STO SW SIDE RD JUNC TK AND RD	259.8	0.5
0728	7055	CUT MARK	CHAP N ANG NW FACE	248.1	0.6
0734	7136	RIVET	STO NW SIDE RD E SIDE JUNC TK	278.3	0.2
0762	7029	RIVET	RIVET **CUCKOO BRIDGE** S SIDE RD C STR	224.7	0.1
0763	6847	RIVET	PARA BR N SIDE TK E BANK STR	211.4	0.2
0784	7159	RIVET	OUTFLOW NW SIDE **BACHELL BROOK** 3.0M SW C BR	234.6	0
0790	6818	RIVET	NBM RIVET CUL SW SIDE RD C STR	209.9	0

There are more than those listed and they can be found by entering the kilometre square reference in the Ordnance survey's Benchmark Locator http://www.ordnancesurvey.co.uk/benchmarks/ from which the above list is taken.
*NBM (*New Bench Mark*) **Rivet** *is a small metal rivet - the head may be seen.*→

LIST of NAMES of PEOPLE
from
The *Homes and People* section pp 168-270

These and other names may also be mentioned when the property has a section in other parts of the book or in Homes No More (cf p 106-7).

Adams *John* 2,Brickyard Cottages 174
  Pippa 2,Brickyard Cottages 174
Antell *Anthony* Cefn Pawl 189
  Elsie Cefn Pawl 189,
  Lisa Cwefn Pawl 189
  Robert Cefn Pawl 189
Barbierato *Mr & Mrs*
   - Garden Cottage (1950-76) 218
   - Home Farm Coach House (1949) 226
Barnsley *Geoffrey* Ventic 261
Bennett *Alice* Llanerchfraith 228
  Alan - Llanerchfraith 228
  Alan, Mrs, Cwm Hir Cottage 202
  Andrew Llanerchfraith 228
  Elizabeth Nanteos (1841) 236
  Ian Llanerchfraith 228
  Ida Llanerchfraith 228
  Ivor llanerchfraith 228
  Jack Llanerchfraith (1931) 228
  John Llanerchfraith (1978) 228
  Martin Llanerchfraith 228
  Megan Llanerchfraith 228
  Miriam Lower Cwmdu Cottage 197
  Olwen Llanerchfraith 228
  Sylvia Llanerchfraith 228
  Tom Lower Cwmdu Cottage 197
Berriman *Abe* Little Plock 247
  Diana - Cross Cottage 193
     - Little Plock 193, 247
  Jake - Cross Cottage 193
     - Little Plock 193, 247
  Reuben Little Plock 247
Bevan Bwlch y Sarnau Manse 187
  George The Happy Union 222
  George The Hall 222
Bowen *Charlotte* The Old School 249
  Emma The Old School 249
  Peter Piccadilly Cottage (1995) 249, 260
  Peter The Old School (2001) 249, 260
  Sandra The Old School (2001) 249, 260
  Sandra Piccadilly Cottage (1995) 249, 260
Brown Forest Lodge 215
  John Llanerchfraith (1841) 228

The centrepiece of the "Spring" tapestry by Mary Strong and Diana Berriman..

  Samuel Llanerchfraith (1851) 228
Brunt *Edward* (19thc) Maesygwaelod 233
  Eliza Maesygwaelod 233
  Mary Jane Maesygwaelod 233
Bryan *Richard* Paddock Cottage 239
Bound *Mark* Cwmydea 204
Cadwallader *Raymond* Cwm Bedw 194
Carlisle *Capt. E P* Pentwyn 204
Chamberlain *Mary* Erw Fair 208
  Mrs The Hall (1950) 220
Coleman *Tom* Broad Oak 176
  Freda Broad Oak 176
Conner *Mrs* Piccadilly 188
Coward *Roger* Cwm Bedw 194
  Sandy Cwm Bedw 195
Davis *Mr & Mrs* 1, Cwm Hir Cottage 201
Davies *Albert* Upper & Lower Esgair 209
  Anne Fishpools 213
  Austen Pryce Vaughan Beili Bog 172
  Austin Upper Esgair 209
  Ceinwen Fishpools 213
  Edward Meredith Beili Bog 173
  |*Elizabeth Miss* The Ventic 261
  Evelyn Beili Bog 213
  Evelyn Fishpools (1958) 213

Davies continued
  Glenys Upper Esgair 209
  Glyn Upper Esgair 170, 208, 209
  Gwen Fishpools 213
  Jacqueline Cefn View Bungalow 186, 208
  James Arthur William Cwm Bedw 194
  John Beili Bog 173
  John Coedglasson (1623) 190
  Joyce Pengeulan 213
  Joyce Fishpools (1958) 213
  Ken Upper Esgair 170, 208, 209
  Leslie Upper Esgair 209
  Mary Beili Bog 173
  Medina Beili Bog 172
  Michael Cefn View Bungalow 186, 208
  Miss Mill Cottage (1964) 235
  Mr & Mrs O.P. Gorffwsfa 219
  Mrs Cwmdu 198
  Muriel Upper Esgair 208, 209
  Nathan Cwmfaerdy 199
  Owen Beili Bog 172
  Owen Meredith The Dafan 206
  Rose (Rosebury) Upper Esgair 170, 208
  Rhydian Thomas Owen Beili Bog 172
  Rhydian Thomas Owen The Dafan 206
  Sarah Ffynongarreg (1927) 212
  Shirley Upper Esgair 209
  Teresa Valerie Beili Bog 172
  Teresa Valerie The Dafan 206
Thomas Beili Bog 173
  Thomas Cwmpoeth (1851) 227
  Tommy Upper Esgair 209
  Valerie Medina The Dafan 206
  William Ffynongarreg (1927) 212
Day Mill Cottage 235
Dexter *Stephen* Lower Cwmdu Cottage 197
Dummer *Andrew* Paddock Cottage, 239
  Claire Paddock Cottage, 239
  Peter Paddock Cottage, 239
  Suzanne Paddock Cottage, 239
Edwards *Doris Violet* Cwmydea 205
  Elizabeth (Snr) Ventic (Fanteg) (1841) 261
  Elizabeth Ventic (1841) 261
  Glyn Cwmydea 205
  Jamie Forest View 216
  John (Snr) Ventic (Fanteg) (1841) 261
  John Ventic (1841) 261
  Richard Ventic (1841) 261
  Sarah Anne Trinnant 256
  Thomas Ventic (1841) 261

Eley *Peter* Cross Cottage 193
Evans *Andrew* Keepers Lodge (Cottage) 227
  Andrew New House 237
  Andrew Nanteos 234
  David Clewedog Bungalow 191
  David Gorffwsfa 219
  Gayle Clewedog Bungalow 191
  Glyn New House 237
  Ivor, Mrs & Mrs 1,Cwm Hir Cottage, 201
  John Raymond Nanteos 234
  Julian James Nanteos 234
  Julie Clewedog Bungalow 191
  Julie Gorffwsfa 219
  Julie School House 191
  Lil New House 237
  Lucy New House 237
  Marc Clewedog Bungalow 191
  Mr & Mrs Cross Cottage 192
  Rosemary Olwen (*Morris*) Nanteos 234
Fenner *Mr* The Hall 220
Fowler *Richard* Devannor (Tyfaenor) 207
Froggat *Dennis J* Bryncamlo 181
  Henry Bryncamlo 181
  Lucy Bryncamlo 181
  Patricia Bryncamlo 181
George *David John* Bryncamlo 181
  Evan Pant y Rhedyn (1841) 241
  Mary Pant y Rhedyn (1841) 241
Gibberd Cross Cottage 193
Gilbert *Robert Greenway* Cwmtelma 204
Greenaway *J.L.* Bryncamlo 181
Gregory *Henry* 199
  Peter Cwmfaerdy 199
Griffiths *Brenda* Tyn y Coed (2001) 260
  Brenda Devannor 207
  Clarice Devannor 207
  David William (Dr) Devannor 207
  Diana Devannor 207
  Douglas 2,Piccadilly Cottage (1990) 260
  Evan Devannor 207
  Gwyn Tyn-y-Coed 246
  Heather Cwmpoeth 203
  Jack Devannor 246
  James John Devannor 207
  Joanne Cwmpoeth 203
  Jonathon Devannor 207
  Leonard Thomas Cwmpoeth 203
  Margaret Hazel Cwmpoeth 203
  Margaret Hazel Ventic 203
  Mercy Piccadilly Cottages (1959/73) 245, 260

Names Index

Moslyn Penbwlch 243
Puline Cwmpoeth 203
Sarah Devannor 207
Susan Cwmpoeth 203
Tom Cwmcringlyn (1975) 196
Tom Tyn y Coed (2001) 260
Thomas Devannor 207
Haggety *Gary* 2,Piccadilly Cottage 2(2000) 60
   Rachel 2, Piccadilly Cottage (2000) 260
Hall Fred *Bryncamlo* 181
   Mr & Mrs Penbwlch 244
Hamer *Anita* Home Farm 226
   Anita 2, Paddock Cottage, 239
   Caroline Rhiw Gam (1996) 247
   Charlotte Annie Frances (1911) Penbryncennau 242
   David Trinnant 256
   David Thomas Trinnant 256
   Dorothy Ffynongarreg 212
   Ellen School House (1957) 251
   Evan Joseph Nantmel 204
   John Alfred Coedglasson 204
   Melwyn Home Farm (1976) 226
   Melwyn Neuadd Fach 226
   Melwyn Brynrhyg(1939) 226
   Melwyn 2,Paddock Cottage (1974) 226, 239
   Ray School House (1957) 251
   Rhiannon Home Farm 226
   Stanley *Coedglasson* 204 **Hamer continued**
   Susannah *Coedglasson* 204
   Vernwyn Thomas Trinnant 256
Hamer-Evans *Marc* Clewedog Bungalow 191
Hardiman *Jim* Foresters House 214
   Susan Foresters House 214
Hardwick *Brenda* Cwmgringlyn 196
   William Cwmcringlyn (1957) 196
Harries *Kerrie* The Smithy (2008) 252
Herbert *Nigel* Llwynonn 232
Hitchcock *Harry* 1,Cwm Hir Cottage 201
Hope *Mrs* Maesgwaelod 233
Hughes
   David Hendy Farm 224
   David Cwmcringlyn 196
   Dennis Hendy 224
   Dilwyn Measgwyn 234
   Doreen 1, Wenallt Cottage 267
   Elsie Cefn Pawl 188
   Elwen Lower Cwmdu Cottage 198
   Elwyn Hendy View (1988) 224
   Ewan Maesgwyn 234
   Harold Cwmcringlyn 196

   Harold Neuadd Fach (1951) 236
   Hazel Hendy Farm 224
   Helen Measgwyn 234
   Hugh Hendy Farm 224
   Janna Rhiw Gam (1996) 247
   Jean Neuadd Fach 236
   Jean Cwmcringlyn 196
   Jim 1, Wenallt Cottage 267
   Julie Garden Cottage 218
   Malcolm Garden Cottage 218
   Martin Neuaddfach 236
   Matthew Rhiw Gam (1996) 247
   Megan Hendy Farm 224
   Myfanwy Hendy View 224
   Owen Maesgwyn 234
   Thoa Neuadd Fach 236
   Rhian Maesgwyn 234
   Van Lower Cwmdu Cottage 197
Humpherston *Paul* The Hall (1997) 220
   Victoria The Hall 220
Humphrey Forest Lodge 215
Humphries *Richard* Ffynongarreg 211
Ingram *Edward* Llwynneuadd (1860) 231
Jones *Adrian* Forest View 216
   Annie Bryneithin 185
   Cliff Brondrefawr 182
   Dai Llwynonn 232
   David John The Happy Union (1963) 222
   Deiniol Llwynonn 232
   Dorothy Llwynonn 232
   Edward J Harwood (1978) Penpentre 244
   Graham Llwynonn 232
   Jane Forest View 216
   Jason Brondrefawr Bungalow 184
   John The Happy Union (1995) 222
   John Thomas The Happy Union (1937) 222
   Joseph Graham Brondrefawr 182
   Karen The Happy Union 223
   Lauren The Happy Union 223
   Lewis Rose Villa (1960) 248
   Luke The Happy Union 223
   Mandy Llwynonn 232
   Margaret Ivy Brondrefawr 182
   Meryl The Happy Union 222
   Pugh Brondrefawr 182
   Rachel Llwynonn 232
   Sarah Ventic (Fanteg) (1841) 261
   Tommy 2, Brickyard Cottages 174
   Violet The Happy Union 222
   Yvonne The Happy Union 222

Kirk *Peter* Sunnydale (2007) 254
   Wendy Sunnydale (2007) 254
Kosek *Lillie* Glan yrAfon 219
Peter Glan Yr Afon 219
   Wendie Glan Yr Afon 219
   William Glan yr Afon 219
Knox *Mr* The Old School (1972) 249
Layborn *Louisa Livingstone* Bryncamlo Farm 181
Leggatt *Barry* Garden Cottage 218
   Jackie Garden Cottage 218
Lewis *Aelwen Hamer* Cwmtelma 204
   Alan Rhiw Gam 247
   Angela Cwmffwrn 169, 200
   Ben Cwmffwrn 200
   Brian Maesgwalod 233
   Caroline Rhiw Gam 247
   Cweridwen Maesgwalod 233
   Chris Penbwlch (1988) 243
   Clarice Devannor 207
   Clive Maesgwalod 233
   Daniel Cwm Bedw 194
   Donna Cwmffwrn 200
   Dylan Penbwlch 243
   Edward Cwm Bedw 194
   Edward Joseph Brondrefawr 182
   Edwin Maesygwaelod, Vron 233

   Elinor Cwmffwrn 200
   Elizabeth Anne Cwmtelma 204
   Elizabeth Anne Coedglasson 204
   Ellis Lynn Cwmtelma 204
   Evan Thomas (Meurig) Maesygwaelod 233
   Family Llanerchfraith 228
   Gaynor Maesgwalod 233
   Howell Vivian Cwmtelma 204
   Ian Cwmffwrn 171, 200
   Idris John Cwmtelma 204
   Joan Elizabeth Price Maesygwaelod 233
   Joe Penbwlch 243
   Maglona Maesgwalod 233
   Margaret Elizabeth Jane Maesygwaelod 233#
   Maureen Maesgwalod 233
   Philip Maesgwalod 233
   Robert Maesgwalod 233
   Robert Tynpistyl 171
   Rosie Cwmffwrn 200
   Sam Penbwlch 243
   Sarah Penbwlch(1988) 243
   Sheila Maesgwalod 233
   Stephen Maesgwalod 233

   Susan Maesgwalod 233
   Sylvia Maesgwalod 233
   Thomas Cwm Bedw 194
   Thomas Edward Maesygwaelod, Vron 233
   Violet Tynpistyl 171
   Vivienne Hamer 204
   William Esgairwy 210
   (1889) Troedrhiwfelen 257
   (pre 1889) Tynyberth 257
Linden *Henry Radcliffe* (1888) Flying Gate 213
Lovell *Julian* T'yr Ehedydd/2,Piccadilly Cott (2007) 260
Lowe *David* Flying Gate 214
   Gorran Flying Gate 214
   Joseph Flying Gate 214
   Peter Flying Gate 214
   Sara Flying Gate 214
   Susan Flying Gate 213, 214
Lydiate *Danny* Tynyberth 259
   Jack Tynyberth 259
   John Tynyberth (1994) 259
   Lynne Tynyberth (1994) 259
Madeley *Ellen* Cwmcringlyn 196
   Kirsty Cwmcringlyn 196
   Timothy Cwmcringlyn 196
   Wendy Cwmcringlyn 196
Mansell *Catherine* Bryncamlo 181
Manual *Bill (William)* Ffynongarreg 212
   Dorothy Ffynongareg 212
Marsh *Brigit* Llywy Cottage 230
   Christel Llywy Cottage 230
   Christiane Christinnecke Llywy Cottage 230
   Elisabeth Llywy Cottage 230
   Henry Llywy Cottage 230
   Laurence Llywy Cottage 230
   Norman Stayner Llywy Cottage 229
Matheson *Neil (Matty)* The Smithy (2008) 252
McDonagh *Mr A J* Ventic 261
Meredith *Family* Hendy Farm 224
Micheson *Lilly* New House 237
Millward *Mrs* Neuadd Fach (1909) 236
Morgan *David* Coedglasson 190
   Hugh Coedglasson 190
Morris *John* Ffynongarreg 211
   Nita Morris Mill Cottage 235
   Sandra Ffynongarreg 211
   Vera Ffynongarreg 211
Newton *Janice* Hazeldene 223
   Richard Hazeldene 223
Nichols *Sam* 1, Brickyard Cottages 175

Names Index

Richard Hazldene 223
Violet 1, Brickyard Cottages 175
North *David* Gorffwsfa 219
Gail Gorffwsfa 219
Jamer Gorffwsfa 219
Phil Goreffswa 219
Nuttal *Margaret* Pant y Rhedyn 241
Jenni Pant y Rhedyn 241
Neil Pant y Rhedyn 241
Ruth Pant y Rhedyn 241
Thomas Pant y Rhedyn 241
Parfitt *Brian* Mill Cottage 229, 235
Della Mill Cottage 235
Isambard Mill Cottage 235
Maxine Mill Cottage 235
Parkin *Amy Claire* Sunnydale 253,254
Angela Claire Sunnydale 253,254
Robert Sunnydale 253,354
Payne *Kerry* 1,Cwm Hir Cottages 201
Shaun 1, Cwm Hir Cottage 201
Tom 1, Cwm Hir Cottages 201
Peel *Darren* Ty Nant (2008) 258
Eloise Ty Nant 258
Ethan Ty Nant 258
Kieran Ty Nant *258*
Maria Ty Nant (2008) 258
Richard Llwynneuadd 258
Petch *John* Higher Cwmdu Cottage 198
Jonathan Higher Cwmdu 198
Matthew Higher Cwmdu 198
Sara Higher Cwmdu 198
Sandra Higher Cwmdu Cottage 198
Philips *Colonel* The Hall 220
The School (1868) 249
Major The Hall, Esgairwy 211
Mary Beatrice The Hall 220
Philips Family *220*
Philips The Old Vicarage/Brynmoel 261
Phillips *Albert* 2,Cwmhir Cottages 202
Mandy 2,Cwm Hir Cottage 202
Mary 2, Cwm Hir Cottage 202
Powell *Angela* Esgairwy 210
Aubrey Llwynneuadd 231
Cara Llwynneuadd 231
Carys Henfryn 225
Christine Ty Cartref (1977) 258
David J Henfryn (1989) 225
David J Cwmfaerdy (1966) 225
Diane Cwmfaerdy 199
Dora Cwmfaerdy 199

Edwyn Esgairwy 210
Eithyl Ty Cartreff 258
Eileen Waun Farm (1965) 269
Elizabeth (1841) Nanteos 234
Glyn Waun Farm (1977) 269
Graham Cwmfaerdy 199
Harry Cwmfaerdy 199
Hayley Cwmfaerdy 199
Jack Cwmfaerdy 199
Jim Cwmfaerdy 199; Esgairwy 210;
   Llwynneuadd 231; Henfryn 225.
John Upper & Lower Esgair 209
Joy Llwynneuadd 231
Kay Llwynneuadd 231
Keith Esgairwy 208
Kinsey Waun Farm 269
Martha-Jane Esgairwy 210
Morien Esgairwy 210
Mrs Flying Gate (1910) 213
Nia Cwmfaerdy 199
Paul Llwynneuadd 231
Richard (1841) Nanteos 234
Sandra Llwynneuadd 230
Trisha Henfryn 225
William Esgairwy 211
Preller *David* Abbey Mill 171
Preller (continued) *Harriet* Abbey Mill 171
Michael Abbey Mill 171
Pat Abbey Mill 171
Sam Abbey Mill 171
Sarah Abbey Mill 171
Price *Alice* Higher Cwmdu Cottage 198
Benjamin Cwmpoeth (1855) 227
Billy The Happy Union (1915) 222
Brett Llwynonn 232
Bridget Bryncamlo Farm 181
Doug Tynyberth 259
Ernie Higher Cwmdu Cottage 198
Jack Llwynneuadd (1960) 231
James Llanerchfraith (1901) 228
Joan Tynyberth 259
John Llanerchfraith (1861/71) 228
Kris Coedglasson 190
Kenward Coedglasson 190
Margaret, Elizabeth, June Maesgwalod 233
Noel Keepers Lodge 227
Noel Broad Oak 177
Richard New House 237
Sally Coedglasson 190
Violet Sunnydale 253

Prosser *David* Troedrhiwfelin 232, 257
   Dorothy Ventic 261
   Ethel Troedrhiwfelin 232, 257
Pugh *Bernard* Troedrhiwfelin (1983) 232, 257
   David The Dafan 206
   Josiah Beili Bog 173
   Karen Troedrhiwfelen (1983) 257
   Mary The Dafan 206
   Miriam The Dafan 206
   Stephen (Rev) Brondrefawr 182
Rees *Adam Mark* Penbryncennau (1987) 242
   Annie Penbryncennau (1914) 242
   Archie Thomas Bwlch y Sarnau Farm 284
   Brian Penbryncenna 242
   Benjamin Brondrefach 178,180
   Ceridwen Ashdale 170
   Ceri Stonesthrow (1992) 253
   Ceridwen Brondrefawr 178
   Charlotte Annie Frances Penbryncennau (1911) 242
   Cherie Stonesthrow 253
   Edward Brondrefach 178
   Elizabeth Brondrefach 180
   Emma Stonesthrow 253
   Gareth Brondrefach 178
   George Thomas Penbryncennau (1911) 242
   Gertie Brondrefach 178
   Gertrude May Bwlch y Sarnau Farm 184
   Gwyn Hazeldene (1973) 223
   Gwyn Stonesthrow (1992) 253
   Harold Ashdale 170
   Harold Brondrefach 178
   Hugh Brondrefach (1835) 178
   Hugh Brondrefach (1961) 178
   Jack Brondrefach 178, 180
   Jacob (Snr) Brondrefach 180
   Jacob (Jnr) Brondrefach 180
   Jane Brondrefach 180
   Janet Penbryncennau (1978) 242
   James Kinsey (1981) Penbryncennau 242
   Jayden Brondrefach 178
   Julia Brondrefach 178
   June Brondrefach 178
   Katie Elizabeth Mary (1982) Penbryncennau 242
   Kaitlyn Brondrefach 179
   Marc Stonesthrow 253
   Mary Brondrefach 178, 180
   Mary Elizabeth Penbryncennau 242
   Nichole Stonesthrow 253
   Raymond Bwlch y Sarnau Manse 187
   Raymond Thomas Penbryncennau (1944) 242
   Richard Brondrefach 178
   Roger Brondrefach 178
   Sian Brondrefach 179
   Sidney Hamer Penbryncennau (1925) 242
   Thomas Brondrefach 178, 180
   Winifred Doris Penbryncennau (1916) 242
Reynolds *Mr & Mrs* The Hall 220
Richards *Dorothy* Forest Lodge 215
   Lewis Forest Lodge 215
Rowlands *Dick 2,* Paddock Cottage 240
Sale *Janet* Coedglasson 190
Sermukslis *Elmars* Bachel Brook Caravan 170
   Marjorie Bachel Brook Caravan 170
Scheeder *Patrizia* Devannor 207
Sims *Mr & Mrs* Brondrefawr 182
   Cliff Brondrefawr 182
   Pugh Brondrefawr 182
Sinnock *Catherine* (nee Sinnock) Ventic 262
   Jean (nee Sinnock) Ventic 262
   Madge Ventic 262
Stanton *Mrs* Llwy Cottage 240
Stephens *Gwynne* Avalon 170,208
   Shirley Avalon 170,208
Stock *Anne* The Smithy (1987) 252
   James The Smithy 252
   Katy The Smithy 252
   Tony The Smithy (1987) 252
Stonebridge *Bryn* Waun Pystill 266
Strong *Andrew* Broad Oak 176
   Elinor Broad Oak 176
   Jacob Broad Oak 176
   Mary Broad Oak 176
Thornicroft *Andy* Rose Villa (1997) 248
   Jane Rose Villa (1997)248
Underhill *Sandy* Cwm Bedw 195
Vaughan *May* 1, Brickyard Cottage 175
Watkins *Alwyn Itol* Pantglas 240
   Elinor Heifena Pantglas 240
   Glenys/ Bronwen Pantglas (1946) 240
   Gwen Eirwen Pantgals 240
   Ithol Pantglas (1946) 240
   Medina Pantglas 240
   Myfanwy Megan Pantglas 240
   Nigel Pantglas 240
Webb *Clinton* School House (1997) 251
   Jamie School House 184
   Valerie School House (1997) 184
   Yvonne School House 184
Webster Forest Lodge 147

Names Index

Went *Jack* (1918) The Smithy(Vulcan Hall) 185
Williams *Averil* 1, Brickyard Cottages 175
 Barry The Old Vicarage (1986) 195
 Carol Bwlch y Sarnau Manse 187
 Charlotte The Old Vicarage 265
 Eirlys 2,Wennalt Cottage, 201
 Eleanor Fronrhydd-Newydd (1816) 149
 Elsie May 2,Wenalt Cottage, 201
 George 2,Wennalt Cottage, 201
 Hilda Fronrhydnewydd 131
 James The Old Vicarage 265
 Jenny The Old Vicarage (1986)195
 Joe Idris 2,Wennalt Cottage, 201
 John Pantglas (1770) 173
 John Wennalt Cottage, 2 201
 Lindsey Bwlch y Sarnau Manse 119, 200
 Lindsey Wenallt Cottages, 2 119, 201
 Lorraine Paddock Cottages, 2 120, 172 (2007)
 Lorraine Bwlch y Sarnau Manse 173
 Margaret Jane George 2, Wennalt Cottage 268
 Margaret 2, Wennalt Cottage 268
 Mary Pantglas (1770) 240
 Mr The Hall 220
 Reg 2, Wennalt Cottage 268
 Reginald Erw Fair 208
 Reginald The Hall 208 *Reginald* Erw Fair 208
 Reginald The Hall 208
 Rosanna The Old Vicarage 265
 Richard 2, Wennalt Cottage 268
 Stanley Fronrhydnewydd 217
 Stephen William Brynmoel (Architect) (1893)262
 Violet Fronrhydnewydd 217
 Violet Tynpistyll 200
Wilson *Thomas* The Hall (1834) 220, 235
Winterton *Angela* The Oaks 238
 Michael The Oaks 238
 Patric The Oaks 238
 Tomas The Oaks 238
Wodehouse
Woodroffe *Joanne* Penpentre (1978) 244
 Helen Marion) Mill Cottage (1964235
Woolley *Margaret* Bryneithin 185,186
 Stephen Bryneithin 185,186
Wozencraft *Amy* School House 251
 Anne Tri Mynydd(1984) 255
 Annie Cefn Pawl 188
 Byron Garden Cottage 208, 218
 Christine Cefn Pawl 188
 Colin Tri Mynydd (1984) 255
 Donna Garden Cottage 218
 Ellen Louise Tri Mynydd 255
 Elsie Ty Cartreff (1978) 258, Cefn Pawl 188
 Flossy Cwmyscawen 227
 Fred Lower Cwmdu Cottage 197
 George Herbert Cefn Pawl 188
 Lesley Cefn Pawl 188
 Meredith Cefn Pawl 188
 Meredith Ty Cartreff (1978) 258
 Meryl Erw Fair, Garden Cottage 208,218
 Meryl The Vicarage, The Happy Union 208
 Michelle Garedn Cottage 218
 Mill School House 251
 Rebecca Erw Fair, Garden Cottage 208, 218
Wozencroft *family* Ffynongarreg 211

This Index was collated by Peter Kirk, (Clerk to the Community Council 2007 -14); Edited by Diana Berriman.

Devannor's Spinner

ABBEYCWMHIR WELSH PLACE NAMES TRANSLATED
including Homes no More

The list below contains most of the Welsh names of properties and geographical features in the Community of Abbeycwmhir with explanations. The alphabetical order here ignores the words 'upper', 'lower', 'little' and the definite articles 'the;' and 'y'. Welsh words in the explanations are italicized, as are versions of Welsh names where the correct Welsh orthography differs from the Anglicized version.. Most of the Welsh-language place-names in Abbey Cwmhir are self evident to Welsh speakers, as is the case throughout Wales, but in the handful of names that are difficult to understand, I have noted the fact. Because the Welsh language changes vowels and consonants in different contexts, the spellings in the place names do not necessarily correspond exactly with the root words in the explanations.

Avalon   E. version of *Afallon*, the Welsh Otherworld or 'Isle of Apples'.
Bachell, stream-name, possibly a 'back-formation' from the little valley it flows through, *bachell*, 'corner', 'nook'
Beilibog = 'Bog Yard', 'Bog Court';; *beili* (= Bailey), 'yard', 'court' + E. bog.
Brondre Bungalow - *Brondre* = 'Hill Dwelling', *bron*, 'hill', 'breast' + *tref*, 'dwelling'.
Brondre Fach = 'Little Brondre'.
Brondre Fawr = 'Big Brondre'.
Bronrevel = 'Smithy Hill', *bron*, 'hill', 'breast' + *yr, '(of) the' + '(g)efail*, 'smithy', 'forge'.
Bryncamlo = 'Camlo Hill'; *bryn*, 'hill' + stream name, *cam* = 'crooked', 'winding' + *llo*, 'calf'. Welsh rivers and streams are often named after unruly animals. In this case the hill is named after the stream that rises there.
Bryndraenog = 'Thorny Hill'; *bryn*, 'hill' + *draenog*, 'thorny. **Not** 'Hedgehog Hill'.
Brynfawr *Bryn Mawr* = 'Big Hill', *bryn*, 'hill' + *mawr,* 'big'.
Bryneithin = 'Gorse Hill' , *bryn*, 'hill' + *eithin*, 'gorse'
Brynmoel = bryn: hill + moel = bare or bald
Bryn y Wyntyll = 'Windle Hill'; *bryn*, 'hill' + *gwyntyll*, 'windle', 'wimnowing fan'.
Buddugre Hill = (possibly) 'Prosperous Hill', *buddug*, 'prosperous', 'victorious' + *bre*, 'hill'.
Bwlchysarnau Farm = 'The Pass of the Roads'; *bwlch*, 'pass', 'gap in the hills' + *y sarnau*, 'the roads', plural of *sarn*, which often means ' (raised) causeway' or 'Roman road' (here probably not the case).
Camlo cf Bryncamlo above
Cefn Crin = 'Dry Hill'; *cefn*, 'hill', ridge' + *crin*, 'parched', 'withered'
Cefn Du = Black Hill; *cefn*, 'hill', 'ridge' + *du*, 'black'
Cefn Dyrys = 'Rough Hill'; *cefn*, 'hill', 'ridge' + *dyrys*, 'tangled' (of undergrowth, etc).
Cefn Lluest = 'Shepherds' Hut Hill'; *cefn,* 'hill', 'ridge' + *lluest*, 'shepherds' hut'.
Cefn Pawl = 'Paul's Hill'; *cefn*, 'hill', 'ridge' + personal name <u>*Pawl*</u>.
Cefn View = *cefn*, 'hill', ridge'.
Clywedog = 'noisy stream'; *clywed*, 'to hear' + *-og*, adjective ending.
Coedglasson = *Coedglason*, possibly = 'green-ash wood', *coed*, 'trees', 'wood' + *glason,* 'green ash'.
Coed Uchaf = 'Top Wood'; *coed*, 'trees', 'wood' + *uchaf*, 'highest', 'top'.
Creigiau = 'Rocks'; *creigiau*, plural of *craig* 'rock'.
Creigiau Hynod = 'Rocks that stand out'; *creigiau*, plural of *craig* 'rock' + *hynod*, 'outstanding', 'remarkable', 'strange'.
Crugyn Llwyd = 'Grey Tumulus'; presumably the hill is named after the cairn at its summmit; *crugyn*, 'hillock', 'tumulus' + *llwyd*, 'grey'
Crychell = 'strong, rippling stream'; *crych*, 'strong', 'bubbling'.
Cwm Bedw = 'Birch Dingle'; *cwm*, 'valley', 'dingle' + *bedw*, 'birch trees'
Cwmcringlyn = 'Valley of Dry Brushwood'; *cwm*, 'valley', 'moor' + *crin*, 'parched', 'withered' + *clun/clyn*, 'heath', 'brushwood'.
Cwm Cwarel = 'Quarry Valley' , *cwm*, 'valley', 'dingle' + *cwarel,* S. Wales form of *chwarel*, 'quarry'.

Cwm Cynydd - *Cwm Cynnydd* = 'Valley of Growth,
Cwm Defaid = 'Sheep Dingle'; *cwm,* 'valley', 'dingle' + *defaid,* 'sheep' (plural)
Cwmderw = 'Oak Dingle'; *cwm,* 'valley', 'dingle' + *derw,* 'oak trees'
Cwmdu Cotttage *Cwm Du* = 'Black Valley'; *cwm,* 'valley', dingle' + *du,* 'black'..
Cwmfaerdy = 'Valley of the Big House'; cwm, 'valley', 'dingle' + maerdy, farmhouse', 'mansion'. The mutation of maerdy to faerdy is interesting.
Cwm Farsley - possibly = 'Marsli's Hill'; *cwm,* 'valley', 'dingle' + *Marsli* (woman's name),. The mutated form (here Marsli > Farsli) is rare, but not unknown, in place-names.
Cwmffwrn = "Oven Valley"; *cwm,* 'valley' dingle' + *ffwrn,* 'oven', furnace', 'hearth'.
Cwm Geifer *Cwm Geifr* = 'Goat Valley'; *cwm,* "valley', 'dingle' + *geifr,* 'goat'
Cwm Hir = 'Long Valley'; *cwm,* 'valley', + *hir,* 'long.
Cwmlliw = *Cwm-Lliw*; *cwm,* 'valley', + *Lliw* 'colourful'. Valley with peat coloured stream?
Cwm Lluest = 'Valley of the Shepherds' Hut'; *cwm,* 'valley', dingle' + *lluest,* 'shepherds' hut'.
Cwm Llygod, possibly = 'Mice Dingle'; *cwm,* 'valley', 'dingle' + *llygod,* 'mice'
Cwm Nant-y-stabl = 'Narrow Valley of the Stream of the Stable'; *cwm,* 'valley', Dingle, *nant,* 'valley', 'stream' + *stabl,* 'stable'.
Cwm Pistyll = 'Spring Valley'; *cwm,* 'valley', 'dingle' + *pistyll,* 'spring', 'well'.
Cwm Pistyll-oen = 'Lamb's Spring Valley' *cwm,* 'valley', 'dingle' + *pistyll,* 'spring', 'well' + *oen,* 'lamb'
Cwmpoeth = 'Hot Valley; '*cwm,* 'valley' dingle' + *poeth,* 'hot'
Cwm Rogue - *Cwm yr Og,* = 'Harrow Valley'; *cwm,* 'valley, dingle, + *yr og,* 'the harrow'.
Cwmtelma - possibly = 'Valley of the Snares, Traps'; *cwm,* 'valley', 'dingle' + *telmau,* plural of *telm,* 'trap', snare'. The -a for -au plural ending is a SE Welsh characteristic occasionally found in Radnorshire.
Cwm-y-dea corruption of *Cwm-du,* 'Black Valley; '*cwm*', 'valley', 'dingle' + *du,* 'black'.
Cwm-yr-hebog = 'Hawk Valley'; *cwm,* 'valley', dingle' + *yr hebog,* 'the hawk'
Cwm yr Og Plantation, see Cwm Rogue
Cwm Ysgawen, Cwm Ysgawen = 'Elder Valley' ; *cwm,* 'valley', 'dingle' + *ysgawen,* 'elder tree'.Elder Flower
Dafarn = '(The) Inn', *tafarn,* 'tavern', inn. Most Welsh place-names in this area are south Walian forms; this name is an exception to that rule, as is *Dafarn Eithin* in Nantmel.
Devannor - *Tŷ Faenor* = 'Manor House'; *tŷ,* 'house' + *maenor,* S Wales word for 'manor', 'demesne', etc.
Dole - *Dôl, dôl;* 'river meadow'.
Upper and Lower Dolau - *dolau,* 'river meadows'
Domen Ddu = 'The Black Mound'; *tomen,* 'mound', 'hillock', 'mixen'. + *du,* 'black'
Dole = 'Meadow'; *dôl,* 'river meadow'.
Erw Fair = '(Saint) Mary's Acre'; *erw,* 'acre' + 'Mair', 'Saint Mary.
Esgair-fawr = 'Great Spur'; *esgair,* 'shank of leg', 'spur of a hill' + *mawr,* 'big'.
Maesgwyn, *Maes-gwyn* = "White field"; *maes,* 'open field' + *gwyn,* 'white'.
Esgairwy - *Esgair-wy*. This appears to be *esgair,* 'shank of a leg', 'spur of a hill' + *gwy,* 'water', but the name is problematic.
Ffynongarreg - *Ffynnon y Garreg* = 'Stone Well'; ffynnon, 'well', 'spring' + *y garreg,* 'the stone'.
Foel fach (Vale fach) = 'The Little Bare Hill'; *moel,* 'bare hill' + *bach,* 'little'
Fron Gwyllt (*Y*) *Fron Wyllt* = 'The Wild Hill'; *bron,* 'hill', 'breast' + *gwyllt,* 'wild'.
Fronrhydnewydd = 'New Ford Hill'; *bron,* 'hill', 'breast' + *rhyd,* 'ford' + *newydd,* 'new'.
Fron Wood - *Fron* = 'the hill'; *bron,* 'hill', 'breast'.
Fuallt = 'The Cattle Wood'; *bu* = 'cattle', 'cows' + *allt,* 'wooded hill'
Garreg Llwyd - (*Y) Garreg Lwyd* = '(The) Grey Stone'; *carreg,* 'stone' + *llwyd,* 'grey'.
Gelynen = '(The) Holly Tree'; *celynen* = 'holly tree'
Glan yr Afon = 'River Bank'; *glan,* 'bank' + *yr afon,* 'the river'.
Glan-Rhedyn = 'Bracken Bank'; *glan,* 'river bank' + *rhedyn,* 'ferns', ' bracken'.
Y Glog = 'The Crag'; *clog,* 'crag', 'cliff'.

Groes = (The) Cross'; *croes,* 'cross'.
Gwar-y-Cae = 'Upper Part of the Field'; *gwar*, 'nape of the neck', 'upper part', 'margin' + *cae*, 'field'..
Gwern garn, see Waun-y-garn.
Hafod-y-ffryd - possibly *Hafod y Ffridd* = 'Summer Dwelling on the Mountain Pasture'; hafod, 'summer dwelling' + ffridd, "sheep-walk', rough mountain pasture'.
Hendy = 'Old House'; *hen*, 'old' + *tŷ*, 'house'.
Henfryn = 'Old Hill'; *hen*, 'old' + *bryn*, 'hill'.
Hirddywel = ' Long View'; *hir* 'long' + *dywel*, 'intensive view'.
Lan-fraith = 'Speckled Bank'; (g)*lan*, 'river-bank' + *fraith*, feminine of *brith*, 'speckled', 'mottled' .
Lan-wen = 'White bank'; (g)*lan*, 'river-bank' + *wen*, feminine form of *gwyn*, 'white'.
Llanerchfraith - *Llannerch-fraith*, = 'Speckled Clearing'; *llannerch*, 'glade', 'clearing', + *fraith*, feminine of *brith*, 'speckled', 'mottled' .
Llidiart = Gate. *Llidiart, llidiard, llidiad* are common forms for 'gate' in this area.
Llidiart y dwr - *Llidiart y dŵr* = 'Watergate' *lidiart*, 'gate' i.+ dŵr, 'water
Llwynneuadd *Llwyn y Neuadd* = 'Hall Grove'; *llwyn*, 'grove', 'thicket' + *y neuadd*, 'the hall'.
Llwybr y Gath = 'Cat Track'; *llwybr*, 'path', trail' etc. + *cath*, 'cat'; road from Bwlchysarnau to David's Well.
Llwyn Hill - *llwyn*, 'grove, 'thicket'.
Llwynonn - *Llwyn-onn* = 'Ash Grove'; *llwyn*, 'grove'. 'thicket' + *onn*, 'ash trees'.
Plock, Little - 'Plock' is a very common old borders English word, also borrowed into Welsh in this area, denoting a small field near the farmhouse, usually set aside for operations like sorting out sheep. The word might also be connected with the W. word *lloc*, 'pen', 'fold'., 'glade' + *tirion*, 'gentle', 'pleasant'. This is also the full Welsh name of the inn in Llandrindod
Llannerch Dirion = 'Pleasant Glade'; *llannerch,* 'clearing'
Llywy = 'Beautiful (Hill)'.; *llywy*, 'beautiful', 'bright'.
Maelienydd, 'The Land of Mael', consists of most of northern Radnorshire. It is supposedly named after Mael ap Cadfael, a tenth century leader, about whom nothing is known, but who was important enough to give his name to different parts of Radnorshire, including the neighbouring parish of Nantmel.Also **Elfael**, = 'Mael's territory'
Maesygwaelod = Bottom Field',; *maes*, 'open field' + *y gwaelod*, 'the bottom'.
Maesyhendy - *Maes yr Hendy* = Field of the Old House'; *maes*, 'open field' + *hen*, 'old' + *tŷ*, 'house'
Marteg, river-name derived from *march*, 'stallion', 'steed' + *teg*, 'fair', 'beautiful'; this river races like a fast horse.
Nanteos = 'Valley of the Nightingale'; *nant*, 'valley' + *eos*, 'nightingale'.
Nant-y-stabl = 'Stream of the Stable'; *nant*, 'valley', 'stream' + *stabl*, 'stable'.
Nant y ffin = nant, 'stream' = ffin = 'boundary'
Neuaddfach *Neuadd-fach* = 'Little Hall'; *neuadd*, 'hall' + *bach*, 'little', 'small'.
Pandy - Fulling Mill (for felted cloth) The stream's name is a 'back formation, from the fulling-mill that used its water, *pan*, '(for) fulling' + *tŷ,* 'house'.
Pant-y-rhedyn = 'Fern Hollow; *pant*, 'hollow', 'dip' + *rhedyn*, 'ferns', 'bracken'.
Pant yr onen, *Pant yr onnen* = 'Ash Hollow'; *pant,* 'hollow', 'dip' + *onnen,* 'ash tree'.
Penbryncenna - possibly *Penbryncenau* = 'Top of the Hill of the Cub'; *pen*, 'top', 'end' + *bryn*, 'hill' + *cenau*, 'cub', 'young animal'.
Penpentre , 'Top of the Village'; *pen*, 'top', 'head' + *pentref*, 'village'.
Penygarreg = 'Top of the stone'; *pen*, 'top', 'end' + *carreg*, 'stone'.
Pen-y-lan = 'Bank Top', + *pen*, 'head', top' + *glan*, '(river) bank'.
Pen-y-llan = 'Top of the Village'; *pen*, 'top', 'end' + *llan*, ' village', 'churchyard', etc.
Pistyll = 'spring'; *pistyll,* **'well', 'spring'.**
Prysg Duon = [x]'Black Scrub-land'; *prysg*, 'scrub-land' + duon, plural form of *du*, 'black.
Pwll-y-Rhos = 'Moor Pool'; *pwll*, 'pool' + *rhos*, 'moor', 'heath'.
Rhiw-gam = 'Crooked Hill',; *rhiw*, 'hill', 'slope' + '*cam*, 'crooked'.

Local Welsh Place Names Interpreted

The Rhos, rhos, 'moor', 'heath'
Trinant = 'Three Valleys'; *tri*, 'three' + *nant*, valley
Troedrhiwfelen = 'the Foot of the Yellow Hill'; *troed*, 'foot' + *rhiw*, 'hill' + *felen*, feminine of *melyn*, 'yellow'.
Rhos,Rhoss = 'moor', 'heath'
Ty Nicholas - *Tŷ Niclas* = 'Nicholas's House; *tŷ*, 'house'
Tynyberth - *Tŷ'n-y- berth* = 'House in the Hedge'; *tŷ*, 'house' + *perth*, 'hedge'
Tynycoed - *Tŷ'n y coed* = 'House in the Wood'; *tŷ*, 'house' + *yn y coed*, 'in the woods, trees'.
Tyr Ehedydd - *Tŷ'r Ehedydd* = 'Lark House'; *tŷ*, 'house' + *'r ehedydd*, (of) the lark'.
Waun Farm = (g)waun, '*moor*'
Waun Gaseg = 'Mare Moor'; (*g*)*waun*, 'moor', 'heath' + *caseg*, 'mare'.
Waun Marteg = 'Marteg Moor'; (g)waun, 'moor', 'heath' + Marteg (q.v.)
Waun Pistyll = 'Spring Moor'; (*g*)*waun*, 'moorland', 'heath' + *pistyll*, 'well', 'spring'
Waun-y-garn = 'Moor of the Cairn'; (g)waun, 'moor', 'heath' + y, 'the' + carn, 'cairn'. This is also known as
Gwern garn = 'Cairn scrub'; *gwern*, 'alder scrub', 'bog' + carn.
Wennallt - Wenallt = 'White Wooded Hill'; *wen*, feminine form of *gwyn*, 'white' + *allt,* 'wooded hill'.
Wern, = (g) *wern*, 'alder scrub', 'boggy land'.
Wern Garrig - *Wern y Garreg* + The Alder-bog of the Stone'; (*g*)*wern*, 'alder scrub', 'bog' + *carreg*, 'a stone'

This list was prepared by Dai Hawkins of Nantmel to whom many thanks.

Oh! Let us never, never doubt

What nobody is sure about!"
- *Hilaire Belloc*

"More Beasts for worse Children"

The first of all commandments is, The Lord our God is one Lord; and thou shalt love the Lord thy God with all thy heart, and with all thy soul and with all thy mind, and with all thy strength; this is the first commandment. And the second is like, namely this, Thou shalt love they neighbour as thyself. There is none other commandment greater than these.
- The Sermon on the Mount (Mark 12:31)

Cefndyrys, Bwlch y Sanau
C 2010

Wishes of an Elderly Man at a Garden Party

I WISH I loved the Human Race
I wish I loved it's silly face;
I wish I liked the way it walks;
I wish I liked the way it talks;
And when I'm introduced to one
I wish I thought *What Jolly Fun!*

- Sir Walter Raleigh (1861-1922)

Marteg Valley
C 2010

The Northern Boundary – Hirddywel - Bounded by Wind

This book may be purchased from the
Abbeycwmhir Community Council
c/o Roger Coward, Cwm Bedw,
Abbeycwmhir, Llandrindod Wells,
Powys LD1 6PH 01597 851021
abbeyhillfarm@gmail.com

Man's days are like those of grass
Like a flower of the field he blooms;
The wind sweeps over him and he is gone
And his place knows him no more.
(Psalm 103)